STRATEGIC MANAGEMENT
for the
XXIst
CENTURY

M. Reza Vaghefi

Alan B. Huellmantel

S^t_L

St. Lucie Press

Boca Raton   London   New York   Washington, D.C.

Library of Congress Cataloging-in-Publication Data

Vaghefi, Mohammad Reza.
    Strategic management for the XXIst century / by M. Reza Vaghefi
and Alan B. Huellmantel.
       p. cm.
    Includes bibliographical references and index.
    ISBN 1-57444-210-4
    1. Strategic planning. I. Huellmantel, Alan B. II. Title.
III. Title: Strategic management for the 21st century. IV. Title:
Strategic management for the twenty-first century.
HD30.28.V33   1998
658.4′012—dc21

                                           98-44194
                                              CIP

No claim to original U.S. Government works
International Standard Book Number 1-57444-210-4
Library of Congress Card Number 98-44194
Printed in the United States of America 1 2 3 4 5 6 7 8 9 0
Printed on acid-free paper

Dedication

This work is dedicated to the memory of our late colleague, Professor Noel B. Zabriskie, who began with us but ...

and

Ray T. Parfet, Jr., former Chief Executive of the Upjohn Company — the real Upjohn planner

Preface

Because the libraries are full of articles and books on strategic management, all new authors should ask themselves, "Why another book?" This preface answers that question for our *Strategic Management for the XXIst Century.*

This book addresses senior management for the next century and how to lead an organization strategically. Following a step-by-step blueprint systematically, a manager will be able to create a strategic planning system and, with a dose of innovative management initiatives, can create competitive strategies that will achieve success in the marketplace. It is the author's firm belief that a corporate planning system should be capable of producing not just a strategic plan but also a strategic planning system composed of individual strategic, administrative, and operations plans. This interrelated set of plans and decisions forms a logical theme that runs through and gives purpose and relevancy to all plans and decisions. In this scheme of operations, the primary and fundamental importance of the strategic plan is in the external environment. The internal environment is the domain of administrative and operational plans which must function flawlessly and be synchronized with the strategic plan. The genesis of this style of planning is the General Electric model of the 1960s which stands today as a state-of-the-art strategic planning benchmark for many corporations.

Other features that differentiate this text with ones already on the market include (1) differentiation of the skills of middle and senior managers, (2) linking long-range strategic plans with today's financial plans and budgets, and (3) evaluation of competitive strategies with market benchmarks. In addition, we have attempted to establish a logical relationship between planning and the structure within which the plans must be implemented, as well as creating a system of strategic planning that can cater to an organization's needs.

In more specific terms, the reader will benefit from this book simply by considering key issues, such as differentiating that which is strategic for the firm from that which is not ... without floundering on issues which at best may divert scarce resources to non-strategic matters. There are plenty of examples in today's world of business where not recognizing strategic issues has had disastrous consequences for the firm, quite often not reversible.

A further new feature found in the text is the linkage between various functions and their contribution to the successful implementation of the strategic plan and how a value system can be created in the organization that would allow a logical flow of ideas and plans for meeting budgets, predicting the future, and by thinking strategically creating the future. In the words of Gluck et al. (*Harvard Business Review*, July/August, 1980), our efforts have been to help managers create "a planning framework that cuts across organizational boundaries and facilitates strategic decision-making about customer groups and resources; (2) a planning process that stimulates entrepreneurial thinking; and (3) a corporate values system that reinforces managers' commitment to the company's strategies."

In this text, we have integrated years of academic and real-world experience, hoping that we can offer potential instructors and students something entirely different and ultimately make the subject of strategic management a more exciting one for all who may use this text. We believe that we have succeeded in this endeavor.

Our efforts would not have materialized had there been no support from our students and all those associated with us, our families and friends. We are especially thankful to Leanna Payne on whom we always counted for last-minute finishing touches. We have dedicated this work to our late colleague Professor Noel B. Zabriskie, who inspired us to begin the text but whose untimely death deprived us of his dedication and professionalism, and Ray T. Parfet, whose planning skills impacted our own thinking.

M. Reza Vaghefi
Jacksonville, FL
Alan B. Huellmantel
Ponte Vedra, FL

The Authors

M. Reza Vaghefi, Ph.D., is Professor of Strategic Management and International Business at the University of North Florida's College. of Business Administration (an AACSB-accredited college). He studied at the American University of Beirut, Lebanon; Stanford Graduate School of Business (ICAME program); and Michigan State University, where he was awarded his doctorate in management. He has written extensively in various journals and has produced many case studies which were previously distributed by Harvard Business School. His most recent research work, co-authored with Alan Huellmantel, appeared in the *International Journal of Strategic Management* (London).

Alan B. Huellmantel is a former planning director at Pharmacia-Upjohn Company, Kalamazoo, Michigan. He studied at Ferris State College and is a graduate of the University of Michigan's executive development program. He is also a graduate of the Stanford Research Institute's program in strategic planning. He has contributed to numerous strategic management journals, to the *Handbook of Modern Marketing* (McGraw-Hill), and to the *Journal of Purchasing and Materials Management*.

Contents

Section 2. The Cases

Section I. The Text

1 The Art of Governing

"One of the least understood aspects of the corporate discipline has to do with corporate governance." (Richard Ellis)

1.1 Introduction

The art of governance, or leadership, is as old as society itself. It has been defined as: "The exercise of authority by an individual, or group of individuals over an organization, its functions, and decisions."[1] The 1990s saw a renewed interest in the subject of corporate governance largely because of one man, Ira Milstein. Milstein, a corporate lawyer, is currently an instructor in corporate governance at Yale University.[2] For the last 20 years, he has been teaching that good governance must start and end with the corporation's board of directors. Above all else they must take responsibility for nominating, hiring, and evaluating the performance of the chief executive officer. Those that are not performing up to the stockholders' expectations, and the board that represents them, must be replaced.

Milstein's involvement with corporate governance began when he was hired as a consultant to the Business Round Table, an assembly of the big company chief executives.[2] From there, he went on to chair a panel formed to draw up performance guidelines for corporate boards. The panel was appointed by the National Association of Corporate Board Directors. Here are a few examples of those guidelines:[3]

1. Every board should have an appointed lead outside director.
2. There should be three yearly executive sessions of only outside directors.
3. The board should make an annual evaluation of the chief executive officer's performance which focuses on the following (although not exclusive) aspects:
    a. Financial performance
    b. How well the objectives in the strategic plan were met
    c. Progress made by the management development programs
4. Decisions pertaining to corporate governance are to be made only by the outside board members.
5. The Directors Affairs Committee of the board will review each member's contributions and continuation every 5 years.
6. If an outside board member's outside duties change, he/she will be required to offer his/her resignation.
7. When a chief executive officer resigns or retires he must offer his/her resignation from the board.
8. The board, not the chief executive officer, will both nominate and select all new board members.
9. Board members should have complete access to the management and books of the corporation rather than being limited to that which is funneled to the board through the chief executive officer.

Milstein's latest, and possibly most important assignment, was as a consultant to General Motors' board of directors. It was he who recommended and motivated them to remove their then chief executive, Robert Stempel. This decision had both domestic and international impacts. In Milstein's own words, "When General Motors went, the dominoes fell. After GM, American Express, Eastman Kodak, Westinghouse, and IBM followed. They did so because GM legitimized an active board."[2]

Between 1989 and 1994, 1,400,000 U.S. managers lost their jobs through board actions. The Germans and Japanese could not understand how this could happen.[4] The explanation lies in the way they finance their businesses and in the make-up of their governing boards. American and British corporations depend on equity capital for their financing, obtained from a large number of dispersed stockholders. Corporate boards serve at the pleasure of these individual stockholders.

By contrast, German and Japanese firms finance their businesses through debt, and their boards are composed of the bankers and workers' representatives that lend them the money. These in-house boards protect corporations from hostile takeovers and board revolts. This structure creates a stable operation and employment, but it has one big disadvantage. Recent records show that managements protected and unchallenged by their stockholders put profit way down their priority list. Not having outside stockholders, who challenge poor performing management teams, could explain why so many German and Japanese companies today find themselves in deep trouble.[4] The German firms operate within a highly regulated environment where the government's role has been a major factor. Additionally, workers are represented on the "works council" which impacts shareholders' profit, not always positively. Japanese firms also operate within a highly regulated and protected environment.

The protection comes by way of *keiretsu*, a celebrated holding company system where sometimes up to 20 companies work within a family of enterprises. Common shareholders' interests receive low priority. It is very much like an organization or brotherhood where big brothers (members of the *keiretsu*) determine what should be done, and small brothers (common shareholders outside the *keiretsu*) have to take what has been decided for them.

Many corporate directors feel that the guidelines drawn up by the National Association of Corporate Board Directors will establish the roadways to be taken by directors and chief executives in the XXIst century. For the role Milstein played in corporate governance during the 1990s, John A. Byrnes of *Business Week* calls him the "Guru of Good Governance". Neil Minow, a principal of the Lens Fund, states that if anyone can be called a statesman in this field, it is Milstein.[2]

And, of course, Milstein is not alone in championing the cause of shareholders. Major pension funds such as Teachers' Insurance and Annuity Association-College Retirement Equities Fund (TIAA-CREF) and California Public Employees' Retirement System (CALPERS) are pursuing the same objective: to find a CEO responsive to shareholders' concern, to trim fat and unnecessary expenses, and to be held more accountable to shareholders. They cite the fact that the more independent a director, usually from outside the firm, the more value will go to the shareholders, and they find a fertile ground in the way the Campbell Soup Company has done it: out of 15 directors, only one is from inside the company and the return to shareholders has exceeded the S&P 500 and is way above Heinz, which is dominated by handpicked board members who are close friends of the CEO.[5]

Others agree that the art of governing, under any of its titles — governor, leader, executive, general manager, etc. — is universal. Its principles and constructs are applicable to governing any and all purposeful organizations.[6,7] Unless organizations have a purpose, there is no reason governors should try to get people to work together.[8] Purposeful organizations come in all types and sizes — small, large, profit, non-profit, economic, domestic, and global.

Regardless of the type or size of the organization, the governor's or leader's responsibilities are the same. While the principles, responsibilities, and constructs remain the same, the scope of activities, cultures, and econo-political situations make some organizations more difficult to govern than others. Large, global organizations are more difficult to govern because every country has its own set of laws, business codes, and cultural variables. The cultural differences, however, are in the environment in which the exercise of authority takes place, not in the act of governing itself. The universal constructs of the art of governing are many and diverse. Constructs are concepts devised to integrate the diverse data of a phenomenon into an orderly process. For planning and governing purposes these constructs can be grouped into two classes: (1) the planning and decisions to make an organization more *efficient,* and (2) planning and decisions to make an organization more *effective.* Decisions for making an organization more efficient allocate resources for improving internal operations, cost-cutting, organizational redesigning, and increasing employee morale. Decisions for making an organization more effective allocate resources externally to gain profitable market shares in today's and tomorrow's markets. The strategic concept is the instrument that governors and leaders use to exercise authority over an organization effectively.

The principles for the strategic concept are embodied in three major decision areas:

Decision Area 1: Establishing long-range objectives — Long-range objectives are directional targets or endpoints derived from the vision of what the governor or leader wants the organization to become.

Decision Area 2: Formulating strategies — Both general and business unit strategies provide the rationale for the resource allocation decisions. Resource allocation decisions are strategic growth decisions made to exploit market opportunities in pursuit of the organization's long term objectives.

Decision Area 3: Designing the organizational structure —Organizational structures can either impede or facilitate the formulation and implementation of the strategies in the strategic plan. To be successful, strategic planning must have an organizational structure that facilitates the planning process.

1.2   Managerial Life Cycles

The recent American Assembly of Collegiate Schools of Business (AACSB) study on business policy makes a clear distinction between the knowledge and skills required of senior and middle management.[9] Middle management is responsible for the day-to-day administrative and operational planning and decision-making required to manage already committed resources to gain market share and profit in today's markets.

Senior management must also be skilled in managing already committed resources, but also must be able to identify and select future markets in which to commit resources. Here a good measure of clairvoyance differentiates the visionary from the run-of-the-mill type executives. In today's global markets, examples of this are abundant and it pays to discern the opportunities. In recent years, according to Porter and van der Lind,[10] "The German and Japanese car makers captured early-mover advantages, but U.S. car makers chose to fight regulations." There is little room for an insouciant executive in today's "global village". Andrew Grove believes that, in his business (high tech), you have to be paranoid. There are decisions that must be made today to be in a position to exploit tomorrow's market opportunities and design organizational structures that can produce and support both the short and long range plans.

The strategic concept blends all three necessary skills — administrative, operational, and strategic — into planning sets, or an interrelated, comprehensive planning system.[11]

The top senior manager or leader in most organizations is the chief executive officer, who is solely responsible for the success or failure of all three sets of plans. The major difference in terms of responsibility is that the administrative and operational responsibilities can be delegated. The strategic responsibilities cannot. The multiple management

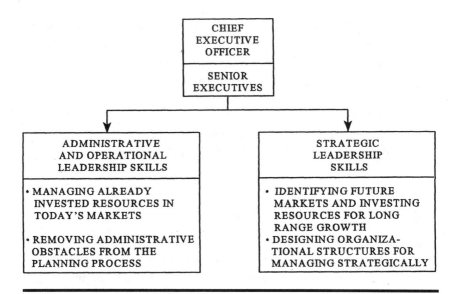

Figure 1.1 Corporate Leadership

or leadership roles can best be visualized by studying the corporate leadership chart shown in Figure 1.1.

Managers, like the products they manage, pass through several levels of management on their way to the top of the organizational chart. These management levels can be classified into three major groups.

Group 1: First-line supervision — Primarily skilled in technical and functional disciplines, such as engineering, accounting, personnel, marketing, etc. These managers usually supervise or manage small groups of workers trained in their own specialized discipline.

Group 2: Middle management — Lead larger numbers of workers and workers with functional training in disciplines other than those of the managers. For example, a manager with an engineering degree manages specialists in production, purchasing, and materials handling. Managing workers with dissimilar functional training requires more in-depth knowledge and skills in human relations, decision-making, problem-solving, delegation, etc., than necessary for the previous group.

Group 3: Senior management; conceptual, strategic, visionary, entrepreneurial leaders — Have the knowledge and skills of manager in Groups 1 and 2 but also know how to research the

Table 1.1 Life Cycle of a Leader

Organizational Level	(1) Technical-Functional (Engineering, Accounting, Marketing, etc.)	(2) Administrative-Operational Planning (Human Relations, Goal Setting, Decision-Making, Problem-Solving, etc.)	(3) Strategic-Entrepeneurial (Strategic Thinking Scenarios, Issue Planning, Strategic Response, Organizational Designs, etc.)	Total
Senior management	10%	20%	70%	100%
CEO, COO Vice president Directors				
Middle management	30%	50%	20%	100%
Department heads Functional managers Product managers Project managers Team leaders				
First-line supervision	75%	20%	5%	100%

future, develop scenarios of future markets, and make resource commitment decisions today to be in a position to exploit tomorrow's market opportunities.

The distinction between the talents required to manage each of these three groups successfully can best be seen by studying the life cycle in the development of a corporate executive or leader (see Table 1.1). According to the AACSB study, the importance of making a distinction between requirements for managing at the various management levels of the organization is that each level calls for separate course materials and a curriculum of its own, taught by instructors familiar with the managing problems at each level.[9]

1.3   Strategic Plans vs. Strategic Management System

As mentioned earlier, for strategic planning to be successful it must be visualized not as a single plan, but as a system of management plans and decisions. The strategic plans address the most important decisions the organization must make; yet, they are the least systematized of all managerial decisions.[12] This lack of systematic thinking can partially be explained by the fact that the terminology of systematic strategic decision-making is relatively new, dating back to the 1960s.[13]

Systems planning has been defined as a set of interrelated decisions that are too large and complex to handle in one plan.[14] The strategic plan itself is not an action plan; it formulates the strategies that will be used to guide the allocation of resources to long-range growth opportunities. It stops short of stating how the strategies will be implemented. The strength of the strategies will determine the organization's potential for profitable growth. This potential, however, will never be reached without administrative and operational plans to execute them. For the strategic management concept to succeed, senior executives, both domestic and global, must learn to couple all three of these plans — strategic, operational, and administrative — into an interrelated planning system.

The strategic planning system is composed of a set of interrelated questions, issues, and decisions that identify and select tomorrow's markets and product offerings. The operational system relates to the questions, issues, and decisions that will be needed to meet today's budget.

1.4   External vs. Internal Issues

The strategic concept for managing resources has been around as a management tool since the late 1950s. The substance of the concept has been extolled, debated, and interpreted by literally hundreds of lectures, articles, and books. Too many of these articles are, in essence, management fads offered as catch-phrased silver bullets that can solve anything that ails the bottom-line of the financial statement.[15]

These silver bullets are very tempting to ambitious managers eager to show they are on the cutting edge of state-of-the-art management. The ideas in and of themselves are not bad; the mistake is in believing that bright ideas and catchy phrases can substitute for the fundamentals of good management. Despite all of the attention it has been given, only a small percentage of today's organizations practice state-of-the-art strategic management.

There are probably many reasons that could be given for this poor success rate, but the one most often heard is that neither the students nor the practitioners understand the concept well enough to practice it successfully.[16] This lack of understanding has been observed repeatedly since the early 1970s when Ackoff, in his now classic book, *A Concept of Corporate Planning*, stated:[16]

> "There is no lack of literature on the subject of corporate planning, nor is there a lack of opportunity for managers to hear lectures on the subject. However, I have the impression derived from discussions with many managers that most of them do not have a clear idea of what corporate planning should be. Most of the literature on the subject tends to be filled with either platitudes or technicalities. Platitudes are easy to understand but generally are useless; the technicalities are useful but less understandable."

This same theme has been emphasized by the McKinsey study in the early 1980s,[14] the Paul and Taylor study in the mid-1980s,[17] and in the 1990s by the Lazer et al.[18] book, *Marketing 2000 and Beyond.* An understanding of the strategic concept must start with the term "strategic". What does it really mean? Strategic to what? Anything that's important? Problem-solving? Re-engineering work groups? Organizational architecture? Changing corporate culture? Long-term profitable growth?

Because the founding fathers of the concept were General Electric, the McKinsey Group, and H.I. Ansoff,[11] it would seem logical to use their original definition for its purpose and meaning. There does not seem to be any disagreement in their minds that the term "strategic" referred to the long-term profitable growth of an organization, to manage the organization's resources strategically. When a firm commits a significant amount of resources to achieve long-term profit, it makes a strategic decision.

This use of the term "strategic" limits its use for planning purposes to those issues that directly relate the organization's resources to opportunities in its external environment, its markets, customer needs, and the competition. All other issues are to be classified as internal issues or problems and addressed in separate administrative or operational plans.

According to Shirley, in the original strategic concept only the issues that meet the following tests are, in a planning sense, strategic issues, and the contents of the strategic plan should be limited to those issues that meet these five tests:[19]

>   Test 1 — Is it directed toward defining the organization's relationship to its external environment: its markets, customer needs, or competition?
>
>   Test 2 — Does it take the organization or business as a whole as its unit of analysis?
>
>   Test 3 — Is it multi-functional in character? That is, does it depend on informational inputs from more than one functional area for its answer?
>
>   Test 4 — Will it provide direction for and constraints on the growth and development of the administrative and operational activities?
>
>   Test 5 — Is it of major importance to the growth and success of the organization? All changes in the environment are not major to the success of the organization even if they meet all four of the above strategic tests.

1.5   Dealing With Strategic and Non-Strategic Issues

Strategic plans are developed to deal with the strategic issues facing an organization. CEOs must resolve many problems and deal with developments as part of their responsibilities, but only those that are truly strategic in nature should be included in the strategic plan; otherwise, the planning will drift from its purpose, lose its focus, and become a less-effective instrument for achieving organization growth. Non-strategic issues should be dealt with by one of the other many company plans, such as the capital budget, the manpower development plan, one of the functional area plans, the research and development plan, and so forth.

An issue is any condition, development, or trend which, if allowed to continue, could have a significant effect on the company's success; however, a strategic issue has even more significant characteristics and consequences. A strategic issue is one that has the potential to change the relationship between the organization and the industry business climate in which it must operate and compete.[19]

Two significant characteristics are contained within the above definition. First, a strategic issue is highly important and must be dealt with (i.e., it cannot be delayed), or the company could be caught in a dangerous misalignment with its environment, and this may cause negative financial consequences. It could mean, for instance, missing the chance to take advantage of an opportunity that has just emerged. Second, the organization's current market share may be affected by the situation. These two characteristics can be used to test an issue to see if it is strategic or not.

Using these two tests, let us separate some hypothetical issues facing a CEO to see which issues are strategic in nature:

Issue 1 — Congress is considering a bill which, if passed, would ban the sale of your brand of a product, but not the brands of some rivals.

Issue 2 — A major competitor has just marketed an improved version of their product which greatly improves the value of their brand to the buyer, as compared with your brand. It will be marketed to the same customers you seek, starting in 3 months.

Issue 3 — One of your major warehouses on the west coast has just burned down. This has completely destroyed 3 months' supply of product inventory, including several of your leading selling brands.

Issue 4 — The chairman of the board of directors insists that the company purchase a new fleet of jets so that less time is wasted by traveling company executives.

Which of these four issues would you judge to be strategic? If you said the first two, you are correct; they satisfy both tests. But, while the company's current market share could temporarily be weakened by issue 3, it would not fundamentally alter the relationship between the company and its business climate. Besides, new inventories would be quickly built to replace the lost products, and future market share would probably be unaffected. Issue 4 is unique because of who suggested the idea. The chairman of the board is the superior of the CEO, and the recommendation must be dealt with. But, the issue does not satisfy either of the tests; therefore, it is not a strategic issue. It would be better dealt with by being included in the capital budget if the idea is approved by the board.

Strategic issues generally have a long-term impact on the future of the firm in question. They could blow away market share, reduce the firm's ability to compete in a fierce battle for long-term survival, and chip away its position in the market. Anytime that a firm has to allocate scarce resources, with the notion of irreversibility (externally oriented) in mind, it is making a strategic decision. Once a scarce resource, such as human or financial assets, is allocated, that resource cannot be deployed for other market opportunities, thus the significance of understanding strategic sense.

To provide a further example of how one can identify strategic vs. non-strategic issues, let us look at a hospital, which like any other business unit has to compete for patients and other clients. The chief executive of this hospital is faced with five issues that need to be scrutinized closely in order to determine the course of action to be taken. These issues appear as critical issues in Table 1.2.

The chief executive discovered from his analysis that three of the issues were strategic and needed to be included in his plan. The other two (a computerized system for the pharmacy and the need for more nurses) were important but not strategic in nature; therefore, they would be dealt with in the hospital's capital budget and manpower plans.

Because planners do not have a crystal ball to tell them what will happen in the future, issues can only be studied in terms of assumptions. Assumptions are used to create a scenario of what tomorrow's industry could look like if the trend continues and the issue emerges. But, in order to do that, the executive needs to have a profound knowledge of the industry in which the firm operates. An analysis of this industry begins with identifying and understanding the participants of that industry followed by in-depth identification of their behavior and the relative strengths and weaknesses of the forces that work within that industry. Every company has to formulate and implement strategies that give it some distinctive advantage that other members of the industry may not have or may not have enough of. Fundamentally, the core of strategy formulation is how to cope with the forces that shape an organization's operations as it relates to its markets it desires to serve. It is not only this feature that determines the level and intensity of competition. The other forces are equally, if not more, important in determining the outcome, i.e., the long-term profitability of the firm. The other forces mentioned above include suppliers of goods or services to the firm, buyers of the goods or services that the firm produces, society's concerns, economic cycles and trends, substitutes that can be used as

Table 1.2 Identifying Strategic Issues for a Hospital

Critical Issues	Does this issue have the potential to change the relationship that exists between the organization and its business climate?	Is this issue of major importance? Will it affect our market share?	Is it strategic or is it non-strategic?
Issue 1. A large, nationally known medical clinic and hospital are reported to be locating a satellite in this area soon.	Yes	Yes	Strategic
Issue 2. A new bill before Congress would decrease Medicare payments.	Yes	Yes	Strategic
Issue 3. The hospital experiences many complaints about its pharmacy service; there is a need for a new computerized drug-dispensing system.	No	Yes	Non-strategic
Issue 4. There is a serious shortage of nurses for the night shift.	No	Yes	Non-strategic
Issue 5. The medical service needs new diagnostic equipment to stay competitive.	Yes	Yes	Strategic

ingredients in the production process, governmental influences, legal system decisions, and the threats that new entrants to the industry may pose. These forces are discussed next to set the stage for the rest of the concepts in the chapters that follow.

In a recent interview with *Fortune* magazine, Louis V. Gerstner, the new Chief Executive Officer of IBM, was asked what he thought of the previous CEO's financial goal for 1992–93 of 18% on equity, 8% on assets plus $4 billion in free cash flow, and a reduction in administrative expenses of 23%. Gerstner replied, "That is the first time I have heard them, so I am not sticking to them. ... I am spending time trying to understand our competitive position, and how we are serving customers. Out of our competitive strategy will come the right set of financial objectives."[20] Additionally, when firms begin to lose the direction they are taking and have no strategic focus (such as Gerstner's focus on serving customers), they tend to take a course of action which has no pilot, no navigator, and no pre-set pattern which can be used to arrive at the correct destination. This is particularly relevant in today's environmentally turbulent times.

For instance, in 1972, IBM, General Motors, and Sears and Roebuck were enjoying market values of $46.8, $23.2, and $18.2 billion, respectively, and were considered to be leading corporate giants in their particular industries of high tech, manufacturing, and retailing. Ten years later, while IBM was still number one in market value, both Sears and General Motors had lost value and ranking. In 1992, they no longer appeared in the top 20 largest global corporations in terms of stock market valuation. All three firms had changed their leaders and were in search of focus and market positions. It took the loss of $4.5 billion in 1991 for GM to wake up and begin a search for new direction. IBM lost close to $5 billion in 1992,[20] and Sears' losses have been so immense that it may never achieve the preeminence that it once enjoyed.

Other changes in the making are seen in long distance communication. In 1984, MCI and Sprint enjoyed 4.5 and 2.7%, respectively, of U.S. market share, with 90.1% being dominated by AT&T. In 1992, MCI and Sprint each had increased their market share to 16.6 and 8.9%, respectively, and AT&T has seen its market share drop to 62.2%. The competition for market share between rivals in an industry has a lot to do with long-term profitability in that industry. The degree of rivalry is a function of many factors, most important among them being long-term profitability. But, this may not always be the same for all industries.

While competition in some industries (such as the airline industry) is very intense, in other industries (such as pharmaceuticals) competition takes a completely different form. The reason is that these two particular industries have different features, and competition is pursued differently and uses different strategies.

In the pharmaceutical industry, competition depends not on price cutting to attract market share, but on the duration of patents on drugs, the need for a high-quality detail sales force, long-term investment in research, and the relative price insensitivity of patients. A typical patient is concerned about relieving pain and gaining good health and not so much with the cost of the medication, because in many cases the cost is borne by the insurance carrier. Due to these production and market features and the fact that any new drug might cost over $100 million to develop and introduce to the market, the pharmaceutical industry has witnessed immense stability, notwithstanding the federal government regulations that are particularly more meticulous in this industry.

1.6 Globalization

For years, many American executives' concerns and objectives were preoccupied only with American markets. However, a number of major events have changed, or will change, this domestically focused outlook. Some of the underlying forces that affect the crafting of a global strategy could be summed up as:

1. There is global competition in the transfer of both high- and low-paying jobs.
2. Automation, which has enhanced productivity at profitable corporations such as Ford, Toyota, Honda, etc., has continued to erode the manufacturing sector's share of the labor force and will continue to impact management decision-making for the rest of the decade of the 1990s and beyond.
3. Many industries are laying off workers at an increasing rate, and high-paying jobs in defense and aerospace are not available anymore.
4. There is increasing evidence of global segmentation and market integration by some companies which tends to impact fundamental management actions such as the search for market

Table 1.3 Employment in the Manufacturing Sector

Country	1961[a]	1991[a]
South Korea	6	25
Taiwan	15	31
Singapore	14	27
Malaysia	6	16
Thailand	3	10
Indonesia	5	10
Japan	21	23
Italy	28	22
Germany	37	32
Canada	22	15
France	28	20
Britain	36	27
United States	28	28

[a]   Percent of total labor force.

Source: Data from *The Economist,* February 20, 1993, p. 15.

opportunities, the making of investment decisions, and, therefore, the scope of strategic planning.

5. The decline of manufacturing's share of gross domestic product
(GDP) in most advanced economies produces additional challenges and opportunities. Over a 30-year period, the manufacturing sector went through some major shifts, although not by
the same percentage in each country (see Table 1.3).

The decline in manufacturing is partially offset by an increase in
some other sectors of the U.S. economy, most notably in the service
sector. During the 1982–1992 time period, the export of services by U.S.
companies increased from 20 to 40% as a share of total U.S. exports.
Services constituted $50 billion of the U.S. total export in 1993. This
increase suggests that there are market opportunities that other companies should identify and perhaps pursue. As countries deregulate their
economies and telecommunications services expand, there appear to be
many opportunities for such services as consulting, accounting, engineering, information systems, and, more recently, medical services provided by the health care sector. All such potential possibilities require

new thinking in market and positioning of resources to enhance market share over time. The top 50 U.S. corporations, which sell products in global markets, accounted for $140 billion of total U.S. exports in 1994. Some earned more than 50% of their revenue in overseas markets. The list includes the blue chips, such as IBM and Boeing, and others such as Gillette, Colgate, NCR, etc.

As a result, many major manufacturing companies now base their investment decisions on worldwide markets. Ford Motor Company's decision to invest $6 billion in England to produce the Ford Mondeo to reach all corners of Europe is a preemptive strategy to establish itself before rivals begin their efforts. With expanding global communications, CNN is now all over the world, and ABC has allied itself with BBC to compete with CNN News and to communicate information faster and more comprehensively than before.

1.7 The Thrust into Global Markets

Although American firms have been selling products in all corners of the world since World War II (for several decades after which such firms had no rivals), their recent thrust into world markets is not necessarily by choice. If they did not, they would lose even their domestic markets. Why? That is a reasonable question, and a typical student needs to know the background for this turn of events.

It all goes back to the beginning of the decade of the 1980s when, according to Bartlett and Ghosal,[21] "the powerful and dramatic impact of foreign competition, particularly from Japan, jolted awake most American managers." The $6 billion investment by Ford in Europe is the direct result of this dramatic event. Of course, that is followed by other giants of the American business sector. And, as pointed out by Luehman,[22] the fact remains that "behind every major resource-allocation decision a company makes lies some calculation of what that move is worth ... and allocation of resources, in turn, is a key driver of a company's overall performance."

What is even more important is that every move that one competitor makes is countered by a move by some other member of the industry. Just recently, Honda Motors Company launched its "global car", the International Accord, based on a single-platform concept adaptable to changes necessary for different markets. The result is expected to reduce the cost of an Accord by 20% for the company and to result in a lower price for the customer.[23]

Concomitant to this rapid move toward globalization of industries over the past few years is the proliferation of strategic alliances, linkages, mergers, and acquisition among firms in the same industry worldwide. These linkages cover mainly three options — capital participation, product supply, or technical tie-ups. By its nature and the intensity of competition, globalization enhances the value and productivity of some capabilities and at the same time diminishes the value of others, not necessarily in the same proportion. A global production scale and innovative ways of producing a product with minimum changes in the equipment that makes it (e.g., global platforms of Honda) are additional features that differentiate the future from the past in the marketplace.

Add to all of these variables the element of culture which, until recently, was not even a part of the calculus in business decisions. But, with business becoming more and more globalized, understanding national cultures and the deep differences that exist among different cultures can become a positive factor in making strategic decisions in the boardroom. It would be a grave mistake to consider such issues as cocktail party chat and not as issues that, once deeply understood and comprehended, can make significant contribution to economic performance of the enterprise.[24]

1.8   Summary

This chapter lays the foundation for the rest of the book. To begin, we could define governance of the enterprise and proceed to see how effectively an organization at the domestic and global markets can function. Harry Pearce, General Motors' general counsel, believes that "the difference is night and day" in regard to recent changes in the ways in which that company is governed. The changes have been brought as a result of dramatic movements in the global markets and pressure on the managers to be more precise about the nature of decision-making which ultimately may tie up scarce resources that, once committed, are not available for other purposes. The next chapter attempts to distinguish among decisions as being operational, administrative, and strategic. Such differentiation facilitates decision-making and down-the-line creation of a more productive organizational infrastructure.

References

1. *Webster's New World Dictionary*, 2nd. college ed., Simon & Schuster, New York, 1982, p. 604.
2. John A. Byrne, "The Guru of Good Governance," *Business Week*, April 28, 1997, pp. 100–101.
3. Robert L. Simison, "GM Board Adopts Formal Guidelines on Stronger Control over Management," *Wall Street Journal*, March 28, 1994, p. A4.
4. Steve H. Hank and Siralan Walters, "Governance," *Forbes*, April 11, 1994, p. 87.
5. John A. Byrne, "The CEO and the Board," *Business Week*, April 28, 1997, pp. 100–101.
6. Thomas J. McNichols, *Executive Policy and Strategic Planning*, McGraw-Hill, New York, 1983.
7. Harold Stieglitz, "The Chief Executive's Job: An International Perspective," *The Conference Board Record*, October 1969, p. 16.
8. Lyndall F. Urwick, *Voice of the Pharmacist*, Vol. VII, American Pharmaceutical Association, Chicago, IL, 1964, p. 1.
9. L.W. Porter and L.E. McKibben, *Management Education and Development*, McGraw-Hill, New York, 1988, pp. 225–229.
10. Michael E. Porter and Class van der Lind, "Green and Competitive Ending the Stalemate," *Harvard Business Review*, September-October 1995, p. 180.
11. H.I. Ansoff, *The New Corporate Strategy*, John Wiley & Sons, New York, 1988, pp. 57–58.
12. T.A. Smith, *Dynamic Business Strategy*, McGraw-Hill, New York, 1979, p. 104.
13. John Garland, Richard Farmer, and Marilyn Taylor, *International Dimensions of Business Policy and Strategy*, PWS-Kent Publishing, 1990, p. 85.
14. Frederick Gluck, Stephen Kaufman, and Steven Walleck, "The Four Phases of Strategic Management," *Journal of Business Strategy*, Winter, 1982, pp. 9–20.
15. Susana Barciela, "Management Fads No Substitute for Business Ethics," *Florida Times Union*, March 6, 1995, Business Section 1.
16. Russell L. Ackoff, *A Concept of Corporate Planning*, John Wiley & Sons, New York, 1970.
17. R.N. Paul and J.W. Taylor, "The State of Strategic Planning," *Business*, January-March 1986, pp. 39–40.
18. William Lazer, Prscilla LaBarbera, James MacLachlin, and Allen Smith, *Marketing 2000 and Beyond*, American Marketing Association, Boston, MA, 1990, p. 229.
19. R.C. Shirley, "Limiting the Scope of Strategy," *Academy of Management Review*, April 1982, pp. 262–268.
20. *Fortune*, August 1994.
21. C.A. Bartlett and S. Ghosal, *Strategic Management Journal*, Vol. 12, 1991, p. 5.
22. Timothy A. Luehman, *Harvard Business Review*, September-October, 1996, p. 132.
23. *Business Week*, September 8, 1997.
24. Geert Hofstede et al., *Strategic Management Journal*, Vol. 12, 1991, p. 165.

2 Strategic Leadership at General Electric: 1947 to 1997

The central focus of management should be "how to allocate resources to profitable global market opportunities."

2.1 Introduction

In the July 7, 1997, issue of *Business Week,* General Electric was cited as the most valuable company worldwide with market capitalization of \$198.09 billion.[1] The purpose of this chapter is to relate the systematic implementation of strategic planning at General Electric to market performance on a consistent basis over a 50-year period.

Before new management concepts are accepted, it seems they must pass through a phase where they are promoted with catchy buzzwords that emphasize certain aspects of the concept or represent a magic code word for improving it. They also must be subjected to attacks from the consulting fraternity, among whom each member attempts to differentiate his or her version of the concept.[2]

Today's strategic planning concept seems to be passing through these stages in its life cycle. It is being attacked as being too bureaucratic and staff oriented, not leveraging its resources, setting short-term incremental goals, focusing only on extent (existing) markets, and not democratizing its creative process. The list goes on.

2.1.1   Planning Buzzwords

Planning buzzwords carry with them an aura of excitement. They offer managers a chance to show their peers and bosses that they are on the cutting edge of change. Such buzzwords have been likened to silver bullets guaranteed to solve whatever ails your company's bottom line. Every year or so brings forth a new set of these silver bullets. Last year's offerings included, among others, re-engineering, restructuring, total quality control, and strategic architecture.

A recent issue of *Business Week* gives us a new set of buzzwords already on the horizon for tomorrow: co-evolution, white spaces, business ecosystems, value migration, strategic intent, and democratized creativity.[3] One expert on buzzwords has gone so far as to give us a series of tests we can use to see if our new buzzwords are really authentic.[4] To qualify, a new buzzword must meet the following five tests:

Test 1 — It must come from what purports to be an *authoritative source.*

Test 2 — It must provide an *instant cure* for your real or imagined problem.

Test 3 — It must cause the hearts of managers to go *pitty-pat* with anticipation.

Test 4 — It must of necessity *obscure the obvious* and at the same time make the uninitiated feel painfully inadequate for not recognizing the brilliant truth encapsulated in the buzzword.

Test 5 — Finally, it must *inspire pseudoactivity;* that is, it must make people think something important is happening while everything remains safely in place.

With this set of criteria managers can decide for themselves whether they are being offered a new, innovative planning idea, or an authentic buzzword.

2.1.2   Criticism: A Reality Check

Most critics target their attacks simply against strategic planning. The reader is left with the impression that there is only one version of strategic planning; unfortunately, there are many. There is the original version formulated at the General Electric Company;[5] the one taught at the business colleges as business policy;[6] the planning, programming, and budgeting version used by the government;[7] and, finally, the numerous hybrids taught by the consulting companies: strategic intent, strategic architecture, etc.[8]

While each of the above versions have their followers, most professional planners consider the original General Electric model to be the benchmark for strategic planning models.[9,10] To be of practical value, any validity check must answer one or more of these three questions:

1. Are these criticisms against the *concept* itself?
2. Are these criticisms against the way the various companies have chosen to *implement* the concept?
3. Or are these criticisms against both?

We started our validity check right at the beginning; we wanted to determine as closely as possible why management at General Electric felt the need to decentralize and adopt a new long-range planning model.

2.2　Planning at GE Prior to the Cordiner Era (1939–1950)

General Electric had its beginning in 1878 when a group of investors joined together to finance Thomas Edison's experiments with the incandescent lamp. The company prospered and grew over the years and by 1939 had $342 million in sales. Its sales volume, because of World War II, increased to $1.4 billion in 1943.

Charles Wilson, GE's Chief Executive Officer during the 1940s, recognized that with growth increases of this scale a new approach to management would be needed. In 1947, he asked Ralph Cordiner, then a young engineer, to study GE's growth problems and make some recommendations.

It was apparent to Cordiner, almost at the outset of his study, that the company needed a more decentralized way of making decisions, a longer range planning system, and more entrepreneurial-like managers to meet the growth challenges. After some soul-searching and thorough thinking, his basic recommendation was that the company decentralize their highly centralized decision-making process; for the organization to succeed, its managers should be endowed with the attributes of entrepreneurial small businessmen who could be held accountable for the results of their performance.

Cordiner defined decentralization as not breaking the company up into smaller, independent pieces, but rather as a way of preserving the strengths of a large company while adding the fast entrepreneurial decision-making of a smaller organization.[11]

GE's planning prior to 1947 and the Cordiner era consisted of an annual plan and capital budgeting to solve internal problems — what the McKinsey Study would classify as Phase I and II of a four-phase strategic planning system.[12]

2.3   Cordiner and the Entrepreneurial Era (1950–1963): Evolution of the Strategic Concept Under Ralph Cordiner

In 1950, Cordiner was made Chief Executive Officer and held this position until 1963.[13] It was during Cordiner's 13-year reign that the nucleus of GE's strategic planning concept was formulated.

A literature search for comments by General Electric officials and their colleagues has provided the authors with the following information about the philosophy and thinking behind the development of General Electric's strategic planning concept and some of the things they have done to implement and improve the concept over the last 50 years.

2.3.1   On the Rationale Behind General Electric Re-Organization

"The underlying rationale for re-organizing the General Electric Company that no organization chart can show is the drive we are trying to instill that will cultivate entrepreneurial decision-makers throughout the length and breadth of this mammoth organization. We want to put all of our managers constantly at risk; we want all of them to be real entrepreneurs."[5]

"The entrepreneurial organization seeks to change, anticipates threats, is opportunity oriented, and searches widely for alternatives. It concentrates on finding the right things to do (effectiveness) whereas the incremental company focuses on operational improvements (efficiency)."[14]

"Far too many of today's companies are filling their top management jobs with managers skilled in problem-solving. What they really need is entrepreneurial problem *formulators*. If corporations are to survive beyond the markets on which they were founded they must be capable of finding *new* markets and *new* customers."[15]

"Planning in many of today's companies has become strictly an administrative task of repeating a process; the creative qualities of strategy formulation have been lost. Imaginative ideas carrying more risk and uncertainty are being cast aside in favor of safer incremental objectives."[15]

"It's the Chief Executive's job to generate this entrepreneurial spirit throughout the organization in order that all managers stay alert for new business opportunities."[16]

2.3.2   On Entrepreneurial/Visionary Strategies

"A strategist first of all generates with his or her associates a vision of the business. That is to say, he or she has a clear picture of the business as it is today, but even more importantly 20 years in the future. Without such a vision to give direction, associates can do no more than drift with the economic current."[17]

2.3.3   On Resource Allocation, Strategies, and Risk

"The resources available (have or can get) to any organization after all are limited, and after his other associates have made a detailed study of the markets in an industry the chief executive must make the big and risky plans and decisions that commit the company's resources to the development or regeneration of its business. It is the responsibility of the chief executive to keep the enterprise profitable both in the short and long term."[18]

2.3.4   On the Marketing Management Concept

Articles on strategic planning rarely comment on the role that the so-called marketing management concept played in the formulation of General Electric's strategic planning concept. It not only played an important role, but was, in fact, the cornerstone on which the concept was built.[19]

Prior to 1957, almost all planning was internally oriented; that is, it was focused on problem-solving and making internal operations more efficient. In 1957, at an American Management Association meeting in New York City, Fred J. Borch announced to the business world marketing's new role at General Electric.[19] In the future, marketing would be both its *corporate philosophy* and one of the *functional disciplines* that would implement that philosophy. He defined corporate philosophy as the broad umbrella that governed all of the company's decisions and activities. By contrast, a *concept* was a recognized way of operating within the climate set by the philosophical umbrella.[19] Under this new philosophy, the customer would become the *pivot point* for all the corporation's activities.[19] As the pivot point around which all planning is done, the customer would now become the *central focus* for not only strategic but also *administrative* and *operational* planning, as well.

In making this announcement, Borch stated that focusing planning on markets and customers was not a new role for marketing. It was returning marketing to its original role under yesterday's owner-entrepreneur.[19] The customer was always the target for their technology and product planning. Yesterday's owner/entrepreneur was his own marketer, technologist, and interpreter of market change. Marketing was chosen as the communication link between the organization and its markets because of its daily contacts with its customers. It was already in position to identify and interpret the impact of change on the marketplace regardless of its source: technological, social, political, financial, or competitive.

2.3.5   General Electric's Marketing Concept

General Electric's new marketing concept was based on two fundamental premises:[21]

Premise 1 — Today's strategic planning lacks a unity of purpose, a central focus or theme, a primacy of decision values. Planning has been defined as the process of weighing the net effect of a set of interdependent decisions.[20] In the case of strategic planning, this would translate into the process of weighing the net effect of a set of interdependent strategic decisions. The marketing concept identifies this set of decisions as the set that allocates resources to market opportunities.

Premise 2 — All new opportunities for corporate growth must have clearly stated market targets.

This second premise stresses the fact that many organizations have grown too large to target their growth strategies at opportunities defined simply as profit opportunities. Strategies such as restructuring, right-sizing, cost-cutting, and divestiture of marginal businesses are certainly growth strategies and, if successful, will produce profit. This profit in turn will improve the organization's balance sheet, but are they truly long-term growth strategies? The answer to this question will depend on what management does with their cost-cutting profits. Only when these new profits are reallocated to market opportunities that produce profitable market share can they truly be called long-term growth strategies.[22]

In 1963, Borch succeeded Cordiner as Chief Executive Officer. From the above comments there can be little doubt that the strategic concept itself was formulated during Cordiner's tenure as Chief Executive Officer with contributions from his top aides, Borch and Reginald H. Jones. The concept had also become central to the core of GE's organizational culture.

The *intent* behind the decentralization and strategic planning concept was the company's drive to create a corporate culture or climate that would encourage entrepreneurial decision-makers and strategic thinkers in its management. The *mechanism* for developing this climate was to be an organized planning system consisting of entrepreneurial/strategic, administrative, and operational plans. Cordiner's successors — Borch, Jones, and John F. Welch, Jr. — have spent their reigns *implementing* the concept with adjustments for changing markets and their own leadership styles. It was hoped that by following the steps in the strategic planning concept, managers and leaders would be developed with the following characteristics:[23]

1. Visionaries, with a commitment to setting both short- and long-range goals
2. Decision-makers, with a willingness to take risks
3. A sense of inquisitiveness about the dynamics of their industries and markets
4. The ability to see implications and utility in shared relationships

2.3.6 Summary

By way of summarizing, the original General Electric strategic planning concept was

1.   Formulated for the purpose of getting its managers to think like entrepreneurs
2.   Based on two older planning concepts: (a) management by objectives, and (b) the marketing management philosophy or concept
3.   Developed to make markets and customer values the central focus for all corporate planning and decision-making: strategic, administrative, and operational
4.   Market focused, creating a set of plans and decisions that allocates resources to market opportunities, the most important decisions the organization makes; in McKittrick's words, "GE's primacy of decision values"
5.   Designed so that all available (have or can get) resources were to be committed (leveraged) in pursuit of the corporate long range objectives.
6.   Designed so that all managers could be evaluated on how well they performed against the intermediate goals set in the long-range strategic plan

General Electric's strategic planning concept was developed by Cordiner and his staff during the 1950–1963 period. His successors, Borch, Jones, and Welch, took the concept and put it into action — by adapting it to their own management styles, the way they liked to make decisions, and according to the changes taking place in dynamic, ever-changing, markets.

Very few, if any, of the following current criticisms of the strategic planning concept apply to the General Electric model:

Criticism 1 — *The concept itself is bureaucratic and staff oriented.* In Cordiner's own words, the purpose for strategic planning was to make GE's line managers entrepreneurial decision-makers. Bureaucratic planning occurs in the way management chooses to organize and implement the concept; if not a deliberate choice, strategic planning is allowed to drift into bureaucracy.

Criticism 2 — *It discourages risk-taking and the leveraging of resources.* The degree of risk in decision-making is a corporate management decision. All planning, including strategic plans, is governed by this corporate policy. Large organizations with tremendous assets can afford to take greater risk in their strategic decisions than can smaller, under-capitalized companies. Again, in Cordiner's own words, GE's planning should commit or leverage all of its available resources — that is, all it currently has or can get.

Criticism 3 — *Incremental profit goals conflict with long-range profitable market share.* Cordiner's line managers were to think and target their vision "as far as 20 years ahead." GE's primary goal under the marketing concept was to achieve a long-range profitable market share. Managerial performance was to be evaluated on how well the intermediate goals in the long-range business plan were met.

Criticism 4 — *Strategic planning focuses only on extent (existing) markets.* The GE strategic planning concept is based on the marketing concept. The marketing concept calls for shifting today's resources to tomorrow's market opportunities, using future market scenarios, competitive information, changing customer values, and market impact studies.

2.4   Borch and the Strategic Planning Era (1963–1971): Implementing the Strategic Concept

When Fred Borch took over from Cordiner, he inherited three major planning problems:

Problem 1 — The marketing concept had to be implemented, activated, and integrated into the strategic planning process.

Problem 2 — There was a need for greater corporate control over the semi-independent action of the 70 divisional vice-presidents. Their plans needed to be blended into an overall strategic plan before they were activated.

Problem 3 — The reviewing and presentation process for the strategic business unit plans were inefficient:
   - There were too many reviewing layers between the strategic business units and top management.
   - The staff planners were policing rather than facilitating.
   - The presentations were time consuming and contained many charts and statistics irrelevant to the strategies.

Because it was in Borch's corporate marketing department under Cordiner that the marketing concept was formulated, it was only natural that his first challenge would be to see that it was implemented properly. The marketing concept, in essence, stated that all planning and decision-making — strategic (entrepreneurial), administrative, and operational — started and ended with customers, their needs, and the competition to provide those needs.[24]

General Electric's size and diversity of its markets made implementing the marketing concept difficult. GE competed in almost every manufacturing industry, made over 200,000 products, and served millions of customers all over the world. The products varied in size and complexity from 10¢ light bulbs to giant steam turbines selling for $10 million.[5]

To help with this problem, Borch hired the McKinsey consulting firm. After studying the problem, McKinsey made two recommendations: add planning teams to the organizational structure and manage similar groups of product lines (businesses) in a portfolio.[25]

2.4.1   Strategic Business Units

Recommendation number one was to use a matrix organizational superimposing a horizontal staff planning team over the traditional vertical line-management organization. These planning teams would be responsible for seeing that long-range strategic planning got done according to the policies and planning model approved by corporate management. Line managers would be responsible for making both the strategic and day to day operational decisions. McKinsey called these planning teams *strategic business units.*

The staff/line relationship would be the same as for the other corporate functions: accounting, finance, legal, etc. The line managers would direct *all* planning activities and make all the decisions. For companies with more than one strategic business unit and where the information in the plans would be aggregated and approved at higher levels, a common model for gathering the information would be necessary. The corporate vice-president for planning would be responsible for developing the model for approval of the Chief Executive Officer. He or she would also be responsible for training the planners, troubleshooting, and checking to see the planning was done according to the model.

GE's new organizational structure was to consist of 10 groups, 50 divisions, 170 departments, and 43 strategic business units. A strategic business unit was defined as a market having sets of interrelated customers, a corporate sub-mission, and its own resources, competitive strategies, and budgets (see Figure 2.1).

2.4.2   Portfolio Management

McKinsey's second recommendation was to manage the 43 strategic business units as a collective group. The only results that counted would be the sum of their total activities. As this approach to managing resources was borrowed from the financial community's portfolio for balancing their investment mix, it was called *portfolio management.*[19]

With 43 business unit managers acting semi-independently to meet not only their own goals but also the goals of the corporation as a whole, some form of centralized control was needed. To fill the void, McKinsey recommended a modified version of the financial community's investment portfolio. The portfolio approach would centralize all resource allocation decisions at the corporate level. For new venture approvals, each strategic business unit would submit their best opportunities for new business with cost/benefit studies to a corporate planning committee. The opportunities would be prioritized according to their merit without regard to the source of the request. Some business units would get multiple approvals; others might get none.

The portfolio was to be a two-axis, nine-box, multi-factored grid. It was a simple method of displaying and prioritizing the business units and their markets according to their potential for growth and the degree of competition expected. The first axis displayed the attractiveness of the market (its growth potential).[26] It stated the stage at which the market was in its life cycle. The second axis stated the strength of the competition for this market (its competitive position; see Figure 2.2).

For the portfolio approach to succeed, each strategic business unit would require:

1.   A "sub-mission" of GE's corporate mission and its own set of financial objectives.
2.   In-depth studies of the markets in each strategic business unit.
3.   Competitive strategies and cost-benefit studies for each major market segment in the business unit
4.   Corporate resources allocated directly for use on approved strategies

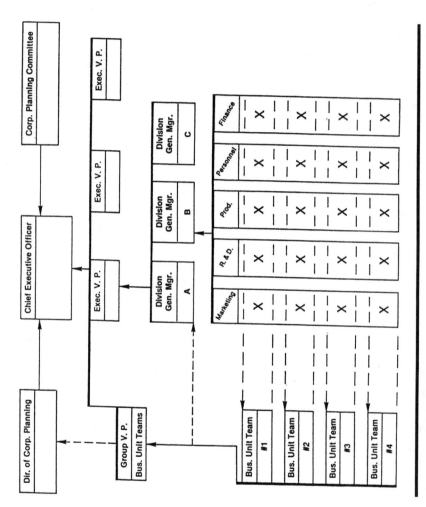

Figure 2.1 A Matrix Planning Structure

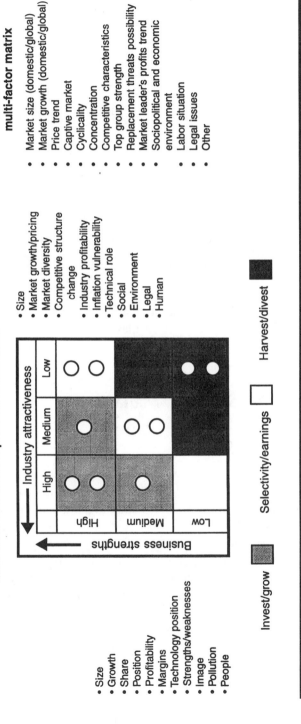

Checklist for a multi-factor matrix

- Market size (domestic/global)
- Market growth (domestic/global)
- Price trend
- Captive market
- Cyclicality
- Concentration
- Competitive characteristics
- Top group strength
- Replacement threats possibility
- Market leader's profits trend
- Sociopolitical and economic environment
- Labor situation
- Legal issues
- Other

GE's multi-dimensional portfolio assessment

- Size
- Market growth/pricing
- Market diversity
- Competitive structure change
- Industry profitability
- Inflation vulnerability
- Technical role
- Social
- Environment
- Legal
- Human

Industry attractiveness

Business strengths

	High	Medium	Low
High	○ ○	○	○ ○
Medium	○	○ ○	
Low			○ ○

Invest/grow · Selectivity/earnings · Harvest/divest

- Size
- Growth
- Share
- Position
- Profitability
- Margins
- Technology position
- Strengths/weaknesses
- Image
- Pollution
- People

Figure 2.2 Nine-Box Matrix. The nine-box matrix is best employed for multi-factor analysis rather than one- or two-dimensional analysis. It is the same basic matrix as in Figure 2.1, but the factors that GE uses to study an individual business' strengths are listed on the left of the box, and the key matching factors for industry assessment are on the right. Note that in all cases the categories correspond exactly or overlap. Cross-matrix analysis is rich in opportunity for suggesting some of the underpinnings of profitability and illuminating strategy options. Matrices need not be look-alikes. Management can decide which factors and how many are relevant for their circumstances; however, this is a useful checklist of factors to be considered as a first step. (Adapted from Bruce Henderson, "Market Share-ROI Corporate Strategy Approach Can Be an Oversimplistic Snare," *Marketing News,* December 1978.)

5.   Intermediate and final goals to be set for each strategy
6.   Performance to be judged not on short-term profits but whether the intermediate goals in the strategic plan had been met

2.4.3   Summary

We can summarize Borch's contribution to GE's strategic planing concept as follows:

1.   The marketing management concept on which the strategic planning concept was based was formulated in Borch's corporate marketing department while Cordiner was Chief Executive Officer.
2.   With the aid of the McKinsey consulting group, Borch developed the technique of implementing the marketing concept with strategic business units.
3.   Again with the aid of the McKinsey group, Borch contributed to the application of the portfolio management technique for managing independent strategic business units as a collective group.

2.5   Jones and the Strategic Management Era (1972–1981): Implementing the Strategic Concept

When Borch retired in 1972, he passed on problems number two and three to his hand-picked successor, Reginald Jones. After studying the problems for six months, Jones was ready to act. He had decided that:

Problem 2 — The lack of corporate control over the divisions and business units was caused by his three vice-chairmen not having line responsibility for the units reporting to them. This issue of control was never more apparent than when GE decided to expand in Europe through acquisitions and mergers. In their haste to get candidates for their divisions, GE's 70 divisional vice-presidents stumbled all over each other without any concern for the corporation as a whole. Jones stated this kind of rudderless, bureaucratic bungling should never happen again.[27]

Problem 3 — The process for reviewing the strategic plans was inefficient, the presentations were verbose, and many of the strategies were lacking in substance. The intermediate layers of management were designed to be transparent for reviewing plans and opaque for control purpose. In practice, they were both translucent. The intermediate layers of management inputs into the plans were supposed to be made during the development stages of the plans.[28]

As for the presentations, they were time consuming and filled with irrelevant charts and statistics, and in many cases the strategies themselves were unimaginative. Jones described the kind of presentations he wanted. The presenters would stand before the reviewers without visual aids of any kind and state their strategies and plans in clear, concise statements.[29]

To attain better corporate control over the actions of the divisions and business units, Jones made his three vice-chairmen responsible for the plans and financial results of all units reporting to them. They had been responsible only for setting general policy (see Figure 2.3). In the new organization, Welch, age 37, became the youngest group vice-president in GE history (see Figure 2.4).[30] The new organization did improve the corporate control problem, and the presentations were better organized, but it did not entirely solve the problems. GE's planning system was still too bureaucratic.

At the 1977 General Management Conference, Jones announced his second attempt to make the system more efficient. Even though GE's corporate health had never been stronger, if the company were to compete successfully in the 1980s, further improvements would have to be implemented throughout the GE system.

He proposed naming five sector vice-presidents, and Welch was one of them. These sector vice-presidents would serve as the spokesmen and worldwide planners for all of the units reporting to them. They would report to two rather than three vice-chairmen. Their first assignment would be to re-assess their strategic plans from a worldwide perspective. This would include industry overlapping, technological needs, market opportunities, and competitive strengths.[31] In the sector concept, strategic business units were flexible; they could be as large as a division or group or as small as a department or product line, depending on market conditions.

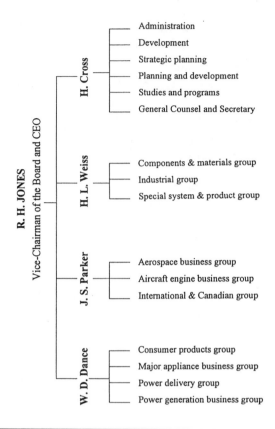

Figure 2.3 GE Organizational Chart

The new worldwide sector assessments led to GE reorganizing its businesses into six broad business arenas:[32]

1. Energy
2. Communication, information, and sensing
3. Energy application — productivity
4. Materials and sources
5. Transportation and propulsion
6. Pervasive services such as financial, distribution, and construction

These six business arenas would be markets in which GE could compete in the 1980s. Because these markets cut across industry lines, Jones declared GE would have to consider co-venturing alliances with

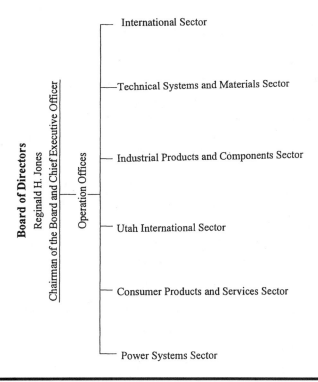

Figure 2.4 GE Organizational Chart

other companies around the world. Co-venturing and working as partners rather than bosses would not come easy for GE's managers, who had been taught to believe that GE could do anything internally (see sector organizational charts).

By 1978, Jones had narrowed down his search for a successor to Edward E. Hood, John F. Burlingham, and John F. Welch, Jr., and all three were promoted to vice-chairmen.[33] In 1981, Jones felt that GE's thrust for the 1980s had been clearly stated:

1. Their overall growth strategy would be to match their technology to markets worldwide in electronics, genetics, and industrial engineering.
2. Their growth would come from concentrating their technology on six specific worldwide markets.
3. GE's strategic planning had reached the stage where the concepts were well grounded; each new chief executive could adapt them to current market conditions and their own management style.

To lead the company into the 1980s, Jones named Welch. When making the announcement, Jones, in true GE tradition, stated that on April 2, 1981, he would retire completely from GE By severing completely his connections with GE, he was sending a message that he fully supported Welch's appointment and the strategies he would pursue in the 1980s.[34] By selecting Welch, he stated he had chosen someone to manage in tomorrow's markets, not today's or those in the past. Upon Jones' retirement, the *Wall Street Journal* had this to say about his leadership:[35]

> "Mr. Jones left a legacy of management skill so respected that other companies paid GE to teach them its management techniques, or better yet wooed away their executives."

Jones' contributions to implementing General Electric's strategic concept can be summarized as follows:

1. His organizational changes did gain corporate control over the plans and activities of the divisions and businesses units.
2. The management layers reviewing the strategic business unit plans were reduced from 43 to six.
3. Strategic planning became worldwide and could cut across industries through the office of sector vice-presidents.
4. The overall growth strategy for the next decade was developed jointly with his handpicked successor, Welch.
5. The length of the presentations and substance of the strategies were still unfinished business.

2.6   Welch and the Strategic Thinking and Visionary Leadership Era (1981–)

When John Welch took over as chief executive, the first thing he did was to make it clear the kind of a leader he wanted to be:[36]

1. *Visionary* — one who leads from a vision of what he or she wants their organization to become
2. *Communicator* — one who can articulate a vision so clearly and logically that the troops not only understand it, but share it.
3. *Organizer* — a leader who can build an efficient, non-bureaucratic organization that can adapt a vision to changing global market conditions, so that it can be implemented successfully

His managers were to be entrepreneurs, not bureaucrats. Decisions were to be made at the lowest possible organizational level. GE would have the speed and agility of a small company, while operating from the strength and stability of a giant organization.[35]

To emphasize how far he would go to get the kind of management he wanted, he stated that everything about GE's management was to be challenged:

1. The way strategic planning was done
2. The way decisions were made
3. The role of corporate staff and the vice-presidents
4. The degree to which external growth (acquisitions, mergers, networking, and alliances) would impact on GE's future

If this sounds familiar, it is. This is the same leadership gospel GE had preached since Cordiner's reign 20 years earlier,[5] the only difference being that Welch's version was delivered with more emphasis and in more detail. His basic objectives for GE were (1) to have all of GE's business units number one or number two in their markets, and (2) to compete in arenas that could be defined simply by drawing three circles of interrelated markets:

Circle 1 — High-technology markets, which then accounted for 33% of GE's business

Circle 2 — Service markets, which then accounted for 33% of GE's business

Circle 3 — GE's core markets: major appliances, lighting, motor transportation, turbines, and contractor equipment, which then accounted for 18% of GE's business.

The remaining 16% of GE's current businesses within a reasonable length of time would have to become number one or number two in their markets or be considered for divestment.

Short-term incremental goal setting was out; long-range stretch goals were in. Incremental goals are internally oriented; they were set as annual increases over GE's previous year's performance. Stretch goals, however, are externally oriented, and they were set to compare GE's performance, not against itself, but against increases in the total market.

Welch defined stretch goals as follows:

1. They should be stated in clear, concise terms.
2. They should be translated into one or two stretch targets.
3. If possible, they should be benchmarked to show that although they are quantum leaps they are not impossible (for example, GE's stretch goal of 23% return on investment was 7.4% higher than GE's present return; however, its chief rival, Westinghouse, had a return for the same period of 22%).

2.6.1   GE's Growth Strategies for the 1990s

To match GE's technology profitability to market opportunities world-wide, GE planned to increase revenue shares in China, India, and Mexico to $20 billion by the year 2000, or 25% of GE's total sales. GE manages markets, not factories. Using a strategy called "smart bomb", GE can investigate potential cities for investment in regard to their having top experts in quality, technology, service, manufacturing, and other skills necessary to provide an infrastructure that could produce a 20 to 25% return on investment (see *Fortune*, July 21, 1997). India met the conditions, but China failed.

2.6.2   Changing a Bureaucratic Planning Process

During his first 4 months in office, Welch traveled and had conversations with managers at all levels of the company. When he finished his travels, he was ready to make his first changes in GE's planning process:[37]

1. To re-emphasize GE's commitment to growth through high technology and the technical service markets, he elevated both to sector-level importance.
2. All business unit presentations were to be limited to the key issues in the plan.
3. The requirement that each business unit have a new competitive strategy each year was dropped. If the strategy were successful, they would only be reviewed every 2 or 3 years.

In 1981, Welch described the history of strategic planning in these terms:[38] "Our strategic planning system was dynamite when we first put it in. The thinking was fresh and the form mattered little. We then hired a head of planning, he hired two vice-presidents, they each hired an assistant, the plan books got thicker and thicker, and the meetings got longer and longer."

In 1985, Welch reduced the layers of management from the corporate offices to the factory floor from nine to four. The 14 strategic business units, each with a planning staff, now reported directly to the chief executive or one of his two vice-chairmen. In total, the planning staffs were cut in half, from 400 to 200.[39]

In 1986, the Executive Council, consisting of the chief executive, the two vice-chairmen, the corporate staff, and 14 strategic business unit managers, was formed to review the strategic business unit plans.[36]

In 1988, Bossidy, one of Welch's vice-chairmen, startled his audience by stating that GE no longer did strategic planning. He hastily added, however, that when they deserted strategic planning, they certainly did not abandon strategic thinking or strategic management. Strategic thinking is thinking about markets, customers, and the competition (the marketing concept).[40]

In 1990, Welch limited the business unit plan presentations to five key issues, each of which was to have only one page of written material:

1. Market conditions
2. Technology
3. Competition
4. Profitability
5. Competitive strategies

In 1993, the strategic business units were reduced to 12 (from 14), and Welch stressed three important themes for GE's management and decision-making:[41]

1. Speed, in everything GE does
2. Stretch, for every goal or target set
3. Boundaryless, in all GE's decision-making and behavior

In 1996, Welch stated GE had four types of leaders:[42]

Type 1 — delivers on commitments and believes in GE's small-company values and is an entrepreneur, a market-oriented risk-taker, and speedy decision-maker; their future with GE: onward and upward.

Type 2 — neither meets commitments nor shares GE's small-company values; their future with GE: won't last long.

Type 3 — believes in GE's values but sometimes misses commitments; their future with GE — usually given second chance.

Type 4 — delivers on short-term results but without regard for GE's values and future; their future with GE: they're out.

Removing Type 4 managers was the ultimate test of Welch's leadership.

In 1997, GE was reported to be the most valuable corporation in the world with a market capitalization of $198.09 billion.[1] General Electric was at the top of the world's industrial enterprises and, in the eyes of the investors, the top of the blue chips.

2.6.3 GE's Growth Strategy for the XXIst Century

GE's overall growth strategy for the XXIst century is[43]

1. To continue to build and hold business outside the U.S., starting with Jones' expansion into Europe in the 1970s and the push for greater market penetration into the Pacific Rim, China, India, and Mexico.

2. To start what Welch called his *third revolution:* the push for a larger share of the technical service markets that spring from GE's core industrial strengths of engines, industrial and health care equipment, etc.

In 1980, GE's service business accounted for only 16.4% of their profit. In 1996, profits from the service sector amounted to 60% of GE's total profit. Profit margins in the service industry were normally 50% higher than for product sales, and revenues from service contracts for maintaining its industrial equipment alone amounted to $7.8 billion, equal to 11% of GE's revenues. These revenues were projected to more than double by the year 2000 to $18 billion.

In 1994, as an indication of its thrust into technical services, GE started signing exclusive multi-year service contracts with large hospital chains and buying up independent service shops. In 1996, GE signed a 10-year, $2.3 billion contract with British Airways to service 85% of the engines in their fleet, which included engines made by GE's rivals Rolls-Royce and Pratt & Whitney. Also in 1996, GE Medical bought National Medical Diagnostics, a leading independent servicer of hospital imaging equipment. GE Medical recently spent $80 million building a state-of-the-art center complete with a television studio to develop educational programs; for fees ranging from $3000 to $20,000, hospitals can tune in to live broadcasts on subjects such as mammography techniques.

GE projects a billion dollar business in the operation and maintenance of power plants for utilities in U.S. and Europe. GE recently signed a contract with the GE/Burlington Northern Railroad to sell and service 150 new DC-powered engines. It is also developing an electronic tracking system to help railroads manage rolling stock more efficiently.

2.6.4 Selecting Welch's Successor

While Welch is set to retire in the year 2000, rumors are flying about who will be his successor.[44] Following in the footsteps of his predecessors and true to GE tradition, this would be a two-step process: (1) Welch and his top management team would conduct research and decide on the overall growth strategy that GE would pursue in the next decade, and (2) the member of his top management team whom he felt was best qualified to implement the new growth strategy would be his successor.

As of May 5, 1997 (*Forbes*),[45] there appeared to be seven candidates for his job:

1. David Calhoun, 40, CEO, GE Transportation Systems
2. David Cote, 44, CEO, GE Appliances
3. Jeffrey Immelt, 41, CEO, GE Medical Systems
4. James McHenry, 47, CEO, GE Lighting
5. Robert Nardeli, 49, CEO, GE Power Systems
6. Gary Reiner, 42, Senior V.P., GE Chief Information Officer
7. James Rogers, 46, CEO, GE Motors and Industrial Systems

Who will ultimately become the fifth General Electric CEO remains to be seen!

2.6.5 Summary

Welch's contribution to improving GE's planning process can best be summarized with his own self-stated three revolutions:

Revolution 1 — successfully penetrating the markets of China, India, and Mexico by matching GE high technology to emerging market opportunities.

Revolution 2 — completing the task started 50 years ago by Cordiner of making entrepreneurs out of GE's managers by removing bureaucracy from the planning process. This can be done in three ways: (1) by making decisions with the agility and speed of a small company operating from the strength of a giant organization; (2) by replacing planning books of statistics, forms, and charts with strategic thinking confined to the key elements of competitive strategy — markets customer needs and the competition response to these needs (a return to GE's marketing concept); and (3) by reducing the layers of management reviewing the strategic plans from the nine to four, with the presentation made on five key issues by the strategic business unit managers directly to the executive council — the chief executive, his two vice-chairmen, the corporate staff, and the 12 strategic business unit managers.

Revolution 3 — Formulating the overall growth strategy for the XXIst century: (1) complete the strategies to penetrate global markets, and (2) sign service contracts with large customers of GE equipment to service not only GE equipment, but also the competitors' equipment (stretch the application of inherent competencies) and to train their personnel in the technique of maintaining GE equipment.

2.7   A Critique of General Electric's 50 Years of Strategic Planning

Reviewing the industry of strategic planning at General Electric reveals hidden truths about their version of the concept and the company culture that developed chief executives that implemented it successfully over a period of 50 years.

The GE company in 1950 under Cordiner did not set out to develop a new planning concept. They were looking for a corporate style of management that would produce managers who could think and make decisions with the agility of small business entrepreneurs. The style of management they selected was their version of the strategic planning concept: an organized approach for developing managerial entrepreneurs.

The question is, then, has their version of the strategic planning concept produced entrepreneurial leaders? Let's look at the record:

1. Cordiner and his team of managers adapted the concept to the 1950s, and GE's profits soared to their highest levels in 65 years.[24]
2. Borch used the same concept adapted to the 1960s and raised profits from $272 million in 1963 to $573 million in 1972.[46]
3. Jones adapted it successfully to the 1970s. Profits rose from $661 million in 1973 to $1514 million in 1980.[46]
4. Welch, with his own unique style of management, completed the job started by Cordiner in 1950; as mentioned previously, GE has been judged the most valuable company in the world with a market value of $198.09 billion.[1] 1996 recorded a net income of $7.25 billion on revenue of about $78 billion.[47]

Up until the 1950s, all planning, including strategic, was *internally* oriented, focused on problem-solving, cost-cutting, and efficiency. GE changed all this in 1957 when they announced a radical change in their planning philosophy. Their new approach would be based *externally* on market conditions. Competitive strategies based on an analysis of markets would be formulated to guide management's commitment of resources to both current and emerging market opportunities.

GE called this new planning philosophy the "marketing concept",[19] and since 1950 all four chief executives — Cordiner, Borch, Jones, and Welch — have based their strategic planning on the marketing concept. To quote Welch, GE's current chief executive, on marketing's importance to strategic planning: "Without marketing's input, strategic planning would not be capable of charting a marketing course, or navigating a successful growth strategy."[48]

Unique features of the GE version of strategic planning, other than the marketing concept, include a disciplined yet flexible concept — disciplined in that certain steps must be followed. The planning information must be gathered in such a way that it can be aggregated and studied at the corporate level. Planning reviews are limited to one-page presentations of the five key strategic issues:

1. Market conditions
2. Technology

3. Competition
4. Profitability
5. Recommended competitive strategies

The concept is flexible in that business unit managers are free to use any methods they choose to analyze markets and the competition: portfolio management, cross-impact analysis, vulnerability assessments, or any other analytical technique.

GE judges and rewards its managers not on short-term incremental increases over the previous year, but rather on how well they have performed against the intermediate goals approved in their long-range strategic plan. Some of these goals are financial, some non-financial.

GE's overall growth strategy for the next decade is a determining factor in the selection of the next chief executive. The strategy is determined first; the executive whose talents best match tomorrow's growth needs gets the job. Welch was selected because he had demonstrated the ability to match GE's core technology to worldwide market opportunities.[49]

True to the McKinsey study model, the GE version of strategic planning evolved over time through four distinct phases culminating in Welch's state-of-the-art, phase IV planning — truly the strategic planning prototype for the XXIst century.[12]

References

1. J. Warner, "A New Breed of Blue Chips," *Business Week,* July 8, 1997.
2. Robert C. Shirley, "Limiting the Scope of Strategy: A Decision-Based Approach," *Academy of Management Review,* 1982, p. 262.
3. John A. Byrne, "Strategic Planning: It's Back!," *Business Week,* Aug. 26, 1996, pp. 46–50.
4. John R. Graham, "Why Business Has So Much Faith in Buzzwords," *Marketing News,* May 10, 1993, pp. 4–5.
5. John Thackeray, "The Management Ways of General Electric," *Dun's Review and Modern Industry,* Nov. 1963, p. 30.
6. L.W. Porter and R.E. McKibben, *Management Education and Development,* McGraw-Hill, New York, 1988, pp. 47–51.
7. Joseph S. Murphy, "The Quiet Revolution in Government Planning Techniques," *Management Review,* April 1968, pp. 4–11.
8. John H. Byrne, "Management's New Gurus," *Business Week,* Aug. 31, 1992, pp. 44–51.
9. Ronald N. Paul and James W. Taylor, "The State of Strategic Planning," *Long Range Planning Journal,* April 1974, pp. 39–40.

10. Steven Rosen, "The Future From the Top: Perspectives on Planning," *Long Range Planning Journal*, April 1974, p. 3.
11. Ralph J. Cordiner, *New Frontiers for Professional Managers*, McGraw-Hill, New York, 1956, pp. 44–46.
12. Frederick Gluck, Stephen D. Kaufman, and Steven Walleck, "Strategic Management for Competitive Advantage," *Harvard Business Review*, July-August 1980, pp. 154–161.
13. Lawrence M. Hughes, "GE Under Decentralization Reaps Record Sales and Profits," *Sales Management*, March 1958, p. 34–35.
14. Patrick Irwin, "Towards Better Strategic Management," *Long Range Planning Journal*, December 1974, p. 65.
15. J.B. McKittrick, "Marketing Precision and Executive Action," The American Marketing Association, Chicago, IL, 1962, pp. 75, 85, 86.
16. L.H. Kurtz, *Reflections on the Art of Administrative Leadership*, issue #37, January 1960, p. 3.
17. L.H. Kurtz, *Reflections on the Art of Administrative Leadership*, issue #37, January 1960, p. 4.
18. John S. McClenahan, "The Finance Man Has Intense Interest in People," *Industry Week*, November 1973, p. 40.
19. Fred J. Borch, *The Marketing Philosophy as a Way of Life*, Marketing Series #99, American Management Association, New York, 1957, pp. 3–4.
20. Wroe Anderson, "A Marketing View of Business Policy," in *Advanced Marketing Efficiency*, American Marketing Association, Chicago, IL, June 1959, p. 118.
21. J.B. McKittrick, "What Is the Marketing Concept?" in *The Frontiers of Marketing Thought and Science*, American Marketing Association, Chicago, IL, December 1957, p. 77.
22. Noel B. Zabriskie and Alan B. Huellmantel, "Marketing Research as a Strategic Tool," *Long Range Planning Journal*, December 1971, p. 112.
23. J. Douglas McConnell, "Strategic Planning: One Workable Approach," *Long Range Planning Journal*, December 1971, pp. 2–3.
24. Lawrence M. Hughes, "GE Under Decentralization, Reaps Record Sales and Profits," *Sales Management*, March 7, 1958, pp. 34–35.
25. Francis J. Aguilar, *General Manager in Action*, Oxford University Press, New York, 1992, pp. 408–410.
26. Bruce Henderson, "Market Share-ROI Corporate Strategy Approach Can Be Oversimplistic Snare," *Marketing News*, American Marketing Association, Chicago, IL, Dec. 15, 1978, p. 7.
27. "GE's Jones Restructures His Top Team," *Business Week*, June 30, 1973, p. 39.
28. Francis J. Aguilar, *General Manager in Action*, Oxford University Press, New York, 1992, p. 411.
29. Francis J. Aguilar, *General Manager in Action*, Oxford University Press, New York, 1992, p. 412.
30. "GE's Jones Restructures His Top Team," *Business Week*, June 30, 1973, p. 38.
31. Francis J. Aguilar, *General Manager in Action*, Oxford University Press, New York, 1992, p. 415.
32. Francis J. Aguilar, *General Manager in Action*, Oxford University Press, New York, 1992, p. 421.
33. Francis J. Aguilar, *General Manager in Action*, Oxford University Press, New York, 1992, p. 419

34. "General Electric: The Financial Wizards Switch Back to Technology," *Business Week,* March 16, 1981, p. 111.
35. Laura Lando, "Electric Switch: GE's Wizards Turning from the Bottom Line to Share of the Market," *Wall Street Journal,* July 12, 1982, pp. 15–16.
36. Russell Mitchell, "Jack Welch: How Good a Manager," *Business Week,* December 14, 1987, p. 96.
37. Francis J. Aguilar, *General Manager in Action,* Oxford University Press, New York, 1992, pp. 424–430.
38. Thomas G. Marx, "Removing the Obstacles to Effective Planning," *Long Range Planning Journal,* August 1991, pp. 21–28.
39. Francis J. Aguilar, *General Manager in Action,* Oxford University Press, New York, 1992, p. 442.
40. Stephen Millett, "How Scenarios Trigger Thinking," *Long Range Planning Journal,* October 1988, p. 61.
41. James Hyall, "GE Chairman Welch Puts Pen to Paper for Annual Address," *Wall Street Journal,* March 7, 1994, p. 10.
42. David Henry, "CEO: Breaking Up Is Hard To Do," *USA Today,* Feb. 2, 1996, p. 8.
43. Tim Stewart, "Jack Welch's Encore: How GE's Chairman Is Remaking His Company Again," *Business Week,* Oct. 28, 1996, pp. 155–160.
44. Linda Grant, "GE: The Envelope Please," *Fortune,* June 26, 1995, pp. 89–90.
45. *Forbes,* May 5, 1997.
46. Francis J. Aguilar, *General Manager in Action,* Oxford University Press, New York, 1992, pp. 408–422.
47. William M. Carley, *The Wall Street Journal,* Jan. 13, 1997, p. A.
48. George S. Day, *Strategic Market Planning: The Pursuit of Competitive Advantage,* West Publishing, St. Paul, MN, 1984, p. 3.
49. Tim Smart, "Jack Welch's Encore," *Business Week,* Oct. 28, 1996, pp. 155–160.

3 Strategic Management for the XXIst Century

"Next to my wife and family, the stock is the most important thing in my mind." (Philip Morris CEO, *Fortune*, June 21, 1997)

3.1 Introduction

Strategic planning in the XXIst century will differ from today's model in several ways:

1. Attempts will be made to standardize planning terminology, at least at the company level. Clarification will start right at the top with the various and confusing planning concepts themselves. Each concept will be defined and classified according to its purpose and the issues it addresses.

2. The National Association of Corporate Board Directors governance guidelines (discussed in Chapter 1) will change the way companies are governed. The outside directors will nominate, select, and evaluate the performance of the chief executive officer. Performance will be judged not so much on today's profit as on how well the intermediate goals in the strategic plan are met. This in turn will make good strategic planning even more important than it is today.

3. The business policy/strategic management courses now taught in business colleges will be updated according to the recommendations made in the American Assembly of Collegiate Schools of Business (AACSB) study.
4. Corporations will be guided by the four-phase approach to state-of-the-art strategic management as outlined in the McKinsey report.

3.2   Standardized Terminology

Confucius is supposed to have said if he were made ruler of the world the first thing he would do would be to fix the meaning of words because definition must always precede action. Strategic management/planning is a team effort. It requires informational inputs from all major units of the organization. Subjects not thoroughly understood can be neither communicated nor acted upon. If Confucius is right, then understanding the strategic planning concept must start with clearly defined planning terms and purpose.

Anyone who doubts that the meaning of planning terms needs to be clarified should try answering these questions:

1. Is the term "strategic management" synonymous with business policy, management by objectives, planning, programming and budgeting, strategic intent, or time-based competition?
2. Are the new management concepts of restructuring, re-engineering, down-sizing, quality control, organizational architecture, and institutional culture offered as replacements for strategic management or are they internally oriented concepts to improve operational and administrative efficiencies?

The confusion over planning terms in one utility company was so bad that, after the planning consultants left, the managers that had been working with them began speaking in tongues, and the other managers felt guilty because they couldn't understand them. Patrick Irwin, a Canadian consultant, states that managerial planning concepts must have a clearly stated purpose and be classified according to the issues they address. Classifying concepts according to the issues they address (strategic, administrative, operational) not only clarifies the issues, but also enables planners to blend similar issues into plans and the plans

Table 3.1 Classifying Planning Concepts According to Issues

Concept	Characteristics of Concepts		
	Strategic	*Operational*	*Administrative*
Strategic planning	X	—	—
Management by objectives	—	X	X
Restructuring	—	—	X
Re-engineering	—	—	X
Business policy	—	—	X
Transforming culture	—	—	X
Competing for the future:			
Strategic intent	X	—	—
Strategic architecture	X	—	—
Strategic management as a corporate planning system	X	X	X

into a comprehensive management planning and decision-making system (see Table 3.1).

3.3   The AACSB Study

The recent study by the American Assembly of Collegiate Schools of Business (AACSB; the accrediting agency of Accredited Colleges of Business) on "Management Education and Development: Drift or Thrust into the XXIst Century?" states that the basic thought running through meetings stressed the need for the current business policy course to be replaced with a more holistic, pluralistic, and systematic approach to integrating an organization's decision-making.

The AACSB study was a 3-year international study commissioned not only by the American Assembly of Collegiate Schools of Business but also by their overseas counterpart, the European Foundation for Management Development. The study's purpose was to establish a generic framework for educating managers capable of functioning in the XXIst century. It was by far the largest and most comprehensive business school study ever attempted. Over 400 business schools and 30 of the world's largest companies participated. The Paris Conference, where the results were discussed, attracted over 600 participants.

The summary report made many recommendations about the direction future business policy courses should take, but stopped short of actually stating what that new direction should be. Well aware of the content of the current business policy and strategic management courses, they recommended, as stated above, that they be replaced with a more holistic, pluralistic, and systematic approach to teaching the strategic concept:[4] *holistic,* in that the functions of business, finance, marketing, personnel, etc. are not taught as specialty subjects operating in separate compartments, but rather as interrelated parts of a corporate decision-making system; *pluralistic,* in that the primary (that is, the most important set of decisions a for-profit organization makes, the so-called set of strategic decisions) requires cross-functional informational inputs for their success; and *systematic,* in that cross-functional decision-making requires a sequential, systematic gathering of functional informational all focused on and supporting the same set of central primary corporate decisions. Today's business policy courses lack a central focus and the unity of purpose for functional planning and decision-making that a primary set of strategic decision provides. The purpose of the current policy course is to show the students how the knowledge and skills they have learned in the functional business courses of marketing, finance, etc., are used in general management's decisions to solve multi-functional problems and exploit multi-functional opportunities.

Strengths of this approach include:

1. It teaches students that many of corporate management's decisions are multi-functional in nature, and multi-functional decisions require informational inputs from each of the specialized functional areas of marketing, finance, etc.
2. It teaches students how to analyze multi-functional problems.
3. It monitors the external environment for trend change and projects their expected impact on tomorrow's markets.
4. It focuses attention on the need for an integrated decision-making approach to managing an organization.

Limitations of this approach include:

1. While it discusses both problem-solving and exploiting opportunities with strategy, its major emphasis is on problem-solving.
2. It emphasizes analytical skills at the expense of synthesizing skills.

3. It teaches a simultaneous rather than a sequential approach to planning and decision-making. All management systems have a definite order in which the information is needed.
4. It teaches policy as a single course rather than a field of study in systematic decision-making.
5. The proliferate use of the term "strategy" has resulted in confusion as to its proper meaning and use in strategic planning and decision-making.

This last point is particularly true when the terms "policy" and "strategy" are used interchangeably. They are two entirely different concepts. Policy decisions have traditionally been considered contingent decisions; that is, they are decisions made in advance and stating the response desired from situations that occur repetitiously. Policy statements such as that of Hanson Industries — "Our growth policy will be to increase market share and control costs" — can be classified and considered a directional statement of strategy but is more a statement of objectives than a competitive strategy. Competitive strategies, by contrast, are formulated from sets of resource allocation decisions that form the central theme on which all other management decisions can be focused.

From the AACSB summary report and the writings of other thought leaders on the subject, we can now draw definite conclusions as to what a new approach to the so-called policy courses would look like:

Conclusion 1 — The vehicle for integrating corporate, functional, and departmental activities into a holistic planning system will be a leadership course in decision-making. Policy, strategy, and plans will be formulated from sets of decisions judged too complex and interdependent to be made individually.

Conclusion 2 — A totally integrated decision system must include not only the decisions that formulate policy, strategy, and plans, but also those that administer and operationalize them.

Conclusions 3 — Any new approach must be taught not as a single course but as a field of study with both overall corporate and functional capstone courses stating the role each should play in corporate decisions.

Conclusion 4 — For management to be taught as a system of decisions, there must be a primacy of decision values; that is, decisions must be classified, grouped, and rated as to their importance. The most important set of decisions automatically becomes the central theme and cornerstone on which the business, functional, and departmental decisions will be focused.

Conclusion 5 — By definition, a system of decisions consists of many decisions built into policies, strategies, and plans in such a way that they create a chain of mutual dependency. Each decision in the chain depends on at least one other decision for its success. Systems of decisions must be developed in an orderly, logical sequential, process or model.

Conclusion 6 — The current emphasis being placed on the importance of visionary leadership requires a broader definition of management than the one that has been accepted traditionally.

Conclusion 7 — Tomorrow's business policy and strategy courses will be taught as courses in organized entrepreneurship, the creative side of leadership that flows from and is derived from the leader's vision.

Conclusion 8 — The most important set of decisions an organization makes will be the decisions that allocate resources to market opportunities at the corporate and business unit levels. This set of decisions will be the central theme and focus for all organizations regardless of the industries in which the operate.

Conclusion 9 — The study of policy and strategy starts right at the top of organizations with the chief executive officers and the visions they have for what they want their organizations to become. Their assignment is to take their organization's resources and make them productive.

In organizations operating in competitive environments, the chief executive officer's responsibilities are somewhat spelled out in this sequence of events:

1. The attorneys draw up the required legal documents and the stock certificates that will be sold to finance the new organization's operations.
2. The public buys the stock certificates.
3. The stockholders then elect a board of directors to represent them and protect their interests.
4. The board, in turn, selects a chief executive officer, who is assigned the task of allocating the organization's resources — money, people, know-how, equipment, facilities, etc. — to

market opportunities in such a way that they are converted into unfilled customer needs at a profit.

5. Resources can only be productive by allocating them profitably to opportunities in the marketplace.

The central theme or thread, therefore, that creates the unity of purpose for the organization's decision system and the instrument that integrates all of the organization's activities into a holistic approach is the set of resource allocation decisions. All other decisions made at the corporate, functional, or departmental levels must contribute to and support the set of resource allocation decisions — both corporate and business allocation decisions and both corporate and business decisions.

3.4 The McKinsey Report

It seems that as soon as a management concept emerges it must go through a stage where it is promoted through the use of catchy buzzwords, generalizations, half-truths, and new interpretations until there are so many versions offered that the underlying substance of the original concept is lost. With business libraries filled with conflicting versions of it, today's strategic management concept seems to be passing through this state in its development.

Regardless of the many titles and catchy buzzwords associated with the strategic concept — strategic planning, strategic management, business policy, visionary leadership, strategic intent, etc. — there does not seem to be any disagreement as to its primary objective: *To convert the organization's resources into unfilled customer needs at a profit sufficient to satisfy the long-term objectives of the stockholders.*

Disagreement exists over what method, process, system, or model to use in making the conversion. The choice of conversion models is unlimited, but for planning convenience they can be grouped into four generalized approaches:

1. General Electric/Ansoff/McKinsey approach: State-of-the-art strategic management and visionary leadership ultimately evolve from the budgeting process into a system of strategic, operational, and administrative plans based on the principle of:
   a. Budgeting for directional and control purposes
   b. Long-term financial profit planning

    c. Futures research with scenario projections of tomorrow's industry markets and unfilled customer needs

    d. Strategies for committing resources to satisfy selective unfilled customers' needs in tomorrow's markets

This approach is the original resource conversion model for developing a strategic management system.

2. Management by objective approaches:

    a. Strategic intent approach — The process is driven by high-risk financial objectives with the primary focus being on techniques to reduce the element of risk through strategic alliances, acquiring key core competencies, and implementation by programs rather than competitive strategies.

    b. Model for non-profit organizations — Very few non-profit organizations attempt to build scenarios of tomorrow's markets, project unfilled customer needs, or judge the strength of expected competition. They are driven primarily by objectives, and respond to trend changes with programs built from experience and intuition rather than strategies based on futures research.

3. Business policy approach: The process is driven by strategies developed through integrated cross-functional planning for the purpose of solving both internal problems and exploiting external opportunities. The strategies are usually developed from extrapolations of current trends and implemented through program planning and budgeting.

4. Non-strategic approach: The planning process is driven by strategies developed by rearranging organizational structures, workforce groups, and other internal maneuvers to gain greater efficiencies through operational improvements and cost-cutting. Using Shirley's five tests as the criteria for strategic plans, only the first of these approaches — the General Electric/McKinsey model — qualifies as a strategic approach. The other three approaches fail to qualify because they are either driven by objectives or implemented with programs rather competitive strategies.

3.4.1 Characteristics of the Original Strategic Concept

The overriding characteristic of the original General Electric/McKinsey strategic model was its evolutionary nature. Starting as an annual budget, it evolved progressively over time into a multi-year, sophisticated, state-of-the-art system for managing the organization's resources strategically (the outcome of which was discussed in Chapter 2). While GE's sales were incomparable to General Motors (less than half), its market value (in the eyes of investors) was more than four times that of General Motors.

Budgets are created by reducing strategies and plans to a set of financial forecasts for the purpose of providing both delegated financial control and a central focus for all of the unit's planning and decision-making. The ultimate goal of strategic management is to create a decision-making system that provides a mechanism for senior executives to meet the vision and financial objectives they have for the organization's future.

The McKinsey Company, one of the founding fathers of the strategic concept, in a 2-year, 120-company, 7-country study, verified that state-of-the-art strategic management evolves logically and progressively from the annual budget. They summarized the results of their study in two major observations:

1.   The strategic process in most successful companies could be divided into four separate distinct steps or phases.
2.   Very few organizations in the world ever reach the fourth phase where they actually practice state-of-the-art strategic management.

The four phases in the development of a state-of-the-art strategic management system according to the McKinsey study are described as follows (see Figure 3.1):

Phase I — The annual budget, a basic financial plan
1.   Most companies trace the start of their formal planning activities to their annual budget where everything is reduced to a financial plan on an annual basis.
2.   The annual budget is derived from implied, but not stated, competitive strategies. The only evidence that strategies exist is found in revenue and earning projections qualified by certain financial and market conditions, such as, debt, sales volume, and profit objectives set as planning targets.
3.   The Phase I annual budget is usually referred to as the basic financial plan.

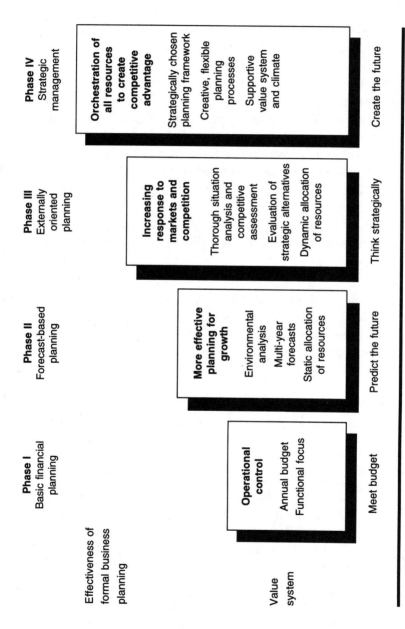

Figure 3.1 Four Phases in the Evolution of Formal Strategic Planning. (Adapted from Gluck, W. et al., "Strategic Management for Competitive Advantage," *Harvard Business Review*, July/Aug., 1980. With permission.)

Phase II — Multiple-year budgeting and business unit planning, forecast-based planning

1. In the early stages, Phase II differs from Phase I planning only in the length of its time frame.
2. Financial planners need multi-year revenue forecasts to use as a base for their capital budgeting. To obtain these forecasts, the treasurer's staff corrects this weakness in Phase I planning by extrapolating past and present revenue trends into the future.
3. Over time, Phase II planning gradually evolves into a crude form of business unit planning. The organization's product lines are segmented into similar markets, customers, and competitive units often referred to as *strategic business units* (SBUs). They are then analyzed individually for their growth potential. Each unit's current market share (its competitive strength) is plotted on a matrix against the unit's market growth rate (its market attractiveness).
4. This two-dimensional matrix is further divided into four sections for the purpose of determining the businesses with strong market shares in growth markets. Unless there are other extenuating circumstances, these are the business units that will have priority on the organization's limited resources (for further information on business unit, portfolio management, see Chapter 6). Phase II business unit analysis has the following major weaknesses:
   a. It is static and deterministic and considers the business' position on the matrix as an endpoint for strategy formation.
   b. It is static in that it focuses on the business unit's current capabilities rather than its potential.
   c. It is deterministic in that the business unit's position on the matrix is assumed to determine the appropriate strategy for the future.
   d. Matrix positioning is regarded as an endpoint rather than the starting point for strategy formation.
   e. Finally, Phase II planning manages its business units as separate, independent businesses. The revenue and profit produced by each unit are allocated only to market opportunities in the unit's own markets.

Phase III — Externally oriented planning. Phase III planning changes the planning emphasis from an internally oriented planning system based on extrapolated projections of past revenue to an externally oriented planning system based on environmental change, trend analysis, scenarios of tomorrow's market, and market impact studies. Where Phase II planning is static and deterministic, Phase III planning is dynamic and creative. It is dynamic in that its matrix analysis is based on changing market conditions, customer needs, market shares, and the strength of the competition, and it is creative in that new innovative strategies are formulated to exploit unfilled customer needs created by a changing, dynamic market. Phase III planning manages its business units not as individual businesses but as a portfolio of businesses. All revenue from the business units are centralized at corporate headquarters and allocated to the best market opportunities they can find worldwide without considering the source of the revenue.

Phase IV — Strategic management. Phase IV, the last step in creating a state-of-the-art strategic management system joins the externally oriented plan described in Phase III with management's day-to-day operational decisions and budgets to form a single short- and long-range strategic planning system. This linkage is accomplished by reducing the strategies in the strategic plan to financial terms and adding them to the revenue expected from current business to form a long-range financial plan. The first year of the financial plan is then detailed and scheduled into an annual operational budget (for more detail on linking strategies to financial plans and budgets, see Chapter 4). Other factors that distinguish Phase IV planning from the developmental phases are

1. Most of the planning information is obtained directly from the functional managers in the line organization.
2. A uniform planning framework or model is used to guide the business unit planning. A planning model of some kind is necessary if similar information from more than one business unit is to be aggregated and studied at the corporate planning level.

3.4.2 Adoption of a Matrix Planning Model

Most corporations are organized around a vertical chain of command. Vertical organizational managers are responsible for everything that occurs in large multi-unit divisions. Many of these divisions will have as many as 20 or more individual business units to manage. To be sure, each business unit receives proper attention and a matrix organizational chart is developed. In matrix organizations, business unit managers are superimposed horizontally across the vertical line organization. Each business unit manager is given his or her own team of specialists: finance, marketing, research, etc. The specialists actually report to the vertical line manager but are on permanent loan to the business unit executive.

3.4.3   Cultural Element in Planning Process

Organizational culture in a planning environment is changed from short- to long-range strategic thinking and decision-making. The overall culture in which the planning takes place is an important factor in Phase IV planning.

In a strategic planning culture, managers view their responsibilities as:

1. Being broader than their own specialized discipline or function.
2. Keeping the planning team informed of major changes taking place within their own specialized functions.
3. Taking a broader, longer view of their assignments and consequently expecting an incentive system that will reward their contributions.
4. Communicating their vision of what they want their organization to become and the model that will be used to make it happen, and to convey this concept to all levels of the organization.

Corporate value system shared by all Phase IV organizations can be characterized by:

1. The value of teamwork
2. Entrepreneurial drive
3. Open communication
4. A shared belief that the corporation can largely create its own future.

For further detail on organizational culture, see Chapter 4.

3.5   Summary

We can summarize this chapter on the future of strategic management by quoting from Peter Drucker's book, *The Age of Discontinuity*. Drucker tells us that we do not have to be a prophet or genius to identify and make assumptions about trend discontinuities. Trend discontinuities are early signs of change taking place. Drucker offers trend analysis as a means of developing scenarios of what tomorrow's society could look like. This same approach can be used for developing scenarios of what the business policy/strategic management concept could look like tomorrow.

Today, we can identify four distinct trend discontinuities in the strategic management field that need to be addressed: (1) the realization by many authors that planning terminology needs to be standardized before the strategic management concept can reach its full potential; (2) recommendations made by the AACSB study commonly referred to as the business college "deans" study to improve the teaching of business policy/strategic management courses; (3) the National Association of Corporate Board Directors' guidelines for board directors; and (4) the study conducted by the McKinsey Company on how strategic planning evolves through four phases, from the annual budget into state-of-the-art strategic management.

From the direction these changes seem to be taking, the most likely scenario for tomorrow could look like this:

1. Attempts will be made to standardize planning terminology at least at the company level.
2. More chief executive officers will be selected for their visionary leadership.
3. The outside board members will determine both the nomination and selection of the chief executive officers.
4. Chief executive officers will not only be evaluated annually by the board, but they will also hold periodic strategic planning sessions with them.
5. Chief executive officers will be evaluated not so much on today's profit but more on whether the intermediate goals in the strategic plan were met.
6. Tomorrow's market opportunities will be identified through futures research; that is, through trend analysis scenarios and market impact studies.

7. Competitive strategies will be evaluated relatively on how much each will contribute to the stockholders' equity, or economic value added (EVA), and market value added (MVA).

The statement at the beginning of this chapter, made by the chairman of Philip Morris, is in many ways an expression uttered by many CEOs, although they shy away from making it so specific. Just look at the second chapter to see what strategic planning can do for your firm if it is systematically conceived and applied. Although we will deal with detail application of these concepts in a later chapter which will also guide the student in implementation of the plans, suffice it to say that the ultimate in strategic planning and management lies in the systematic application of the McKinsey report as described in this chapter and more extensively analyzed later.

References

1. George Steiner, *Strategic Planning*, Macmillan, New York, 1979, p. 12.
2. Paul Theibert, "Eschew that Paradigm! Drop the Jargon," *Wall Street Journal*, Manager's Journal, 1994.
3. Patrick Irwin, "Towards Better Strategic Management," *Long Range Planning Journal*, December 1974, p. 64.
4. Jacques Lesourne, *The Changing Expectations of Society in the Next Thirty Years*, American Assembly of Collegiate Schools of Business, St. George's House, Windsor Castle, February 1979, pp. 32–35.
5. William A. Dymsza, "The Education and Development of Managers for Future Decades," *Journal of International Business Studies*, Winter 1982, pp. 9–19.
6. Hanson Industries, *Interim Report*, New York, May 1994, p. 3.
7. Robert Shirley, "Limiting the Scope of Strategy," *Academy of Management Review*, April 1982, pp. 262–268.
8. Frederick Gluck, Stephen P. Kaufman, and Steven Wallace, "The Four Phases of Strategic Management," *Journal of Business Strategy*, 1982, pp. 9–20.
9. J. Warner, "A New Breed of Blue Chips," *Business Week*, July 7, 1997.
10. Peter J. Drucker, *The Age of Discontinuity*, Harper & Row, New York, 1969) pp. 1–7.

4 Visionary Leadership

4.1 Introduction

As mentioned in previous chapters, today's boards of directors are seeking and selecting visionary chief executive officers.[1] If this trend continues into the XXIst century, and we think it will, we will need a much clearer picture of what is meant by vision.

There seems to be general agreement on what the directors want from their chief executives: a well-thought-out vision, or roadmap, for the corporation's future. While the requirements for a visionary leader are quite clear, what actually constitutes a vision, or how one is acquired, remains unclear to both planners and top management.

As one prominent executive stated his frustration, "I've come to realize that we need a vision to guide us into the future, but I can't get my arms around what a vision is. I've heard it expressed as a mission, purpose, values, a vision statement, strategic intent, etc. Terms like these are of no practical value to me; in fact, I find them to be a boring string of words."[2] Another agrees that "this vision thing is needed whatever it is."[3] Statements of missions and visions are important to define what a business is, but they don't tell us where it wants to go, or how it will get there.

Strategic success, with or without a vision, can never be reduced to a formula or recipe. It can, however, be made an understandable, purposeful activity through programmed strategic thinking. Strategic thinking is about how new ideas are created with which to build strategies (ideation), how to disburse strategies to the troops (communication), and how to create an orderly process to activate the strategies in the strategic plan (implementation).

4.2   Strategic Thinking

In recent years strategic planning has come under fire because it has emphasized form over substance. Form is important, but too much time spent on form results in bureaucratic organizations, red tape, and too much paperwork.[4] What never has been challenged, however, is strategic thinking — the thinking that produces both the analysis of the situation and the creative elements that synthesize the results of the analysis into a successful strategic plan.[5]

Thinking strategically begins by identifying the business units in which the corporation wants to compete and continues through an analysis of the dynamics of the so-called strategic triangle in each business unit:

1. The business unit itself
2. The customer
3. The competition[6]

The purpose of this analysis is to find market opportunities.

Once the market opportunities have been identified, the analysis continues searching for the key success factors in each opportunity. Key success factors are those factors in which business units must excel if the market opportunity is to be exploited.

A senior executive in the lumber business analyzed his industry as follows.[7] In the lumber business, there are two overriding success factors: owning large tree farms and maximizing the yield from each.

1. To own tree farms requires capital.
2. Maximizing yield requires sunshine and water.

In states with sunshine and little water, the key factors are finding trees that require less water and/or getting more water. In states with water and little sunshine, the key factors are fertilizer and/or more sunshine. With water and sunshine, the average length of time required for adequate tree growth is 15 years; without adequate water and sunshine, the average is closer to 30 years.

Recapping, the key success factors in the lumber industry are (1) capital, (2) sunshine, (3) water, (4) fertilizer, and (5) trees requiring less water or sunshine.

In large corporations, there will be many business units, strategic triangles, and key success factors to be aggregated and prioritized into a corporate strategic plan. Gathering the information from the business units in a uniform manner so they can be aggregated at the corporate level will require some form of an orderly process.

4.3   The Creative Process

The current business policy/strategic management courses have been criticized for stressing analytical skills while ignoring the equally important synthesizing skills. A more accurate criticism would be that they stopped thinking strategically after they analyzed the situation. Analysis is the starting point of creative thinking.[8] It gives direction for the synthesizing side of strategic thinking.

One executive stated, "I am against turning creative people loose with no guidelines, no aim. I believe in *directed* creativity, not creativity in the abstract."[9] The S.C. Johnson case study on the strategy they developed to promote their new product, Pledge, is a good example of directed creativity.[9] The success of this product could not have happened without a good promotional strategy. This strategy could not have been formulated without good analysis (market research). The research conducted with women pointed out that they dusted almost daily yet waxed their furniture only once a month. They did not mind dusting, but they hated to wax. The creative team was given the assignment to come up with a promotional strategy that would get their new wax on the daily dust cloth. The creative team given this direction came up with the promotional slogan — "Pledge waxes instantly as you dust" — and the sales success of this strategy is history.

Kerin suggests that leadership is not management, but rather management plus a higher order of capability which he describes as *vision*.[10] Donald Kendall, the chief executive of PepsiCo, agrees with Kerin by stating that visionary skills, not managerial skills, are the essence of leadership.[10]

Recently, the *Investor's Business Daily* asked their panel of chief executives to comment on visionary skills as they pertain to leadership.

They were asked to discuss what a vision is and the skills it takes to be a visionary leader. A consensus of their answers goes something like this: The chief executive's vision mentally reconstructs tomorrow's industry and its future markets, based on signals of change already appearing on the horizon. He or she then repositions each of the company's businesses in their markets.[11] To be able to do this successfully, a visionary leader needs:

1. Industry experience — knowledge of the history and markets in which the company wants to compete
2. Sound judgment and both intuitive and studied insight
3. The ability to conceptualize and think strategically about the future

Can creativity be taught? Probably not. Can it be programmed and cultivated consciously? We think the answer is yes.[12] Not withstanding that most of the major contributions in creative thinking in the business world can be traced to an elite group of geniuses (the Sloans, Fords, Edisons, Gates, etc.), psychologists tell us that all of us have some degree of creative ability. It is senior management's job to find ways to unleash this latent pool of creativity.

Some years ago, Levitt stated there are two major steps to the creative process and both must be understood if we are to program our own creative thinking: ideation and innovation.[13]

4.3.1 Ideation

Ideation is the ability one has to conceive, or recognize through the act of insight, useful ideas. Just as energy is the basis of life, ideas are the source of innovation and entrepreneurship. Theories of how ideas are conceived can be traced to the work of economist Joseph A. Schumpter.[14]

The *Transcendentalist* approach attributes ideation to imagination. Imagination provides the premise and asks the questions from which logic and reason grind out the conclusions. New ideas in this approach are conceived intuitively without logic or precedent.

The second theory is known as the *Mechanism* approach. This theory claims ideas do not spring full blown out of nowhere. They must have antecedents. They are the result of an accumulation of many individual thoughts blended over a period of time.

The third theory, the *Cumulative-Synthesis* approach, states that neither the Transcendentalist nor the Mechanistic approach alone is valid. The Cumulative-Synthesis approach combines the two by stating that ideas are the result of the accumulation of many ideas, but the critical factor is the act of insight in the synthesis. While we may never get agreement on exactly how ideas are created in our brain, we do seem to have general agreement that ideation occurs in four distinct stages.[15]

4.3.1.1   Stage 1: Saturation

Saturation is said to exist when we add things to the point where no more can be absorbed. In the case of ideation, the "things" would be information and library research pertaining to our problem or opportunity. Edison described this point best when he said, "Genius is 99% perspiration and 1% inspiration; I am more a sponge than an inventor."

In this stage, we saturate our subconscious with the elements from which it is hoped that the answers will later spring. Once the saturation stage is reached, we can switch our mind set to other things and let our subconscious take over.

4.3.1.2   Stage 2: Incubation

This is the passive step; we quit thinking about our problem or opportunity and do something else. We walk away temporarily and allow time for our subconscious to convert all the data we have given it into new ideas, concepts, and patterns.

4.3.1.3   Stage 3: Illumination

This is the stage when the lights go on and the flash of inspiration takes place, when the act of insight and recognition of relationships takes place. Galileo was supposed to have been sitting peacefully in a cathedral when he saw a great lamp swinging to and fro and conceived his idea of the pendulum. Newton was loafing under an apple tree when an apple fell and he got the inspiration for gravity.

4.3.1.4   Stage 4: Verification

In this stage, it is time to determine if these inspirations and ideas are practical. Rough, incomplete ideas must be shaped and judged as to their usefulness. One of America's largest engineering firms has a slogan which in one sentence describes the dynamics of the whole creative thinking process: "Let your imagination soar, then engineer it back down to earth."[16]

4.3.2 Innovation

In industry, we must attach a condition of utility to ideas before they can be considered creative.[17] Industrial creativity means a complete process: getting the ideas, communicating the ideas to those who will activate them, and following them through to reality. Levitt tells this story. Suppose you know two artists. One describes to you an idea for a great painting, but he does not paint it. The other has the same idea and paints it. Levitt labels the first a *creative talker*, the second a *creative painter*.[13]

4.4 Barriers to Creativity

The goal of every visionary leader is, or should be, to develop a successful planning process that is flexible enough to be perpetuated over time and generations of managers. Companies that have such a planning process are said to have a planning culture. The dictionary defines culture as "a particular way of thinking, talking, and acting about a subject by a group over a long period of time." The group in the case of a company with a planning culture would be all of its employees.

Brady advises management to start by identifying and removing the obstacles that can stifle creativity. Here are the things he advises to guard against:[18]

1. Within the structure of the organization
   a. Over-structured organizational charts and too many layers of management
   b. Too many procedures
   c. Poor channels of communication
   d. Turfs or fiefdoms
   e. Fear of management
   f. Routine, boring assignments
   g. Undirected creativity
2. Within the individual

    a. Individuals not being aware of their creative potential or how to program their creative thinking

    b. Lack of recognition and reward for creative thinking

    c. Individuals taking unfair advantage of their creative freedom

These obstacles must all be addressed at some time; however, unless the troops are made aware of their unused creative ability and encouraged to reach their full potential, the other issues are irrelevant. It is often said that things we understand we do better, and a better understanding of the creative process should help the awareness problem.

4.5 Converting the Leader's Vision into a Strategic Plan

Visionary leadership in practice can be described as a two-step process in which Step 1 creates the vision, and Step 2 verbalizes the vision and communicates it to the planning team that will make it happen. Because converting visions into strategic plans requires informational inputs from all managers of major units in the organization they, in turn, must be informed of the vision they are being asked to support. It has been said that "the sharpest minds and the most brilliant ideas are prisoners in persons who cannot communicate their genius or musings to others."[19] The vehicle used to communicate the vision and turn it into a long-range strategic plan is usually referred to as the "Corporate Planning Guidelines Memo".[20] The term "memo" may be somewhat misleading, as the visionary message can be delivered in any form the chief executive chooses. For the sake of brevity we are going to refer in this chapter to all written visionary communication forms as the Corporate Planning Guidelines Memo.

Most chief executives share their visions with only their planning team. There is, however, a growing movement led by chief executives at General Motors, Louisiana Pacific, and Glaxo Holdings to make everyone in the organization aware of top management's vision. For example, Glaxo Holdings' Chief Executive, Dr. Richard Sykes, wants no confusion among his employees as to what direction Glaxo's future should take. He considers it his responsibility to "make sure that everyone working for Glaxo has a very clear vision of where the company is going and how it is going to get there."[21]

As mentioned earlier, the vehicle for communicating the leader's vision is usually referred to as the Corporate Planning Guidelines Memo, whether the vision is targeted at just the planning team or to others in the organization. Depending on the audience, this memo usually covers one or more of these three subjects:

1. The *vision* itself, as explained by the chief executive.
2. A planning *model* to provide a framework for gathering the planning information that will be needed.
3. General *instructions* as to how the planning process will be coordinated.

4.5.1 Verbalizing the Vision

Verbalizing the vision consists of the leader discussing, in his own words, the present "state of the organization" — where it is today, some of its problems, changes taking place in the industry, and some of the things that will have to be done to reposition the organization in tomorrow's markets. In brief, it explains where the organization is today and where the chief executive would like it to be in the future.

4.5.2 Planning Format or Model To Be Used

Mental visions are activated through strategic planning and decision-making. Strategic planning cannot be done in a vacuum. It requires informational inputs from all major units of the organization. The first question asked by unit planners from corporate headquarters concerns what information, specifically, is wanted from them.

The simplest way to answer this question is with a verbal model. Verbal models are sets of questions that the plan must answer if it is to be successful. Every organization makes many plans: administrative, operational, and strategic. Each plan will have its own set of questions to answer. In the case of the strategic plan, it would probably include the following:[22]

1. What will be the organization's mission statement (including the vision) and long-range objectives?
2. What will be the scope of its businesses?
3. What external environmental changes have occurred or can be expected?

4. What could be the effect of each change on the industry in the future?
5. What new opportunities and threats could these changes bring?
6. What are our competitors' strengths and weaknesses in response to these opportunities?
7. What are our capabilities relative to the competition?
8. At what customer groups will we target our responses?
9. What will be our competitive strategy in responding to these opportunities and threats?
10. How can we link new strategies to our long-range financial plan?
11. How can we effectively activate the strategic decisions within the operations of our organization?

4.5.3   General Planning Instructions

The first two subjects (a knowledge of the CEO's vision and the informational objectives provided by the set of strategic questions) form a directional framework that guides and unifies all of the organization's planning efforts. The only additional information the planners will need is

1. Whether the planning will be done simultaneously by all units or sequentially; if sequentially, in what order
2. Historical revenue and profit trend tables that can be used for extrapolation and benchmark purposes
3. Dates and location for the planning retreat and the order in which the presentations will be made

4.6   An Example: The Atlantic Refining Company's Corporate Planning Guidelines Memo

The following example of a Corporate Planning Guidelines Memo is based on the thoughts of the chief executive of Atlantic Refining Company (ARC) delivered in a speech to his managers in 1964.[23] President Thornton F. Bradshaw was aware that employees were asking questions about the company's future and its strengths and weaknesses. He decided to share with them the same vision for Atlantic's future he had just given to his planning team.

4.6.1   The State of the Organization

Bradshaw began by stating that as of the first of the year, the company would be recycling their long-range strategic plan. Before starting the new cycle there were several things that he wanted to talk to them about, including some of the company's present problems, the vision he had for its future, and a few instructions as to how the planning information would be coordinated. What follows is excerpted from Bradshaw's presentation.

4.6.2   Atlantic's Major Problem

There are many ways to measure a company's success, but, in the long run, return on employed capital (invested capital plus borrowed money) is the key measurement of an organization's right to stay in business. Atlantic's major problem can be stated simply — in the past it has not earned enough on its employed capital. Last year, for instance, Atlantic earned 6.5% (see Figures 4.1 and 4.2 for operating results for 1954–1963). The 13 domestic companies with whom Atlantic competes earned an average of 8.8%. Our basic vision is to earn 9.0% by the fifth year of our strategic plan. We think this is an attainable goal. If we are to reach our profit goal, we must build on our strengths and be realistic about our weaknesses.

4.6.3   Atlantic's Strengths and Weaknesses Compared to Its Competitors

Atlantic's strengths include:

1. Our reserve of crude oil is better and our rate of return is higher than most of our competitors.
2. The percentage of our gasoline sold through company-owned outlets is in the top half of our competition.
3. Our foreign crude oil production volume is better than most of our competitors.
4. Atlantic's refinery transportation system is well located and adapted to serve our needs.
5. Our pool of technical and supervisory people is among the best.

Atlantic's weaknesses include:

1. The R&D efforts to support our oil producing efforts have been underfinanced.

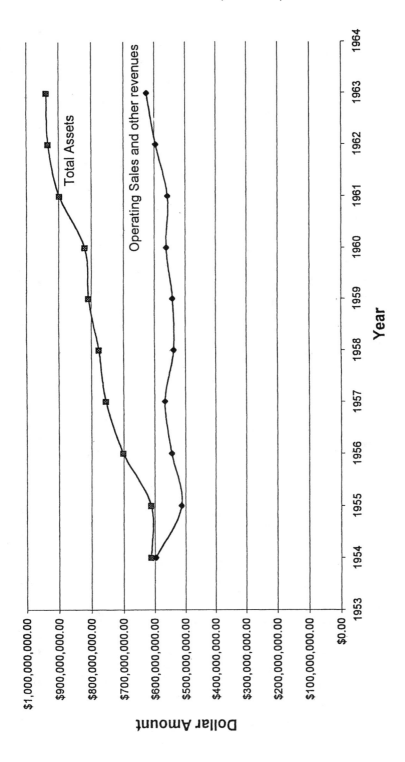

Figure 4.1 Sales and Total Assets, 1954–1963 (Based on raw data from *Atlantic Magazine,* 1964, pp. 1–6.)

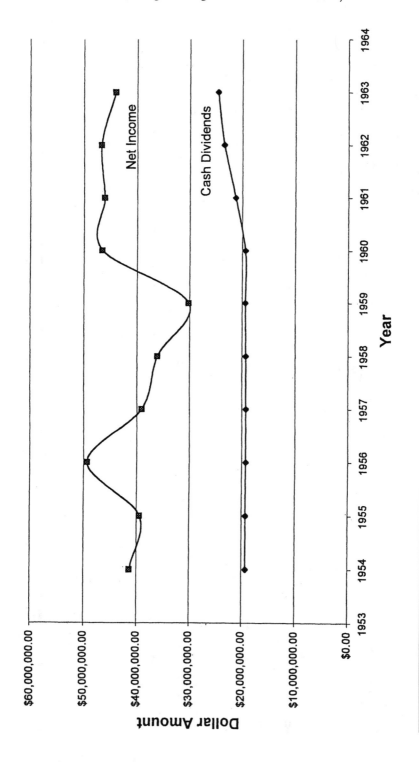

Figure 4.2 Cash Dividends and Net Income, 1954–1963 (Based on raw data from *Atlantic Magazine*, 1964, pp. 1–6.)

2. We have overemphasized our drilling efforts in the continental U.S. at the expense of offshore exploration.
3. The profit from the manufacture and sale of our domestic gasoline and furnace oil is considerably less than that of our competitors.
4. We need to put greater emphasis on, and apply more financing to, our exploration and oil drilling efforts.
5. We need a more aggressive marketing program, based on better market analysis of our past successes and failures.

4.6.4 What Kind of a Company Do We Want Atlantic To Become?

This is the vision that corporate management has for Atlantic's future:

1. A company that concentrates on things it has proven it can do well, such as (a) finding crude oil at home and abroad, (b) refining crude oil into products that can be sold at a profit both at home and abroad, and (c) developing petrochemical products from our own technical competence.
2. A company that maintains a balance between present and future profits.
3. A company right-sized down to fighting weight, whose staff services are essential, rather than luxuries.
4. A company whose basic objective is to improve its profit on its employed capital.

4.6.5 Atlantic's Profit Centers

The Atlantic Refining Company is organized around two profit centers, one is domestic and the other foreign. Both profit centers are in the business of discovering and producing crude oil, refining, and selling light fuel oils in the form of gasoline and furnace oil and manufacturing and selling petrochemical products.

4.6.5.1 The Domestic Profit Center

In regard to the crude oil business unit, we know how to find crude oil and refine it profitably; this isn't one of our problems. This division, however, does have some problems and decisions to make, and following are a few of them.

Should the division sit on its hands and take the profit from its past investments, or ask for additional resources to pursue the expensive hunt for more crude? If it decides to stop exploring, its short-run profit picture will be much improved, but what about the future? Will it have enough crude oil to satisfy the needs of the gasoline and furnace oil business units over the next 5 years? This is a question that the crude oil business unit cannot answer until they receive a copy of the strategic marketing plans of the gasoline and furnace oil business units. If the domestic oil needs in these units are greater than our present yields, then the division will be faced with these questions:

1. What additional resources will be needed for exploration to meet these new demands?
2. Where should the new exploratory efforts be concentrated? In the continental areas of the U.S.? In offshore drilling in Louisiana, Washington, Oregon? In Alaska, where we own acreage in Cook Inlet and on the North Slope? In Canada, where we have almost tripled our production in recent years? In none, or some combination, of the above? Any recommended drilling sites should be accompanied by an annual cost/return study over the next five years.

In regard to the domestic gasoline business unit, as mentioned earlier, one of Atlantic's weaknesses is its return on employed capital. In the gasoline business, our return is considerably less than that of our competitors. From our marketing research reports we know that we make money selling gasoline when we operate in regions:

1. Where we have a significant share of the market
2. Where our sales per station are high
3. Where we have a high concentration of lessee dealers
4. Where our dealer outlets are located strategically in or near metropolitan areas

Conversely, we lose money in areas in which the above factors are not present.

We know from the most likely scenarios we have projected of tomorrow's oil industry that future success will belong to those companies that are fully integrated and can operate profitably. We have made a corporate decision that we want to be one of those companies. That leaves the domestic gasoline business unit planners to decide how, and at what costs, this growth in market share and profit will take place by answering the following questions:

1. In which of the regions where we now have a significant share of the market do we attack first?
2. Where, when, and at what cost and projected return do we increase our lessee dealers?
3. Which new regions should we target first for expansion over the next five years?
4. In what order, at what cost, and what returns could we expect from the new lessee dealers in these regions?
5. In which regions where our volume and profit per station are low do we abandon our efforts, and in which do we pursue a holding operation?
6. What additional resources (money, personnel, equipment, etc.) will it take for the unit to meet the long-range annual objectives that have been set for each of these regions and markets?

It will be from the answers to these questions that we will decide how much additional crude oil will be needed over the next 5 years. The Crude Oil Division will obviously need this information before they can pursue their own planning work.

In regard to the domestic furnace oil business unit — again, before we can make corporate decisions about resource allocations for growth — we will need several recommendations from domestic furnace oil. We are now selling in a non-growth market and our profits are at best marginal. Do we get out of the business and improve our short-term profit, or are there legitimate reasons for us to sell furnace oil under these conditions? As mentioned earlier, the decision has been made that Atlantic should remain and compete in the future as a fully integrated oil company. These, then, are the questions that we will need answered by our furnace oil plan:

1. Given the company's decision to stay a fully integrated oil company, what alternative strategies do we have to improve our present profit growth?
2. Which of the above alternative strategies do you recommend?

3.   What additional new resources will be needed annually to activate each of the recommended strategies, and what returns could we expect from each?

In regard to the domestic petrochemical business unit, taken as a group, our chemical products do not make a profit for us. Individually, however, each product does cover its own cash costs. Because we are not actually losing money on any one product, we plan no withdrawals. What we would like to do with these products in the future is to reduce our costs, increase sales where we can, and periodically review and assess our progress.

We also want to continue to search for chemicals that will give us unique, profitable products in the petrochemical markets. To this end, we intend to increase our R&D budgets.

We will continue to manufacture and sell detergents, alkylates, ultra wets, ammonia products, and the output of the BTX plant as aggressively as we can. To help us with our long-range plans for the chemical business unit, here are some recommendations we will need:

1.   Where, when, and how much can we cut costs and/or increase sales in our present line of chemical products?
2.   Where are the *unfilled* needs and *growth* markets in the petrochemical industry?
3.   Where should we target our research for new petrochemical products?
4.   What additional annual resources will be needed for our R&D budgets over the next 5 years?

4.6.5.2   The Foreign Profit Center

In regard to the crude oil business, our foreign operations were originally confined to searching for crude oil in Venezuela. Our goal was to provide additional crude to support our domestic needs. These operations have been successful, and we now have enough crude to support our needs for years to come. At this point in time, we at the corporate level must reconsider the role that we want our foreign operations to play in our overall vision for the company: Should we stop searching for foreign crude and increase our short-term profit margin by $5 to $10 million a year, or continue to invest in foreign explorations?

Our most likely scenario of tomorrow's oil industry projects a growing demand for energy in third world countries. Because of these projections, we have decided that Atlantic should continue its search for additional crude supplies. Wherever we can, we shall proceed from a base of cheap crude and enter the retail gasoline and furnace oil markets in the region of the oil supply.

Given this corporate decision, we will need help in deciding:

1. If and where we should start our exploration in offshore Libya
2. If we should look for new drilling sites in the North Sea
3. If we should bid on new drilling sites in the Persian Gulf

In regard to the foreign gasoline, oil, and petrochemical business units, we need to ask in what countries and markets should we start looking for retail service stations? For furnace oil business?

4.6.6 *Additional Planning Instructions*

To be successful, every plan must answer certain specific planning questions. The following is a sequential set of planning questions which acts as a verbal model of what we want our strategic plan to accomplish. Let the following questions guide and focus you as you develop your planning information:

1. What external environment changes can be expected that are relevant to your industry?
2. What could be the effect of each change on the industry business climate?
3. What new market opportunities and threats could these changes bring?
4. What are our competitor's strengths and weaknesses to respond?
5. What are our capabilities to respond relative to the competition?
6. What will be our competitive strategy in responding to these opportunities and threats?
7. At what group of buyers will we target our responses?
8. What costs, returns, and risks can be expected with each strategy annually over the 5-year period?

We will use the same format this year as we did last year for submitting cost/return projections and financial plans. The key dates to remember are

1. By March 30, all business units are to complete their planning work.
2. By June 30, all divisions are to submit their planning work to the top Corporate Planning Committee.
3. By October 15, all short-range annual plans are to be submitted to the divisional general managers for their review and approval.
4. By November 15, all annual plans and their budgets are to be sent to corporate planning for review.
5. By December 20, all approved plans are to be ready for implementation on January 1.

4.6.7 The Outcome: Atlantic Refining's Growth Record Under Its 1965 Strategic Plan

Today's chief executives must not only be visionary leaders in the sense that they can create and communicate logical visions of the future, but they also must be held accountable for the results of their visionary leadership. The 1965 strategic plan that resulted from Bradshaw's visionary leadership was responsible for the successful growth record of improving return on assets from 6.5% in 1965 to 15.5% in 1979 as reported in *Forbes* magazine in 1988.

4.7 The Role of the Annual Budget in Implementing the Strategic Plan

Many strategic plans fail because they never get implemented. Drucker has said strategy is nothing until it degenerates into work.[24] This can be translated literally to mean that strategy is nothing until it is implemented. Strategic leaders implement their strategies the only way they can be implemented — first, by forecasting the expected costs and returns of each one and, second, by working them into the budgeting system (both the long-range financial plans and the annual operational plans).

Budgeting is an integral part of the strategic planning process, something planners often forget. Seymour Tilles of the Boston Consulting Group calls this one of the forgotten truths about planning. To quote him directly; "One of the curious aspects of budgeting is that it seems to be designed to keep basic assumptions about future growth plans implicit while giving a great deal of attention to their quantitative implications. Thus, most budgets focus entirely on numbers and rarely on the assumptions and strategies on which the numbers are based. The strategic planning process focuses attention on the assumptions and strategies, as well as the numbers, in the budget."[25]

Linking the strategies to the budget requires two steps. First, the long-range financial and capital budgeting plans lay out the multi-year costs and returns expected from the strategies in the plan. Second, when approved, the first year of the approved strategies is detailed into assignments, resources, schedules, etc. which become part of the annual operational plans (see Figure 4.3).

4.8   Measuring the Relative Values of Competing Strategies

While all elements in a strategic system are important, two are absolutely essential if the system is to be successful. The first of these two is the creative element that determines the competitive advantages and the potential the business has for growth. The second is the element of forecasting to determine the relative value expected from the competitive advantages built into each strategy or business unit.

The importance of the creative element (that is, the art of developing competitive strategies) has been well documented above. Forecasting, the art of projecting the revenue and profit expected from each strategy or business unit, is seldom addressed in any detail by strategists. Two strategists who have written extensively on the subject of forecasting revenue and profits are Robert S. Weinberg, a former professor of economics at MIT and a strategic planner at IBM,[26] and Alford Rappaport, a former Director of Accounting Research at Northwestern's J.L. Kellogg Graduate School of Management.[27]

Weinberg developed a simple verbal model that could be used to project the built-in advantages in a strategy into expected market share, revenue, and operating profit. He builds his model on what he states are the "seven structural determinants of short- and long-term profits." When the questions about these seven variables are answered properly he has all the information he needs to predict, or forecast the relative profit potential for each competition strategy. The seven so-called determinants or building blocks for predicting operating profits are

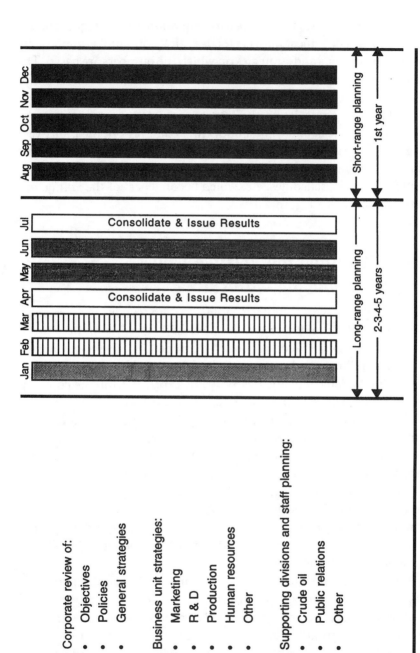

Figure 4.3 Annual Planning Timetable

1. Total market potential
2. Market development rate
3. Market realization rate
4. Competitive impact factor
5. Pricing factors
6. Variable cost factors
7. Fixed cost factors

Here are the questions Weinberg wants answered about these profit variables:

1. What is the total potential for this market?
2. At what rate can the total market be turned into real potential (today's potential)?
3. At what rate is today's potential currently being sold?
4. What share of this market (in units) can this company expect, based on the competitive advantages built into each strategy?
5. How should the products or services in the strategy be priced to attain the highest possible profitable market share?
6. What are the fixed costs of activating the strategy?
7. What are the variable costs?

While the Weinberg model gives the strategist all the information necessary to make the strategic decisions, the substance and success of the decisions will depend on the strength of the competitive advantages built into the strategies (see Figure 4.4).

As early as 1981, Rappaport was championing "economic value added" as the technique of choice for deriving shareholder equity contribution from operating profits. The economic value added (EVA) technique is the only profit concept that measures both the impact of dividend payouts and capital gains. EVA has received wide adoption in business because of its simplicity and the real visible value that it adds to the shareholders' wealth, the latter becoming increasingly important to the investors in general and institutions in particular. EVA is a simple method to measure the real profitability of an operation. The distinctive feature of this method is its all-inclusive feature that considers all the capital tied up in the operations (namely, all the heavy and light equipment, real estate, and components of the working capital such as cash, inventory, securities, and receivables) to generate the amount to be used as a true measure of a firm's profitability.

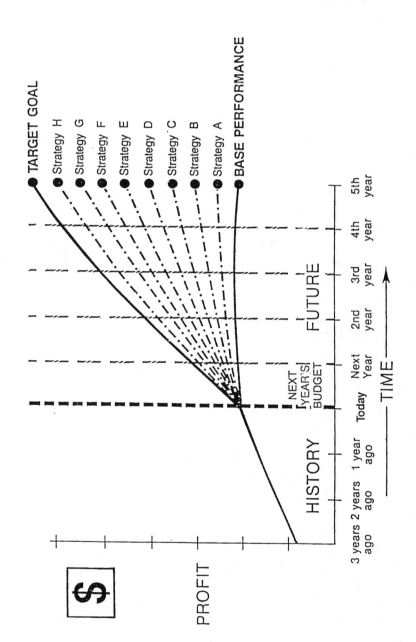

Figure 4.4 Long-Range Financial Plan (links strategies and returns from multi-year strategies).

Let us use some sample figures to determine the economic value added for a typical firm. Mr. X borrows $10,000 from a bank in order to invest in a small business. The charge for using this capital ($10,000) is 5%; therefore, the after-tax interest on the loan is $500. At the end of the year, the business has earned 15% profit, thus this net operating profit after tax amounts to $1500. The next step is to subtract the interest charge on the borrowed money from the earned profit: $1500 – $500 = $1000. This amount is Mr. X's economic value added. Simplifying the formula, we could say that:

Net operating profit after taxes – charge for the capital
= economic value added

Many companies have eagerly adopted the concept of EVA, and from all indications they feel they are responding more to the actual capital investment than before. The concept takes into account the total cost of the operation's capital. Many companies that have used the concept, such as Coca Cola, CSX, AT&T, Quaker Oats, Briggs and Stratton, and many more, do realize its value in determining the market value of their respective firms. What is even more significant is the correlation between EVA and stock price: "It seems that stock prices track EVA far more closely than they track such popular measures as earning per share or operating margins or return on equity."[28]

4.9 Directing and Controlling the Strategic Planning System

Chief executives do not have to be specialists in strategic planning to qualify as visionary leaders. What they do have to know is how to control the planning and keep it on track. Functional managers often fill their plans with interesting but irrelevant information, charts, and statistics.

Nothing promotes bureaucracy more than planning information that contributes nothing to answering the strategic questions. Strategic questions are those questions the plan must answer if it is to be successful (see Table 4.1 for the list of strategic questions). Strategic planners, however, do have to be planning specialists. They must know all aspects of the planning model to be used, be able to explain it clearly, and to troubleshoot wherever needed.

Table 4.1 Core Questions of Strategic Planning

Eleven Core Questions of Corporate Strategic Planning	Marketing Director	Field Sales	Logistics	Sales Admin.	Advertising	Pricing and Catalog	Product Mgmt.	Marketing Research
Question 1. What will be the organization's mission statement and long-range objectives?	X							X
Question 2. What will be the scope of its business?	X						X	X
Question 3. What external environmental changes can be expected?	X	X	X				X	X
Question 4. What could be the effect of each change on the industry and its markets?	X	X	X				X	X
Question 5. What new opportunities and threats could these changes bring?	X	X	X				X	X
Question 6. What are the competitors' strengths and weaknesses?	X	X	X				X	X

	100%	64%	55%	0	0	0	82%	100%
Question 7. What are our capabilities relative to the competition?	X	X	X				X	X
Question 8. What will be our competitive strategy in response to these opportunities and threats?	X	X	X				X	X
Question 9. At what target groups will we target our response?	X	X					X	X
Question 10. How can we link strategies to our long-range financial plans?	X							X
Question 11. How can we activate our strategic plan?	X						X	X
Contribution of each marketing function to strategic planning	100%	64%	55%	0	0	0	82%	100%

Source: *International Strategic Management Journal*, Vol. 27, No. 1, 1994. With permission.

4.10 Summary

It is often stated that an entrepreneur is visionary and an excellent manager is missionary. In order to inspire his subordinates (and, in the late Sam Walton's terminology, "associates"), the chief executive officer must have the confidence and an inspiring attribute all summed up in a "vision" for the future — a vision based on a future, part of which the rank-and-file can see or "touch" and a part that can only be explained by the leader in order to energize them all to help him achieve the goals and objectives of the organization. Furthermore, the chief executive officer should not only be able to achieve those goals, but also, once achieved, be able to enjoy the fruits of their efforts no matter how small. Mankind can accomplish a lot if motivated in the right way and able to partake in the fruits of success.

References

1. Kevin Maney, "IBM's Quest for Visionary," *USA Today*, February 5, 1993, p. 1.
2. James C. Collins and Jerry I. Porras, "Organizational Vision and Visionary Organizations," *California Management Review*, Fall 1991, pp. 31–33.
3. Gilbert Fuchsberg, "Visionary Mission Becomes its Own Mission," *Wall Street Journal*, January 7, 1994, p. B9.
4. Francis J. Aguilar, *General Managers in Action*, Oxford University Press, New York, 1992, pp. 408–410.
5. Michael Porter, "Corporate Strategy: The State of Strategic Planning," *The Economist*, May 23, 1987, p. 18.
6. Kenichi Ohmae, *The Mind of the Strategist*, McGraw-Hill, New York, 1982, p. 7.
7. Kenichi Ohmae, *The Mind of the Strategist*, McGraw-Hill, New York, 1982, pp. 84–85.
8. Kenichi Ohmae, *The Mind of the Strategist*, McGraw-Hill, New York, 1982, pp. 4–12.
9. *Handbook of Advertising*, McGraw-Hill, New York, 1960, pp. 14-4–14-5.
10. Roger A. Kerin, Vijay Mahajan, and R. Rajan Varadarajan, "Organization Renewal," in *Contemporary Perspectives on Strategic Market Planning*, Henry Reece, Ser. Ed., Allyn & Bacon Co., Boston, 1990, p. 419–420.
11. Farrell Kramer, "Vision: Can Your Enterprise Live Without It?," *Investor's Business Daily*, January 13, 1993, p. 4.
12. Laurie Tema-Lyn, "Creativity Can Be Taught," *Marketing News*, May 8, 1989, p. 4.
13. Theodore Levitt, "Creativity Is Not Enough," *Harvard Business Review*, May-June 1963, pp. 72–83.
14. John J. Corson, "Innovation Challenges Conformity," *Harvard Business Review*, May-June 1962, pp. 67–74.
15. Helen Rowan, in *Think* magazine, November-December 1962, IBM Corporation, New York, pp. 7–15.

16. Wilfred A. Peterson, *Ideas: The Beginning of All Things*, The Jaqua Company, Grand Rapids, MI.

17. Richard H. Harris, "A Creativity Training Program," *Michigan Business Review*, May 1956, p. 27.

18. William T. Brady, "The Management of Innovation," *Business Topics*, Spring 1961, pp. 7–14.

19. Betty Castor (Education Commissioner, State of Florida), "New State Test Finds Mediocre Writing Skills," *Florida Times-Union*, May 20, 1993, p. B-1.

20. Rochelle O'Conner, *Corporate Guides to Long-Range Planning*, Report #687, The Conference Board, New York, 1976, p. 1.

22. Stephen D. Moore, "Glaxo's Prescription: Get Back to Basics," *Wall Street Journal*, April 21, 1993, p. A5D.

22. Noel B. Zabriskie and Alan B. Huellmantel, "Developing Strategic Thinking in Strategic Management," *Long Range Planning*, December 1991, pp. 25–32.

23. Thornton F. Bradshaw, "Our Plans and Our Hopes for the Future," *The Atlantic Magazine*, November-December 1964, pp. 9–16.

24. Peter Drucker, *Marketing Management*, Fifth ed., Prentice-Hall, Englewood Cliffs, NJ, 1984, p. 71.

25. Seymour Tilles, *Making Strategy Explicit* [client briefing], Boston Consulting Group, April 1970, p. 1.

26. Robert S. Weinberg, "Top Management Planning and the Computer," CMA-Paper 520, presented at the Chemical Marketing Research Association annual meeting, Cleveland, OH, November 1965, pp. 1–14.

27. Alford Rappaport, "Selecting Strategies that Create Shareholder Value," *Harvard Business Review*, May-June 1981, pp. 139–149.

28. *Fortune*, September 20, 1993, p. 40.

5 Finance-Marketing Interface

"Today's management lacks a unity of purpose, a central focus, a set of primary decisions to guide its planning and decision-making." (J.B. McKitterick)

5.1 Introduction

As many as 60% of strategic plans have failed because the strategies in them could not be implemented profitably. Even the best operational people cannot implement broad, generalized strategies not expressed in competitive terms. Generalized strategies are not targeted at any particular competitor, nor do they contain elements of competitive advantages. Providing competitive information for strategy formulation is a job for the marketing and finance directors, properly supported by information from the marketing research department and financial markets. Competitive strategies must be derived from resource strengths and the advantages built on these strengths, but matching resource strengths to market opportunities requires research about changes occurring in the environment, scenario projections about the future, and market impact studies. Organizations operating successfully in the XXIst century will require marketing and finance research departments capable of providing these services.

5.2 The Challenge for the XXIst Century

During the 1970s and early 1980s, many converts were made to this new growth concept. By the mid-1980s, however, many of these converts were having second thoughts about its usefulness.[1] They were discovering that it was much easier to recognize and accept the value and logic of a concept than it was to execute it successfully, because concepts that have no relevance to reality and cannot be executed successfully are not of much practical value. The challenge to chief executives and their marketing and finance directors for the XXIst century will be to find a way to bridge the gap between *formulating* and *implementing* strategies.

Harvard University's Michael Porter, commenting on today's strategic planning problems, concluded that the need for and substance of strategic planning have never been challenged. What *has* been challenged are the skills of the planners and the methods they have used to develop their strategies.[2] In other words, the strategic concept itself is a sound concept and is here to stay. It is up to the organization's planners to sharpen their skills and gain the experience necessary to formulate competitive strategies that can be implemented profitably.

Formulating competitive strategies starts with the marketing directors and their planning staffs. They are the organization's specialists in monitoring and interpreting trend changes in the external environment that could affect markets. Trend changes in the environment offer new opportunities for changing the company's market position.

The opportunities presented by these changes are matched against each competitor's resource strengths. These strengths provide the building blocks for competitive strategies. The secret to formulating strategies that can be implemented lies in the ability of the planners to judge the strength of their strategies relative to that of their competition. Organizations that lack outstanding strengths cannot expect their market planners to formulate anything but weak strategies, and weak strategies cannot be implemented profitably no matter how talented the operational people may be.

How skillful are today's marketers in fulfilling this responsibility? Do Porter's comments apply to them? Are most chief executives satisfied with the strategic side of their marketing plans? A survey by former American Marketing Association President Joseph H. Rabins found that only 15 out of 50 top executives were satisfied with their strategic marketing. Only eight were satisfied with the strategic information they received from their marketing departments.[3]

More recently, a survey of 94 companies by David Reid resulted in him bluntly concluding that:[4]

"The quality of strategic marketing planning in the sampled companies was *poor*. This is partly due to *ignorance*, but more closely linked to an *absence of vision* which results in a lack of motivation to *acquire* and *interpret information*. In short the process of strategic marketing is weak." [emphasis added]

Ignorance is being used here in the best sense of the word — to denote a lack of knowledge and understanding of the subject matter. Reid seems to be telling us that the marketing directors in the organizations he surveyed lacked vision and did not understand the subject matter of the strategic planning concept well enough to formulate strategies that could be implemented successfully.

If the strategic side of marketing planning is to improve, the marketing directors who are also the chief marketing planners must:

1. Have a clearer understanding of the purpose for the corporate strategic planning concept they are being asked to support.
2. Recognize the marketing concept as marketing's "bill of rights" and license to become a legitimate member of the corporate planning team.
3. Identify the specific questions the strategic plan must answer to be successful.
4. Realize that a great deal of the strategic marketing information required to answer these questions can only come from a XXIst century strategic marketing research group within the marketing research department.

The purpose of this chapter is to clarify these requirements and to suggest what many top marketing managers need to do to strengthen their contributions to the company's strategic planning.

5.3   The Concept and Purpose of Corporate Strategic Planning

Some time ago the *California Management Review* carried an article stating a fundamental truth: it is impossible to understand or improve sub-systems of concepts without first having a clear understanding of the larger system which the sub-systems support.[5] For example, to improve a carburetor (a sub-system), an engineer must first understand the operation of the engine that the carburetor supports (the larger system). Because strategic marketing is a sub-system of strategic planning, it should follow that marketing planners cannot fully understand marketing's role without first understanding the corporate strategic planning concept itself. An overview of the concept can be visualized by examining Figure 5.1, which emphasizes that the real purpose for the strategic plan is to allocate (and reallocate) the organization's resources to fill the revenue and profit gap between where the organization is and where it wants to be. The study of strategic planning does not start with corporate planning staffs or marketing planners. It starts right at the top of the company with the chief executive officer's financial objectives.

In most for-profit organizations, the stockholders elect a board of directors to represent their interests. The board, in turn, selects a chief executive officer (CEO) to manage the organization for them. The CEO is given the assignment of taking the organization's resources and, within the limits imposed by the board's policies, allocating them to growth opportunities that will produce revenue and profit sufficient to meet the organization's long-range financial objectives. The corporate strategic plan provides the process by which the chief executive fulfills this assignment.

The strategic plan is the organization's lead plan, but it is not the only plan that organizations make. Every organization makes many plans, many of which support the strategic plan. Shirley classifies all of these plans into one of three groups; strategic, administrative, or operational.[6] The groupings are based on the type of issues and decisions addressed by the plan. These plans and their major characteristics are shown in Figure 5.2

Strategic plans and their issues are directly concerned with the relationship between the organization and the external environment within which it must compete. These are the issues that determine the effectiveness of the organization. They answer the questions that blueprint the route to be taken, the strategies to be used, and the work to be done to reach the organization's long-range financial objectives. All other plans support the strategic plan, either by removing administrative issues that could be obstacles to its success or by identifying and

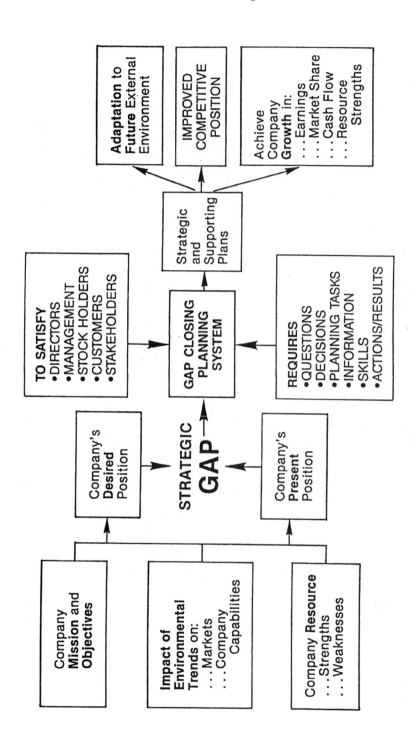

Figure 5.1 Strategic Planning Concept

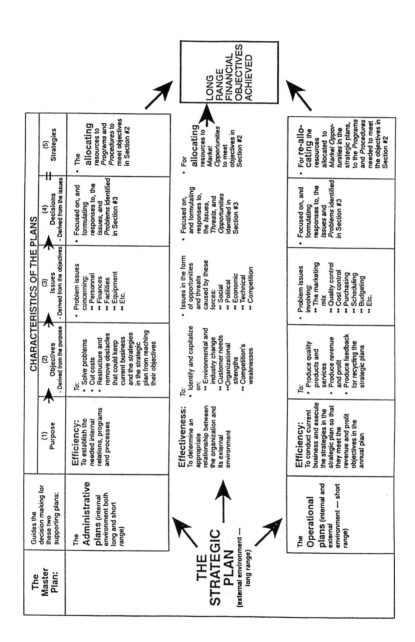

Figure 5.2 Corporate Planning System — Strategic Plan and Supporting Plans

detailing the operational issues necessary to implement the plan. These supporting plans determine how efficient the organization will be in performing the work required to implement the strategies in the strategic plan.

Often the term "strategic" is used in connection with the administrative and operational plans to denote the importance of the issues in those plans. This indiscriminate use of the term has made it difficult for many planners to differentiate between strategic and non-strategic issues and plans.

The process for developing a strategic plan suggested by Shirley consists of four separate but interrelated sections:[7]

Section 1 — Establishing mission statements and setting long-range objectives

Section 2 — Producing strategies and programs to achieve the objectives which include a general statement of strategy, competitive market strategies, and the programs necessary to activate the competitive strategies

Section 3 — Projecting the expected costs and revenue from the competitive market strategies by (1) prioritizing and stating where the funds and other resources will come from to activate the market strategies, and (2) integrating the approved and funded market strategies into the long-range financial plans and budgets

Section 4 — Implementing the competitive market strategies by detailing the first year of the long-range financial plan into operational schedules and budgets

All of the above sections are important, but Section 2, strategy formation, is the key to the success of the strategic plan. It is the key because it is the determining factor in the success of the execution steps, Sections 3 and 4. Unless the general statements of strategy in Section 2 are reduced to market strategies and directed at specific competitors, revenue forecasts and market shares cannot be estimated with any degree of accuracy. Without reasonably accurate revenue forecasts the relative strengths of alternative strategies cannot be measured, nor can they be projected into the long-range financial planning and budgeting system.

For example, how can market planners calculate and project revenue estimates from such vague general statements of strategy as:

"The organization's long-term growth objectives will be achieved by increasing R&D funding, by expanding research efforts overseas, and by consolidating the U.S. consumer goods operations and increasing their budgets."

Generalized statements of strategy such as the above cannot be implemented simply by designing programs and scheduling dates for completion. Programs by definition are sets of decisions outlining the work needed to activate the strategies.[8] They have nothing to do with competition and can never be a substitute for the innovative, creating thinking that must go into formulating competitive market strategies.

Marketing planners cannot pick market share, revenue, and cost projections out of the air; they must be derived from, and be based on, the assumptions made about the competitive advantages built into the strategies. No plan, regardless of its nature (strategic, operational, or administrative), can be implemented without its being quantified and put into the financial plan and annual budget.

Seymour Tilles of the Boston Consulting Group calls this need to base budgets on strategies one of the forgotten truths in planning. To quote him directly: "One of the curious aspects of budgeting is that it seems to be designed to keep basic assumptions about future growth plans implicit while giving a great deal of attention to their quantitative implications. Thus, most budgets focus entirely on numbers and rarely on the assumptions and strategies on which the numbers are based. The strategic planning process focuses its primary attention on the assumptions in the strategies from which the numbers are derived."[9]

How can marketing directors improve their inputs into the corporate strategic planning system? For one thing, they could have a better understanding of the purpose for the plan, the questions the plan must answer if it is to be made successful, and the decisions that will be made from the market information they submit. Once they understand the purpose for strategic planning, they and their staffs can better innovate and be creative about the market information they submit for the strategic decisions. A blueprint for this information was given by the marketing management concept articulated by J.B. McKitterick many years ago. This became the foundation for what is now referred to as strategic marketing.

5.4 The Concept and Purpose of Strategic Marketing

Prior to the 1950s, marketing's planning role was strictly an operational-level function. The marketing director's planning concern was to gather and package market information for his own decisions and those of his operational peers. In 1957, J.B. McKitterick of General Electric Corporation changed all of this when he stated corporate management's need for strategic marketing inputs with his paper, "What Is the Marketing Management Concept?"[10] He explained, in general terms, the impact that market information has on strategy formation and corporate growth decisions, and he stated emphatically that changes in the external environment, not internal factors, would in the long term determine the organization's growth.

However, knowledge of external change by staff specialists is not useful unless this information gets into the planning system and is put into focus for decision-making purposes. The question that puts change into focus for decision-making is, "What impact could this change have on tomorrow's customer needs and company market position?" The marketing management concept assigns the responsibility for answering this question to marketing, and this makes the marketing director a full-fledged member of the corporate strategic planning team.

McKitterick based his marketing management concept on two fundamental premises:

Premise 1 — *Today's strategic planning concept lacks a unity of purpose, a primacy of decision values to guide its strategy formation.*[10] To be successful, strategic planning must have inputs from all major functions of the organization. This premise simply states that all contributors must furnish information to support the same set of strategic decisions, and this set of decisions must have a primacy of decision values, the most important being the set that allocates corporate resources to long-range growth opportunities. All other planning decisions must be secondary or supportive to this set.

Premise 2 — *All opportunities for corporate growth must have clearly stated targets.*[10] This second premise stresses the fact that many organizations have grown too large to target their growth strategies at opportunities defined simply as profit opportunities.

Strategies such as restructuring, right-sizing, cost-cutting, and divestiture of marginal businesses are certainly growth strategies, and if successful they will produce profit. This profit, in turn, will improve the organization's current balance sheet, but are these truly long-term growth strategies? The answer to this question will depend on what management does with their cost-cutting profits. Only when these profits are re-allocated to market opportunities that produce profitable market share can they be classified as long term growth strategies.

In summarizing the marketing management concept's impact on marketing, we can say that the corporation's economic mission is to define and satisfy a set of wants for a defined group of consumers or customers. To this end, marketing research must be used to provide the strategic marketing information that market planners will need to fulfill their assignment. The organization structure must be such that the corporation can respond quickly to market changes and be sensitive to its target markets. To do this, marketing research must be given a new role.

5.5   Role of Marketing Research in Strategic Marketing

A number of thought leaders in planning have long championed the role of marketing research as an important element in the gathering and interpreting of information for strategic marketing, as reflected in these observations:

1. "Top management must believe that significant progress can be made by involving marketing research in strategic issues."[11]
2. "In the future, marketing research will enjoy an executive function image as opposed to the green eye shade image that has too long prevailed in many companies."[12]
3. "In the future, market researchers will have to take a broader view of themselves and help a beleaguered top management cope with a stormy external environment. They will have to develop a more strategic vision of what they are trying to accomplish."[11]

4. "Market research has a twofold relationship to strategic marketing and the marketing management concept. Market considerations are now moving to the center of the corporate management stage. Marketing research should provide the inputs of information and analysis that are the basis for the rational decision-making implied by the marketing concept."[12]

It is not enough to have a few planning authorities aware of marketing research's importance to strategic marketing. Nothing is going to change until the practitioners themselves (that is, the chief executives, marketing directors, and the marketing research directors) get the message.

Marketing research departments can be thought of as having life cycles in their development, just like products, managers, markets, and the planning process itself. Most departments start by gathering information and acting as fact-finding agencies. The second level in their life cycle starts when they are asked to contribute inputs into operational planning and problem solving. The final phase in the development starts with futures research, scenario projections, and market impact studies for corporate-level strategic planning and decision making. This departmental evolution can be seen in Figure 5.3.

After years of reviewing the output of research departments the authors estimate that only approximately 5% have yet reached the third level in their life cycle. This brings up the question of why. Why, after over 30 years of intense interest in the subject of strategic planning, are so few marketing research departments doing useful futures research?

Although there may be others, there are at least three possible reasons. First, the academic discipline of marketing research has traditionally been highly preoccupied with improving research methodology and ways of furnishing information for tactical decisions and brand management.[13] To this day, there exists almost no acknowledgment of marketing research's responsibilities in the support of strategic planning in any of the leading American university-level marketing research texts.

Second, neither the American university business schools nor the American Marketing Association have done enough to stress the importance of futures research studies to the success of strategic planning. As recently as 1988, the American Marketing Association's *Survey of Marketing Research* did not even include futures research in the spectrum of marketing research responsibilities.[14]

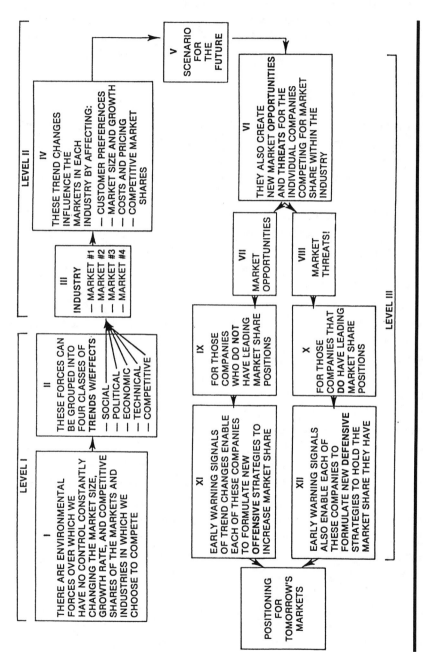

Figure 5.3 Environmental Trends and Their Effect on the Industry's Markets

Third, much of the market research done to aid strategic planning is done without the benefit of a planning focus, or even worse, from the wrong focus.[11] To be relevant and useful, market research contributions must be guided by and fulfill the information needs of the planning model being used to develop the competitive strategies for the strategic plan. These planning models affect the gathering of market research information in three ways (see Figures 5.2 and 5.4):[13]

1. In the validity of the futures information gathered for the planning decisions
2. In financial reality, as to how the financial analysis will be linked to the competitive strategies
3. In administration reality, in the form of cost/effectiveness studies on proposed strategies

5.6 Level Three Marketing Research Departments

In reviewing the work of marketing research departments, we find many references to, and attempts at, level three research. The research is labeled with the correct terminology, is interesting, and reads well. The only problem is that the outcome of the research in many instances does not help management make better strategic decision about the future (see Figure 5.5).

Stephen Millett of the Batelle Institute sums it up best by stating that the research is too abstract. It is not focused on the correct questions and does not produce the hard answers necessary for growth decisions.[15] Two companies have been recognized by the American Marketing Association for their outstanding level three research departments: the Singer Company of Stamford, CT, and the Johnson Wax Company of Racine, WI. By reviewing the papers presented by officials from these companies we can give some insight as to why they were chosen.

Alfred S. Boote, Marketing Research Director at the Singer Company, described the relationship of marketing research and strategic planning in their company as being symbiotic, a partnership with both units having definite roles to play. Strategic planning provides the framework within which marketing research information is needed. This framework limits the scope of, and gives a focus to, the research.[13] The

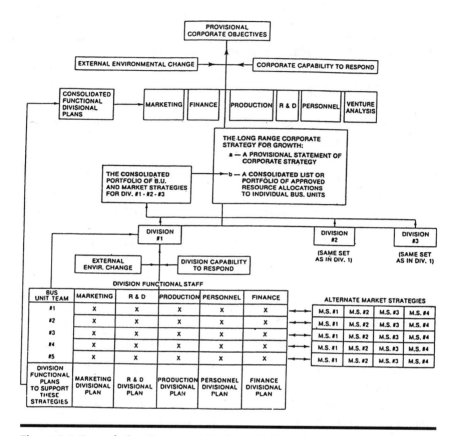

Figure 5.4 Formulating Corporate, Business Unit, and Market Strategies

framework takes the form of informational objectives. These informational objectives are usefully expressed as questions that the plan must answer if it is to be successful. Identifying the correct questions to ask and developing the correct answers from the research information represent the creative side of strategic planning — creative because it determines the substance of the growth strategies in the plan.

The informational objectives at Singer, according to Boote, require marketing researchers' involvement at all levels of the strategic planning process, specifically by:

1. Basing the long-range financial objectives on market opportunities in tomorrow's markets

2. Defining the scope of the organization's businesses, based on competitive market information

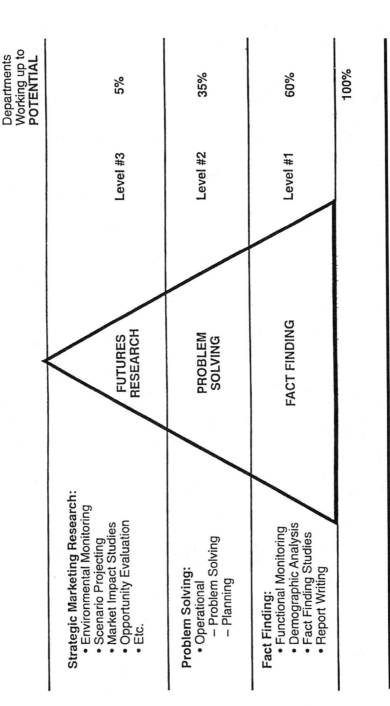

Figure 5.5 Development Life Cycle of a Marketing Research Department

3. Projecting scenarios of tomorrow's markets, based on trend changes already appearing on the horizon
4. Evaluating the marketing strength of possible competitors for new market opportunities
5. Building the company's marketing strengths into competitive strategies
6. Identifying the customer groups that will be targeted for each approved competitive strategy
7. Projecting outcome expectations of revenue and marketing costs for each competitive strategy for use in long-range financial planning
8. Detailing the first year of the long-range financial plan with schedules, time tables, assignments, etc. into the annual operational plan, the plan that activates the strategies in the strategic plan

Strategic Planning Director H. David Glatzel of Johnson Wax states emphatically that resource allocation decisions must be based on market research if they are to be successful.[11] He agrees with Boote as to the value of informational objectives by stating that most strategic planning fails because the proper questions were not researched and, worse yet, were never asked. At Johnson Wax they ask the questions that identify the major planning issues, then both the strategic planners and marketing researchers focus on the same issues. The techniques and methods, such as market segmentation, product positioning, scenario projections, etc., will be dictated by the questions and issues selected.

Johnson Wax has three organizational levels of marketing research:

Organizational Level 1 — Responsible for the research for decisions relating to sales and brand management, new product development, pricing, advertising, etc.

Organizational Level 2 — Confines their research to decisions concerning market growth, market share, profitability studies on market segments, competitive intelligence, customer satisfaction, product quality, etc.

Organizational Level 3 — Concentrates on research for corporate and business planning and growth decisions, which are the major resource allocation decisions that must be made today to be in position to exploit new opportunities in tomorrow's market. Level three research includes some form of environmental monitoring, trend analysis, scenario projections, market impact studies, opportunity evaluation, etc., as suggested by Figure 5.3.

5.7 Marketing: The Gatekeeper for External Changes

All relevant external trend changes must be evaluated for the impact they could have on the organization's market position. In a sense, this makes marketing research's market impact studies a screening gate, through which all trend changes, regardless of their source, must pass.

Consider, for example, a prediction by the chief financial officer that, based on emerging trends in the economy, there could be a 10% drop in national disposable income in the third year of the strategic plan. Could this have an impact on future market share and revenue? It certainly could; the U.S. Department of Commerce reported that all industry revenues are affected to some degree by changes in disposable income, and it has provided marketing researchers with a table of sensitivity indices for all U.S. industries. This table indicates that for every 10% annual change in disposable income, changes in industry revenue will vary from 3.2% for the boat and aircraft industry to 0.6% for prescription drugs.[16]

Let us take another example. Suppose that the director of purchasing reports that a raw material shortage is predicted for one of the organization's leading products and that substitute materials will be substantially more expensive within 2 years. Could this change have an impact on future revenue? It certainly could; any significant change in production costs, or product quality, could have a major impact on market response and therefore future revenue if alternative sources or replacement materials are not found in time.

In addition to providing strategic marketing information for corporate growth decisions, marketing research plays a major role in the strategic thinking that precedes strategic planning and decision making. Former president of the American Marketing Association, William Later, writing in *Marketing 2000 and Beyond,* makes it quite clear that CEOs expect marketing directors to be visionary leaders and to think more about today's decisions that will shape tomorrow's market position.[17]

How and where do corporate and marketing executives acquire vision? Visionary leadership, sometimes referred to as entrepreneurship, is acquired through a combination of experience, intuition, and the use of futures market research. Research on future markets is rightfully a responsibility of marketing research.

A recent article in *Long Range Planning* states that the simplest way to approach the strategic planning process is to answer 11 core questions.[18] By answering these 11 interrelated, sequential questions, planners would have automatically developed a corporate strategic plan. It is interesting to note that informational inputs from marketing research are required to answer not only questions 4, 5, 6, 7, and 8, which determine the substance of the competitive strategies, but all of the other questions as well. Marketing research is the only department in the entire organization that can make that statement.

5.8   The Interface

The bridge between planning for the markets in which a corporation wants to be 5 to 20 years from today and meeting the corporation's long-range financial objective lies in the relatively new planning technique called portfolio management. This approach blends the individual market strategies and their financial outcome into a set of business unit strategies for the future. This technique is particularly useful for solving the unique planning problems of multi-business unit organizations that stress more than one dominant corporate objective.

In the past, growth rate has been the dominant objective, with market share providing the central thrust for strategic planning.[19] Sources of capital to finance this growth have been of secondary importance. This traditional approach has now been seriously challenged by financial planners, and for sound reasons. Moreover, both the marketing and financial areas have been criticized by top management for taking the traditional functional or parochial approach, rather than a "holistic" approach to their planning.[20] Top management's solution to the problem is to "... make *business* men out of the marketing and financial vice presidents."[21]

The uncertain business climate of recent years with its volatile interest rates, persistent inflation, and scarce working capital has also forced many companies to re-assess their planning objectives. The policy of growth at any cost is being replaced by one where growth is limited to those opportunities which can be largely financed internally.[22] This change in corporate philosophy, although apparently simple, is making the job of strategic planning much more complex for several reasons:

1. Planners no longer have one dominant corporate objective to meet; they now have three: growth rate, cash flow, and earnings on equity.
2. These three objectives are highly interrelated and must be met with limited resources, especially cash.
3. In organizations with more than one business unit or major product line, market strategies must now be formulated to generate growth, cash flow, and earnings simultaneously.
4. Strategic management requires effective interplay between portfolio inputs and outputs.

In the portfolio management concept, the inputs involve identifying market opportunities, formulating competitive strategies, and making assumptions and options on which the strategies are based. These are, and will continue to be, basically marketing contributions. The outputs of the portfolio involve the evaluation, ranking, and balancing of alternate investment strategies. These will remain financial contributions. Between these two different viewpoints lies an interface of gray areas where the two sets of responsibilities have been shared by marketing and finance.

Until recently the marketing and finance officers have taken responsibility for their own functional contributions. The shared informational inputs which constitute the interactional interface between the two are those which allowed both to escape being held accountable for results. This has not worked in the sense that some CEOs are not now willing to accept this state of affairs.

In order to understand what information falls into this interface, a visualization is needed. The questions that usually occur in portfolio management demonstrate who contributes which information input into it. Table 5.1 illustrates the interrelated questions that form the thread of interaction that runs through the portfolio management concept.

Notice in Table 5.1 that there are four questions early in the thinking for which marketing's expertise is needed. Finance also has four that are its unique contribution; however, there are seven questions where *both*

Table 5.1 Marketing and Financial Planning Contributions in Portfolio Management

Primarily a Market Contribution	The Marketing-Finance Interface	Primarily a Financial Contribution	A Set of Essential Marketing and Finance Questions for the Corporate Approach to Portfolio Management
X	—	—	*Question 1.* Can we identify the economic and social trends that could affect the markets in which we want to complete 5, 10, 20 years from now?
X	—	—	*Question 2.* Can we relate any major changes in the above trends to either opportunities or threats to our selected industries and markets?
X	—	—	*Question 3.* Can we define the businesses and markets in which we want to compete in the future?
—	X	—	*Question 4.* Can we appraise our own resource strengths and weaknesses that determine our ability to respond competitively to the discontinuities in these trends?
X	—	—	*Question 5.* Can we formulate sets of effective competitive market and business unit strategies for these opportunities?
—	X	—	*Question 6.* Can we *prioritize* the list of our market opportunities based on our capability to compete successfully?

Question			
Question 7. Do we have the resources to activate one or more of these strategies?	X	—	—
Question 8. Can we convert more of our idle assets into cash?	X	—	—
Question 9. Can we extend the time of our accounts payable?	X	—	—
Question 10. Can we reduce our cash dividends?	X	—	—
Question 11. Should we sell off any of our poorly employed assets for cash?	—	X	—
Question 12. Could we generate more cash by redeploying some of our present assets?	—	X	—
Question 13. Could we spin off part of a division or subsidiary to obtain cash without sacrificing its functioning viability?	—	X	—
Question 14. Can we obtain cash or debt capacity by acquiring another company?	—	X	—
Question 15. Does our portfolio of market and business strategies balance out to meet the multiple long-term financial objectives of the corporation as well as sales growth?	—	X	—

experts must make a joint or shared contribution in order to address the question adequately. Both viewpoints are necessary to produce the balanced portfolio which top management needs to achieve the simultaneous objectives of earnings, cash flow, and growth for the total organization.[23] It is these questions, where a mutual sharing of inputs occurs, that an interface can be said to exist. The extent to which this interface occurs in a company will largely determine the speed with which a business viewpoint, as opposed to a functional viewpoint, develops in the minds of both executives.

5.9   Marketing's New Responsibilities

While the interface is necessary in planning, CEOs are saying that they want accountability for results as well. Consider these recent samples of what is being said around the country about the chief marketing officer:

1. "Companies of every stripe are looking for managers, presidents, or chief executive officers who can not only develop long-term product strategies but also instill an entrepreneurial spirit into corporations that, more often than not, practice risk avoidance."[24]

2. "Corporate board rooms are making marketing the number one business priority. In a recent study conducted jointly by the marketing consultants at Coopers & Lybrand and Yankelovich, Skelly, and White, more than half of the polled executives at 250 corporations ranked marketing as the most important strategy of the 1980s."[25]

3. "In an increasing number of firms, the chief marketing executive is directing the strategic planning of the strong market-centered focus of strategic planning."[26]

What is being suggested in these statements is that top management is now expecting their marketing vice-presidents to be held accountable not only for effective market and business unit strategies in the portfolio, but also for their financial implications. On this point David Cravens has this to say about strategic marketing:[26]

"Marketing's new financial responsibility can be described as follows: In order to respond to these (new environmental) pressures positively, marketing managers need a better understanding of accounting and financial management than their predecessors did. The characteristic marketing manager's emphasis in analysis and action on sales volume, gross margin, and market share must be replaced by a more general management focus on bottom-line profitability and return on investment."

Given that this is true, what form should the marketing-finance cooperation take? The evidence suggests that it should *not* be an equal sharing of responsibility. Rather, marketing must be dominant in evaluating and recommending markets and strategies the company should be investing in. This will involve more risk-taking than CEOs have been accustomed to; however, if a recommended opportunity is funded, the CEO will hold the marketing executive accountable for total results.

This is not to imply that the financial officer's role in portfolio management has declined. It is still a vital role where valuable information and evaluative perspective is supplied to assist the marketing officer and the CEO in their roles. However, it must be a supporting role, as CEOs will hold their marketing executive responsible for profit. The interface is more important than ever, but the chief marketing officer must be the one to recommend market strategies, and his CEO will hold him accountable for profit results.

5.10 Functional Strategic Planning

All functional vice-presidents have one thing in common. They are line managers to the people who report to them and staff advisors in their functional specialty to top management. The contributions of marketing and finance are the most critical functional inputs to the strategic plan, and they have been discussed extensively in the planning literature. Very little, however, has been written about the contributions expected from the lesser known functions, such as human resources and purchasing (see Chapters 7 and 8).

5.11 Summary

We have tried to point out in this chapter that the act of formulating competitive, winning strategies is the weakest link in the corporate strategic planning process, because weak strategies cannot be implemented profitably, and in too many of today's organizations marketing is contributing to this weakness.

Steven Harrell, Manager of Strategic Planning at General Electric Corporation, sums up this problem by stating that most organizations have been through the planning process several times by now and probably have enough corporate strategies formulated to last for years. What they need now are market planners that understand the planning process well enough to reduce these generally stated, unfocused growth strategies into competitive strategies with built-in advantages that can be focused on specific competitors.[27] These competitive strategies can then be prioritized for top management approval with cost/benefit studies and placed in the long-range financial plans and annual budgets.

To effect these changes, marketing directors will have to:

1. Have a better understanding of the purpose of strategic planning and how the strategic marketing information they submit to top management will be used
2. Focus their strategic marketing inputs on only one set of decisions: the set that allocates corporate resources to market opportunities
3. Develop their marketing research departments so that they are capable of producing strategic marketing research — this means futures research, based on environmental monitoring, scenario projections, market impact studies, and other types of research necessary for corporate planning and making growth decisions.

If these changes occur in companies, Lazer's predictions will come true:

> "The future will see a significant reorientation in marketing management priorities and outlook ... marketing will be seen as a change agent — a means of continuous adjustment and adaptation. ... The future will occupy a far more prominent position in both (marketing) management deliberations and research concerns. Future thinking will become a normal consideration — a basic input, a regular building block — for the most critical management activities of tomorrow."[28]

References

1. See, for example, "The New Breed of Strategic Planner," *Business Week*, September 14, 1984, pp. 62–65; Barrie G. James, "Strategic Planning Under Fire," *Sloan Management Review*, Summer 1984.

2. Michael Porter, "Corporate Strategy: The State of Strategic Planning," *The Economist*, May 23, 1987, pp. 17–22.
3. Joseph H. Rabin, "Top Executives Have Low Opinion of Marketing Research and Marketer's Role in Strategic Planning," *Marketing News*, October 16, 1981, pp. 1, 5.
4. David M. Reid, "Where Planning Fails in Practice," *Long Range Planning*, April 1990, pp. 85–93.
5. Dow Votah and S. Prakesh Seth, "Do We Need a New Corporate Response to a Changing Social Environment?" *California Management Review*, Fall 1969, pp. 3–16.
6. Robert C. Shirley, "Limiting The Scope of Strategy," *Academy of Management Review*, April 1982, pp. 262–268.
7. Robert C. Shirley, "Limiting The Scope of Strategy," *Academy of Management Review*, April 1982, pp. 64–66.
8. *Webster's New World Dictionary*, 2nd college ed., Simon & Schuster, New York, 1982.
9. Seymour Tilles, "Corporate Strategic Planning — The American Experience," client briefing, The Boston Consulting Group, April 1970, p. 73.
10. J.B. McKitterick, "What Is the Marketing Management Concept?" in Frank M. Bass, Ed., *The Frontier of Marketing Thought and Science*, American Marketing Association, Chicago, IL, 1975, pp. 71–81.
11. H. David Glatzel, "Marketing Researchers Must Start Contributing to Strategic Marketing," *The Marketing News*, February 19, 1982, p. 11.
12. Wendell R. Smith, "The Future of Marketing Research," a presentation at the September 1959 meeting of the Western Michigan Chapter of the American Marketing Association.
13. Alfred A. Boote, "Include Marketing Research in Every Level of Corporate Strategic Planning," *The Marketing News*, September 18, 1981, Section 2, p. 8.
14. Ann R. Root, in *1988 Survey of Marketing Research*, Thomas C. Kinnear, Ed., American Marketing Association, Chicago, IL, 1989, pp. 41–44.
15. Stephen M. Millett, "How Scenarios Trigger Strategic Thinking," *Long Range Planning*, 1988, pp. 61–68.
16. Clement Winston and Mabel A. Smith, "Income Sensitivity of Consumption Expenditures," *Survey of Current Business*, U.S. Department of Commerce, U.S. Government Printing Office, Washington, D.C., 1950, pp. 17–20.
17. William Lazer, Priscilla LaBarbere, James M. MacLachlan, and Allen E. Smith, *Marketing 2000 and Beyond*, American Marketing Association, Chicago, IL, 1990, pp. 225–229.
18. Noel B. Zabriskie and Alan B. Huellmantel, "Development Strategic Thinking in Senior Management," *Long Range Planning*, December 1991, pp. 25–32.
19. Robert E. MacAvoy, "New Rules for Strategy and Planning," *Management Review*, June 1976, pp. 4–5.
20. Herman H. Pohl, "The Coming Era of the Financial Executive," *Business Horizons*, June 1976, p. 16.
21. Bill Abrams, "Top Executives View Marketers as Myopic and Unimaginative," *Wall Street Journal*, October 9, 1980, p. 31.
22. Louis V. Gerstner, Jr., and M. Helen Anderson, "The Chief Financial Officer as an Activist," *Harvard Business Review*, September-October 1976, pp. 36–37.
23. George S. Day, "Diagnosing the Product Portfolio," *Journal of Marketing*, April 1977, p. 29.

24. William Lazer, "The Systems Concept in the Evolution of Marketing Management Thought," *American Marketing Association Annual Conference Proceedings*, 1962, p. 117.

25. "To Market, To Market," *Newsweek*, January 9, 1984, p. 70.

26. David W. Cravens, "Strategic Marketing's New Challenge," *Business Horizons*, March-April 1983, pp. 18–24.

27. "Panel Sees a New and More Vigorous Role for Marketing in Strategic Planning," *The Marketing News*, American Marketing Association, Chicago, IL, August 22, 1980, p. 1.

28. William Lazer, "The Systems Concept in the Evolution of Marketing Management Thought," *American Marketing Association Annual Conference Proceedings*, 1962, p. 229.

6 The Planning Organization

"Capable people working together in a well-designed organizational structure produce state-of-the-art management. Having both, you can't miss; with only one, you are seriously handicapped; without, either, God help you!" (Lounsbury Fish[3])

6.1 The Role of the Organizational Structure

The organizational structure has often been called the mechanism by which management directs, coordinates, and controls the firm's activities.[1] It provides a framework within which groups of specialists can work efficiently towards common goals. The key word here is "efficiently"; the better the organizational design, the more efficient the operation.

Years ago, Lounsbury Fish, of Standard Oil Company, stated that poorly designed organizational structures were responsible for much of an organization's bureaucratic problems: excessive paperwork, unnecessary committee meetings, etc. He also stated that most of the friction and frustration that creep into an organization are not so much the fault of people as the house they live in.[2]

In designing organizational structures, management should be guided by these six tenets:[4]

1. Each component should be organized around the achievement of a specific purpose.
2. Each component should comprise a logical separable field of responsibility.
3. Each component should represent a clear-cut section of the company for which the manager can be held accountable for results.
4. All of the elements necessary to achieve the goals of the assignment must be included in the component.
5. The managers of the compartments should have access to, and working relations with, managers in other compartments vital to their success.
6. There should be as few management layers as possible.

Strategic and operational assignments serve different purposes and have different objectives; therefore, they require separate organizational structures. In summarizing the role of organizational structures in planning and management, it can be said, generally speaking, that (1) unimaginative strategies are responsible for ineffective management plans, and (2) poorly designed organizational structures are responsible for inefficient, bureaucratic management plans.

Global organizations normally evolve over time through five progressive phases:

Phase I — Most organizations start out as small, one-country, domestic companies.

Phase II — Over time, an export department is added to sell their product lines out of the country through export brokers.

Phase III — If the export department is successful, a separate international division is formed with its own marketing organization, and they may or may not do some of their own manufacturing.

Phase IV — Again, if the international division is successful, it is replaced with a multi-national organization consisting of a staff at corporate headquarters and overseas functional operations in marketing, manufacturing, and possible research units.

Phase V — The final step in the evolution of a state-of-the-art global organization occurs when the multi-national organization rules all geographical areas through policy, strategy, and control mechanisms set at corporate headquarters. All resources are centralized at headquarters and allocated on a global basis wherever the best market opportunity presents itself. All geographic areas compete among themselves for the organization's limited resources.

6.2 Organizational Planning

Each generation of chief executives must study and redesign their organizational structure to meet the needs of their times. As management practices and markets change, so too must the organizational structures. The goal of organizational planning is to make and keep organizations efficient. As stated earlier, poor organizational structures encourage bureaucratic inefficiencies.

Earlier chief executives, in response to the increasing complexities of business and the growth in size of corporations, added line-staff relationships and decentralized organizations to strengthen their decision-making. Since the early 1950s, chief executives have been responsible for not one, but two, major assignments, and to make matters more complex, they must be accomplished simultaneously. Their first assignment is to meet today's budget with already committed resources. Their second assignment is to acquire and allocate resources to be in position to take advantage of tomorrow's new business opportunities. To meet this challenge, they have designed two new organizational forms.

The first of these new forms has been called the free-form organization. It offers management a more flexible, informal structure. Louis F. Hackman, an expert in both organizational theory and Greek philosophy, modeled the free-form organization after Aristotle's classic means-ends treatise: purpose-function-structure.[5] Under the free-form concept, the objectives (what the organization wants to achieve) are derived from its purpose. An executive is then given full responsibility for the decisions needed to achieve each objective — both the planning and the execution of the plan. Each executive is free to form teams of specialists to help with gathering the information and making the necessary decisions. The teams are formed and dismissed at the will of the executive.

Polaroid Corporation's founder and Chief Executive, Edwin Land, once described Polaroid's version of the concept as being similar to the solar system with its sun and satellites. The executive in charge represents the sun, and the supporting teams are the satellites in Polaroid's decision-making system.[5] In actual practice, companies using the free-form concept become conglomerated. They direct and control their semi-independent organization by clear company policies and corporate strategic plans.

The second structure of recent vintage is the so-called matrix organization. The matrix organization is formed by superimposing a horizontal organization over the traditional vertical structure. Matrix organizations operate with teams of specialists similar to the free-form structures. They differ, however, in that the decisions are made not by the executive in charge of the team but by the vertical line managers. Matrix organizations offer the following advantages over a single vertical structure:

1. They remove the two major complaints against vertical organizations — organizational and functional parochialism.
2. They address the needs of both meeting the annual budget and planning for the future.

Key elements of a good matrix organization include (see Figures 6.1 and 6.2):

1. The company is organized around its markets (businesses) rather than its functions.
2. Business teams are focused on the corporation's long-range strategic plans.
3. The organization offers fewer layers of management.
4. The feedback from the marketplace drives the performance of the vertical organization.
5. Performance rewards are based not on individual but on team results.
6. Every functional specialist on the team contributes information for the decisions from their own discipline's frame of reference (finance, engineering, production, etc.).

6.3   The Chief Planner and the Planning Team

6.3.1   Introduction

Chief executive officers are not only the organization's chief line managers, they are also the chief planners. They manage the strategic planning

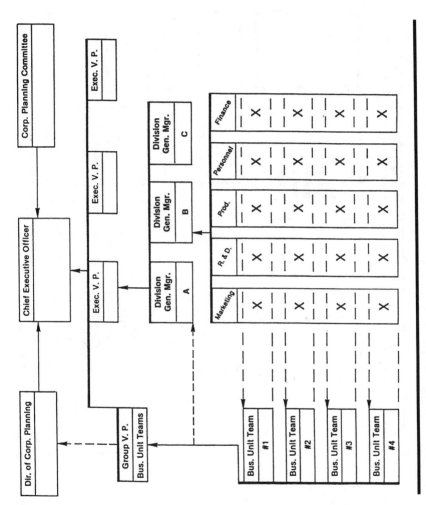

Figure 6.1 A Matrix Planning System

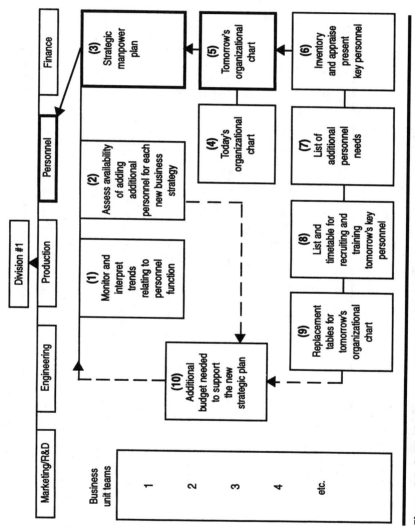

Figure 6.2 Strategic Personnel Planning

function in much the same way they manage the other specialized functions of the organization: finance, accounting, marketing, etc. To manage the specialized functions, chief executives need not have in-depth knowledge of each function. They do, however, need to have a clear picture of the role and contribution function each must make to their organizations if they are to be successful.

In the case of strategic planning, he or she must know enough about the purpose of the strategic planning concept to state clearly what they expect the planning to accomplish. The simplest way to state these expectations is with a list of the questions the plans were designed to answer.[6] A list of clearly stated questions not only offers a simple, easily understood control mechanism, it also provides a benchmark against which to judge the performance of each element in the planning process.

Most chief executives readily accept their role as chief planner. Few, however, feel as comfortable with it as they do in performing their line management duties, and for good reason. Most chief executives climb the organization ladder through line management assignments. Very few come from the planning ranks, nor have they had time to keep up with the state of the planning art. The purpose of this section is to analyze the implementation process of strategic management and synthesize the pivotal role of the chief executive officer in the process.

6.3.2 The Planning Team

One of the most important decisions the chief executive must make is to select a corporate planning director. This is a personal decision, as the success of the plans developed will depend entirely on the decisions the chief executive makes. Designing the strategic planning system and determining how the information will be packaged for the chief executive's decisions is the responsibility of the corporate planner. The association and trust are often so close between the corporate planner and chief executive that if the chief executive is replaced, so is the corporate planner.

Most chief executives consider the terms "domestic" and "international" inappropriate when applied to planning; in fact, they are misleading. They base their opinion on their belief that the principles of the strategic planning concept are universal. They do, however, readily admit that there are many differences that must be given consideration when planning the future of a global organization over that of a single country or geographical area. Some of the more common differences are

1. Languages
2. Way in which the country is governed
3. Culture and value systems
4. Legal and monetary systems
5. Level of economic development
6. Structure of the business organizations
7. Transportation systems
8. Methods and channels of distribution
9. Availability of information about markets, customers, and competition

The Kono Studies comparing U.S. strategic planning with the Japanese version offers a good example of how these differences affect planning systems. Because of the culture and business traditions, Japanese strategic planning up until the 1990s was highly centralized, with both objectives and strategies formulated from the top down by the chief executive, senior management, and the planning staff. Their purpose for planning was stated as "to solve corporate problems worldwide." This contrasts greatly with the U.S. approach of decentralized, guided, bottom-up planning for the purpose of "developing strategies to guide the allocation of resources to new market opportunities." The study states, however, that beginning with the 1990s Japanese planning has become much more decentralized and more closely resembles the U.S. approach.[7]

6.3.3   The Corporate Planning Director

There are two important aspects of any planning system: the process that develops the plan and the substance of the plan itself. The substance of the plan will depend entirely on how successful the line officers are in creating competitive advantages in the strategies they select. The design and effectiveness of the planning process are the responsibility of the corporate planning director. W.C. Roney breaks the corporate planning director's responsibilities into four dimensions:[8]

1. Architectural — as mentioned earlier, the corporate planner is the architect of the planning process and system.

2. Directive — in his directive role, the corporate planner acts on behalf of the chief executive in supervising all planning activities.

3. Monitor the line managers to see that they adhere to the planning format designed by the corporate planner but approved by the chief executive.

4. Check to see that the information being gathered for decision-making is gathered in a uniform manner throughout the organization so it can be aggregated and evaluated at higher planning levels.

5. Negotiate and persuade the line managers to conform to the planning process and schedules. Deviations from the approved planning process not settled through negotiations are reported to the chief executive to whom the corporate planner usually reports. It is up to the chief executive to see that compliance to the planning process is adhered to.

6. Supportive — in his supportive role the corporate planner is a teacher, trainer, consultant, and troubleshooter. He must be capable of performing and advising on all of the tasks necessary to assure that the process produces the best planning information possible.

7. Administrative — as the administrator of the plan, the corporate planning director monitors the progress of the plan, keeps procedures on schedule and communications fluid, and stays current on state-of-the-art planning methods and models.

6.3.4 *The Corporate Planning Committee*

The corporate planning committee in practice resembles more of a team than a committee. The chief executive officer is chairman, and the corporate planning director acts as its secretary. The members of the team are the top line officers in the organization as well as the marketing and finance officers. Each member brings a specialized functional or geographical viewpoint of the organization's present operations. Every member of the organization reports to (and is represented directly or indirectly by) one of the team members.

The committee has two primary duties. The first is to assist the chief executive in developing his or her version of what they want the organization to become. The vision as stated above blueprints what tomorrow's industries could look like based on change already appearing on the horizon. All of the objectives, strategies, opportunities, and plans are based on the scenario of tomorrow's industries. The second duty is to review the sector or divisional plans as they are presented to the chief executive. They evaluate and prioritize them according to their relative value. The final decision is made by the chief executive officer. This is not a democratic committee in the sense that votes are taken, because the chief executive as the team chairman is solely responsible for the decisions in the strategic plans.

The committee often meets in so-called retreats. These retreats, however, are not to do the planning, but to review and evaluate the strategies and plans that have been developed from lower planning levels, bottom-up.

6.3.5   Sector Level Vice-Presidents

Only large, worldwide organizations with many divisions and business units have sector vice-presidents. They and their planning staffs act as lower level corporate planning committees. Each sector vice-president supervises, reviews, aggregates, prioritizes, and recommends the strategies and business unit plans for several divisions. General Electric Company, with 90+ business units, was the first to use sector-level planning. The purpose for having this additional planning level is to cut down the amount of work and to speed up the work of the corporate planning committee.

6.3.6   Divisional Vice-Presidents

Divisional level planning is the highest planning level where meaningful competitive strategic inputs are made. Planning done above the divisional level is too far removed from the marketplace to keep current on new customer needs and the competition. In a practical sense, each division operates as a separate company guided only by broad corporate objectives and basic financial objectives. These guidelines permit corporations to decentralize their operations without losing control of their overall purpose and goals.

6.3.7   Strategic Business Unit Managers

Up until 1970, the formal planning levels stopped with the divisional vice-presidents. Divisional strategies are, by nature, broad, general strategies having as their purpose to give guidance as to how the corporation's resources will be committed to future market opportunities. Organizations of any size, however, are made up of multiple product/market segments. Each of these segments offers opportunities based on its own individual competitive environment, including such factors as:

1. Unfilled customer needs
2. Unique growth opportunities
3. Competitors
4. Resource requirements

The 1970 planning process offered no formal means of converting these broad divisional strategies into specific competitive strategies for each product/market segment.

In 1971, General Electric decided it was time to correct this deficiency. As one General Electric executive expressed it, they needed to get their planning down to where the strategies were more specific, where the managers could get their arms around them and accept responsibility for their success or failure.[9] Guided by a task force of general managers and assisted by a team of McKinsey consultants, they divided the corporation into product/market segments having similar economic and cultural characteristics. For planning purposes these segments were called strategic business units. They then appointed a planning manager for each business unit. To provide uniformity, the task force also developed a process for each manager to follow in their planning. The process was adapted from the portfolio approach used by the financial community for making investments. It worked this way:

1. Each business unit was to be clearly defined as to its purpose and the scope of its operations.
2. Scenarios of tomorrow's industries were to be projected based on changes already appearing on the horizon.
3. Each scenario was to be analyzed for the unit's current competition position and growth potential.
4. Long-range competitive strategies were to be formulated to exploit both today's and tomorrow's opportunities in each product line.
5. The approved competitive strategies were to be implemented and performance reviewed, with strategies being adapted and recycled.

To summarize, the task force divided the corporation into product/market segments, and similar product/market segments were grouped into strategic business units. Each strategic business unit was given a planning manager, who was given a uniform planning process to follow in analyzing his product/market segments and developing competitive strategies. This process was given the name of portfolio management.

6.3.8   Product, Brand, or Market Managers

The origin of the product management function can be traced to an attempt by the large, complex global organizations to get their planning closer to the customer and to capture the creative, innovative leadership that the entrepreneurial owners of smaller companies give to their line of products. A good example of this entrepreneurship was E.H. Stuart, who launched Carnation Evaporated Milk by acting as his own strategist, production man, market researcher, promotion specialist, and distribution manager.[10]

The first organized approach to reproducing entrepreneurship was made by the Proctor and Gamble Company in 1928, when they appointed C. C. Uhling as brand manager for their Lava Soap products.[11] The title given to such a manager will vary with the type of products the organization markets. The title of "product manager" or "brand manager" is usually used by companies marketing different products to the same set of customers or market segment. The term "market manager" is used by companies marketing the same or closely related products to more than one set of customers or market segments.

The primary responsibility of product managers under any of their titles is the same — to provide the creative, innovative thinking necessary to produce competitive advantages. Demonstrable competitive advantages are the building blocks of successful strategies. In recent years, because of disappointing experiences, the product management concept seems to have fallen out of favor in the U.S. It seldom appears in the planning literature, nor is its importance emphasized in the marketing curriculum. This, despite the fact that no less an authority than Proctor and Gamble traditionally selects its future top executives from among the product managers. When the concept fails to produce the desired results, it is usually not the fault of the concept, but the way it was implemented.

Product management failures can almost always be traced to one of these four fundamental errors:[12]

1. Clear-cut responsibilities and assignments have not been spelled out by top management.
2. Administrative and budget control tasks are emphasized at the expense of conceptual, creative, strategic thinking.
3. The product managers are not given enough authority to do their jobs. Too often the work degenerates into low-level clerical work and progress reporting.
4. The product managers are assigned to the position based on their administrative rather than their creative skills and knowledge of the marketplace.

According to one publication, product managers in Germany are held in much higher regard than they are in the U.S.[11] This may be due to the fact that U.S. companies do not export the concept until they have worked out all the bugs and can practice it successfully in the U.S.

As mentioned above, all organizations have growth product lines that produce negative cash flows. They also have mature product lines that produce positive cash flows. The tasks and skills for product managers assigned to each of these product lines will be the same. The only difference will be in the resources and financial goals they are given (see Figure 6.3).

6.4   Summary

Most organizations have some sort of planning, as they are all faced with a finite amount of resources. In order to prioritize, given the limited resources, organizations must plan and must also make sure that planning is integrated within the organizational culture, and there must be a faith in it to make it happen. The source of information for the planning function is the functional manager, the field representative, and all others who are in touch with the consumer for whom the product is being produced. Add the field experience to the vision of the CEO and a sense of discipline in adhering to the rules of the game, and you will find a planning system that can be a major contribution to the outcome of the organizational effort. Planning done in a vacuum would end up on a shelf somewhere to collect dust. Planning done in collaboration with as many people as possible and with as much input as possible will find a fertile ground for implementation.

A. Product managers are the answer when multiple products flow into a single market.

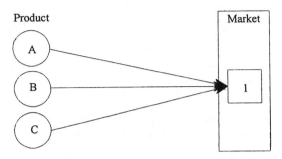

B. Market managers get the nod when a single product flows into multiple markets.

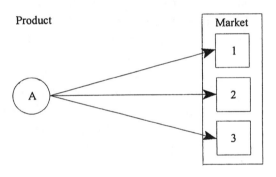

Figure 6.3 Product Manager Responsibilities

References

1. Lounsbury Fish, *Organization as the Mechanism of Management: Top Management and Control,* Standard Oil Company, San Francisco, CA, 1941, pp. 5–6.
2. Lounsbury Fish, *Organization as the Mechanism of Management: Top Management and Control,* Standard Oil Company, San Francisco, CA, 1941, pp. 15–19.
3. Lounsbury Fish, *Organization as the Mechanism of Management: Top Management and Control,* Standard Oil Company, San Francisco, CA, 1941, p. 30.
4. David I. Cleland and William R. King, "Organizing for Long Range Planning," *Business Horizons,* August 1974, pp. 26–27.
5. Louise Hackman, "Free Form Management," *Duns Review and Modern Industry,* December 1964, pp. 31–56.
6. Noel B. Zabriskie and Alan B. Huellmantel, "Developing Strategic Thinking in Senior Management," *Long Range Planning Journal,* December 1991, pp. 25–32.
7. Kono Studies on Japanese Planning.

C. Neither approach is suitable when products and markets criss-cross.

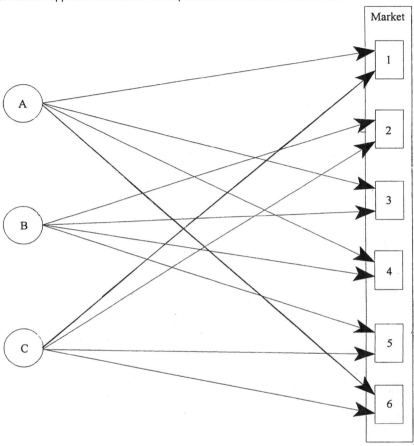

Figure 6.3 (continued)

8. W.C. Roney, "For the Chief Executive Organizing and Directing the Planning Function," *Managerial Planning,* March-April 1977, pp. 1–13.
9. Kevin Maney, "Secrets of Outliving Competitors," *USA Today,* October 28, 1996, cover story.
10. Stephens Dietz, "Get More Out of Your Brand Management," *Harvard Business Review,* July-August 1973, pp. 127–135.
11. Robert M. Fulmer, "Product Management: Panacea or Pandora's Box?" *California Management Review,* Summer 1965, pp. 63–73.
12. B. Charles Ames, "Payoff from Product Management," *Harvard Business Review,* March-April 1964, pp. 141–152.

7 Strategic Management in Human Resources

7.1 Introduction

Traditionally, the job requirements for the human resources executive have called for an understanding of the needs and desires of the workforce, skills in labor relations, enhancing the productivity of workers, managing benefit plans, and a bundle of operational tasks such as supplying cafeteria services, travel arrangements, training programs, and so on; however, the signs are now pointing toward an entirely different breed of human resources manager. Corporate management is beginning to expect the new breed to do all of the above functions in addition to contributing strategic input to corporate plans. They will also be expected to implement these contributions once they are approved and put into the strategic plan.

One of the big advantages of monitoring the signs that signal trend changes is the lead time it provides to prepare for them. If the current signs are correct, then human resources management should be addressing two major questions:

1. What are the specific ways human resources should be contributing to strategic planning and management?
2. What steps should they take to formulate an acceptable strategic manpower plan which will be needed if tomorrow's strategies are to be successful?

The purpose of this chapter is to point out the three major strategic dimensions to the human resources manager's job, to explain how each dimension is linked to the other, and how each will contribute to the business and corporate plans.

7.2   Strategic Planning

Before the strategic dimensions of contributions expected from the new breed of human resources (HR) officer can be discussed, it is first necessary to summarize the strategic planning process itself. Just what is it that the HR officers are being asked to support?

Strategic planning is the instrument used by top management to position the organization in tomorrow's business environment. The planning process supplies the information on market opportunities and threats. These opportunities and threats are created by changes taking place in the external environment, especially in the market place. This is not something new; management has always been faced with this challenge. What *is* new is the strategic approach.

The strategic approach demands an external focus. Many company planning approaches are internally focused; that is, they gather information to use in improving operational problems (e.g., in facilities, efficiencies, organizational structure changes, product modifications, etc.) with little or no concern for the changes taking place outside the company. This is putting the cart before the horse. External, not internal, change will decide the future of the organization.

Strategists further insist that strategic decisions, not plans, decide the future for an organization. The highest order of strategic decisions are those that allocate resources to emerging market opportunities. To make these decisions wisely, the chief executive must have timely information inputs from his major functional specialists: marketing, production, human resources, finance, and others, as needed.

These informational inputs must not only be timely, but they also must be gathered in a certain sequence, according to need. For example, marketing information on market opportunities and threats is needed first, as the purpose of strategic decision-making is to invest company resources for growth. After marketing contributes their information, the other functional areas can incorporate their plans by determining the support that they can give each strategy.

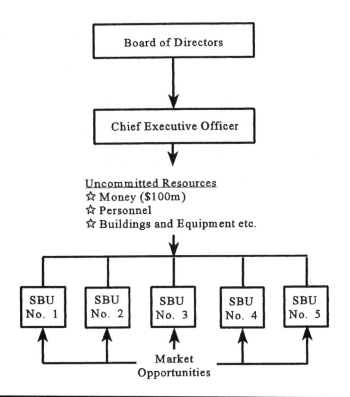

Figure 7.1 Resource Investment Strategic Decisions

Many organizations are now converting their planning structure to the strategic business unit (SBU) concept for gathering their strategic information. In this method the organization is segmented into sub-units on the basis of markets and product groups. Within each SBU is a team of planners composed of specialists from the major functional areas.

Figure 7.1 illustrates the resource investment aspect of strategic planning and the process of investing resources in market opportunities identified during the planning process by the SBUs. The drawing further suggests that uncommitted resources of several types are available for each planning cycle.

To be successful in developing the correct information, strategic planning must have inputs from both the corporate managers and the SBU planners. The corporate level inputs include resource appraisal, corporate missions, objectives, and strategies. The SBU consists of a team of planners who are to identify and evaluate market opportunities with creative, competitive strategies.[1] Team members from each functional area sequentially provide information on the support they can supply for each strategy and market opportunity or threat.

The idea of having an SBU team of planning specialists set up as a team for sequential planning is visualized in Figure 7.2. To illustrate the sequential performance of the team members, assume in Figure 7.2 that the marketing representative of SBU No. 1 has identified a market opportunity during the planning cycle and that each opportunity has four potential strategies for development. The other functional representatives (engineering, production, human resources, etc.) would then sequentially evaluate all four strategies to determine the extent to which each could currently be supported, what new resources would be needed, and what the costs would be. Human resources would be one of the last functions to add input to a strategy, as the other functions must first indicate their personnel needs. Finance would be the last functional representative on the team to contribute, by financially evaluating each strategy. When all SBU team members have thus evaluated each strategy, the planning information would be forwarded to top management for their approval and the allocation of resources to the most attractive opportunities and strategies.

To conclude, the failure of the strategic planning concept to live up to its full potential in the 1970s is being attributed partially to the failure of top management to involve functional line managers in the development of the planning information. This is an essential requirement.[2]

7.3   Three Strategic Dimensions of Human Resources Management

If it is true that a firm is actually strategic (as opposed to relying upon internal problem-solving) and if the planning process requires line managers to contribute information when strategies are being developed, then it becomes evident that HR management has three major strategic dimensions to their job. They are

1.   Continual monitoring of trends relating to the human resources function
2.   Assessment of the staffing needs and costs for each new business strategy developed during the strategic planning process

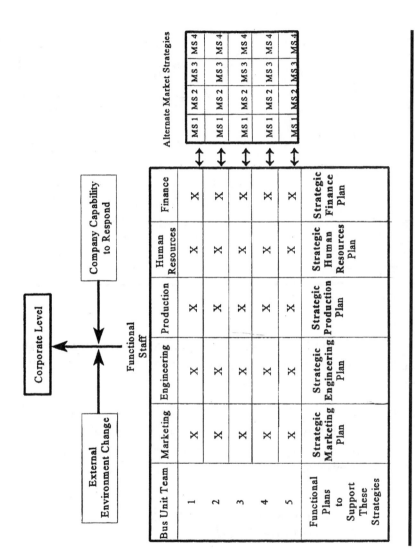

Figure 7.2 Augmentation of Human Assets

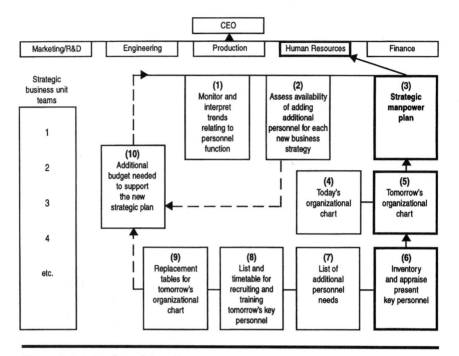

Figure 7.3 Interplay of Functions

3. Development of a strategic manpower plan after the strategic investment decisions have been made in order to prepare the organization for the future

Steps 1, 2, and 3 in Figure 7.3 depict these three dimensions. The dimensions are linked, indicating that they are sequential, interrelated activities. Steps 4 through 10 elaborate on the development of the strategic manpower plan.

7.3.1   Strategic Dimension 1: Monitoring and Interpreting Trends

Human resources managers possess a unique understanding that is vital to the success of an organization: identifying and interpreting the implications of trend changes and the appearance of new personnel methods (e.g., cafeteria-style fringe benefit plans) in terms of their potential impact on the firm. This is called "environmental scanning" and should be an ongoing part of human resources management, not just during the planning cycle.[3] This process appears as Step 1 in Figure 7.3, the first and fundamental strategic dimension of HR management. Environmental scanning involves both the monitoring of trends, which includes identifying and watching them, and the interpretation of changes in them (discontinuities) which may have an impact on the industry and company.[4]

Human resources management should make their environmental scanning expertise (step 1) available to top management in two ways. The information can be worked up and played into the business unit planning team by the HR representative on the team during the planning cycle. Alternatively, if the planning cycle is not active at the time a discontinuity is identified, a proactive approach can be taken by directly offering the information to corporate management or the affected business unit planning team leader. As one HR executive states it, "We are paid to take things to top management. If they have to come to us, we must ask ourselves why we have failed."[5] A study by A.T. Kearney found that the most productive and profitable companies have their senior human resources managers working closely with top management in this way.[6]

7.3.2   Strategic Dimension 2: Contributing to New Business Strategy Planning

The second strategic dimension of the human resources management's job occurs during the strategic planning cycle. Step 2 of Figure 7.3 suggests that a two-way linkage exists between the SBU planning team and human resources management. On the one hand, the HR function is affected by the strategies approved by the CEO, and, on the other, human resources influences the strategies by the input of information to strategies that are developed *during* the planning cycle. In a recent study, only four of the ten companies studied had achieved this two-way linkage.[7]

If the company employs the SBU planning team method of building their strategic planning information on market opportunities and strategies, then HR management should have a representative on the planning team along with the other functions shown at the top of Figure 7.2. Notice the left side of the drawing. It shows that some organizations have several business unit planning teams. Each SBU would have a team consisting of representatives from all major functional areas. Using this approach, the chief HR executive would appoint one of his specialists to each team. Each team member would keep him informed of their team planning work.

Both strategic dimensions 1 and 2 are illustrated by a planning situation that an American ethical drug firm experienced. During the early 1970s the trademarked prescription products in the ethical drug industry were facing a market challenge from generic drugs. Within the health care industry, several converging trends were altering the future business climate. The federal government agencies and health insurance companies were paying for an increasing number of prescriptions, centralized buying of drugs on bids was increasing, and many individual states were considering setting up drug formularies. Drug formularies would mean that all prescription drugs paid for by the state agencies would have to be listed in the formulary, and most drugs would be listed under their generic names. They would be purchased on bids which meant heavy price competition, and trademarked drugs would be at a great price disadvantage.

Generic drugs were produced by companies where low costs were a necessity, such as those that had no research expense, minimum Food and Drug Administration (FDA) production and control standards, warehouse-like manufacturing facilities, minimum salaries and benefits for employees, and so forth. These factors enabled them to charge relatively low prices. The questions asked of the HR representative on the business planning team were these:

1. Would trends in FDA regulations, OSHA requirements, and labor laws over the next few years force the cost of producing generic drugs more in line with the cost of producing trademarked drugs, or would they continue to be much lower?
2. If a generic manufacturer were acquired and the difference in labor costs were projected to hold at a much lower level, could the corporation maintain two different levels of salaries and benefits for employees doing the same jobs without causing morale or labor law problems?

After studying both federal government and industry production trends, the HR representative conferred with the vice-president for human resources. The conclusions supplied to the business unit planning team were:

1. There was a high probability that governmental regulations over the next few years would place stricter manufacturing controls on generic drugs, resulting in higher labor costs. Generic production costs could be expected to approximate trademarked drug costs in this time period.

2. If the company did acquire a generic manufacturer and attempt to maintain two levels of compensation for personnel doing the same work, within 2 years low employee morale and major labor problems could be expected to develop with personnel in the acquired company.

Based on the input from human resources and other cost projections, the strategy of acquiring a generic manufacturer was dropped. Instead, the company chose to meet the generic drug challenge with products manufactured in their existing plants.

The bottom of Figure 7.2 shows that each functional area has a strategic plan (strategic marketing plan, strategic engineering plan, and so on). After the team planning process is complete and the information is forwarded to the CEO for the strategic decisions, each function has a plan of proposed strategies with the support required to execute them. Whichever strategies the CEO approves, the executive of each function area knows what his function has said it could do to support them and what it must do for implementation of its part of the strategic plan.

These two dimensions — monitoring trends and making inputs to the strategic planning process — occur prior to the decisions on resource allocation that appear in the strategic plan. However, after the decisions have been made, the third dimension must be performed: a strategic manpower plan to implement the strategic plan effectively.

7.3.3 Strategic Dimension 3: The Strategic Manpower Plan

Today's organizational structure must be adapted to fit the changes in the new strategic plan. As a result of adding products, seeking new markets, or significantly changing strategies for existing products and markets, the organizational structure and staffing needed in the future

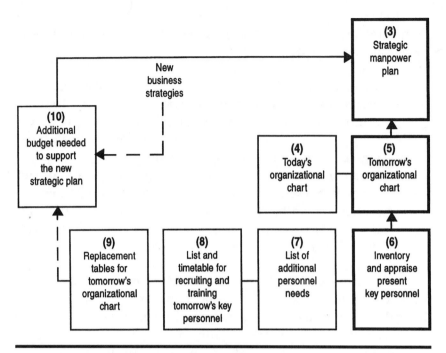

Figure 7.4 Elements of Strategic Manpower

to execute these strategies will be different from today's. This is the primary purpose of the strategic manpower plan: to assure the staffing and structure for effective performance.[8]

Given the above, what must be done, and in what order, to create an effective manpower plan? Figure 7.4, a portion of Figure 7.3, suggests that there are seven steps involved (boxes 4 through 10). Because most of the components of manpower planning are well known to human resources executives, this discussion will concentrate on the links between them and the strategic nature of each one.

7.3.3.1 Organizational Charts

Because most companies have an existing organization chart showing how the functional areas are currently executing today's strategy, step 4 may already be done. In step 5, the key question that human resources executives must answer to the satisfaction of top management is what the organization will look like 3, 5, and 10 years from now as it enters new businesses, drops existing businesses, and phases the organization into the future? This requires conceptual thinking.

Put another way, it must be determined how supporting the approved strategic plan will alter staffing patterns, work habits, and reporting relationships while achieving greater productivity and profitability. Several organizational charts reflecting the evolution of the company 3, 5, or 10 years from now may have to be developed. These should then be presented and explained to top management for their input and approval. The approval at this time can only be preliminary, as much additional work must be done on staffing and budgeting. The importance of the work done in steps 5 and 6 of the manpower plan is suggested by the extra-heavy dark lines shown in Figure 7.4.

7.3.3.2 Key Personnel Appraisal and Inventory

In step 6, the attention shifts to management succession planning. The focus is on identifying the most crucial management jobs in the division or company. These are the ones that, if left unfilled or filled with incompetent people, might substantially lessen the success of strategies and therefore future profits. These key people usually amount to about 10% of the managers.

It is important to appraise the key people in terms of their potential to assume enlarged responsibilities and to inventory them for either lateral transfers or upward moves to higher positions. Most firms have an appraisal system and determine the performance of people in their current jobs and the additional preparation needed to make them more productive. However, in strategic manpower planning it is the future organizational job requirements that must be considered. Therefore, the appraisal system must consider the job requirements of the positions in future years.

After the appraisals, the next task is to create a managerial inventory by deciding which managers are already able to take larger assignments and which ones will need more training before being moved. It should also be determined what additional training will be needed. One successful system for providing all of this information is the manpower appraisal and inventory process.[9] With the information developed in steps 5 and 6, it is possible to determine the staffing, training, and budget portions of the strategic manpower plan.

7.3.3.3   Future Personnel and Budget

It may have become evident during the previous step that additional or new types of people will be needed; therefore, in step 7 the work is to develop a list of the additional key personnel that will be needed. In step 8, the recruitment and training timetable for adding the additional personnel is developed for each of the future years. Any additional training needed by these people can be determined by the job requirements of the position and assignment.

Steps 5, 6, 7, and 8 can be illustrated by a large American regional hospital which recently completed this managerial appraisal inventory to prepare for several strategies aimed toward neurological and open-heart surgery market opportunities. To implement their newly formulated strategic plan, the hospital would need to strengthen several areas in their present organizational chart.

To make the strategies workable, several key personnel would have to be added. First, a corporate vice-president for marketing with skills and experience in monitoring environmental trends and analyzing market segments for new growth opportunities in these areas of surgery would be needed. A new combination nurse/social worker specialist would also be needed to strengthen the home-care services for discharged patients.

The success of the strategies also depended on having an insurance expert in health care services and a medical/contract negotiator person. The marketing insurance section would need to add someone with expertise in medical services that could be offered to large companies who might be expected to self-insure the health care needs of their employees. Therefore, the human resources department would need to add an experienced physician/contract negotiator who could develop the contracts for their HMO/PPO organization.

The hospital then reviewed the information on personnel from their personnel appraisal and inventory system (step 6 in Figure 7.4) to determine if existing employees could fill their needs. The review revealed that there were no acceptable candidates among present employees for the corporate vice-president or the insurance positions, that there was an experienced physician/contract negotiator on staff not now being used in this capacity but available and ready to assume the responsibility, and that 12 months of training would be required to prepare an available nurse for the nurse/social worker position.

The summary results from the strategic manpower plan showed that over the next 2 years several actions must be taken:

1. A new corporate vice-president for marketing would have to be hired from outside the organization.
2. Additional training would have to be provided over the next 12 months for a currently employed nurse/social worker in order to assume the role of home-care specialist.
3. A new insurance specialist would have to be brought into the organization from outside as quickly as possible.
4. Finally, the new organizational position of physician/contract negotiator could be filled immediately from the medical staff.

In this way, the manpower needs to make the strategies successful were identified and action steps to be taken by the appropriate sections were assigned.

For step 9 (replacement tables for tomorrow's organizational chart), reference must be made to the inventory information developed in step 6. At that time it was discovered who among existing personnel were ready to be given a different assignment. In developing replacement tables, two or three candidates for each job are entered under each key position. For example, under Vice-President of Engineering would be listed two or three people who would be qualified for the job in the future, along with a statement of readiness or additional training needed.

The final step, step 10, is creating the budget that will enable tomorrow's organizational chart to function. The major cost information inputs come from the estimates of the costs of supporting business strategies that the HR representative on the business team developed during the strategic planning process. Other costs will become evident from the work done in steps 7, 8, and 9. Therefore, the budget for the strategic manpower plan should reflect all of the future costs (for each year of the strategic plan's time frame) of recruiting, training, compensating, fringe benefits, space, equipment, and support needed by the key personnel to function productively in tomorrow's organization.

When these seven steps are completed, the HR executive will have a plan that enables the transition of company management organization from today into tomorrow's business by properly supporting the strategic decisions in the company's strategic plan.

7.4   Summary

The human resources function in large companies is changing dramatically. In addition to the traditional personnel planning necessary for training, wage and salary administration, lay-offs, recalls, recruitment, industrial relations, and a host of other operational responsibilities have recently been added three strategic dimensions. At this point in time, evidence from studies of companies suggest that both top management and human resources executives are still having difficulty in relating these responsibilities to the corporate strategic plan and the information building process that enables it.

While there may be numerous strategic responsibilities, it appears that three are critical if top management's expectations of the enlarged human resources' job responsibilities are to be satisfied. These three are related to each other and if done sequentially enable the company to obtain and productively use the right people in the right ways for the company's future sales revenue, profit, and growth.

To perform the strategic dimensions of the HR executive's job properly, three changes will have to occur in many companies:

1.   The chief HR executive must be made a regular member of the corporate and divisional planning and review committees, in addition to one of his managers becoming one of the members on the strategic business unit planning teams.

2.   The chief human resources executive must be given new responsibilities: (a) Monitoring and interpreting the impact of environmental trend changes related to working conditions, employees' rights, and employment, information that should be available to both top management and the SBU planning teams; and (b) during the strategic planning process, furnishing information to the SBU team through the HR representative about the availability and cost of staffing additional personnel so that each new strategy can be properly evaluated and prioritized at the SBU planning level.

3.   The chief human resources executive must accept the responsibility for developing a strategic manpower plan that will enable the organization to evolve into the organization required for future business. Included in this plan should be an inventory and appraisal system, future organization charts, and replacement

tables based on the strategic plan. Plans for recruiting and training key personnel, career development programs, and replacement tables are also part of this responsibility.

These three dimensions of the human resources management job are not discretionary; they are interrelated and necessary for effective long-range corporate planning. Top management can ignore this at the peril of having neither good planning nor the proper personnel to implement strategies when the time is right. Conversely, human resources executives in some companies will have to take the initiative in making their top management aware of the need for a new breed of human resources manager and the role they should perform in planning.

References

1. Loyd Baird, Ilan Meshoulam, and Ghisland Degive, "Meshing Human Resources Planning with Strategic Business Planning: A Model Approach," *Personnel*, September-October, 1983, pp. 14–25.
2. Frederick N. Gluck, Stephen P. Kaufman, and A. Steven Walleck, "Strategic Management for Competitive Advantage," *Harvard Business Review*, July-August, 1980, pp. 154–161.
3. Robert E. Sibson, "Strategic Personnel Planning," *Personnel Administrator*, October, 1983, pp. 39–42.
4. Subhash C. Jain, "Self Appraisal and Environmental Analysis in Corporate Planning," *Managerial Planning*, January-February, 1979, pp. 20–26.
5. "Job Title Not All That Has Changed for Personnel," *The Florida Times-Union*, January, 1983, pp. B-11, 21.
6. Kenneth F. Misa and Timothy Stein, "Strategic HRM and the Bottom Line," *Personnel Administration*, October, 1983, pp. 27–30.
7. Karen A. Golden and Vasudevan Ramanujam, "Between a Dream and a Nightmare: On the Integration of HRM and Strategic Planning Processes," *Human Resource Management*, Winter 24(4), 1985, pp. 429–452.
8. Julia R. Galosy, "Meshing Human Resources Planning with Strategic Business Planning: One Company's Experience," *Personnel*, September-October, 1983, pp. 26–35.
9. This is a process developed in the 1970s for the Upjohn Company of Kalamazoo, MI, by Alan Huellmantel to meet the strategic human resources requirements of their strategic plan.

8 Strategic Purchasing Planning

8.1 Introduction

Several decades ago, Bruce Henderson postulated that purchasing would gain increased importance in corporate planning activities in the years ahead,[1] and now many corporate executives agree that purchasing is indeed making valuable contributions to the long-range plans that corporate management must develop.[2] More challenges lie ahead, according to Zenz,[3] who predicted that the management of materials would receive escalating emphasis through the 1980s and beyond, accompanied by "an increase in the use of purchasing backgrounds to fill the materials management position."

To illustrate the importance of purchasing's role in corporate planning, consider the following episode that happened at a well-known pharmaceutical firm. Based on market research information, corporate management made the decision to introduce a new product in a relatively new market within the next several years. Laboratory research revealed that a new formulation of chemical compounds offered not only improved therapeutic value but an advance in production techniques as well. After 3 years and a multi-million-dollar research investment, however, purchasing discovered that no supplier (or group of suppliers) could provide one of the key ingredients in the quantity or at a cost that would permit the new product to be priced competitively in the marketplace. As a result, 3 years, much work, and a large amount of money were wasted; "poor planning" was cited as the culprit. Obviously, purchasing should have been asked to study key supply markets and to furnish this critical piece of information much earlier in the corporate planning process.

A number of signals are evident today which indicate that supply-related considerations are recognized increasingly as essential inputs for corporate planning activities. A recent advertisement in the *Wall Street Journal* sought a materials manager for "the development of a 'Class A' manufacturing resource planning system at the corporate level."[4] Other evidence includes the increasing frequency of articles about strategic planning issues appearing in the *Journal of Purchasing and Materials Management* during the past 7 or 8 years.[5] The *New Study Guide* briefly discusses strategic planning and its linkage to purchasing strategy.[6] Additionally, the Purchasing Executive Seminar conducted at the Harvard Business School includes instruction on corporate planning and strategy. Clearly, many believe that purchasing has an important new role to play in corporate management and that strategic planning skills should be an integral part of the new professional purchasing manager's talents.

Adamson summed up this issue in a recent article and raised two important questions that should be of concern not only to purchasing managers but to strategic planners as well:[7]

1. What techniques can be used to tie purchasing and planning together?
2. How can purchasing provide inputs to the preparation of corporate strategy?

The purpose of this chapter is to provide some answers to these two questions. First, a structured model of strategic planning is discussed to reveal ways to tie things together. Second, four strategic inputs, or contributions, that purchasing can make to corporate planning are presented.

8.2   The Strategic Planning Process

Only one set of decisions concerns the entire organization and its future — these are the long-range strategic decisions. The sole purpose of strategic planning is to provide the necessary inputs — in the proper

A. THE STRATEGIC PLANNING SYSTEM —

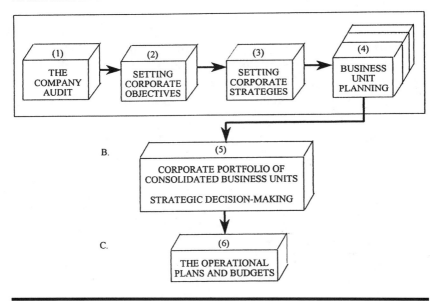

Figure 8.1 Simplified Strategic Management Model

form, to the right people, at the right time — so that the "best" strategic decisions can be made and efficient operational plans and budgets can be developed to implement them.

The chief executive officer is responsible for seeing that the organization grows profitably, generates a sufficient cash flow to finance most of this growth, and produces annual earnings that meet the financial objectives of the organization. The simplest way for the leader to approach this task is to ask the correct questions about the organization. These might be called the "strategic questions", of which there are six. Answering these six questions is the essence of the concept of strategic management.[8]

To help visualize this concept and to guide the discussion, a simplified model of the strategic management process is shown in Figure 8.1. Notice that the model contains six steps. These steps correspond to the six strategic questions. Notice also that the model has three levels (A, B, and C). These levels equate to the three principle elements of strategic management: strategic planning, strategic decisions, and operational plans and budgets, respectively.

8.2.1   Level A

Level A is the strategic planning element of strategic management and contains four steps. The company audit asks the question, "What are the strengths and weaknesses of the organization?" It is here that distinctive competencies are initially discovered by studying the characteristics of the organization that are of major importance to its profitable growth, financial security, and competitive advantage. Long-term supply contracts, stockpiles of critical materials, a strong network of qualified suppliers, and a highly skilled and well-managed purchasing function are a few of the strategic strengths that could provide the company with a clear competitive advantage.

Setting corporate objectives involves answering the question, "What objectives (or targets) are appropriate for this organization?" This is essentially a mission statement about the scope of businesses (activities or product lines) the organization should be in, what these businesses should become in 5 to 10 years, and the financial objectives of the organization. Given the fact that many firms pay out one half or more of their sales dollar to outside suppliers, the purchasing function has a substantial impact on what can and cannot be accomplished.

Setting corporate strategies requires answering the question, "How can this organization achieve its objectives?" Commonly, this is a relatively brief strategy statement concerning "the schemes whereby a firm's resources and advantages are managed (or deployed) in order to surprise and surpass competitors or to exploit opportunities."[9] A main pillar in Toyota's corporate strategy, for example, is "just-in-time" materials scheduling. Obviously, the purchasing and materials management function is a strategic element in this scheme.

The most critical and challenging part of strategic planning is business unit planning. Here is asked the question, "Which of the organization's current, or proposed, business units holds the most potential for growth, cash flow, and earnings?" Management must designate the strategic business units (SBUs) that make up the company, both present and proposed. Ideally, an SBU has these characteristics:[10]

1.   It is a single business (activity or product line) or collection of related units with an identified market(s).
2.   It has a distinct mission which uses corporate resources and generates revenues.
3.   It has its own competitors.

4. It has a unique set of competitive characteristics.
5. It consists of one or more program and functional units.
6. It can benefit from strategic planning.
7. It can be planned independently of other operating units.

Each SBU must have its own individual plan. Because most firms are involved in more than one business endeavor, there are often a relatively large number of business unit plans requiring evaluation. For example, Eaton Corporation has over 400 SBUs, General Electric claims 300, and Mead Corporation has 24, each of which is managed by a business unit manager. The key point is that each business unit plan identifies market opportunities with proposed strategies for exploiting them. Business unit strategies refer to the separate planning associated with each kind of business in which the corporation is involved.[11]

Each business unit plan must now be evaluated by each functional leader within the firm. The functional leader provides expert advice, from his or her functional perspective, on the feasibility of each business unit plan. This is developed around two basic questions:

1. From the point of view of our specific functional expertise, how many of these market opportunities seem practical?
2. If practical, what would it require in additional resources (money, personnel, equipment, facilities, etc.) to support each market opportunity?

It is here that provisional functional strategies are first developed. Functional strategies refer to the planning efforts of the chief specialties — or functions — within the business (e.g., purchasing, marketing, production, personnel, finance, etc.) which support the corporate and business unit strategies.[11]

It is at this point that the pharmaceutical company mentioned earlier went astray. Without purchasing's expert advice on these two questions, the business unit plan resulted in a meaningless and wasteful investment alternative.

8.2.2 Level B

The planning staff then compiles every functional leader's evaluation of each plan, eliminates those plans judged impractical, and prepares the business unit portfolio for top management's decisions. Top management must now make the strategic decisions by answering the question, "Does the cumulative effect of the individual business unit strategies provide a balanced portfolio?" (balanced in the sense that the company can meet all of its objectives). More specifically,[12]

> "Strategic decisions are those decisions that allocate company resources in and out of company strategic business units (SBUs) in an attempt to meet the company's financial objectives. They are the most important decisions the chief executive officer makes because they determine where the company's future earnings, cash flow, and growth will come from."

8.2.3   Level C

The question then becomes, "What annual operational plans and budgets will be needed to implement each of these approved business unit strategies?" Essentially, these are the familiar work assignments detailed in the annual plan. There is an important difference, however. These operating plans and budgets are based on a solid strategy that is consistent with the corporate objectives, with a specific plan of action, and with a timed sequence of resource commitment assignments. A prime benefit of strategy-based plans and budgets is that they can be subjected to a meaningful investment analysis of the company's strategic resources. Budgets then become much more than cost control devices or exhortations to try harder — they can be used to appraise the efficacy of the entire planning process.

The purchasing function must now do its own detailed planning for the next year so that it can fulfill its responsibilities in executing the first year of the corporate strategic plan. All the planning, decisions and strategies must be made functionally operational, or, as suggested by Drucker,[13] they "must degenerate to work to be meaningful."

8.3   Purchasing's Contributions to Strategic Planning

The purchasing function clearly has important contributions to make to any company's strategic planning effort. There are at least four broad areas of strategic significance:

1. Monitoring supply market trends
2. Interpreting the meaning of these trends to the firm
3. Identifying the materials and services required to support company and SBU strategies
4. Developing supply options

Each of these strategic issues is addressed in the following sections.

8.3.1   Monitor Trends

A host of factors can affect the business environment of supply markets. Commonly cited are political and legal, economic, technological, natural, and social factors. The purchasing executive must determine which trends are relevant to current and planned company operations and monitor them. Secondary economic data sources are plentiful for this purpose.

There are innumerable private and governmental sources of secondary data. Every bureau of the government, almost without exception, publishes data of some description. These data are presented and indexed in the monthly catalogue of the U.S. Government Printing Office. This catalogue is available on subscription from any field office of the Department of Commerce or Government Printing Office agency. The most commonly used of these sources by businessmen include the *Monthly Labor Bulletin,* which is a publication of the Federal Reserve Board and contains a wide variety of financial and economic statistics, and the *Survey of Current Business,* which is the official monthly publication of the Department of Commerce. It contains 40 pages of data including literally hundreds of different statistical series.[6]

8.3.2   Interpret Trends

The purchasing function is the prime authority in determining what supply market trends mean and how they impact corporate objectives and strategies. Appropriate trends should be extrapolated into the future, and their influence on supply market conditions should be evaluated. Supply market scenarios (shortages, surpluses, stable or rising prices, new technologies, and the like) can then be developed and examined for their impact on corporate objectives and strategies.

Purchasing research can enhance the purchasing executive's judgment in a variety of ways. Time series analysis can reveal much about the behavior of historical data. Trends, seasonal movements, cyclical variations, and irregular occurrences can often be estimated accurately enough to permit reasonable forecasting. Correlation or regression analysis can be used to investigate and determine associative relationships and may be useful in developing a mathematical forecasting model. Judgmental methods such as the Delphi technique and Bayesian analysis can also be useful at times in trend interpretation.

8.3.3 Identify Needs

An estimate of current and proposed material needs of each business unit must be made on a continuing basis. These projections should be compared with the scenarios developed previously to evaluate such factors as availability, prices, sources, lead time, and so on. If similar requirements cut across several business units, it obviously is desirable to consolidate them and repeat the evaluation. PERT, MRP, and similar planning techniques offer a viable framework for conducting the evaluation of future positions. Quantity and time estimates for required materials should be plotted into the future and compared with expected conditions, and critical events or potential problems should be identified. The purchasing executive can then provide realistic answers to questions such as: "What material alternatives exist?" "What alternative market and purchasing strategies may be possible?" "Is a given approach practical, and, if so, what additional resources are needed?"

8.3.4 Competitive Purchasing Strategies

If the results of the preceding step indicate that present purchasing strategies are capable of fulfilling the company's needs, then continuance of past practices would be appropriate. In today's turbulent supply markets, however, such an event may be the exception rather than the rule. As a result, incumbent purchasing professionals are called upon more and more to develop options which will help business units remain competitive in the marketplace.

Purchasing literature contains a vast array of tools and techniques that can be used to develop alternative competitive procurement strategies.

Several dozen can be gleaned from most reliable books in the field. Investigation of the following possible courses of action illustrates some of the key creative approaches:

1. Make-or-buy analysis of selected requirements
2. Value analysis of selected requirements
3. Development of a standardization program
4. Utilization of the learning curve concept in pricing
5. Development of specialty suppliers
6. Utilization of international sources
7. Negotiation of long-term contracts
8. Employment of hedging techniques
9. Development of a comprehensive forward buying program
10. Utilization of the stockless purchasing concept

All of these have clear and far-reaching implications for maintaining the competitiveness of business units and may favorably impact the corporation's growth, cash flow, and earnings potential.

In the final analysis, if purchasing does not provide the strategic inputs just discussed, where does the corporation get this information? At first, one might think that such information simply is ignored. However, careful analysis reveals that such an explanation generally is naive and erroneous, because resource market information is simply too important for most firms to ignore.

A more plausible response is that some other functional executive furnishes it, or worse yet — assumes it. This mode of operation is unacceptable for two reasons. First, the corporate planning process is not getting critical strategic information on supply trends and competitive options from the most logical source where that expertise resides — the purchasing function. Corporate strategies and business unit strategies may consequently be based upon faulty information and may subsequently prove difficult or impossible to implement. Second, the purchasing executive will ultimately have to conduct essentially the same type of analysis in developing and implementing purchasing strategies, based on someone else's information and decisions. Hence, if such activity is to be conducted by purchasing, it obviously should be conducted at the point in the process that produces the greatest value to the total organizational effort.

8.4   Some Observations

In this last section, some thoughts on a few pertinent questions about strategic purchasing planning and the future of the purchasing professional are suggested. These questions and comments are by no means exhaustive or mutually exclusive but cover selected points that are important.

Is the purchasing executive the only functional leader with both a strategic and an operational side to his or her job? Absolutely not. Any functional specialty within the corporation that has direct responsibility for supporting business unit plans has both a strategic and an operational job to do. That is, without the particular function in question, the business unit cannot be planned and operated. In addition to purchasing, some commonly cited dual-role functions in modern complex organizations include marketing, production, finance, research, engineering and development, and personnel.

Is strategic planning an "all or nothing" alternative for the organization? Not at all. In fact, too rapid a movement into a more complex corporate planning system can generate more problems than solutions. Substantial time is required (years, as a rule) to evolve from an annual budget form of management to strategic management. This evolutionary process has been chronicled into four major episodes and is a distinct advantage for the purchasing professional because it permits personal growth over time, one requirement of professionalism.[8]

Is a background in research techniques and mathematical procedures necessary for a line purchasing manager involved in strategic planning? Not necessarily. An understanding of what these specialized topics can offer in terms of inputs for planning and decision-making is quite adequate. Far more critical skills include asking the proper questions and accurately interpreting the answers. Strategic planning is more an art than a science; personal judgment is the paramount variable.

8.5   Summary

Would knowledge of strategic planning enhance a person's career opportunities in the purchasing field? Poor sales and profit performances in troubled economic times have caused many CEOs to look for improvements in a heretofore unexplored area. Some have apparently discovered that well-known axiom expressed in purchasing literature — a dollar saved in the acquisition of material produces the same profit as a $20 increase in sales for a firm with a gross margin of 5%.[14] Job opportunities and advancement potential in purchasing are running well ahead of many other fields. In fact, it has been estimated that over 20,000 purchasing positions were available each year throughout the 1980s, and these new positions demanded higher educational requirements.[15] Other evidence suggests that career opportunities in purchasing are accompanied by better than national average income levels and increases.[16]

Is it absolutely necessary to know something about strategic planning to gain advancement opportunities in purchasing and materials management? Not all career advancements require knowledge of strategic planning. But with purchasing's definite movement toward the upper levels of the organization chart, strategic planning skills are becoming more important for the purchasing professional at or near the top of the purchasing function. Coe[17] found that many purchasing executives are making contributions to their company's strategic planning efforts because of their own self-involvement. And to be truly professional in any field, one must become involved.[18]

References

1. Bruce D. Henderson, "The Coming Revolution in Purchasing," *Journal of Purchasing and Materials Management*, Summer 1975, pp. 44–46 (reprinted from *Purchasing Magazine*, April 20, 1964).
2. Paul V. Farrell, "When Top Management Makes a Commitment to Better Purchasing," *Purchasing World*, March 1982, pp. 30–33; Paul V. Farrell, "Purchasing at Anheuser-Busch: Way Up the Corporate Ladder," *Purchasing World*, February 1982, pp. 30–32; Harry Holiday, "Your Basic Function Is Managing Money: A CEO Talks About the Major Concerns in Purchasing," *Purchasing World*, January 1982, pp. 74–75; Michael D. Webber, "Now Is the Time for Strategic Materials Planning," *Purchasing World*, November 1981, pp. 55–57; I. Robert Parket and Joseph Eisenberg, "The Industrial Purchaser: New Star on the Organization Chart," *Business*, January-March 1982, pp. 27–32.
3. Gary J. Zenz, "Materials Management and Purchasing: Projections for the 1980s," *Journal of Purchasing and Materials Management*, Spring 1981, p. 20.
4. Such ads are common in the *Wall Street Journal*; this particular reference is from the August 25, 1981, issue.
5. Joel Adamson, "Corporate Long-Range Planning Must Include Procurement," *Journal of Purchasing and Materials Management*, Spring 1980, pp. 25–32; Robert E. Spekman and Ronald P. Hill, "Strategy for Effective Procurement in the 1980s," *Journal of Purchasing and Materials Management*, Winter 1980, pp. 2–7; David H. Farmer, "Seeking Strategic Involvement," *Journal of Purchasing and Materials Management*, Winter 1980, pp. 20–24.

6. Edward J. Bierman, Ed., *The New Study Guide*, New York National Association of Purchasing Management, 1980, p. 148.

7. Joel Adamson, "Corporate Long-Range Planning Must Include Procurement," *Journal of Purchasing and Materials Management*, Spring 1980, p. 25.

8. Frederick W. Gluck, Stephen P. Kaufman, and Steven Walleck, "Strategic Management for Competitive Advantage," *Harvard Business Review*, July-August 1980, pp. 19–26.

9. David J. Luck and O.C. Ferrell, *Marketing Strategy and Plans*, Prentice-Hall, Englewood Cliffs, NJ, 1979, p. 6.

10. Philip Kotler, *Marketing Management*, 4th ed., Prentice-Hall, Englewood Cliffs, NJ, 1980, p. 76.

11. David J. Luck and O.C. Ferrell, *Marketing Strategy and Plans*, Prentice-Hall, Englewood Cliffs, NJ, 1979, p. 20.

12. Noel B. Zabriskie and Alan B. Huellmantel, "Strategic Marketing's Four Basic Tasks," *Marketing News*, June 26, 1981, pp. 4–5.

13. Peter F. Drucker, *Management: Tasks, Responsibilities, Practices*, Harper & Row, New York, 1973, p. 128.

14. Gary J. Zenz, *Purchasing and Materials Management*, 5th ed., John Wiley & Sons, New York, 1981, p. 8.

15. Larry Ziunipero and Gary Zenz, "Impact of Purchasing Trends on Industrial Marketers," *Industrial Marketing Management*, February 1982, pp. 17–23.

16. "Profile of the Purchasing Professional — 1981," *Purchasing World*, October 1981, pp. 76–77.

17. Barbara J. Coe, "Industrial Marketing Executives Determine Purchasing Agent's Role in Strategic Planning," *Marketing News*, June 26, 1981, p. 11.

18. John M. Browning and Noel B. Zabriskie, "Professionalism in Purchasing: A Status Report," *Journal of Purchasing and Materials Management*, Fall 1980, pp. 2–10.

9 Non-Business Strategic Planning

9.1 Introduction

Strategic planning in most business organizations has become a fairly sophisticated operation, with specialized staffs to do the planning work and make studies about the future. Contrast this with most non-business organizations, without staffs and relying on committee members and volunteers to do the staff work that all planning efforts require.

Given the nature of most non-business organizations — social, health care, fundraising, trade associations, universities and colleges, etc., board members usually consist of lawyers, physicians, professional social and health-care workers, housewives, etc. These are all very important elements of a board of directors, but few of these people, if any, have sophisticated training or experience in the art and techniques of planning.

To further compound the problem, a review of the planning literature reveals many articles and books to help business planners, but very few that address the problems of planning for non-business organizations. The purpose of this chapter is to help fill that void. Most of our knowledge about strategic business planning has been adapted from the art of military planning. The next step in this evolutionary process should be to adapt business to non-business strategic planning.

Table 9.1 The Concept of Strategic Management

The concept applies to *all* organizations, profit or non-profit, that operate in *competitive* situations.

It is a *decision-making* concept. The planning process is the mechanism we choose to develop the information on which to base the decisions.

The most important decisions any organization makes, its *primary* set of decisions that all other decisions support, are those *decisions that commit resources today* to put the organization in position to exploit the opportunities in *tomorrow's* markets.

The strategic concept in practice is not a single plan but a corporate planning and decision-making *system*. It consists of *strategic, administrative,* and *operational* plans.

Planning *issues* are defined as the problems and opportunities that *could* have a *major* effect on the organization's future if not addressed.

All planning issues are *not* strategic in character any more than they are all administrative or operational.

The *strategies* formulated in the strategic plan are only concerned with *strategic issues.*

A logical place to start any study is with a clearly stated definition of the subject. In the case of non-business strategic planning, this would be with a definition for non-business planning. Because we are borrowing our concept from the business world we must first understand what business planning is all about (see Tables 9.1, 9.2, and 9.3):

> Strategic business planning is a process that uses competitive strategies to allocate its resources to projects that can exploit industry opportunities or defend threats caused by change in the marketplace for the purpose of meeting the long-range objectives of the organization.

Without too much trouble we can paraphrase this definition for use by non-business planners as:

> Strategic non-business planning is a process that uses competitive strategies to allocate its resources to projects that can exploit opportunities to fill the unfilled needs of its clients, patients, or members for the purpose of meeting the long-range objectives of the organization.

The biggest single difference between strategic planning and other long-range planning concepts such as capital budgeting, management by objectives, issues management, etc., is that in strategic planning,

Table 9.2 Strategic Management: Profit vs. Non-Profit Organizations

	Profit Organizations	*Non-Profit Organizations*
The concept of strategic management itself	Strategic issues the concept addresses defined narrowly as external issues only	Strategic issues the concept addresses defined broadly as both internal and external
Terms used to guide the planning process: ■ Mission ■ Vision ■ Definition of scope ■ Strategies ■ Objectives	Distinctly separate steps for instructing those who will do the planning; planning process driven by strategies	Often duplicate or overlap each other; platitudes rather than helpful instructions; planning process driven by objectives and programs
Decisions and plans based on a static (no change) and a dynamic (changing) marketplace	Decisions and plans based on scenario projections of tomorrow's marketplace developed from change already appearing on the horizon	Decisions and plans based on scenarios of tomorrow's marketplace developed by extrapolating today's trends into the future; no projections in practice equate to extrapolations
Strategic management as an evolutionary process	State-of-the-art strategic management evolves from the annual budget in four distinct phases	The evolutionary process seldom identified or understood

resources are allocated directly to the projects the organization wants to achieve, rather that to the programs that are to deliver the strategies for achieving the projects. The programs then compete against each other for the resources to activate them based on the strength and innovativeness of their strategy. Management then selects the set of one or more programs it will activate to achieve each project.

The programs selected derive their importance and relevancy from the specific projects they are trying to improve. By allocating resources directly to projects rather than to programs, the planners have a built-in a method for evaluating the success of each program: either the program improved the project or it didn't.

Let's take as an example a project the Arthritis Foundation might select as an unfilled need regarding the care and treatment of arthritis:

Table 9.3 Static vs. Dynamic Markets

Strategic decisions and plans made today are futuristic in that they must be made against a backdrop of scenario projections of tomorrow's markets.

Static markets are markets where no change is expected during the planning period. Scenarios of what the industry could look like tomorrow can be developed by extrapolating market conditions into the future.

Dynamic markets are markets where change is already appearing on the horizon. Scenarios of what the industry could look like tomorrow can be developed in one of three ways:

1. With a crystal ball or guru to help develop scenarios.
2. The changes can be ignored, and today's market conditions can be extrapolated into the future.
3. By using state-of-the-art tools for developing scenarios; futures research

The need of certain arthritis sufferers to improve mobility and muscle tone and to learn techniques for relaxing. One of the best ways known to improve mobility and muscle tone in arthritis sufferers is through disciplined exercise — that is, exercise that puts minimum stress on the inflamed joints. The question now becomes one of alternatives, which set of exercises to choose. Cost/benefit studies can be run on all proposed exercises: aquatics, ballroom dancing, aerobic dance, mild forms of sports, etc. Finally, a set of programs will be selected and the resources that have been allocated to the project will be re-allocated to a set of programs. The programs will then be evaluated based on their effectiveness. If not effective, they will be discontinued, and the resources will be re-allocated to new programs and approaches until the mobility project improves.

9.2 The Executive Summary

The executive summary is just that — it is the essence of the strategic plan in brief outline form for executive reading. After glancing at the summary statements, busy executives can read as little or as much of the full report as they desire.

9.3　The Purpose for a Strategic Plan

A strategic plan is just one among many plans every organization must make. Plans are in reality nothing more than a series of interrelated decisions. These decisions can be made in formal written plans or informally, but regardless of the form they take they must be made. Plans and planning decisions can be classified into three groups: strategic, operational, and administrative. Each plan has its own purpose and its own set of questions that must be answered if it is to be successful. The strategic plan monitors the change taking place in the industry. It is the lead plan that sets the future direction for the organization. The other two plans either implement or support it. It describes in broad terms how the organization will allocate its resources to compete in tomorrow's non-business climate, the clients it wants to serve, the geographical limits of its operations, and how it intends to identify and serve the changing needs of its client group.

9.4　The Planning Audit

The planning audit answers the question, "Where are we today?" It furnishes management with an appraisal of current operations. Management can extrapolate current operations into the future to see where they probably will be if they continue to operate as they have in the past. If they are satisfied with this growth, then there is no reason to change the strategic plan. If management desires more growth, they can use the audit as a base or springboard from which to exploit new opportunities for change until they reach the growth objectives they desire. But, they should also define the issues (Table 9.4).

9.5　Thinking "Strategically" About the Future

Organizational leadership begins with planning, and planning in turn begins with strategic thinking. Strategic thinking is considered the prelude to strategic planning. It provides the leader with a mental blueprint, a vision of what he wants the organization to become. This vision is expressed as a verbal model containing the questions the plan must answer if it is to be successful. Strategic thinking is based on the premise that organizations must be led. They cannot be permitted to drift into the future.

Table 9.4 Planning Terminology

Mission (purpose): What is our purpose? Why were we organized? To do what?

Vision (futuristic thinking): What does top management want this organization to become, and why?

Definition of operations (scope): What is the scope of our operations, in terms of the geographical areas and publics (customer groups) we want to serve?

Profit organizations (health care publics)
Arthritis
Diabetics
Cardiovascular
Allergies

Non-profit organizations (university publics)
The young who need to be prepared for entry-level employment as specialists
The mid-career specialists who have proven their competence and need periodic updating in their specialty
The mid-career specialist who desires to become a candidate for management
The middle manager who desires to become a candidate for senior (general) management

---

The chief executive officer, president, or board chairman must provide this leadership. In order to do that, he must ask some of the basic questions that could provide the "core" of a strategic planning and management of a non-profit organization. The fifteen "core" strategic questions that make up the non-business verbal model for strategic planning are

Question 1. *What will be the organization's mission statement and long-range objectives?* The mission statement provides the reason why the organization exists and what it wants to become. It is a general statement of purpose which gives the organization a framework within which to select its long-range objectives and the working tasks that must be accomplished if the mission is to be successful. The long-range financial and other major objectives are listed as targets against which to measure success.

Question 2. *What is the geographic scope of the organization's responsibilities?* This question simply states the geographical area in which the organization will operate during this planning period.

Table 9.5 Market Size

Potential Users of Our Service by Age Groups	1996[a]	1997	1998	1999	2000	2001
0 – 5						
6 – 18						
18 – 50						
50 – ?						

[a] Actual.

Table 9.6 Location

Potential Users of Our Service by Age Groups	Duval	St. John's	Clay	Nassau	Etc.
0 – 5					
6 – 18					
18 – 50					
50 – ?					

Question 3. *What is the size of the organization's market in this geographic area?* Using a chart similar to Table 9.5, identify the potential users by age groups over the next 5 years. Using a chart similar to Table 9.6, indicate the number of these potential users that are located outside the local county (list by age groups). Using a chart similar to Table 9.7, identify how many of these users the organization will try to serve over the next 5 years (list by age groups).

Question 4. *What is the organization's general statement of strategy?* Strategies, by definition, are sets of decisions for guiding operational behavior toward achieving objectives. Strategic plans determine the course of action that an organization undertakes. The role of objectives in strategic planning is to give the planners pre-stated direction and end-results against which to evaluate the success of these strategies. The statement of strategy describes the overall approach the organization will take for its

Table 9.7 Number of Users

Potential Users of Our Service by Age Groups	1996[a]	1997	1998	1999	2000	2001
0 – 5						
6 – 18						
18 – 50						
50 – ?						

[a] Actual.

growth. It applies to *all* of the organization's growth projects. The set of competitive strategies are developed to achieve specific growth projects or opportunities. They are innovative strategies that build in the advantages each program could have over the current programs now in use, if there are any, or that competitors could develop. (Using the following example as a guide, write a general statement or strategy for your plan.)

> *(example only)* The Northeast Florida Chapter of the Arthritis Foundation's general statement of strategy for achieving its long-range growth objectives will be accomplished by: (1) enlarging the base of arthritis sufferers that it serves and creating a better quality of life for them, (2) expanding the use of volunteers, (3) adding more arthritis sufferers to current programs, (4) extending programs now being offered in the county to selected other counties in northeast Florida, (5) increasing membership in the Chapter, (6) increasing financial contributions so the Chapter can offer new and improved programs.

Question 5. *What external changes now on the horizon could affect future operations in this industry?* (The industry for non-business organizations would be the social, health care, trade association, etc., field in which they operate.) Basically, strategic planning is an exercise in decision-making. It is about making decisions today, to be in position to take advantage of tomorrow's opportunities. It requires some insight into what tomorrow's non-business climate could be like. Because the non-business leaders that must make these decisions are not clairvoyant and do not have crystal balls, they must rely on futures research and their own experience and intuition. Futures research is a tool of the planning trade that monitors the changes already appearing on the horizon that could affect tomorrow's non-business environment. These changes are then projected into scenarios of what tomorrow's industry could look like. Management then selects the most likely scenario and studies the new opportunities it could bring, along with the tasks necessary to exploit them. Include in your plan any major changes, if any, you think could change your industry over the next 5 years and give the year you think the change will take place. For an example of external changes now on the horizon, see Figure 9.1 on the following page for proposed changes in the health care field.

Question 6. *What could be the effect of these changes on tomorrow's industry?* Once major changes have been identified, they must be studied as to the impact each could have on tomorrow's industry. Include in your plan how you think these changes, if any, could affect the industry.

Question 7. *What new opportunities or threats, if any, could these changes bring to the industry?* There are five major types of opportunities or threats: (1) social, (2) political, (3), economic, (4) technical, and (5) competitive. Include in your plan any new opportunities or threats you think the above changes could bring to organizations in your industry. (If no major changes are expected, then questions 5, 6, and 7 may be skipped.)

Question 8. *If we have competitors, what will be their strengths and weaknesses for responding to both new or current industry opportunities and threats?* Could these opportunities, if there are any, take advantage of these opportunities to fill client needs better than we could? In your plan, list your competitors and their strengths and weaknesses.

Question 9. *If we have competitors, what are our capabilities relative to theirs?* Name the specific capabilities and strengths your organization may have relative to the competition for exploiting each new opportunity, if there are any.

Question 10. *Based on what tomorrow's industry could look like, what projects and programs will be needed to fill unfilled client needs?* This question is to remind us that planning focuses on the future, and the opportunities and new projects available to our

CONFUSED ABOUT HEALTH REFORM PLANS? | Here's a Guide: ▼▼▼▼▼▼▼▼

Americans agree overwhelmingly that the U.S. health-care system is not doing its job of providing affordable care to all, young and old alike, as readers have told the Bulletin (see page one article). Three crucial problems afflict the system: uncontrollable costs, the growing number of persons without health insurance and the lack of a long-term-care program.

Congress is considering more than 30 health-care reform proposals, divided into three main groups: market-based proposals to assist some people now without insurance to purchase it, "pay-or-play" plans whereby employers either provide insurance to employees or pay taxes to finance an alternate public system, and proposals for a single-payer health-care system like Canada's. Below are several major proposals receiving congressional scrutiny.

Most plans aim to hold down soaring costs of health care and to enable the estimated 34 million Americans now without health insurance to have access to the health-care system. A smaller number would insure the costs of long-term care.

Almost all of the proposals would require new financing to meet start-up expenses or shifting of costs from the private to public sector. The sponsors claim that many have the potential of reducing the total cost. For instance, the plan of Sen. Bob Kerrey, D-Neb., reports the largest need for new revenue—$246 billion in taxes the first year. But Kerrey holds that his plan would save $11 billion in America's total health care costs the first year, and more than $150 billion over the first five years, because of overall savings it would make in health-care costs.

	PRIVATE (Market-based reform)		EMPLOYER-BASED ('Pay or play')			GOVERNMENT SPONSORED (Single payer)		
	Rep. Nancy Johnson (H.R. 1565)	Sen. John Chafee (S.1936)	Sen. George Mitchell (S.1227)	Rep. Dan Rostenkowski (H.R.3205)	National Leadership Coalition for Health Care Reform[15]	Rep. Pete Stark (H.R. 650/651)	Rep. Marty Russo (H.R. 1300)	Sen. Bob Kerrey (S. 1446)
Eligibility	16	16	Universal	Universal	Universal	Universal	Universal	Universal
Mandated basic benefits (acute care)[1]	Yes	No	Yes	Yes	Yes	Yes	Yes	Yes
Preventive care	Yes	Tax incentives; Public health programs	Yes	Yes	Yes	Children and pregnant women only	Yes	Yes
Pregnancy-related care	No	No	Yes	Yes	Yes	Yes	Yes	Yes
Well-child care	No	No	Yes	Yes	Yes	Yes	Yes	Yes
Outpatient prescription drugs	No	No	No	No	Yes	Low-income only	Yes	Yes
Long-term care services (LTC)[2]	No	No	No	No	No	Yes	Yes	Yes
Medicare	Remains intact	Remains intact	Remains intact	Enhanced benefits Expanded to include 60-64 year olds	Remains intact	Expanded to all ages	Replaced	Replaced
Medicaid	Remains intact	Unchanged (Optional state programs up to 200% of poverty)	Replaced except for LTC benefits	Replaced except for supplemental optional services and LTC	Replaced except for LTC benefits	Replaced	Replaced	Replaced
Copayment (what you pay)	Not addressed	Not addressed	Acute - 20%	Acute - 20%	Acute - 20%	Acute - 20% Home and community-based services - 20% Nursing home (after deductible) - 20%	No	Acute - 20% Physicians visits $5 illness LTC - 80% of social security benefits
Deductibles	Not addressed	Not addressed	Individual - $250 Family - $500	Individual - $250 Family - $500	Individual - $200 Family - $400	Acute - $500 Nursing home - 2 mos.	No	Individual - $100 Family over 2 - $300
Caps on personal out-of-pocket expenses (acute care)	Not addressed	Not addressed	$3,000	Individual - $2,500 Family - $3,000	Individual - $1,500 Family - $3,000	$2,500	Not applicable	Individual - $1,000 Family of 2 - $1,500 Family, 3 or more - $2,000
Financial protections for low-income	No	Tax credits	Yes	Yes	Yes	Yes	Yes	Yes
New revenue needed[17]	Not addressed	$150b over 5 years	$6b first year	$80b first year	$34.7b first year	$125b/year	**	$246b first year
Major financing sources	Not addressed	Not addressed	**	9% income surtax Increase Medicare payroll tax Increase Medicare tax wage base to $200,000	1% payroll tax	4% income tax $1,000 annual premium	8% payroll tax $57 month health and LTC premium in '92 Increased taxes on personal, corporate, Social Security income	5% payroll tax Excise taxes Increased taxes on personal, corporate, Social Security income
Cost containment	3,4,5	3,4,12	3,4,6,7,8,9	7,8,9,11	3,4,6,7,8	9,10,11	7,8,9,10	8,9,10
Quality assurance	Data collection Demonstrations Reform Medicare peer review	Not addressed	Medicare mechanisms	Medicare mechanisms	13,14	Medicare mechanisms	Medicare mechanisms	State quality commissions
Small business insurance reform	Yes	Yes	Yes	Yes	Yes	Not applicable	Not applicable	Not applicable
Malpractice reform	Yes	Yes	Yes	No	Yes	No	No	Yes

1 Includes hospital, physician and mental health services
2 Includes nursing home, home health and community-based services
3 managed care
4 malpractice reform
5 reduced benefit mandates
6 outcomes research/practice guidelines
7 national health expenditure targets/caps
8 negotiated payment rates
9 administrative simplification
10 single-payer financing
11 Medicare payment rules
12 emphasis on prevention
13 National Quality Board
14 technology assessment
15 not yet introduced in Congress
16 expands access but does not require that all Americans have coverage
17 estimate from a variety of sources, some independent, some from sponsors
** plan is not specific

Figure 9.1 Proposed Health Care Reform Plans

organization must be based on what tomorrow's industry could look like. It also relates to the programs we will offer to accomplish these projects. Each program in turn must be based on a strategy that is innovative and creative enough to fill the need better than the present program in use or ones which our competitors could offer. In your plan, list the projects and

Table 9.8 Additional Personnel Requirements

Projected New Employee Needs	1996[a]	1997	1998	1999	2000	2001
Full-time						
Part-time						
Volunteers						

[a] Actual.

programs by age group and years that could be needed over the next 5 years.

Question 11. *At what client group will we target our program's responses?* Rather than "shotgun" our programs at all clients, the programs should be "rifled" at those who can most benefit from the programs. In your plan, list each such group.

Question 12. *What additional personnel will be required to offer the new programs listed in Question 10 above?* Using a chart similar to Table 9.8, include in your plan your need for full-time and part-time employees and volunteers, per year, over the next 5 years

Question 13. *What resources, other than personnel, will the organization require over the next 5 years?* Using a chart similar to Table 9.9, list, by year, each new resource that will be required, such as vehicles, computers, equipment, facilities, etc.

Question 14. *Where will the money come from to provide these new resources and fund the new projects?* Sources of funds could include: United Way, grants, dues, private donations, promotions, fashion shows, golf tournaments, walk-a-thons, and others. Using a chart similar to Table 9.10, list the expected sources of revenue on an annual basis for the next 5 years.

Question 15. *How can we link our new strategies and programs to our long-range financial plan and budgets?* Budgeting is an important part of a planning system (see Tables 9.11 and 9.12). The long-range financial plan for strategic planning purposes consists of both capital and direct expenditures. Until the strategies and programs get into the organization's budget, they are nothing more than paper plans. Following are some helpful comments about the importance of linking strategies to the organization's financial plan and budgets.

Table 9.9 Other Resource Requirements

Projected New Resource Needs	1996[a]	1997	1998	1999	2000	2001
Vehicles						
Computers						
Equipment						
Facilities						
Other						

[a] Actual.

Table 9.10 Source of Funds

Projected Funding Sources	1996[a]	1997	1998	1999	2000	2001

[a] Actual.

9.6 Linking Strategies to the Financial Plan and Annual Budgets

Many strategic plans fail because they never get implemented. Drucker has said strategy is nothing until it degenerates into work. This can be translated literally to mean that strategy is nothing until it is implemented. Strategic leaders implement their strategies the only way they can be implemented: first, by forecasting the expected costs and returns of each strategy, and, second, by working them into the budgeting system (both the long-range financial plans and the annual operational plans).

Budgeting is an integral part of the strategic planning process, which is something planners often forget. Seymour Tilles of the Boston Consulting Group calls this one of the forgotten truths about planning. To quote him directly:[1]

Table 9.11 Five-Year Financial Plan

Item (Totals Only)	1996[a]	1997	1998	1999	2000	2001
Revenues						
Total revenues						
Expenditures						
Direct expenses						
Capital expenses						
Other expenses						
Total expenses						
Gain or loss						

[a] Actual.

"One of the curious aspects of budgeting is that it seems to be designed to keep basic assumptions about future growth plans implicit while giving a great deal of attention to their quantitative implications. Thus, most budgets focus entirely on numbers and rarely on the assumptions and strategies on which the numbers are based. The strategic planning process focuses attention on the assumptions and strategies, as well as the numbers, in the budget."

Budgeting is one of the tools management uses to delegate and still keep control over subordinates' work priorities. When organizational leaders approve the annual budget, they are telling the subordinates that they are free to activate and spend the money for these programs without further approval.

Table 9.12 The Annual Operational Budget

Items	Actual (1996)	Projected (1997)
Revenues (detailed by source)		
Total revenues		
Direct expenses (detailed by expense)		
Capital expenditures (detailed by expenditure)		
Other expenses		
Total expenses		
Gain or loss		

There are two traditional methods of developing budgets, neither of which is acceptable to strategic planners:

Method 1 — Extrapolate last year's budget figures into the future; that is, project them based on past experience.
Method 2 — Management selects revenue and expenditure figures for the budget in advance, and the planners then must tailor the budget to fit these figures.

Strategic planners build their budget by projecting both current and new programs into the future based on the customer needs in the scenario of *tomorrow's* industry. Linking the strategies requires two steps. First, the long-range financial and capital budgeting plans lay out the multi-year costs and returns expected from the strategies and programs in the plan. Second, when approved, the first year of the approved strategies and programs is detailed into assignments, resources, schedules, etc. and becomes part of the annual operational plans.

9.7 Summary

When we deal with business organizations for which the motive is to make profit in the market place, the tools of analysis are clear and well established. Whoever uses the tools more effectively is going to be ahead of others in reaching the organizational goals. The not-for-profit organization does not have the luxury of such clear-cut tools of analysis. It must depend, by its nature, on voluntary work by people of good will. But, after this first phase is completed, the organization must deal with the same issues that a business organization faces: markets, clients, donors, competition with other not-for-profit organizations pursuing the same resources that similar organizations are. Therefore, it becomes essential to establish and structure a planning system that will be used to achieve the objectives of the organization and create the capabilities that will allow the not-for-profit organization to survive and serve a particular group or community.

Reference

1. Seymour Tilles, *Corporate Strategic Planning — The American Experience* [client briefing], Boston Consulting Group, April 1970, p. 73.

10 Implementation of Strategic Plan

"A leader knows what's best to do; a manager knows merely how best to do it." (Ken Adelman)

10.1 Introduction

Our main objective in this book is to teach students and other readers how to lead an organization strategically — the best way to utilize the resources of the firm and achieve the outcome necessary to stay ahead of the competition and how to identify strategic vs. non-strategic issues so that resource allocation decisions are as sound as possible, because once such decisions are made they may be irreversible. The purpose of this chapter is to introduce the necessary conceptual and analytical framework to make this happen. In order to do this we will take you, the reader, on a tour of steps necessary to arrive at the critical moment when you have to make a decision, factors that you have to consider, analyses that you should have made, and the scope of work and the extent to which you should have scanned the environment and the sensitivities that you should have exercised within the organization in order to make things happen as intended.

This book is about strategy and strategic management of resources in order to create the best circumstances. In Robert Grant's words, "Strategy is the unifying theme that gives coherence and direction to the individual decisions of an organization or person."[1] The objective of such a unifying theme is, of course, to bring about the conditions that are most favorable to the organization over a sustained length of time. The question, then, is how does one strive to achieve a favorable position over a sustained length of time?

There are a number of critical elements that will facilitate the process. It must be understood that successful results for organizations are not the outcome of random actions of the leadership in that organization. This is precisely why we decided to incorporate the experience of General Electric right at the beginning of the text. Had there been major strategic shifts in the implementation of the planning process, the company may not have achieved the status that it so well deserves. A thorough study of the second chapter reveals that the General Electric leadership succeeded in instilling the following in the core managers and to the fullest extent possible throughout the organization:

They established the goals that were long term in nature, simple, and consistent. It must be observed that stating the goals and objectives in simple terms and putting a time horizon on them did not come out of nowhere. A great deal of analysis was conducted before they arrived at such goals. The feasibility, practicality, and achievability of such objectives were subjected to rigorous analysis and then put into effect.

The leadership at General Electric had a profound knowledge of the changing and competitive environment. The important and significant issue here is that this understanding led to appropriate decisions that laid the ground rules for later success. Hesitation and procrastination would have had disastrous results. If you look around, you will notice some obvious examples. Where is Montgomery Ward? The status of Sears has changed from being the top national retailer to one trying to catch up with Wal-Mart. Apple Computer once held a leading position in the personal computer market, but due to internal issues and lack of focus, it lost that position and has yet to re-emerge as credible computer maker.

The third component in this process is a profound unbiased and rational appraisal of the resources at the disposal of the firm. These could be financial resources or human assets, at times more important than the financial assets. Later on we will have an opportunity to discuss strengths or weaknesses and opportunities or threats that any sizeable organization faces. But, at this time, we would like to stress the significance of understanding the depth and breadth of the resources at the disposal of the firm. There should be no illusion on the part of management that surviving in the competitive world of business today is like engaging in a constant battle where scenarios shift, loyalties are not durable, and tools of analysis need continuous improvement. One misstep is all it takes to fall behind and never be able to gain the high ground that one had before losing the competitive battle.

The fourth component, but the most important in the process, is effective implementation of the plans. According to Kenichi Ohmae,[2] "In business as on the battlefield, the object of strategy is to bring about the conditions most favorable to one's own side, judging precisely the right moment to attack or withdraw and always assessing the limit of compromise correctly." There are many great strategists in American business, past and present, who marshaled the resources and set the goals to be achieved by utilizing those resources: Billy Durant, the genius organization builder at General Motors, and Alfred P. Sloan, another great mind who created a huge empire during his 40 years at the top of General Motors. In recent years, one should notice the role that Lee Iacocca played in revitalizing a collapsing Chrysler Corporation and making it a competitor with the other two major automakers. And, of course, there is Henry Ford, who created the Model T which set into motion Detroit becoming the Mecca of the automobile industry for so many decades. All these people had strategies that, with exceptional situations, worked well.

More recently, we can observe how Bill Gates has energized the high-tech industry by his constant quest to lead this sector and to impact businesses and households worldwide. All these leaders of American business seem to have two common features, according to Ohmae:[3] intuitive quality and analytical capability, both "based on the real nature of things, and imaginative reintegration of all the different items into a new pattern, using nonlinear brain power. This is always the most effective approach to devising strategies for dealing successfully with challenges and opportunities in the market arena as on the battlefield." All successful executives share what is expressed in Figure 10.1 — the capability to visualize and the ability to communicate their vision to the implementers and then direct their activities to fruition.

Communicating the Leader's Vision to the Troops

It has been said that "the sharpest mind and the most brilliant ideas are prisoners in a person who cannot communicate that genius or musings to others." Strategic leaders must be able to *communicate*, as well as *create visions*. Nothing happens until the planning team receives and develops a plan to exploit the leader's vision.

Figure 10.1 Communicating a Vision (Quote attributed to Bette Castor, President of the University of South Florida, in the *Florida Times Union,* May 20, 1993.)

10.2   Step 1: The Purpose of the Plan

The purpose of any firm in the long run is to create the results that meet the long-range objectives of its stakeholders. The group of stakeholders includes the owners of shares of the firm, the customers who will ultimately buy its product, employees who have a tremendous stake in the viability of the firm on which their livelihood depends, the suppliers who provide the ingredients that go into the production process and whose future for growth and prosperity depends on that particular firm and the like, the location and the community in which the firm has established business, the country at large, and, of course, the industry as a whole that may need muscle to survive.

In order to achieve his company's purpose, the chief executive officer has to be vigilant and continuously scan the environment (both domestic and global) in search of clues that may have to be incorporated in the strategic plan for implementation. This feature — searching for clues — is where a first-rate CEO can differentiate himself from those who are second rate. The chances are that the first-rate CEO can create a lot more value for the stakeholders by simply letting his vision work its way into the future (see Figure 10.2). According to Hamel and Prahlad,[4] "If managers don't have detailed answers to questions about the future, their companies can't expect to be market leaders." Additionally, if they are reluctant to be decisive, to lose a battalion in order to save the division, and "have no stomach for emergency-room surgery, like John Akers at IBM or Robert Stempel at General Motors, they soon find themselves out of a job."[5] The reader is directed to look again

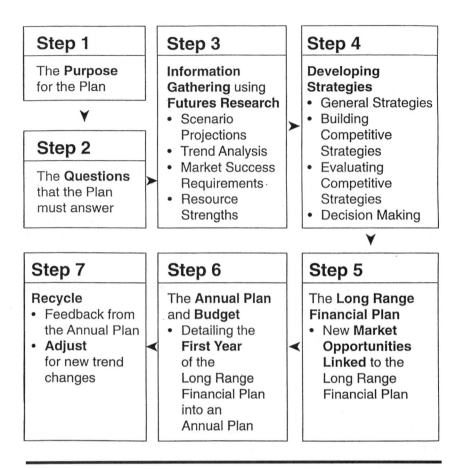

Figure 10.2 Directing and Controlling a Strategic Plan

at Chapter 5, Figure 5.6, where we have spelled out the details of the core questions that a strategic plan must answer

10.3 Step 2: The Questions the Plan Must Answer

Step 2 is most vital in the sense that the managers must critically question the underpinnings and assumptions of the strategic plan. It is important to question whether the plan creates the necessary ingredients and capabilities which, if followed zealously, would provide a sustained competitive advantage for the firm. Also, such questioning as determining whether the plan differentiates between strategic and non-strategic issues would test the depth of thinking and readiness of top management as well as middle managers. Also to be considered is whether the plan has the support of the key personnel who may have to share its vision and assumptions in order to make it work.

10.4   Step 3: Information Gathering Using Futures Research

This step is very critical in the sense that it provides the underpinnings of what comes out in Step 4, the stage where strategies are developed. The first act, then, is to write down a scenario of events that would possibly take place in your business or industry or in the economy as a whole. For instance, if a firm is operating in the health care market, the rapid changes that are taking place in the society, the diminishing role of the federal government, the increasing role of the states, and the institutional changes (hospitals and insurance industry) should be the focus of scenario building. One can almost foresee even a change in the student population, which may turn away from medical schools toward the engineering field or various business management disciplines simply because, looking down the road, it may not seem too cost effective to study medicine, go through all sorts of hurdles during training, face yet more obstacles, and then make just enough money to pay back what you borrowed to go to medical school.

The most frequent questions that students raise regard how we can predict the future and then plan our operations on such unknowns. To answer this question we would like to refer to the comments made by the management guru Drucker,[6] who says, "In human affairs — political, social, economic, or business — it is pointless to try to predict the future, let alone attempt to look ahead 75 years. But it is possible — and fruitful — to identify major events that have already happened, irrevocably, and that will have predictable effects in the next decade or two. It is possible, in other words, to identify and prepare for the future that has already happened." Let us see what happened to Big Blue, IBM, which ignored something that had already happened.

In 1993, IBM was in big trouble. The company had been flattened by the desktop revolution and had almost written off the mainframe computer. The former CEO had decided to divide the company 13 ways and was considering spinning off some of the parts. The stock had collapsed. After decades of dominating the market, IBM was being destroyed by internal inertia. The company's perfectionism was so intense it was difficult to get products out of the labs, which lost $1 billion of their research budgets. The company's lifetime employment was no longer in effect. The workforce had been cut dramatically —by 187,000 — and there was a $20 billion write-off. No one wanted to save this company. Finally, on April 1, 1993, one man took the challenge, Lou Gerstner, former chairman of R.J.R. Nabisco and one of the successful managers at McKinsey.

Gerstner entered the arena full speed ahead. Within 90 days, he had made critical decisions. He would keep the company together and put his money on mainframes. (See Figure 10.3.) It was a very daring and unpopular decision. The other people wanted to disaggregate everything. He began cutting costs, restructuring, and weeding out disbelievers. Jolting the staff with shock therapy, he acted as cheerleader during the overhaul and revival of the mainframe, stoked the service businesses, and brought IBM back to the party in PCs.

He came up with a vision to lead big companies into the brave new networked world. IBM would devise their technology strategies to build and run their systems and ultimately would become the architect and repository for corporate computing, tying together entire industries. Gerstner is taking IBM back to the future, back to what it was in the good old days: the information technology for corporate America. The rise of the Internet has given that role new glamour and meaning. By refocusing IBM's resources and outlook, the company has energized many at its labs in Silicon Valley, New York, and Switzerland, and the latest discoveries indicate that the company is focused on products and customers, the way it should have been a long time ago.[7]

Market success requirements are dependent on the actions of the leadership and the resources that the leadership will deploy to achieve the intended results. The best way to discuss this component is to have a look at the conditions at ENI, one of the biggest Italian oil companies. This company, like many other business firms in Italy, had been bleeding for many years. Due to the fact that the Italian economy had to open up because of its membership in the European Union, many commercial firms went through some serious restructuring. ENI was lucky, because in 1992 the task of reorganizing the company went to Franco Bernabe. In less than 5 years' time, from 1992 when he was appointed

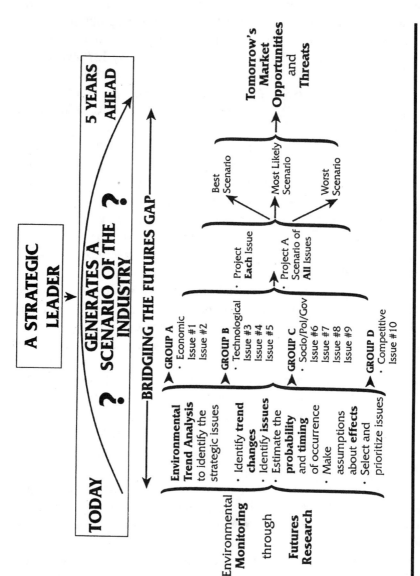

Figure 10.3 Futures Research

as Chief Executive of the company, he took ENI from being a money-losing political financing machine to the world's fifth most profitable publicly listed oil company. When he stepped in, the state-owned company was in chaos. (See Figure 10.4 and Table 10.1.) The former chairman, Gabriele Cagliari, was in jail for corruption, all of the top executives had been arrested, and there was not even a board of directors.

In 1992, the company was in the red by $623 million and had a net debt of $19 billion. As of 1996, the company had cut its debt in half, and net earnings were $3 billion. This success is due to the fact that Bernabe was well prepared when he took over. He had been studying the strengths and weaknesses of the company for 6 years prior to his appointment. He was fully aware of the terrain and the strengths and weaknesses.

10.5   Step 4: Developing Strategies

It may help us understand the issues if we define and differentiate the words that may impact our analysis. A policy statement refers to some principles or ongoing courses of action that guide decision-making. Growth strategies are sets of decisions that will guide future actions toward achieving greater market share or higher revenue, profit, or market share.

Generally there are two kinds of growth strategies. General statements of strategy refer to broad strategies that indirectly affect the unit's growth in terms of revenue and market share. The competitive strategies are market strategies that are directly aimed at the unfilled customer needs for the purpose of gaining revenue and market share. Of course, market opportunities are industry-wide and open to all competitors. Here is a good example of industry opportunity (Table 10.2). The battery industry is experiencing tremendous growth worldwide. Global battery sales are estimated at $41 billion per year and are expected to increase 50% over the next 5 years. As a result, many believe that the battery industry is in the early stages of a revolution. The primary force pushing the industry's expansion is the explosive demand for the new generation of portable consumer and industrial products. These products include mobile telephones, camcorders, cameras, and laptop and hand-held computers. In Eastern Asia, quickly expanding economies and rapidly rising incomes are also creating a high demand for portable tape players and radios.

Industry Trend Changes Now on Horizon	Probability of Occurrence	Year when Industry Effects could Occur 1	2	3	4	5	Expected Impact on Industry	Rank of Importance	Scenario — Projections based on the most Important Trend Changes
1. Social Environmental, Health, Energy, Lifestyles, etc.									
• Trend #1	80%		X				Major	1	
• Trend #2	20%			X			Medium	—	
2. Political Regulatory, Monetary, Fiscal Policies, etc.									
• Trend #3	60%	X					Major	3	
• Trend #4	50%	X					Minor	—	
• Trend #5	40%				X		Minor	—	
3. Economic Taxes, Interest Rates, Credit, etc.									
• Trend #6	70%		X				Major	2	
• Trend #7	40%			X			Major	—	
• Trend #8	10%	X					Medium	—	
4. Technological New Products, Processes, Materials, etc.									
• Trend #9	70%			X			Minor	—	
• Trend #10	30%			X			Minor	—	
5. Competitive New Competitors, Promotions, Prices, etc.									
• Trend #11	80%	X					Major	5	
• Trend #12	60%	X					Major	4	

Best Case Scenario

Most Likely Scenario

Worst Case Scenario

Figure 10.4 Trend Analysis

Table 10.1 Differentiating Among Growth
Strategy, Policies, and Programs

These Companies Will Achieve Their Long-Range Objectives by:[a]	Long-Term Growth	Policy Statements	Programs or Work To Be Done
Winn-Dixie			
Selling only for cash		X	
Never buying real estate		X	
Streamlining food distribution system			X
Warner Lambert			
Increasing advertising budget	X		
Consolidating divisions A & B			X
The Southern Company			
Maintaining competitive prices		X	
Providing unsurpassed service		X	
Kelsey Hayes			
Exporting anti-lock brake system to Far East markets	X		

[a] General statements by top management.

Another key factor in the industry's growth is rapid development in microelectronics and electric motor and display technologies. These technological advances have reduced the power requirements of many electrical systems. This makes it possible to run devices that use low-voltage batteries, such as telephone handsets and personal infusion pumps for drug treatment.

In addition, a battle is going on between the largest U.S. and Japanese companies for commercial dominance in the battery industry. The two biggest U.S. battery companies are Duracell and Ralston Purina, owner of the Energizer and Eveready brands. Exide is another large U.S. company that is dominant in lead-acid batteries used for vehicles. Matsushita, owner of the Panasonic battery brand, is the final member of the "big three" battery companies worldwide. Other Japanese players are Sony, Sanyo, Toshiba, Asahi Chemical, and Japan Storage. These Japanese companies are leading the way in the newer types of rechargeable batteries, used in consumer products such as mobile telephones.

Research and development costs are another important factor behind the battle between U.S. and Japanese battery companies. New

**Table 10.2 An Example of Matching Success Requirements
With Resource Strengths: The Electric Car Market Opportunity**

Market Success Requirements	Resource Strengths[a]		
	General Motors	Ford	Chrysler
Ability to develop effective battery system	Lead-acid battery?	Sodium-sulfur battery?	Nickel-iron battery?
Access to key suppliers (metal, glass, components, etc.)	10	10	10
Have labor skilled in mass production and assembly	10	10	10
Have distribution system for delivering cars	10	10	10
Established buyer confidance for service and industry experience	10	10	10

[a] Each rated on a scale of 1 to 10 in strength.

electrical and chemical technologies require huge investments in research and development. In many of these technical fields, Japanese firms are dominating the market. This success stems from the fact that Japanese battery companies are working in close association with leading Japanese makers of electronic consumer goods.

In consumer batteries, established alkaline and zinc batteries still dominate the market. Approximately 20 billion of these general-purpose batteries are sold worldwide. Because zinc batteries store less power and are cheaper, they outsell alkaline batteries in less developed countries, while the opposite is true in high-income regions such as the U.S.

Another important segment of consumer batteries is the newer, high-power-density and rechargeable batteries. Sales of rechargeable batteries are $5 billion per year and are expected to double by 2001. Automotive and industrial batteries, with sales of $21 billion a year, make up the remainder of the battery industry. Particular growth is also being seen in reserve power backup for industries such as medical, power generation, computers, and telecommunications.

Another potentially large market for new batteries is being created in the U.S. Approximately $500 million is being spent by the government and automotive industry on research into low-pollution, electrically

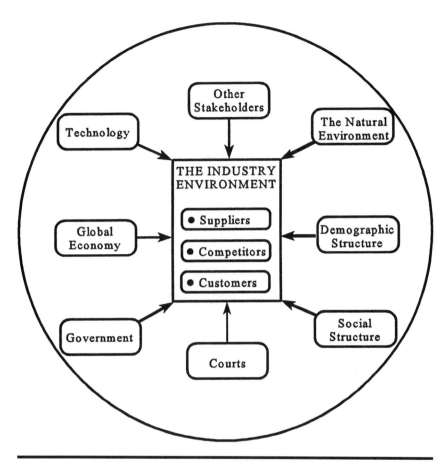

Figure 10.5 Constituents of a Firm

driven cars. By early next century, up to 500,000 electrically powered cars could be in use in the U.S.; however, many technological barriers will have to be crossed before these high-efficiency batteries are a realistic means of powering the next generation of cars.

Strategies, as mentioned earlier, provide the necessary coherence so that actions of the firm are based on well-thought-out mapping of the future course of action. Figure 10.5 provides a general picture of the various constituencies which the firm has to deal with and be concerned about, as well as whose demands the firm must be sensitive to. In addition to the above forces that impact the decision of the executive, in recent years Michael Porter has introduced what has become known as the "five forces", which are shown in Figure 10.6.[8] Porter's pioneering

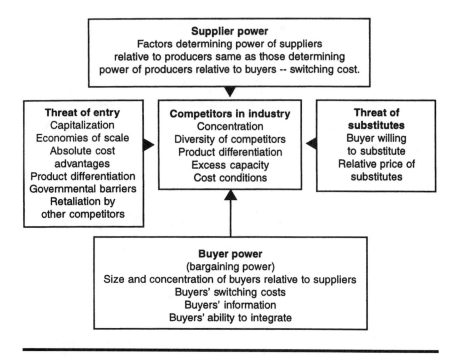

Figure 10.6 Porter's Five Forces (Adapted from M.E. Porter, *Competitive Advantage,* The Free Press, New York, 1985.)

study of the market structure, influenced by industrial economics and the structure of the American economy, has provided an easy map by which to see the forces at work in a daily battle for profit and market share.

The corollary to the "five forces" is the kind of strategy a firm may adopt to beat the competition. Here, Porter advocates two strategies: cost and differentiation.

10.5.1   The Sources of Competitive Advantage

The starting point for identifying the sources of competitive advantage should be, it seems, understanding the industry in which a hypothetical firm should compete. The industry's potential for growth is the most important indicator of the extent and intensity of rivalry among firms in that industry. If the firm can produce high-quality product coupled with superior customer service and has built-in mechanisms to produce a given product at a lower cost than rivals, the firm has the necessary conditions to reap above-average or premium profits in the long run.

However, this is not a complete blueprint for sustained competitive advantage. In order to out-compete rivals over the long run, the process should begin with ingredients that go into the production of parts, a design that will outperform competitors' product, and, most importantly, the reliability that will provide an undeniable value and make a long-lasting impression in the mind of the customer.

A firm may be able to establish itself as provider of superior product if it can meet the above prerequisites. Once this has been established, the chances are that disposable incomes at the consumers' command will flow its way. In the automotive industry, most consumers look for value for the money they spend on cars, in part due to competition from the Japanese big three (Honda, Nissan, and Toyota), but also because some customers still harbor the view that American-made auto parts are of inferior quality. This view is continuously substantiated by the resale prices of U.S.-made cars which indicate substantial differences between domestic and foreign cars.

10.5.2 The Core of Competitive Strategy

In an industry crowded by many rivals, each determined to capture a sizable share of the market, the one firm that has something special to offer, over and above what the rivals offer, will be able to achieve that goal. In a competitive market, the standard practices may be inadequate to achieve prime objectives. Management needs to be innovative and make sure that the implementation of its competitive strategies are articulated in a fashion that provides the customer an opportunity uncovered by rivals.

While Porter emphasizes that there are essentially two approaches to competitive strategy, there is a third which recent experience has shown to be a viable opportunity: the entry into the American market by the Honda Civic, which exhibited and combined *both* elements of Porter's favorite strategies, low cost and highly differentiated qualities. It shows that it is possible to be a low-cost producer and yet still offer the customer value, especially in a market where there is a void to be filled with such product.

10.5.3 Evaluating Competitive Strategies

For the purpose of decision-making, each competitive strategy must be evaluated on a relative basis according to the contribution it is expected

Table 10.3 SWOT Analysis

Internal Strengths	Internal Weaknesses
Adequate financial resources?	No clear strategic direction?
Well thought of by buyers?	Lack of managerial depth and talent?
An acknowledged market leader?	Missing any key competencies?
Well-conceived functional area strategies?	Poor track record in implementing strategy?
Access to economies of scale?	Plagued with internal operating problems?
Insulated (at least somewhat) from strong competitive pressures?	Too narrow a product line?
Proprietary technology?	Weak market image?
Cost advantages?	Below-average marketing skills?
Product innovation abilities?	Unable to finance needed changes in strategy?
Proven management?	No R&D capability?
Highly differentiated product?	

External Opportunities	External Threats
Serve additional customer groups?	Likely entry of new competitors?
Enter new markets or segments?	Rising sales of substitute products?
Expand product line to meet broader range of customer needs?	Slower market growth?
Diversify into related products?	Adverse government policies?
Add complementary products?	Growing competitive pressures?
Vertical integration?	Vulnerability to recession and business cycle?
Ability to move to better strategic group?	Growing bargaining power of customers or suppliers?
Complacency among rival firms?	Changing buyer needs and tastes?
Faster market growth?	Adverse demographic changes?
Other?	Other?

to make to the long-range financial objectives. A thorough comparison must be made between the given company's position and the competition. Additionally, it may be helpful to look at what has become the norm in the analysis process, the strengths/weaknesses/opportunities and threats factors (SWOT; see Table 10.3).

10.6   Step 5: Long-Range Financial Plan

In a free-enterprise economy, companies are created for the purpose of responding to a consumer's unfulfilled need. It is obvious that there must be a reward for risk taking, and executive actions are driven that way. Companies that have risen to prominence in the domestic and global markets have been able to marshal resources and invariably began with ambitions that were out of all proportion to their resources and capabilities. At the global level, Honda comes to mind. From a humble beginning, it has achieved prominence second only to Toyota. At the domestic level, all you need to do is look at the daily paper and the name of Microsoft's Bill Gates appears somewhere. The college dropout is the wealthiest man on earth, and he has yet to achieve his goal.

The goal is not financial success. After all, what will you do with billions of dollars in your bank account or in stocks? The strategic achievement itself becomes the ultimate goal, not the monetary reward that follows such success. In order to achieve that level of success, a business leader needs all the necessary resources that he can muster. These resources are, at times, people. A simple look at the United Parcel Service (UPS) proves the point. It is the total familiarity with UPS' operations by every driver who distributes the packages on a daily basis that provides UPS with speed and accuracy in the delivery system. At times, billion dollar acquisitions are made simply for the human assets, because similar grooming of new personnel may be more costly, and the firm may, by the time it has groomed enough, have lost the market opportunity that it once had. The ultimate in strategic management is to follow a path that will allow a manager to create the future through orchestration of all resources to create a sustainable competitive advantage. Strategic decision-making is a combination of intuitive judgment and analysis of hard facts and then arriving at decisions that may at times prove extremely difficult to make; however, if a manager is on continuous alert and is cognizant of what is taking place in the external environment at the global level, his life is made easier by not having to make those hard decisions, be it called Christmas massacre or whatever else.

Today we live in a global economy. As market performance in the last few months of 1997 has shown, there is tremendous linkages between the economies and, by the same token, the management of firms that compose those economies. The days of looking at the home market and counting market share are gone, having been replaced by various global economies that are intertwined. But, if managers follow the steps provided thus far religiously and with a deep sense of commitment, the chances are that they may not be taken off guard, because success depends on a host of factors, human assets, financial assets, and, more than anything else, the products that customers want. To have successful strategic management, a manager should understand and firmly believe that the *customer is still the king.*

10.7   Strategies for Competitive Advantage

The principal job of a manager is to *allocate scarce resources to profitable market opportunities.* The resources could be financial, human, or physical assets. The goal is "profitable market opportunities". In pursuing this goal systematically and analytically, the chances are that the manager will indeed succeed in satisfying the stakeholders and sustaining their loyalty over time. This should be done through analysis of competitive advantage. Competitive advantage grows fundamentally out of the value a firm is able to create, for its buyers, that exceeds the firm's cost of creating it. Because there are many firms that interact with each other in an industry (and that is why we are addressing the issue of competitive advantage), we also have to address the question of how a firm can outperform its rivals and establish a different position and sustain it for the long run.[9] In Kenichi Ohmae's words (from his book, *The Mind of the Strategist*):

> "What business strategy is all about is, in a word, *competitive advantage.* ...
> The sole purpose of strategic planning is to enable a company to gain, as efficiently as possible, a sustainable edge over its competitors. Corporate strategy thus implies an attempt to alter a company's strength relative to that of its competitors in the most efficient way."

According to Porter, a firm can achieve competitive advantage, essentially, in two ways. It can produce a product or service at a lower cost than its rivals, or it can produce a differentiated product in such a way that the customer is willing to pay a premium price for it. In the lower cost strategy, a firm must establish itself as a cost leader and convey the message in no uncertain terms to the public. Take the case of Compaq, the leading low-cost producer of personal computers. "Compaq has become one of the world's most successful companies and today leads the computer industry in market share performance and balance sheet strength. ... We have achieved this by consistently executing our strategic

Table 10.4 Allocating Scarce Resources to
Profitable Market Opportunities (ASTOMO)

The ASTOMO model is a method used to forecast the results expected from exploiting a market opportunity. The model breaks total market opportunity into segments:

1. The total potential of a market
2. The undeveloped market
3. The saleable market
4. Current industry sales, according to competitors' market share vs. our current share, if any

Competitive strategies are developed for each market opportunity, and forecasts are made based on the strength of the strategy for:

1. Market share gain
2. Unit and dollar sales
3. Operating profit

---

plans ... striving to provide customers with the highest levels of innovation and flexibility at the lowest total cost of ownership."[10] By executing a low-cost strategy, Compaq made it possible for the shareholders to enjoy a 24.8% rate of return on equity in 1997, 20% more than in 1996.

The second strategy is differentiation, when the firm produces a product for which the consumer is prepared to pay a premium price. The whole strategy begins with creating value for the consumer that justifies higher price. The most basic tenet here is to ensure that such values are communicated to the consumer. Windows 95/98 exhibits these features beautifully.

The customer is prepared to pay for the product because from the beginning Microsoft established the fact that it was providing a valuable product that the consumer could use effectively. In order for a firm (in this case Microsoft) to sustain its differentiation strategy and be able to charge a premium price, it must constantly innovate and create new features for the product. Once a manager decides on the type of strategy that the firm may adopt, the firm would then look at the market in which management is considering investing resources. Table 10.4 provides a blueprint by which an investigation of the market potentials should direct itself.

The industry in which the firm is interested is the starting point of analysis. To make wise investment decisions, a manager has to have a thorough understanding of the structure of the industries they want to enter (or are in) and in which they want to compete for market share. It is also very important for the manager to understand the underlying competitive forces active in that industry. Each industry is different and requires close scrutiny, because it is important to comprehend which competitive forces are more significant. The preponderance of the force will determine where strategic attention has to be focused. Managers must also understand that their action may change the course of operation of an industry. When AT&T introduced its Universal Card, it made a major decision by requiring no annual fee, which the customers loved. This action introduced a new element to the market in that other credit card companies realized they would lose market share if they did not adopt the new policy. So, today, most credit cards have no annual fee. The ones that do charge an annual fee, such as American Express, have to offer some distinctive advantages to offset the annual fee, and the advantage must be more than enough to the job. It is also very critical that strategies adopted be tested so that the attractiveness of the industry is not undermined.

10.8   Evaluating New Business Opportunities

Table 10.4 provides a good example of how to approach a new market using the "allocating scare resources to profitable market opportunities" (ASTOMO) model. Of course, the firm in this case has to offer something over and above the competitors in the market to win market share. The best example that comes to mind is the automobile industry and how the Japanese manufacturers entered the U.S. market. In the early 1970s, they came in with small cars that did not seem to attract much attention. Americans had been used to big cars for such a long time that to them the small car looked unreliable, unsafe, and inefficient. However, the first waves of the energy crisis changed the whole picture and something that seemed so unattractive all of a sudden looked reasonable and even desirable. A combination of factors helped establish the Japanese presence in the U.S. marketplace, probably forever.

Some of the Japanese manufacturers practiced Porter's low-cost strategy, and some others followed a combination of differentiation (high quality) and low-cost strategy. In the latter case, Honda comes to mind, as low cost and high quality became the hallmarks of the Honda Civic. The car has maintained that reputation ever since its introduction. The Japanese car makers came in and attacked an undeveloped market — the demand for a small, gas-efficient car — and established their name and reputation. Once in the saddle, they gradually moved into other more profitable markets and more expensive cars which exhibited many innovative features that American cars completely lacked. Today, they have more than 30% of the U.S. market, and two of their cars, the Toyota Camry and Honda Accord, are favorites of the American consumers, as reflected by being named the number one and two sellers for 1997 in *Consumer Reports* magazine.

10.9   Manager's Job: Decision-Making and Resource Allocation

The marketplace is where actions take place, where the resourceful and insightful entrepreneurs survive and prosper, and where the slow, too-conservative managers are brushed aside. Just about 10 years ago, the Sears' operations, annual sales, and, at times, monthly sales were indicators of the movement of the economy. Because Sears lost its focus and failed to act upon the fundamental changes taking place in society, new champions stepped in to take over Sears' share of the market. Today, Wal-Mart is the standard for sales performance, the prosperity of the economy, and consumers' mood.

This is why we have decided to take you, the reader, on a step-by-step process of *resource allocation to profitable market opportunities.* Although simple reading of the exhibits would prove to be self-explanatory, we feel that such a tour in decision-making warrants some narrative to help understand the process. We begin, in this section, with the ASTOMO model provided previously in Table 10.4. Every new business opportunity can and should be studied carefully, and with adequate data it is possible to determine the potentials of different market segments. Fortunately, most such data are either available in usable form or can be collected from different sources to give us a picture of what a market is. Understanding the industry well will help determine the total market, the undeveloped part of it, and the potential amount of sales for which investment decisions have to be made. Figure 10.7 provides a

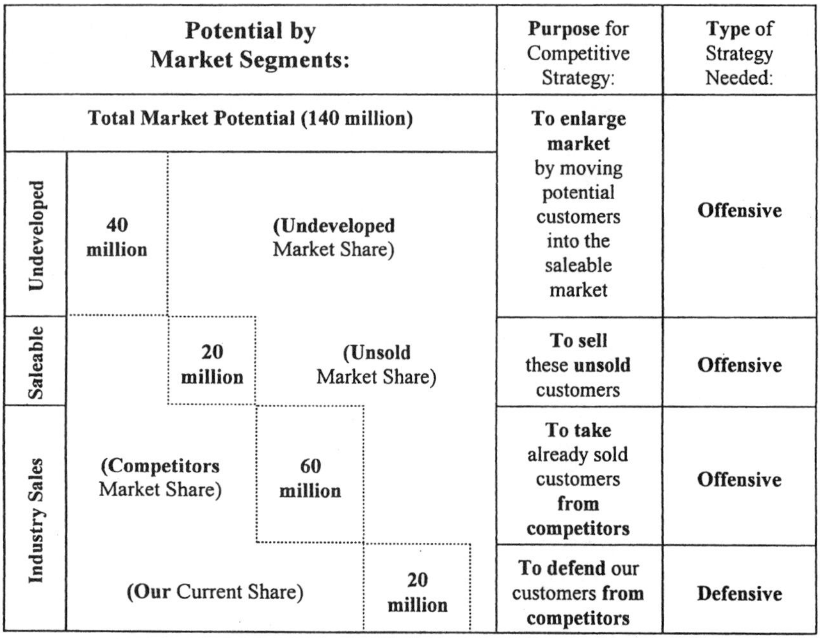

Potential by Market Segments:			Purpose for Competitive Strategy:	Type of Strategy Needed:
Total Market Potential (140 million)			To enlarge market	
Undeveloped	40 million	(Undeveloped Market Share)	by moving potential customers into the saleable market	Offensive
Saleable	20 million	(Unsold Market Share)	To sell these **unsold** customers	Offensive
Industry Sales	(Competitors Market Share)	60 million	To take already sold customers **from competitors**	Offensive
	(Our Current Share)	20 million	To defend our customers **from** competitors	Defensive

Figure 10.7 Evaluating New Business Strategies

picture of how to proceed with determination of total market potential and the purposes of the organization's competitive strategy.

10.10 An Example

Assume that the market investigators have done their job in regard to an oral anti-diabetic drug and have provided management with an analysis of the market. A scenario can be created similar to that shown in Table 10.5. Once management is equipped with this data, then further market analysis can be made for subsequent years which would make it possible for management to create a strategic planning process by which resources can be procured for investment decisions down the road, as reflected in Table 10.6.

10.11 Application of Economic Value Added

The economic value added (EVA) is generally applied to an ongoing operation to determine if the previously policies and strategies have

Table 10.5 Evaluating New Business Strategies

The market opportunity: An improved oral anti-diabetic drug

The competitive strategy: Built around the advantages of (1) lowering blood sugar and (2) fewer side reactions

Sales and profit forecasts:

1.	Total market potential (developed and undeveloped)	6 million patients
2.	Total undeveloped market	3 million patients
3.	Total saleable market (as of today)	2 million patients
4.	Current industry sales	1 million patients
5.	Forecasts for first 5 years	
	First year (for example):	
	Expected market share (25%)	250,000 patients
	Sales forecast (units)	75 million tablets
	(300 tablets per year per patient)	
	Average selling price	$.50 per tablet
	Sales forecast (dollars)	$37.5 million
	Operating costs	
	Fixed	$3.0 million
	Variable	$12.0 million
	Operating profit (before taxes)	$22.5 million

added value to the enterprise or the shareholders. For this purpose, we would refer the reader to Figure 10.8, where the formula is provided, as well as an example of how to apply the concept of EVA. The technique can be applied to a corporation as a whole or its components. It requires rigorous accounting data to determine the exact figures and accounting information to come out with the necessary input, but once the data are there, relatively accurate calculation can be made as indicated by the example of Anheuser-Busch (see Figure 10.8). The same technique can be used for every market opportunity, and with some degree of accuracy the management can determine a future course of action as far as allocation of scarce resources to market opportunities is concerned (see Table 10.7).

From Figure 10.8, it should be quite evident that it is possible to apply the concept to an entire organization, but it is also applicable to *units* of the organization to give management a clearer picture of how

Table 10.6 Evaluating New Business Strategies

The market opportunity: (?)

The competitive strategy: Built around the advantages of (1) ?, and (2) ?.

Sales and profit forecasts

	Number of Patients (by year)					
	1	2	3	4	5	Total
1. Total market potential (developed and undeveloped)						
2. Total undeveloped market						
3. Total saleable market (as of today)						
4. Current industry sales						
5. Forecasts for first 5 years						

Expected market share
Sales forecasts (units)
Average selling price
Sales forecast (dollars)
Operating costs:
    Fixed costs
    Variable costs
Operating profit (before taxes) $200M

profitable such units are. This is extremely helpful in determining not only the leadership capabilities of different managers but also in determining fair compensation for more productive managers and establishing an equitable system within which ambitious managers can sketch their future. To provide a further example of how to use EVA, Table 10.8 is provided.

As we have emphasized in the previous pages, strategic management is about allocating a significant portion of the firm's scarce resources to new market opportunities or enhancing the capabilities of the present productive system. In either case, Figure 10.9 will illustrate why such exercise is essential. Such an exercise should lead to creating a long-range financial plan which, over the years, would provide management with a road map of the financial flow and how such a flow would affect the liquidity and financial viability of the enterprise (see Figure 10.10). And, once such steps are taken, they can be recycled with the added benefit of correcting the mistakes made or optimism that may have affected such allocative behavior.

The **EVA Model (Economic Value Added)** is a method for evaluating the worth of a business unit, or activity, to the stockholders:

- A corporation
- A division
- A plant
- A business unit
- New products
- Acquisitions
- Competitive strategies
- Etc.

EVA equals:

Annual operating profits over 5 years	– Taxes –	Weighted cost of employed capital including debt	×	Total capital and debt employed in the activity

After-tax operating profit	minus	Cost of capital	equals	EVA

Anheuser-Busch

$1756 million operating profit	11.3% weighted average cost*	Anheuser-Busch's
–$617 million taxes	× $8.0 billion total capital	positive EVA
$1139 million minus	$904.0 million equals	$235 million

* 67% equity @ 14.3%; 33% debt @5.2%

Figure 10.8 What Is EVA?

10.12 Summary

Strategic management of resources depends on rigorous exercise of strategic planning (see Figures 10.11 and 10.12). The best way, to date, to do the job is to follow the four phases of the evolution of formal strategic planning (provided in Figure 3.2 in Chapter 3) to see how a firm can create a value system which will begin to meet the budgetary restraints, can perform an analysis of the environment in order to predict the future, and in the process can think strategically about allocation of resources in order to create the future. As Drucker states, at the beginning of the present chapter, it is possible to create the future. All one needs to do is to increase the necessary response to markets and competition and orchestration of all resources to create competitive

Table 10.7 Prioritizing Market Opportunities Using the EVA Model

Market Opportunity	Total Capital Employed	5-Year Operating Profit	Economic Value Added (EVA)	Remarks
Market opportunity 1				
Market opportunity 2				
Market opportunity 3				
Market opportunity 4				
Market opportunity 5				
Market opportunity 6				
Market opportunity 7				
Market opportunity 8				
Market opportunity 9				
Market opportunity 10				
Total				

Table 10.8 Evaluating New Business Strategies

Total employed capital (corporate level) = $4.6 billion
Total capital invested = $2.6 billion, at 13.0% rate of return
Total debt invested = $2.0 billion, at 6.5% interest rate

Weighted average annual rate of return = 10%
Current corporate tax rate = 28%

Market opportunity 1: Improved oral anti-diabetic drug

Competitive strategy: Built around the advantages of (1) lowering blood sugar, and (2) fewer side reactions

Financial forecasts (first 5 years)
1. Operating profit (before taxes)   +$200.0 million
2. Taxes   −$ 56.0 million
    Net   +$144.0 million
3. Cost of employed capital = 10%
4. Total employed capital = $50 million
    $50 million × 10% =   −$ 5.0 million
5. Economic value added (EVA)   +$139.0 million
    (to current shareholders' value)

How will the **revenue** and **profit forecasts** for **new market opportunities** be linked to the **long-range financial plan**?

1. By **extrapolating** the organization's current momentum over the next 5 years to form a base budget.
2. By **incrementally adding** the forecasted revenue and profit for each approved new market opportunity or strategy to the base formed by the above extrapolation.
3. **Current momentum** equals the trend of currents business — what the revenue would be if no new business opportunities were added.

Figure 10.9 Strategic Planning

Creating new strategic plans from "scratch" every year is a waste of time and money.

Once a strategic plan is approved and implemented, it can be kept current based on feedback from the annual operational plans and new industry changes appearing on the horizon.

Figure 10.10 Recycle

Managers and leaders have career life cycles, just as products and markets do.

At the top of the cycle, senior management adds another dimension to middle management.

This "added dimension" is the strategic (visionary, conceptual, institutional, entrepreneurship) side of managing or leading.

This "added dimension" has as its primary objective repositioning of the organization's resources in tomorrow's markets.

The basic theme of strategic leadership is to procure, evaluate, and systematically allocate resources to market opportunities for the purpose of meeting the organization's long-range objectives.

Figure 10.11 Summary

advantage for the firm. A look at the U.S. market today shows us a number of firms that lead the wave in creating the future. Such firms — for example, Microsoft, General Electric, Merck, NUCOR, and Toyota — are creating the future that the next century will inherit.

References

1. Robert M. Grant, *Contemporary Strategy Analysis*, 3rd ed., Blackwell Publishers, Malden, MA, 1997, p. 9.
2. Kenichi Ohmae, *The Mind of the Strategist*, McGraw-Hill Company, New York, 1982, p. 13.
3. Kenichi Ohmae, *The Mind of the Strategist*, McGraw-Hill Company, New York, 1982, p. 15.
4. Gary Hamel and C.K. Prahlad, "Competing for the Future," *Harvard Business Review*, July-August 1994, p. 126.
5. Gary Hamel and C.K. Prahlad, "Competing for the Future," *Harvard Business Review*, July-August 1994, p. 24.
6. Peter Drucker, *Harvard Business Review*, September-October 1997, p. 20.
7. *Wall Street Journal*, October 6, 1997, p. 1.
8. Michael E. Porter, *The Competitive Advantage*, The Free Press, New York, 1985.
9. Michael E. Porter, "What is Strategy?" *Harvard Business Review*, November-December 1996, p. 69.
10. Compaq, Annual Report, 1997.

Section 2. The Cases

I n this section we will introduce the second part of the text, the cases that will help students apply their knowledge of strategy. Each case reflects some separate issues. Some are more complex than others and require more analysis and discussion. In order for the reader to understand each case, we urge you to read the next section on the "Case Method". When you have studied that section and absorbed the message in there, then we would like you to read the section on "Financial Analysis". The purpose of this section is to help readers analyze financial data in order to comprehend fully the financial situation that a given company is faced with. It is extremely important that students understand the financial map of a particular business and specific company so that the recommendations that they may offer are based on solid facts and not some imaginary situation.

11 Objectives and Philosophy of the Case Method

For many readers, the use of case studies will be something new and different from the conventional study of business courses, and some comments about the philosophy, objectives, and merits of such a method may be informative before undertaking "case study" courses.

The technique of using actual business problems (cases) as an educational and analytical instrument was developed early in the 1920s at Harvard Graduate School of Business Administration. Although Harvard Business School was an innovator and pioneer in using the case method as a tool for educating managers, the actual use of a "case" as a tool for educating students goes further than that. It grew, to some extent, from the practice of teaching law by studying past legal cases, and obviously in medicine through the use of clinical work, but such methods are centuries old. What we consider innovative about Harvard Business School's method was their new way of applying the case concept to the business school environment.

What is a case? What does it entail? What do we want to accomplish through cases that cannot be accomplished through conventional methods of teaching business management? A business manager is a decision-maker. In order to make proper decisions, the manager should be able to recognize the facts, to reason out the connection with existing circumstances and conditions, and to set out a plan of action. The astute manager is the one who is able to assess the surroundings and the uniqueness of particular problems and to apply appropriate analytical tools toward their solution. A case is, or should be, based on a real

211

business situation which includes not only the facts, but generally some additional information on the company and possibly the industry with sufficient data to reflect the decision to be made and the setting in which the decision-maker finds himself.

An additional objective of the case method is to provide the reader with an opportunity to combine a general business education, which could be at times theoretical, with the practical side of business. This will allow students a valuable opportunity to develop their own conceptual framework. If this technique is used correctly, the chances are that students will become more practical and down-to-earth in summing up business problems and making decisions.

While business schools such as Harvard make great use of the case approach, many others have attempted a reasonable combination of theory and practice. The theory is based on the stock of knowledge gathered through research and involves models of components of the business management function, while the case method draws heavily on the practices of business for the issues and "tools" for classroom study.

A more significant objective of the case method is to sharpen the student's analytical ability to separate fact from fiction, the relevant from the irrelevant, and trivial information from that which is vital to his decision-making action. When attempting to achieve this objective in an uncertain environment, the case-study student will be less afraid of uncertainty and become more confident in new situations; he will be more aggressive in expressing his views, all the while learning the tools of his trade. "Because wisdom can't be taught,"[1] for a lasting impression one should learn more by being actively involved in a given case, by "empathetic" observation of what is going on, and by benefiting from other participants in a given situation.

Finally, a case provides an atmosphere in which students can recognize and identify the problem at hand, analyze the interrelated facts, and come up with a range of alternatives of which one may be superior to others. No principle, concept, or theory is a substitute for an actual business experience.

11.1   Case Relevance to Manager Development

It would be appropriate to say that outstanding traits of a successful manager are his ability to analyze situations, make decisions, and take definitive action. In the action-oriented world of business, avoiding a tough decision will often have disastrous results for the manager or his firm, or both. One could become labeled as an ineffective and inefficient manager by avoiding decision-making responsibilities.

There are, however, various bases for making decisions. Some managers will make a decision in a way that they feel conforms with the wishes of their superiors. Some make what are primarily intuitive decisions. Still others look at the easily accessible and available information, identify the immediate problem, and decide on that basis. Many managers are more adept at analyzing situations than at the ultimate selection of the best alternative. The effective managers, however, gather as much information as can be found within the limits of permissible time and cost, analyze the data, explore the various alternative methods of solving the problem, accept the uncertainties, select the best method, and immediately lay out a plan of action to implement their solution.

Studies in business administration should, therefore, involve the student in exercises which prepare him for this kind of responsibility. The best way that has been established to accomplish this goal is through the study and analysis of cases. Through practice with a series of cases, the "student manager" is able to develop a procedure — an approach — for analyzing problems in a firm which will arise as part of his own career activities. When a well-defined method of case analysis is used and a large number of cases are analyzed, the student becomes adept at analyzing complex problems and acquires the skill and the habit of viewing management problems from an analytical and critical point of view.

A dexterity or "skill" is developed largely by doing, rather than by reading about how someone else did the job or by idealizing an unreal setting. One cannot learn to play football by reading a book or listening to a lecture; even watching others do it is not enough. One must actually play — one must become involved — in order to learn. A case gets the student involved in the business problem and forces him to analyze it and make a decision (for better or for worse).

Also, having analyzed a series of cases concerning firms with different types of products and problems and operating in different environments, the student will be better prepared, in the future, to deal with the problems of his firm as it grows and takes on new products, and as the political, economic, and cultural environment surrounding his firm changes.

A case is a real-life situation. It actually happened. It has been researched, structured, and written by a scholar in such a way as to include the pertinent facts about the company, the environment, and the people involved so that the reader can visualize the situation and actively participate in the original experience. The usual case contains information which covers the background and development of a situation for which the reader realizes that a decision must be made and some action taken. Sometimes the problem will not be clear. Often a problem will be apparent but it will not be the basic problem. The student is challenged to locate the basic problem and then determine the hierarchy of problems which spring from it. The basic problem is usually of a strategic or policy nature.

There is often a tendency for students to read the text material in a case and ignore, or only glance at, the tables, balance sheets, and other tabular data. This tendency must be overcome. The analysis of the hard data included in a case is an important part of the learning experience and usually permits the student to infer far more about the company and the situation than is stated in the text.

In a real-life situation, a manager may not have access to all the information he would like prior to making a decision. The collection and analysis of all necessary information would almost always cost too much, and by the time all the desired information is gathered it would be too late. Hence, most decisions must be made with incomplete information. To this extent, a case study simulates real life. The student will usually feel that the case does not contain enough data; however, a careful study of most cases will permit the student to infer or assume a considerable amount of additional information. In other words, a student will gain a certain amount of experience in dealing with uncertainty that does not accrue to the student in "lecture" courses.

Uncertainty is closely associated with the essence of the case method, and the case study pedagogist believes uncertainty to be an important contributor to the learning process. As Kenneth Andrews stated, the case method of learning is intended to evolve "a way of thinking which does not collapse before the demands of concrete experience."[2] Most of the teaching techniques students are accustomed to in colleges and universities are deductive in nature, starting with a generalization and using examples or problems for illustration. Much of the uncertainty and frustration associated with the case method results from a reversal of the process. The cases, if used in the traditional manner, are not presented as illustrative of either good or bad administrative policies or practices; rather, they depict the situation as it actually is and the student is left to determine the rightness or wrongness of the situation and to make a decision, usually in the form of a set of recommendations. The case method and the emphasis upon inductive reasoning requires the student to use the same thought processes he must exercise as the manager "on the spot". He has to develop his own generalizations through experience rather than have someone (e.g., the professor) present the generalizations and then illustrate them deductively.

11.2 Case Analysis

The use of cases in the learning process, from the student's perspective, should be viewed in several stages — analysis by the student independently, analysis by students in study groups, and presentation of the case analysis in the form of written reports or through class discussion. By systematically analyzing a large number of cases on his own, before subjecting his work to a study group, the student earns a high degree of self-confidence over time. Then, by comparing notes with colleagues in the study group, the logic of alternatives can be tested, and the less useful alternatives can be either discarded or reduced in importance. Finally, through class discussion, the weighty matters related to the most feasible alternatives can be explored in depth without wasting class time on obviously weak recommendations and without misdirecting the class toward unimportant matters.

11.3 Student's Independent Analysis

When first approaching a case, the student is advised to quickly skim through the opening paragraphs, review the headings or subtitles, and then evaluate the quality and quantity of information contained in the tables and appendices. This will give him a framework into which he can fit his analysis.

The student should then read the case slowly and thoroughly, making notes of pertinent facts and ideas. By the time he has completed the reading he should have formulated some idea as to the problems involved. He will know what data are needed and can go on to a thorough study of the tables and appendices.

Quite often, identifying the problem(s) also suggests possible solutions or courses of action, particularly after the student has had considerable experience with cases or with the decision-making process "on the job". Even if this does happen, it will be beneficial to the student to look to other sources for insight into the particular problem posed by the case and for an understanding of the management "tools" required to resolve the problem. Textbooks can be used for these purposes, but the student should bear in mind that the textbook presents the views of the author(s) which almost always reflect his bias. Other alternatives should be explored through other readings and, if possible, through conversations with managers who have been confronted with the same issue. Most important, however, is to be certain that all the data of the case have been analyzed and understood. Whether the case deals with specific techniques of accounting or broad statements of objectives in corporate strategy, there are insights to be gained from all the data available in the case, and the astute student will learn to use the data.

It is only after one has assimilated all the available information from these sources that he is in a position to make assumptions concerning the need for further data. Can one rightfully make assumptions about inflation as of the date of the case without having checked inflationary levels at that time through any one of a number of sources? Can one assume that stockholder's sole interest in the firm is in dividends without reading some of the many studies on this subject? The answer to these obvious questions leads quickly to an appreciation of the burden placed on the student by the case method. His recommendations must stand the test of evaluation by his peers when compared with similar action taken by the managers in the past and when trends in management practices are observed. Having to make assumptions is not merely a defect in the case method's lack of information, for in the real world of managers the lack of information is a constant companion but decisions still must be made.

The student should go through the process of selecting the best alternative for the situation stated without help from his classmates before participating in the study group. At first he may be apprehensive about his own recommendations when compared with others, but in time he will observe that the uncertainties that bother him also bother other members of the group and gradually he develops the confidence to present his views without fear and defensiveness. He learns that judgment is not always a matter of "right vs. wrong" but is a matter of selecting the best alternative in specific situations — and sometimes this means selecting the least detrimental alternative.

11.4   Study Groups

Each student should go through the initial process alone, so as to exercise his own powers of analysis and his own decision-making ability. But, the next important step is to get together with one or several of his colleagues, who have similarly prepared their own individual analyses of the case, for an informal discussion. Each person has the opportunity to present and justify his analysis, his decision, and his recommended plan of action. He must, however, be able to assimilate, with an open mind, the arguments of colleagues who disagree with him and to change or modify his solution if necessary: It is most essential that the student maintain an open mind. Dogmatism will not take him far in a management career and will hinder the decision-making process, not only in his study group but also later in his management career.

Having followed the above procedure, the student arrives in the classroom well prepared for a class discussion of the case. He has a clear grasp of the facts of the case and has arrived at a defensible solution. It is, of course, not the final solution. New approaches or insights will be presented by other students. Again, each student must be able and willing to accept new facts (which he missed) or more realistic assumptions, which may lead to a different solution.

The student should be cautioned that there is not usually a "final" or "best" solution. Do not expect the instructor to identify the "correct" analysis. The objective of a case analysis is not to determine the correct solution. Rather, it is to permit the student to exercise his analytic competence and logic and to make decisions that are consistent with his analysis.

In summary, the purpose of the study group is to provide a sounding board for ideas, to test the choice of alternatives in an environment in which final evaluation is not a factor, to sharpen the student's powers of persuasion, and to instill an air of confidence into the student that will carry over into his management career. The major tools of management are the communicating skills, and the study group should provide a means of testing these skills in a "committee" type environment.

After the student has made appropriate refinements of his analysis, as a result of discussion in the study group, the analysis process is basically complete and he should begin thinking about the other major process in case study — class or report presentation.

A thorough review of the analysis steps may be helpful before leaving this part of our treatise in case study pedagogy. As a student gains experience with the case method, he will no doubt refine and amplify these steps to suit his own style and assignments but five steps are suggested as follows:

1.   Receive the case material.
2.   Complete the case information.
3.   Evaluate the current situation.
4.   Evaluate alternatives for future action and reach a decision.
5.   Review the recommendations critically.

11.4.1 Receive the Case Material

Before the student can start any analysis he must develop a receptive attitude toward the case. Malcolm McNair[3] calls this "a willing suspension of disbelief." He further describes it as "the willingness to take at face value the situation which the case presents, forgetting that this is artificial, so to speak, forgetting that this is a case, forgetting that this is a classroom, being willing to take the situation at face value and become the person concerned with it." This attitude is necessary from the start. If a student cannot conceive of a case as containing a real problem, not an imagined one, he will not be able to analyze it effectively. It may be difficult at first for a student to see himself as a participant in a case, but he must make every effort to take the case seriously and to become as involved with it as he would with any real decision.

All students at one time or another are stricken by an acute time problem and this can lead to the temptation to merely read the case in a superficial manner without hard analysis or to scan the text matter and skip the quantitative data. This should never be done. It can be assumed that the case writer has given enough information for considerable analysis, but there is no guarantee that the information has not been cleverly disguised. In order for the analysis to be effective and efficient, the student must carefully analyze the case before proceeding.

There are several things the analyst should look for when reading the case. Often, driven by a need for specific information, the analyst will completely ignore the "big picture". This error leads to conclusions inconsistent with economic conditions, corporate objectives, etc. While looking for these kinds of information, the student should take care to discriminate between fact and opinion. He must adopt a critical and questioning attitude toward all inputs.

The student should keep in mind that he is acting in the role of a participant in the case and as such his need for more information has to be interfaced with its cost and the urgency of the decision. A good student will state "specifically what further information he desires, why it is significant to the problem, and how they would have gone about obtaining it."[4]

When adopting the role of a participant in the case, the student must keep in mind that administrators cannot use such generalizations as "in the long run" or *ceteris paribus* as an excuse for incompetent decisions. Hindsight is also an invalid input. This information was clearly not available to the people involved in the case and it violates the basic concept of a case education. The use of hindsight is, in effect, an attempt to turn an issue case into an appraisal case. As such, it subverts the original purpose of the assignment.

11.4.2 Complete the Case Information

The information provided in the case will never be complete. In order to proceed with the analysis, the student will have to attempt to augment those areas which he feels are deficient. This may or may not be possible. There are two ways he can supplement the data in the case. The first is by inference. Any inference must be carefully structured from the case, as pointed out previously. As the student grows more adept with the analysis, he will become more adroit at defining what inferences can be made. In the early stages of his analysis he will have to evaluate carefully the information given and decide what can be inferred from it.

The second way he can augment the case information is by research. The purpose here is not to find out what actually happened, but rather to fill in the gaps so that the information available for the student's decision-making process is that which an executive would have had at the time of the case. It is important for the student to recognize that the goal of the case method is a pattern of thinking, not specific case solutions; consequently, the research should be directed toward obtaining supporting data for the analysis rather than toward determining the decision made by the manager in the actual situation.

Secondary research often will be concerned with the industry involved. No firm operates in a vacuum. In order to analyze a company's performance it is often necessary to compare it with other firms. General sources of financial records are very useful both in the investigation of competing firms and the industry as a whole. The student should be able to evaluate the company in relation to other companies and to general trends in the industry.

Finally, certain types of cases involve specific tools or knowledge before a decision can be made. Accounting and financial management cases are examples of business functions that utilize a body of knowledge that must be understood by effective managers in these areas. The case method handles this problem by requiring the student to research the body of knowledge and acquiring as much of an understanding as possible on his own. Quite often the study groups can be used to discuss particularly difficult concepts and techniques that the student needs help with. Beyond this, the professor has to be viewed in part as a resource person to refer the student to sources of understanding on the concepts or techniques in question. In a graduate class utilizing the case method, however, these activities should and do take place outside the classroom, leaving class time free for case discussion.

11.4.3 *Evaluate the Current Situation*

Once the problems have been identified, the analyst should determine the firm's background to the problem situation. This step is more important in broader corporate strategy issues than in some accounting cases, but background should never be ignored.

Three components of the business picture require specific attention. These are the corporate environment, the corporate strategy or segments thereof, and the roles of the participants. A thorough understanding of the company's environment is essential to the analysis of a business policy case. The environment is composed of technological, economic, social, and political elements.

Although the technological elements are the most rapidly changing, they are also often the easiest to identify. The economic segment covers both the general macroeconomic picture and the specific markets involved. The social aspects of a company's environment are perhaps the most overlooked. They are as essential as any of the other elements. The emphasis required by the political segment will often be determined by the type of industry involved and by the scope of the company. Certainly a large firm with international involvements must be more sensitive to the political climate than a small firm dealing in an unregulated area.

The analyst should also attempt to identify the corporation's strategy or that portion relevant to the issue of the case. It is very probable that the company will not have a clearly stated strategy, but that should not dissuade the student from defining it for himself. A strategy formulation will be necessary as a reference point for the decision-making process. It can be most easily identified by comparing the company's market opportunities with its specific actions.

The particular people involved in the case are of great importance to the analysis. The student must examine each character and role to the extent allowed by the data in the case. He must be careful to take the identity of the character and not force himself into the case under the name of the character. As the student, Price, says, "I see now that in analyzing the case I should have tried to be Joe Longman. Instead, I assumed that Joe was me ... I never really looked at Joe."[5] The student should be careful to understand the motives behind the actions in the case. When he analyzes his recommendations, he will have to interpret whether or not they are consistent with the motives displayed by the characters. If they are not, some changes will have to be made.

Beyond the investigation of each character's individual role, the analyst often must also investigate the group behavior. Interaction between the characters in the case can be as revealing as the actions of any one character, and the student should examine the functioning of the group process. The analyst must be aware of the pitfall of responding emotionally to a particular character. He must remain objective and attempt to afford each character the impartial attention which is dictated by his place in the case.

11.4.4 Evaluate Alternatives for Future Action

The first step in evaluating alternatives is to identify viable opportunities open to the company. Andrews[6] lists five questions to guide the student in this task:

1. What are the essential economic and technical characteristics of the industry in which the company participates?

2.   What trends suggesting future change in economic and technical characteristics are present?

3.   What is the nature of competition both within the industry and across industries?

4.   What are the requirements for success in competition in the company's industry?

5.   Given the technical, economic, social, and political developments that most directly apply, what is the range of strategy available to any company in this industry?

While all of this may not be appropriate for every type of case, analysis along the lines suggested by these questions will lead the student to an outline of the alternatives available to the firm.

The student must tread a fine line between overburdening his analysis with unfeasible alternatives, on the one hand, and stunting his analysis by severely limiting the alternative spectrum, on the other. Fuller, in his discussion of unsatisfactory written cases, states that a failing student "characteristically thinks in terms of limited alternatives."[7] The neophyte analyst would, therefore, be advised to overestimate the possible alternatives rather than to run the risk of falling into the "failing student" pattern. As the student becomes more familiar with the case method he will become skilled at balancing his alternatives with the time available for analysis.

The next step for evaluation of these alternatives is to define the competence areas of the company. This can best be approached by investigating the strengths exhibited by past performance. It should be obvious to the student that some of these strengths will be more easily identifiable than others.

Careful comparison of the company's opportunities and its competence areas will allow the student to narrow the field of alternatives available. He should then proceed to choose a specific alternative — *make a decision.* It is not enough to pick an alternative. The student must be prepared to defend his choice from the standpoint of a participant in the case. Consistency between the analysis and the ensuing decision is vital to the learning process.

11.4.5   *Review the Recommendations Critically*

After the student has determined what his specific recommendations will be, he must critically evaluate them to determine their strength and validity. The first question he should ask is whether or not the recommendations solve the problem he has identified. If they do not, he must either modify his problem statement or renovate the recommendations. It is entirely possible that in the course of the analysis, the student's estimation of the problems has moved away from the original statement. If he feels that this change is valid, then he should restate the problems. If, on the other hand, he feels that his original problem statement is correct he will have to rework his recommendations.

The second question he should ask is whether or not his recommendations are feasible. The importance of hard analysis prior to a decision cannot be overemphasized at this point. Feasibility of alternatives cannot be determined without it. But ultimately the decision rules supreme. It should result from the analysis and reflect a clear course of action that is possible.

11.5   Case Presentation

In recent years, management in business has seen the rise of two different types of professionals — the decision-maker and the analyst. Perhaps it is inaccurate to say that these two types have developed in recent years, but certainly the magnitude of the divergence has become more pronounced. The size and complexity of large corporations, and even some medium-sized firms, has accelerated the emphasis upon staff analysts who feed information to the decision-makers.

It is apparent from this trend that the effectiveness of the analyst's work depends on his ability to communicate his findings to the decision-maker. It is equally important for the analyst to be adept in the various communicating skills as it is for him to have the technical ability to analyze varied problems in the management of businesses. The case method recognizes both of these needs; the analytical skills have already been emphasized, and now the relevant communicating skills require attention.

Defining the necessary communication skills poses a number of difficulties, as the presentation may be an oral one, to a small or large group, or it may be written and addressed to one or more individuals. Then, too, the peculiarities of the decision-maker to whom the presentation is directed create a problem for the analyst. Some managers may wish to hear or read the report in a manner that allows them to evaluate the analysis before considering recommendations. Then, some managers do not wish to receive one recommendation; rather, they prefer several alternatives presented in a manner that allows them to make the appropriate selection. Generally, however, business managers assign the responsibility to their staff to study a problem as well as make a recommendation for its resolution. Managers are busy people who do not wish or simply cannot afford to take the time to study all the analytical work. They want to see recommendations early in the report and study the analysis only if they feel the recommendations require reinforcement. As the decision-maker becomes more confident in the work of his staff he tends to read less of the supporting analysis.

Generally, case presentations take this latter approach — recommendations early in the report with supporting data following, but the student should be cautioned that he must know his audience. Recent events in both government and business raise certain danger signals that the analyst should bear in mind. There is considerable evidence that decision-makers in large organizations often tend to put more confidence in the analyst than is prudent. Instead of reports that present recommendations supported with analysis, the decision-maker allows the analysts freedom to take action and then report his efforts. As the decision-maker becomes more and more confident in the work of his staff he gives them greater freedom to act on his behalf rather than report findings to him along with recommendations. A logical extrapolation of this practice is staff people acting in a manner they feel protects the decision-maker from unnecessary details, and many decisions are made without his knowledge or approval. From this point, the next logical step may be staff members interpreting rather important matters to be unnecessary details and the accountable administrator ultimately answering for decisions he knew nothing about.

It is readily apparent, therefore, that presentations or reports, either written or oral, involve more than merely good grammar and organization; these are expected, but the reports also require recognition of the decision-making process. The decision is left to the decision-maker, and he must be supplied with sufficient data to evaluate recommendations offered by staff analyst.

To accomplish this in a case study course, it is imperative that the student accept the role of one of the participants in the actual situation. Sometimes, this will be the decision-maker, and at other times it will be the analyst. Ironically, even as the analyst, there is a decision to be made — what to recommend as a course of action. If the supporting analysis is inconsistent with the recommendation or if there are gaps that seem to imply lack of consideration of certain issues, the result may be poor decisions as well as poor evaluations of the analyst by the decision-maker.

As a result of experiences in previous courses, students often attempt to make written reports on cases in the form typically used for academic research, which requires that the scope and methodology of the research be carefully described before the findings are presented. This practice is intended to develop the student's ability to do academic research and present it to an audience of academic peers. In contrast, business managers are not as much concerned with how a recommendation is reached as they are with simply reaching it. This notion can be overemphasized, however. As we have already stated, recommendations must be accompanied by sufficient analysis to make them acceptable to the decision-maker which implies some concern with how the analyst approached his assignment. At least there is concern that all relevant factors were considered in reaching the decision, but it is the recommendation itself that is of most concern to the business manager.

Because of the different interests of the business manager, the structure of the reports, either written and oral, is usually different from that of a thesis or dissertation. Recommendations are made early in the report so that it does not read like a mystery story, withholding the findings for a big climax. Often students tend to resist this type of presentation because it forces them to state their position (the recommendations) without the benefit of prior disclaimers, qualifications, etc. It forces the student to state his recommendations in a way that is logical and can be readily justified by the ensuing data. He has to take a position.

The correct use of vocabulary, grammar, and punctuation is an absolute necessity. It is expected that reports will reflect a command of the communicative skills, and no amount of brilliant analysis can overcome deficiencies in the use of this important management tool. It is not enough to have correct analysis; the presentation must also comply with standard and not dramatic language form. It should use words the meaning of which cannot be misinterpreted, and it should be concise, tending away from verbosity. The major tool of management is communication — one should learn to use it well.

References

1. Charles I. Gragg, "Because Wisdom Can't Be Taught," in *The Case Method of Teaching Human Relations and Administration*, Kenneth R. Andrews, Ed., Harvard University Press, Cambridge, MA, 1960, p. 3.
2. Kenneth R. Andrews, Ed., *The Case Method of Teaching Human Relations and Administration*, Harvard University Press, Cambridge, MA, 1960.
3. Malcolm McNair, "McNair in Cases," reprinted from the *Harvard Business School Bulletin*, July-August, 1971.
4. Stephen H. Fuller, "What Is an Unsatisfactory Examination Paper?," in *The Case Method of Teaching Human Relations and Administration*, Kenneth R. Andrews, Ed., Harvard University Press, Cambridge, MA, 1960, p. 125.
5. Harrier O. Ronkin, "What Our Student Learned," in *The Case Method of Teaching Human Relations and Administration*, Kenneth R. Andrews, Ed., Harvard University Press, Cambridge, MA, 1960, p. 59.
6. Harrier O. Ronkin, "What Our Student Learned," in *The Case Method of Teaching Human Relations and Administration*, Kenneth R. Andrews, Ed., Harvard University Press, Cambridge, MA, 1960, pp. 78–80.
7. Stephen H. Fuller, "What Is an Unsatisfactory Examination Paper?," in *The Case Method of Teaching Human Relations and Administration*, Kenneth R. Andrews, Ed., Harvard University Press, Cambridge, MA, 1960, p. 127.

12 Key Financial Ratios: How They Are Calculated and What They Indicate

Profitability Ratios

1. Gross profit margin	(Sales – cost of goods sold)/sales	Indication of the total margin available to cover operating expenses and yield a profit
2. Operating profit margin	Profit before taxes and before interest/sales	Firm's profitability from current operations
3. Net profit margin	Profit after taxes/sales	After-tax profits per dollar of sales
4. Return on total assets	Profits after taxes/total assets *or* Profits after taxes & interest/ total assets	Measure of the return on total investment or assets
5. Return of stockholders' equity (or return on net worth)	Profits after taxes/ total stockholders' equity	Measure of the rate of return on the stockholders' investment

6. Return on common equity	(Profits after taxes – preferred stock dividends)/ (total stockholders' equity – par value of preferred stock)	Net return on the investment which the owners of common stock have made
7. Earnings per share	(Profits after taxes – preferred stock dividends)/number of shares of common stock outstanding	Earnings available to the owners of common stock

Liquidity Ratios

1. Current ratio	Current assets/ current liabilities	Extent to which the claims of short-term creditors are covered by assets
2. Quick ratio (or acid-test ratio)	(Current assets – inventory)/ current liabilities	Measure of the firm's ability to pay off short-term obligations
3. Inventory to net working capital	Inventory/(current assets – current liabilities)	Measure of the extent to which the firm's working capital is tied up in inventory

Leverage Ratios

1. Debt-to-assets ratio	Total debt/total assets	Measures use of borrowed funds to finance the firm's operations
2. Debt-to-equity ratio	Total debt/ total stockholders' equity	Measure of funds provided by creditors vs. funds provided by owners
3. Long-term-debt-to-equity ratio	Long-term debt/ total stockholders' equity	Leverage used by the firm

4. Times-interest-earned (or coverage) ratios	Profits before interest & taxes/ total interest charges	Firm's ability to make interest payments
5. Fixed-charge coverage	(Profits before taxes & interest + lease obligations)/ (total interest charges + lease obligations)	More inclusive indication of the firm's ability to meet all of its fixed-

Activity Ratios

1. Inventory turnover	Sales/ inventory of finished goods	Effectiveness of the firm in employing inventory
2. Fixed-assets turnover	Sales/fixed assets	Effectiveness of the firm in utilizing plant & equipment
3. Total-assets turnover	Sales/total assets	Effectiveness of the firm in utilizing plant & equipment
4. Accounts-receivable turnover	Annual credit sales/ accounts receivable	How many times the total receivables have been collected during the accounting period
5. Average collection period	Accounts receivable/ (total sales/365) *or* Accounts receivable/ average daily sales	Average length of time the firm waits to collect payment after sales

Shareholders' Return Ratio

1. Dividend yield on common stock	Annual dividends per share/ current market price per share	Measure of the return to owners received in the form of dividends

2. Price/earnings ratio	Current market price per share/after tax earnings per share	Faster growing or less risky firms tend to have higher price/earnings ratios than more risky firms
3. Dividend/ payout ratio	Annual dividends per share/ after tax earnings per share	The percentages of profits paid out as dividends
4. Break-even analysis	Fixed costs/(contribution margin/unit = selling price/ unit – variable cost/unit)	Measure of how many units must be sold to begin to make a profit

Case 1. Southeastern Shipyards, Inc.*

The Background

The history of Southeastern Shipyards, Inc., dates back to 1875, when the Mercury Dry Dock Company was formed on the north side of the St. John's River in downtown Jacksonville, FL. It began operations in the construction and repair of small- to medium-sized ocean-going vessels and enjoyed moderate success. In 1911, the Gables Corporation was formed on the opposite side of the St. John's and operated primarily as a builder of medium to large ships. Both of these companies operated successfully through World War II, although neither enjoyed substantial growth or had significant profits. During the war, both companies assisted in the effort with the construction of victory ships and with repair work required by the U.S. Navy. They returned to normal operations at the conclusion of the war, and no significant developments took place until 1955, at which time the Gables Corporation went through reorganization, necessitated by mismanagement rather than economic conditions. Mr. Gables, the founder, died in 1951, and the resulting management team, headed by his son, was

* This case was prepared by James V. Knutzen in cooperation with Drs. M. Reza Vaghefi and William H. Tomlinson of the University of North Florida's College of Business Administration, as a basis for classroom discussion and not to illustrate either effective or ineffective handling of an administrative situation.

unable to direct operations properly. Aero General, Inc., obtained control during the reorganization and attempted to put the Gables shipyard on the south side of the river back on its feet during the next 2 years. Meanwhile, the Mercury Dry Dock Company, across the river, was sold in 1959 to a Jacksonville financier, G.R. Harrell, who had gained 100% control by 1965. During this period, under Harrell's control, the name was changed to Southeastern Shipyard, Inc., and the shipyard became very profitable, with earnings in the $1-million range each year. At the same time, the shipyard on the opposite side of the river was floundering under Aero's control, and in early 1965 Harrell expanded his operations by acquiring the entire southside yard from Aero General. From 1965 to 1969, this consolidated shipyard in downtown Jacksonville was known as Southeastern Shipyards, Inc., and enjoyed profitable though not spectacular success.

During this period in the late 1960s, a large number of international companies were diversifying and expanding, and conglomerates and holding companies were becoming fashionable. Consequently, Harrell decided that it may be a good time to put his ownership of the shipyards on the open market and realize a substantial capital gain. This is exactly what transpired, and in 1969 the Frankfurt Company, primarily a manufacturer of truck trailers in Detroit, MI, purchased 100% of the outstanding stock of Southeastern Shipyards from Harrell. Operations were not disrupted, and the only change Frankfurt made in the management was to bring in D.L. McFarland from Maryland Shipyards, Inc. (another subsidiary of Frankfurt) as president. Under Frankfurt policy, McFarland was given essentially a free hand in his running of the shipyards and was able to obtain huge company loans for purposes he felt were critical to the shipyard's growth. McFarland stated that, "... most of the equipment in the shipyards was of World War II vintage when we purchased it in 1969, and it repairs more tankers than any other yard in the United States." Consequently, he embarked on an ambitious expansion program, and subsequently stated in 1971 that, "... Southeastern Shipyards, Inc., is now one of the best-equipped yards in the country." The basis for this statement was the fact that during those 2 years the shipyards were thoroughly modernized with the addition of two large new dry docks, each capable of handling ships up to 18,000 tons. In addition, mobile cranes were purchased, and a 27,000 square-foot building was constructed to house the metal trades at the yards. As a result of these and other improvements, "... business was expected to increase by some

50% by 1973 to $48 million," according to a statement made by McFarland in 1972.

As the year 1972 came to a close, the financial statements revealed that it was a record year both in terms of revenues and earnings, although the growth was not as spectacular as McFarland had projected. Following is a table of pertinent financial highlights for the period 1965 through 1972.

	1965[a]	*1968*[a]	*1970*[a]	*1972*[a]
Quick assets	$8222	$8010	$12,593	$8350
Current assets	9418	10,624	14,202	9846
Total assets	15,029	16,299	20,406	28,979
Current liabilities	10,566	8126	2917	4513
Non-current liabilities	2735	1508	654	206
Equity & parent company loans	1728	6613	15,835	24,260
Revenues	28,601	35,856	36,722	38,344
Earnings before taxes	2221	2900	2565	2832
Taxes	1175	1571	1261	1392
Earnings	1042	1329	1304	1440

[a] In thousands.

Frankfurt was satisfied with the performance of McFarland and the shipyard since 1969 and continued to give McFarland a free hand as 1973 approached. At this point, Southeastern Shipyards, Inc., was one of the largest employers in the city of Jacksonville, employing almost 3000. Four separate yards were in operation, three along the northern bank of the St. John's and one across the river. The primary source of revenue was repair and maintenance work on medium- to large-sized ships, and to perform this the shipyards had six dry docks in use, four on the north side and two across the river. Late in 1972, McFarland had been successful in acquiring some waterfront property adjacent to the docks at the northside yard and decided to consolidate operations by closing the southside yard and moving those two dry docks to some of the waterfront space obtained by the acquisition. This move was expected to result in the sale of all real estate on the south side, which would realize several million dollars.

In order to better understand the operations and use of dry docks by Southeastern Shipyards, Inc., a short examination of dry-docking reveals that it is a technique used to remove a ship from the water so that the underwater portion can be inspected, repaired, maintained, or altered. The three primary reasons for dry docking are (1) to remove marine growths which cause fouling, (2) to prevent hull erosion, and (3) to make repairs or alterations. Fouling is caused by barnacles, mussels, and other marine organisms attaching themselves to the ship. This fouling seriously impedes the ship's speed, thereby increasing the cost of operations. Corrosion of the underwater hulls of ships is caused by electrochemical reactions. Paint or other cover materials applied periodically to the hull will protect the steel as long as the material remains intact. Periodic and casualty repairs to the underwater hulls of ships are required for propellers, shafting, rudders, and sea connections. Alterations are sometimes made to obtain more speed, use less horsepower to obtain the same speed, or to improve maneuverability.

The frequency with which a ship requires dry docking is governed by the five following factors: (1) preservation of the hull of the ship; (2) accidents necessitating repairs to the hull; (3) regulations of the U.S. Coast Guard for all American ships; (4) regulations of classifications, such as the American Bureau of Shipping, Lloyd's Register of Shipping, and Bureau Veritas, for ships which are inspected and classed by them; and (5) the trade in which the ship operates. Most owners dry dock their ships yearly for inspection, cleaning, painting, and routine repairs. Some owners find it economical to do this semi-annually.

Dry docks can be of four different types: marine railway, floating, graving, and mechanical lift. Floating dry docks have become more popular in recent years because they can be constructed in sections and can accommodate larger ships. Southeastern Shipyard facilities presently include six of these floating-type dry docks, as mentioned earlier. To operate this kind of dry dock, the dock is first submerged by partially filling the tanks with water to provide the required depth of water over the keel blocks. The tanks of the dock are then rapidly pumped out; as soon as the ship is positioned by powerful pumps located within the dock walls, the ship is lifted out of the water. The water within the cell of the dry dock spills out of the opening of the dock as the dock rises out of the water. The floating dock has several advantages, such as lower initial cost, greater mobility, and greater size, as they can be constructed in sections and hinged together. The six floating dry docks that the shipyards were operating at the end of 1972 were all in sound working order and could be expected to provide several more years of service with proper maintenance.

The management of the shipyards was a finely structured hierarchy with McFarland at the top. He was highly qualified for this position, having been the president of Maryland Shipyards, Inc., for several years prior to his coming to Jacksonville. The organizational chart in Figure 1 reveals the other people in key positions. Substantially all of these individuals were long-standing employees who had worked their way up the ladder, which is the normal method of filling positions at the shipyard. All key personnel were compensated solely by a yearly fixed salary with the exception of McFarland and Shapiro, who received bonuses determined by the profitability of the yard. Salaries were substantial, and the motivation and morale of management appeared to be high. One unique fringe benefit of the shipyard was a special dining room/bar called the "Blue Room" where 20 designated key employees could gather for drinks and lunch. This was considered to be a motivating factor for those intent on reaching management positions. The only employee other than those shown on the top management line allowed in the Blue Room was the controller, Bob Jayson. The Blue Room was also used extensively to entertain potential customers, port and city officials, and others during the week. Essentially all employees other than management and office personnel were represented by an industrial union, which negotiated a contract with the company every 3 years. The average hourly rate for these semi-skilled and skilled workers was $4.25 per hour. As a result of heavy work loads, a large portion of the workers earned significant amounts of overtime at time and a half, and the wages were considered good in the community. Consequently, the company has never had any serious labor problems and expected negotiations in 1973 to run smoothly when the 3-year contract expired; however, the shipyard constantly had trouble obtaining and retaining highly skilled workers in the machine trades.

Due to the nature of the ship repair industry, Southeastern Shipyards did not require the intricate sales and marketing staffs that most businesses do. Competition for repair work was such that the few facilities in existence in the U.S. had all the work that they could handle, and the shipyard had no active sales force to speak of. Rather, future business and sales depended on maintaining strong customer relations and on being fair in price negotiation and in giving excellent and prompt service. The normal way in which an individual job proceeded was for a ship representative and a shipyard "estimator" to sit down and determine the extent and scope of work and the scheduling. Then, at the

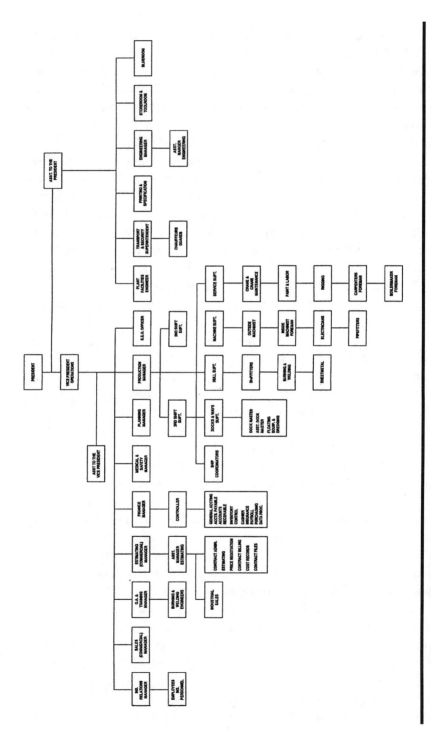

Figure 1 Southeastern Shipyards, Inc., Organizational Chart

completion of the work, the same two people would sit down and negotiate a settlement based on direct labor, materials, overhead, and normal profit margin. These negotiations are conducted in a firm but flexible manner, as both parties are dependent on each other.

The projected sale of real estate on the south side of the river, as was mentioned earlier, was expected to realize several million dollars for potential use by the shipyard. McFarland was already given the verbal go-ahead by Frankfurt to examine investment opportunities for the expected available cash. The planning function at the shipyards was not highly structured, although a planning department, headed by R.M. Cocker did exist. McFarland sought various ideas from management for areas in which to expand or diversity in late 1972, and three projects were finally decided on as definite possibilities for expansion based on preliminary studies: (1) purchase a giant floating dry dock at a cost of approximately $15 million which would accommodate super tankers, (2) purchase a shipbuilding company in Jacksonville at a cost of approximately $3 million, and (3) purchase an engineering firm in Houston, TX, for approximately $2 million. It was not decided whether one, two, or all of these projects should be undertaken, and detailed feasibility studies were made of all three. The first form of expansion would require a tremendous investment, and its success was dependent on many factors, such as the (1) harbor and port facilities of Jacksonville, (2) resources and economy of Jacksonville, (3) sales and market potential, and (4) availability of skilled workers and harbor space.

The other two projects were much smaller in magnitude and represented different types of expansion. Purchase of a shipbuilding company was one form of vertical acquisition, as Southeastern Shipyards repaired ships. The other, purchase of an engineering firm, was another form of vertical integration, as this acquisition was expected to replace the substantial sandblasting work performed at the shipyard and being subcontracted. The results of the company's research on these three projects is highlighted in the following paragraphs.

Purchase of Giant Dry Dock

The shipyards felt four areas as mentioned in the preceding paragraph would be critical in making a final decision as to this purchase. The company's research in these four areas is revealed as follows:

Harbor and Port Facilities

Jacksonville is sometimes referred to as the "gateway to the Southeast". The Jacksonville Port Authority has a progressive attitude toward expansion of the harbor facilities, and the port is in the process of becoming truly a deep water ocean port. Since the creation of the Jacksonville Port Authority in 1963, the primary wharves and docks at Talleyrand have experienced a complete transformation. These facilities now include 3964 linear feet of marginal wharf, 611,000 square feet of covered storage, and extensive support and maintenance equipment. The Port Authority is also proud of its facilities at Blount Island, which is strategically located in the St. John's River, halfway between Jacksonville and the Atlantic Ocean. The island facilities include 2600 linear feet of marginal wharf and 360,000 square feet of warehouse space, and with the completion of a 45-ton, twin-light container crane in 1972, the Blount Island container terminal had become the most modern in the Southeast. This improvement and expansion program was continuing as 1973 began, and the Port Authority was financing construction of a new steel and concrete bridge from Heckscher Drive to Blount Island, to help move cargo from the rapidly expanding complex.

The port of Jacksonville, FL, lies along the lower 24.5-mile stretch of the St. John's River, 145 nautical miles south of Savannah, GA, and 345 nautical miles north of Miami, FL. The deep-water entrance and channel lead west from the river's mouth to the Florida East Coast Railway Bridge (24.5 miles above mouth) in downtown Jacksonville. As a result of the various River and Harbor Acts of Congress since 1880, the entrance and channel have been maintained in a manner to accommodate ocean-going vessels. The River and Harbor Act of October 27, 1965, provided for a deepening of the present channel from 34 to 38 feet to accommodate large, supercargo-type vessels. This project was now in progress and was a vital necessity if Southeastern Shipyards, Inc., was to capture its portion of the repair and maintenance work on these large ships. At the end of 1972, the 38-foot channel reached the halfway point, and bids for extending the improvement already had been received by the Army Corps of Engineers.

It was apparent that the Jacksonville Port Authority had every intention of making Jacksonville a modern and truly deep-water port essential for Southeastern Shipyards, Inc., in the years ahead.

Jacksonville's Resources and Economy

The resources of Jacksonville, including the availability of skilled workers, growth of the economy, and inland transportation facilities, would play a vital role in determining the advisability of Southeastern Shipyards, Inc., making this acquisition. The proposed dry dock would require in excess of 400 skilled workers for operation, which the labor market in the Jacksonville area would have to absorb. The continued growth of Jacksonville, both in terms of economic output and transportation facilities, would be a necessity for the years ahead, also.

The population of Jacksonville had increased from 455,400 in 1960 to its current level of almost 600,000. This trend was expected to continue in the future, with a projection of over 700,000 by 1980 and over 1,000,000 by the year 2000. Over 60% of the people in this area earned a living by wages or salaries, as opposed to proprietor's income, property income, or transfer payments. From the expected trend in population and the evidence of a large and stable work force in Jacksonville, it appeared that an available supply of workers would be available in this area.

The year 1972 could be considered possibly the most important year in the history of Jacksonville's economic growth as a result of the decision of Westinghouse-Tenneco to locate their joint venture, Offshore Power Systems (OPS), on Blount Island. This development was expected to provide massive economic stimulus to the area for many years ahead. An impact of the growth that had been taking place could be seen by comparing general cargo imports from 1966 to 1971. In this relatively short period of 5 years, the total tonnage handled increased from 638,729 tons to 1,307,759 tons, or had roughly doubled.

Inland transportation represented a significant portion of the total operating cost for industry and was of primary concern to shippers. The cost of moving freight throughout the Southeast was related to affluence and population concentrations, as well as the geographic distances between communities. In comparing Jacksonville to cities in the industrial crescent, it was determined that a shipper serving the Southeast could cut his transportation costs by more than 50% by originating his shipments in Jacksonville. In addition, this location had been improving with time because the majority of growth (both in population and income) in the southeast was taking place in Florida.

All of these statistics and studies on the resources of Jacksonville reached the same conclusion: The city was a dynamic and growing area on the verge of becoming the major seaport of the region.

Sales and Market Potential

Southeastern Shipyards, Inc., presently had six floating dry docks in use. The largest of these had a lifting capacity of 18,000 tons, was 622 feet long, and had a width of 93 feet. The proposed new dry dock would have a lifting capacity of 40,000 tons, a length of 827 feet, and a width of 144 feet. In other words, the proposed "super dry dock" would accommodate ships over twice as big as those currently being handled. To determine the number of ships presently in operation which were too large for the 18,000-ton-class dry dock, the company obtained a list from Lloyd's Register of Shipping of world fleet totals. This list, as of February 1972, was as follows:

Tankers	1210
Ore and bulk carriers	760
General cargo and passenger	80
Total	2050

A determination was made by the company that approximately 500 of these vessels traded on the east coast of the U.S. at one time or another. According to the sales department, on numerous occasions during 1972 the company had been approached from both domestic and foreign ship owners and operators, offering ships that could not be dry-docked with present facilities. During January and February 1972, alone, 12 vessels were refused service at Jacksonville because of size.

An estimate by the company that sales could be increased by $10,000,000 a year could be substantiated by analyzing current company sales. In 1971, the largest dry dock at Southeastern Shipyards, Inc., realized sales of $5,500,000. The dry dock was occupied 239 days during the year, which means that the average daily sales were approximately $23,000. Because the proposed new dry dock would be expected to handle ships over twice as large as those presently docked, the proposed dry dock would anticipate fees of $50,000 a day. Assuming a minimum of 200 days of utilization a year, this would produce an increase in sales to the company of at least $10,000,000 per year.

Most of the large flag ships now trading on the east coast were now being repaired in foreign countries because of the lack of facilities in the U.S. At the time, only two dry docks existed on the eastern seaboard which were of the large variety required, but neither of these was handling the tanker and cargo ship repair business. Sun Shipbuilding on the Delaware River could not compete with the climate, location, and lower billing rates of foreign ports; the other, in Newport News, VA, was restricted because of heavy Navy activity. In addition, both of these yards were used primarily for shipbuilding, rather than repair work.

Overall, the shipping and market potential for repair work on the large ships appeared to be plentiful and on the increase on the east coast of the U.S.

Availability of Skilled Workers and Harbor Space

An equally important consideration was whether resources could be provided in the Jacksonville area to accommodate this type of expansion. As pointed out, over 400 workers would be required to operate the proposed dry dock, most of them skilled; yet, the shipyard already was having trouble finding and keeping qualified people for existing positions and had resorted to company training programs to create new skills in workers.

The port and harbor facilities of Jacksonville had been expanded and updated significantly, as was brought out earlier. Continued development of the port and the deepening of the channel to 38 feet were critical to the long-range future of the company, according to Jayson. However, he felt that the existing facilities were more than adequate to ensure that the large super-tankers would be accessible to the company. He pointed out that the bulk of the shipping trade in these ships took place between the oil fields and refineries of Texas and Louisiana and the commercial markets in the northeastern U.S. The ships must pass Jacksonville on their return voyages to the oil refineries. Because the vessels were empty at this time, Jayson indicated that the present channel of 34 feet would be satisfactory.

Purchase of Shipbuilding Company

The shipbuilding company that Southeastern Shipyards was considering acquiring was a long-standing firm in the Jacksonville area and consisted of a single location on the intracoastal waterway at Atlantic Boulevard. The facilities permitted construction of only one to three small- to medium-sized ships at a time, each of which took 12 to 18 months to build. Ferries and ocean-going research vessels were typical of the ships produced.

The company usually realized a profit of 10 to 20% on these contracts which averaged out to approximately $200,000 a year before taxes for the years 1965 to 1972. Following is a copy of the company's balance sheet at December 31, 1972:

Assets
Current assets

Cash	$194,460
Accounts receivable, less allowance	$205,604
for doubtful accounts of $2980	
Costs and estimated earnings in excess of collections	$190,941
on progress billings on uncompleted contracts	
Inventory of materials and supplies	$66,143
Other	$1412
Total current assets	$658,560
Property, plant and equipment	$1,365,150
Total assets	$2,023,710

Liabilities and stockholders' equity
Current liabilities

Notes payable, bank	$430,000
Accounts payable and accrued expenses	$313,470
Accrued payroll and amounts withheld from employees	$70,595
Amounts due an affiliated company	$5560
Current portion of long-term debt	$24,996
Total current liabilities	$844,621
Long-term debt	$33,813
Stockholders' equity	
Common stock, $1 par value; authorized, issued,	$10,000
and outstanding (10,000 shares)	
Retained earnings	$1,135,276
Total stockholders' equity	$145,276
Total liabilities and stockholders' equity	$2,023,710

Southeastern Shipyards felt that this acquisition would enable them to enter a related field in which they had know-how and job-related experience.

Purchase of an Engineering Firm

The third possibility for expansion under consideration by Southeastern Shipyards was the acquisition of Key Houston, Inc., in Houston, TX. The company was in the business of developing, constructing, and marketing abrasive blasting and recovery equipment used extensively in the shipbuilding and ship repair industry. They had a reputation in the ship-repair industry of marketing a superior product and had done extensive business with Jacksonville Shipyards over the years. This business consisted primarily of selling sandblasting equipment, which Southeastern Shipyards used extensively to clean the hulls of ships of barnacles, mussels, and other marine organisms prior to the painting of the hulls. Key Houston had been a leader in its industry for years and had enjoyed financial success, realizing after-tax profits in the $150,000 range for the 4 years prior to 1973. Following is a balance sheet of Key Houston at August 31, 1972, which reveals their strong financial position.

Assets

Current assets

Cash	$31,875
Accounts receivable, less allowance	$151,002
for doubtful accounts of $2300	
Inventories	
Raw materials	$171,191
Work in process and finished goods	$49,600
Total inventories	$225,791
Deferred federal taxes on income	$28,000
Prepaid expenses	$621
Total current assets	$437,288

Other assets

Patents	$10,266
Investment in Key Europe, Ltd.	$4162
Total other assets	$14,428

Property and equipment

Land	$350,000
Buildings	$450,000
Equipment on rental	$93,000
Automobiles	$20,496
Furniture and equipment	$19,544
Property and equipment	$933,040
Less	($134,289)
Total property and equipment	$798,751
Total assets	$1,250,467

Liabilities and stockholder's equity

Current liabilities

Accounts payable — trade	$63,298
Accounts payable — stockholder and officers	$79,922
Accrued expenses	$8960
Deferred income	$47,099
Federal income taxes payable	$109,600
Payments due within 1 year on long-term debt	$16,802
Total current liabilities	325,681

Long-term note payable, less portion due within 1 year	$77,036
under original repayment plan, included in current liabilities	

Stockholder's equity

Common stock, par value $1 a share; authorized	$10,000
(100,000 shares); issued and outstanding (10,000)	
Retained earnings	$837,750
Total stockholders' equity	$847,750
Total liabilities	$1,250,467

Southeastern Shipyards president McFarland stated that "… Key Houston would be a good vehicle with which to enter a field directly related to the company's activities, and would afford the opportunity to lead in a phase of shipyard work which has been troublesome and costly to every shipyard, domestic and foreign."

Appendix A

In regard to the purchase of a shipbuilding company and engineering company, some considerations by management not presented in the case study include:

1. The shipbuilding company also performed ship repair services on small vessels. This segment of the business was in competition with Southeastern Shipyard's St. John's Division.
2. Southeastern Shipyard's St. John's Division (small vessel repair services) could be relocated to the shipbuilding company's site.
3. St. John's Division could be used as an overflow for large ships from the main facility. The properties are adjacent to each other. Additional wet berth space along St. John's River is necessary for future growth of repair services to the larger ships.

4. The engineering company operation could be relocated to vacant land owned by the shipbuilding company which is adjacent to the present shipbuilding and small vessel repair sites.
5. A joint labor force for the shipbuilding company and the engineering company could be maintained. Because customer orders are heaviest from April to October at the engineering company, the labor force from the engineering company could be utilized by the shipbuilding company or for small vessel repair during the off season.

Southeastern Shipyards, Inc. Balance Sheet

	1970[a]	1971[a]	1972[a]
Current assets			
Cash	1034	992	506
Accounts receivable	11,623	11,167	8000
Inventories	1545	1,510	1340
Total current assets	14,202	14,119	9846
Plant, net	6164	6774	19,120
Non-current assets	40	65	13
Total assets	20,406	20,958	28,979
Liabilities			
Current liabilities	3917	3440	4513
Non-current liabilities	654	441	206
Loans from parent company	13,219	13,355	19,098
Stockholder's equity	2616	3722	5162
Total liabilities & stockholders' equity	20,406	20,958	28,979
Revenues			
Ship repair	36,140	38,345	37,852
Ship construction	0	989	0
Industrial work	582	759	462
Total revenues	36,722	40,093	38,344
Cost of sales	34,157	37,939	35,512
Earnings before taxes	2565	2154	2832
Taxes	1261	1048	1392
Net income	**1304**	**1106**	**1440**

[a] In thousands of dollars.

Case 2. Matsushita Electrical Industrial*

Brief History

Matsushita Electrical Industrial Co., Ltd., is one of the world's leading producers of electric and electronic products. The company was incorporated in Japan in 1935 as successor to a manufacturer of electrical equipment for household use founded in 1918 by the late Konosuke Matsushita. Its business grew rapidly after World War II to meet the rising demand for consumer electric and electronic products, including washing machines, black and-white televisions, and refrigerators. The product range was expanded in the 1960s and 1970s to include color televisions, hi-fi components, air conditioners, microwave ovens, industrial equipment, communications and measuring equipment, and videotape recorders. In the 1980s, the company extended its operations on a global scale to meet the worldwide demand for products based on sophisticated electronics and precision technology. The 1990s have brought about a focus on semiconductors, electron tubes, and lighting products. Most of the company's products are sold throughout the world under the names Panasonic, National, Technics, Quasar, Victor, and JVC.

---

* The case was written by Dr. M. Reza Vaghefi, assisted by Mark Puskar, for discussion purposes only.

Consumer Electronics Industry

Once a decade, the consumer electronics industry, those manufacturers who have given people the means to enjoy live and recorded entertainment at home, has come up with a blockbuster of a new product. First, there was the gramophone, with its heyday in the 1920s. Next came radio (1930s). After the second world war came black-and-white television (1950s), then color television (1960s), followed by hi-fi equipment (1970s). In the 1980s, there was the videocassette recorder (VCR). Most recently, there is the compact disc player of the 1990s. Before the virtual reality machine can become the breadwinner for industry, probably in the early 2000s, history suggests there will be a blockbuster product in between.

One thing is certain: any new entertainment gadget for the home will have to be more of a "computer in disguise" than a record player, tape recorder, or television set. Digital techniques are now being applied to every other appliance in the industry's workshop. The digital audiotape (DAT) recorder promises the same leap in performance for the lowly cassette recorder. Digital tricks are also being used to brighten up the television's colors and to make the picture appear sharper. These, however, are mere Band-Aid solutions until the fully digital television arrives in the with the introduction of cinema-like, high-definition television (HDTV).

The trend toward digital appliances has set two headstrong industries on a collision course. To squeeze all the information for HDTV's vastly more detailed picture into the limited space on the airways depends on the software skills honed in the computer industry, along with lots of computer memory chips and quick microprocessors. For their part, the consumer-electronics makers see machines such as HDTV set as a platform on which to build all manner of other digital gadgets for consumers: perhaps a home newspaper press, a set of talking and illustrated encyclopedias, or a virtual-reality machine itself. The industry's giants are grabbing all the computer know-how they can find so as not to become dependent on the computer industry for vital components. Sony has been selling its own version of an engineering workstation since 1987. Philips has been in the computer business even longer. Matsushita has recently taken up licenses on a couple of America's most popular workstation designs.

The cost of staying competitive in consumer-electronics is about to become prohibitive for all but a handful of firms. Companies that want to keep up with the leaders will have to spend at least 7% of their net sales on research and development (R&D). Sony and Matsushita have been consistently investing even more than that in R&D. Three things are essential for companies wishing to stay in the race. First, they have to produce their own semiconductor chips. Second, they must have the know-how for making computers and telecommunications equipment as well as consumer products. And, third, they must have strong and cooperative management linking the technical, production, and marketing departments, along with a clearly defined plan detailing where the company intends being in 5 years' time.

Manufacturers are trying to create new variations from old themes. Half the television sets being sold in Japan have screens bigger than 32 inches — and fatter profit margins. The trend to jumbo televisions is repeating itself in the U.S. Another new fad, at least in Japan, is to build the tuner for receiving satellite broadcasts into the television set itself, or even into a VCR. Some manufacturers have started selling VCRs that automatically skip the advertisements. Others have been playing tricks with the television's brightness and color signals to make bigger pictures appear clear. All the liquid-crystal screens in pocket-sized televisions are now colored. Compact optical discs are now writable just like a tape.

For the time being, it looks like the breadwinner will be the electronic components segment: the manufacturing expertise that Matsushita has developed in the electronics industry is allowing them to sell more and more components to other companies for use in their products. For example, Matsushita has just developed a laser-detector-hologram unit for use in computer disk drives, and laser driver IC's for rewritable optical disks.

Internal Environment

Locals have traditionally called Matsushita the "Maneshita" (from the Japanese word for "imitation") because of the way it has let others pioneer new products and then used its own superb manufacturing skills to come out with cheaper models a year or so later. With the help of its 25,000 company-owned shops, it could flood the domestic market and crush the competition. Where Sony has concentrated more on selling goods to affluent individuals, Matsushita has looked toward families with modest means and little technical interest. Products with Matsushita names are easy to use and self-contained. For instance, while Sony offers its customers a satellite tuner for them to plug into their television sets and wire into their stereo systems, Matsushita simply builds the satellite tuner into the television itself.

Matsushita is not more brawn than brain. Rather like IBM, the Osaka-based company has cultivated the air of a corporate conservative, preoccupied with mundane manufacturing, marketing, and the bottom line, leaving fanciful things such as innovation to others. That is only part of the picture, however. Just like IBM, Matsushita actually pours billions into R&D — in fact, around $2.4 billion during the 1990 financial year.

Rather like IBM a decade ago, Matsushita has traditionally invested in R&D for defensive purposes. It has had little interest in producing gadgets that went beyond tried and true, but it was always determined to have the necessary inventive know-how, should it ever be needed.

With its dominance at home, Matsushita has been slower to turn itself into a global company, but since Akoo Tanii became president in 1986, Matsushita has embarked on an ambitious plan to clone itself abroad. Its first objective is to create a corporate giant in the U.S. as big as the parent company in Japan. Within the past 3 years, Matsushita has increased the number of its plants in the U.S. from 14 to 23 and employs 16,000 workers in the U.S. alone. Its long-term plan is to have 50% of the products it sells in the U.S. made in this country (up from 35% today). The U.S. sales volume reached $7.3 billion in 1996.

In Matsushita's book, "going local" also means developing joint ventures and original equipment manufacturing (OEM) arrangements with local manufacturers. For instance, it makes batteries with Eastman Kodak. But, the company is still more of an international, rather than a multi-national, company.

The transformation of Matsushita from an electric company to an electronic company started 10 years ago with its restructuring. The former president, Yamashita, launched the Action-61 Movement in 1983 by stating that, because the electric-appliances industry had matured, Matsushita had to become an electronic company by entering into such businesses as semiconductors, computers, office automation, and home automation. In line with this policy, wealthy Matsushita, which is often called the Matsushita Bank, invested considerable money in those businesses.

Matsushita's decisions, however, were late compared to their competitors, and it could not link its strategy with effective measures for organizational activation. The ultimate reason behind the two factors is that Matsushita has been unable to overcome the limits of its famous departmentalized system. This system was very effective in the home electronics business, in which each department specialized in a specific appliance. Within this business environment, there were no serious reasons to cooperate among departments, but what was eventually required was an activated organization which could quickly grasp the needs of the market and produce inexpensive products with high quality. That was exactly what Matsushita had thus far achieved, but it was not without a price. Strong sectionalism developed among departments and weakened the company's ability for strategy development and its implementation. However, the electronics business requires quick and risky decisions by top management with close collaboration among existing departments.

Matsushita has built the global leadership position of its well-known Panasonic and National brands on its ability to control its global strategy from the center in Japan, yet it has been able to implement it in a flexible and responsive manner throughout its worldwide operations. Three factors are important in explaining the achievement of strong central direction and control without becoming inflexible or isolated: gaining the input of its subsidiaries into its management process, ensuring that development efforts are linked to market needs, and managing responsibility transfers from development to manufacturing to marketing.

If Matsushita is the champion of efficient, centrally coordinated management, its Netherlands-based competitor, Philips, is the master of building effective national operations worldwide. And, just as Philips' managers envy their Japanese rival's ability to develop product and strategies in Osaka that appear to be implemented effortlessly around the globe, their counterparts in Matsushita are extremely jealous of Philips' national organizations that are not only sensitive and responsive to their local environments, but are also highly innovative and entrepreneurial. Philips' first color television set was built and sold not in Europe, where the parent company is located, but in Canada, where the market had closely followed the U.S. lead in introducing color transmission. Also, the first stereo color television set was developed by the Australian subsidiary. The list of local innovations and entrepreneurial initiatives by Philips is endless.

While Matsushita's localization program was triggered by political pressures to increase local value added in various host countries, the company had also hoped that the decentralization of assets would help its overseas units achieve a greater measure of local responsiveness, self-sufficiency, and initiative. To management's frustration, such changes were slow in coming.

Matsushita bought MCA so as not to be left out, because at that time Sony believed that the key to selling more video and audio equipment was to own a Hollywood studio and a recording company; they also bought CBS Records and Columbia Pictures. According to this argument of synergy, if you can flood the market with your own brands of software (movies and recorded music), you will then sell more of your own brands of hardware (machines for playing videos, CDs, and tape cassettes). Matsushita paid $6.1 billion in 1990 for MCA Entertainment, a deal which included Universal Studios. "The software and hardware sides of the business," said a pleased Akio Tanii, Matsushita's chairman, "are like the wheels of the same car."

If anything, the synergy argument is nothing more than a *post hoc* justification. Sony has always blamed its crushing defeat in the video wars on the paucity of movie titles for its brand of videocassette machines. Actually, the fight between the Matsushita camp's VHS recorders and Sony's Betamax machines ended when video-rental stores around the world decided that they could no longer afford to carry two lines of the same titles, one for each format. They opted for VHS because by then it had penetrated three times more homes. That had nothing to do with the availability of software. It was simply the result of Matsushita and its JVC subsidiary's greater willingness to make their VHS components and know-how available to other manufacturers.

Little practical evidence can be found to support the synergy argument. The best thing that can be said about Matsushita's takeover of MCA is that at least it bought a profitable company. As a percentage of sales, MCA's operating profit in 1990 was 14.5%, practically double Matsushita's 7.5%. MCA had been turning results like that for 5 years.

The Future of Electronic Products: DAT, DCC, and HDTV

The digital audiotape (DAT) records sound as a (digital) stream of coded beeps rather than as a not-too-faithful (analog) copy of the sound waves themselves. There is no way for stray noise to creep in during a DAT recording. A digital signal is either there or not there; it cannot be partly there (that is, in a slightly degraded or distorted form) as in the case of an analog recording on a cassette tape. Also, the slightest fraction of digital sound that may have been missed during recording is instantly "recalculated" from the adjacent bits of sound code. The result is an exact replica of the original.

The magnetic recording method that is totally pirate-proof has yet to be invented. This, plus the lingering threat of court action by the copyright holders, has made consumer electronics companies leery about tooling up for DAT in a big enough way for prices to fall to popular levels. The cheapest DAT recorder currently sells for around $500.

There is a growing feeling that DAT may have now missed the boat. Industry folklore suggests that, to become a hit product, any new gadget has to be embraced by hardcore enthusiasts while it is still a novelty and then raved about in the press. Mass production, distribution, and advertising do the rest. For novelty seekers in Japan, DAT's arrival was delayed so long that it became yesterday's news before hitting the streets. Besides, DAT now has competition. Its most serious rival looks like Philips' recent DCC (digital compact cassette) recorder. This provides the same CD-like sound as DAT but on much less expensive tapes — and in a machine that not only uses an inherently simpler recording method but which can also play ordinary cassettes in the bargain.

To mollify the music industry, Philips has built serial-protection circuitry into its new DCC — and has sworn to grant licenses only to manufacturers that agree not to tamper with it. Several record companies have already endorsed the DCC format. The first Japanese licensee looks like it could be Matsushita. The Japanese giant is rumored to have been closely working with Philips on the development of DCC. To many, the thought of Matsushita throwing its enormous weight behind DCC — in a direct challenge to Sony's preeminence in DAT — suggests a rerun of the video wars.

Japanese manufacturers have gone further than anyone else in turning high-definition television (HDTV) into a commercial reality. Work on the Japanese version began 20 years ago at NHK, the country's public broadcasting corporation. Over the years, NHK has worked closely with Japanese industry, orchestrating the development of "Hi-Vision" and hammering out the broadcast standards. With its 1125-line screen and 16-×-9 proportions, Hi-Vision is the most mature of the various proposals for HDTV around the world. More importantly, Japanese industry is further ahead in working out how to make the components at realistic prices. It has designed most of the essential chips needed and is now producing them in trial quantities. Meanwhile, NHK has been transmitting an hour of Hi-Vision broadcasts every day to help stir up interest.

There is a penalty, however, for being first. With its ancestry in the 1970s, Hi-Vision remains an awkward hybrid: part old-fashioned electronics and part computer-like digital electronics. As it stands, a Hi-Vision set with its aerial dish is chained to broadcasts from communications satellites. Privately, Japanese manufacturers worry that they may have been saddled with an obsolete system — while Europe and the U.S. are adopting more advanced forms of HDTV.

For the past 3 years, the European Commission has been backing a "super-telly" called HDMAC that was spawned originally by Britain's Independent Broadcasting Authority. Unlike Japan's Hi-Vision, HDMAC has the attraction of being compatible with existing television sets. In Europe, people with conventional televisions will also be able to watch the new HDMAC broadcasts, albeit without the high-definition quality (though with a considerably better picture than they normally receive). The system, which is based on a 1250-line screen, has suffered a number of delays. Meanwhile, Japanese firms have been quietly hinting that they have a lot of HDTV experience to offer the Europeans if they would like to cut them in on some HDMAC know-how in exchange.

But, both Hi-Vision and HDMAC look like they are being eclipsed by recent developments in the U.S.. After looking as though it was out of the running altogether, the U.S. has bounded back with no fewer than six contenders in the HDTV stakes. All of them are fully compatible with the analog television system known as NTSC. Best of all, five of the six manage this compatibility trick without making the slightest sacrifice of the broadcast industry's analog past. Being totally digital, they offer viewers the chance to experience on the television screen what they so far (thanks to CD players) have only been able to hear: absolute purity of signal.

With the consumer market stalled, Sony and Matsushita are trying to recoup by turning to industrial markets. New niches for HDTV gear range from electronic publishing and teleconferencing to medical training systems and supercomputer graphics used by scientists. The most promising such market for HDTV is as a scientific and engineering tool. Unlike workstations, which were not designed to capture or display real images, HDTV combines camera, recording, and display technologies.

For supercomputer researchers, HDTV's chief attraction is increased size and brightness of display. At Hitachi, HDTV is used in combination with a supercomputer to produce dazzling simulations of silicon crystal growth. Designers of automobiles and other products are now using HDTV together with computer-aided design (CAD) tools to speed up product development. HDTV lets one take a realistic, computer-generated rendering of an automobile and weave it together with real images so that it appears to be driving through a desert or down a crowded city street.

Financial Highlights

There has been no major change in the percentages of different sales categories at Matsushita. By 1996, the communications and industrial equipment category constituted 32.48% of sales. Second was video equipment sales with 17.49%. Electronic components was the third major category, with 13.75% of the sales. Home appliances was fourth, with 6.16% of the sales (see Tables 1, 2, and 3, next page).

**Table 1 Sales Categories (in billions of yen)
for Fiscal Year Ended March 31**

	1996	%	1995	%
Video equipment	1342.40	17.49	1225.20	18.03
Audio equipment	576.30	7.50	517.70	7.62
Home appliances	1026.40	13.37	914.00	13.45
Communications and industrial equipment	2492.90	32.48	2012.60	29.62
Electronic components	1055.80	13.75	1020.50	15.02
Batteries and kitchen-related products	471.90	6.16	404.80	5.96
Other	710.20	9.25	700.10	10.30
Total	7675.90	100.00	6794.90	100.00

**Table 2 Sales by Geographic Markets (in billions of yen)
for Fiscal Year Ended March 31**

	1996	%	1995	%
Japan	6137.00	70	5653.50	73
North America (U.S. and Canada)	2682.10	30	2126.00	27
Eliminations	(1143.20)	–15	(984.60)	–14
Total	7450.00	100	6599.00	100

**Table 3 Sales By Business Segments (in billions of yen)
for 1996 and 1997**

	1997	1996
Audiovisual and home appliances	3556.0	3260.3
Information/communications and industrial products	4575.6	3970.2
Total	8131.6	7230.5
Eliminations	(455.7)	(435.6)
Consolidated totals	7675.9	6794.9

Case 3. McDonnell Douglas — Turning the Corner?

On August 21, 1992, McDonnell Douglas Chairman and CEO John McDonnell reported some bad news to the financial community:[1]

"McDonnell Douglas Corporation had net earnings of $1.00 per share in the second quarter of 1992, down from $2.01 per share in the second quarter of 1991. Operating earnings fell in all three aerospace segments. In the military aircraft segment, there was a $34 million pre-tax charge reflecting increased costs and higher reserves in the C-17 program. In the commercial aircraft segment, earnings were reduced by a $29 million increase in development expenditures, mostly as a result of developing the concept of the MD-12, a proposed four-engine airliner. Because costs on the MD-11 have not declined as rapidly as planned, the corporation raised its cost estimate for the total program and reduced the rate at which it is reporting earnings. On June 30, 1992, total aerospace debt was $2845 billion, compared with $2940 on June 30, 1991, and $2386 billion on December 31."

Because the mean of Wall Street analysts' projections for the quarter was $2.43 per share, the announcement triggered a massive sell-off of the company's common stock.[2] Paul Nisbet, a broker for Prudential securities, told his clients "that the second-quarter report, with several factories contributing to the disappointing earnings, had severely strained any buildup of management credibility that had been taking place" over the last year.[2]

Of course, the financial community has been known to overreact to poor short-term announcements, but the underlying causes of the company's substandard performance held disturbing implications. In the commercial aircraft segment, revenue increased from $1.80 billion to $2.15 billion in the past year, but operating earnings fell more than 62% over the same time frame.[3] In the military aircraft segment, operating earnings dropped 44%, mostly due to yet another significant write-off on the C-17 transport program.[4] As C.J. Lawrence, Inc., analyst Howard Rubel said, "The issue is not so much the horrific earnings, but looking forward, the quality of the balance sheet and the ability of the company to recoup investment in the MD-11."[3]

Clearly, McDonnell Douglas Corporation (MDC) was facing some difficult challenges ahead, induced by the amazing changes that occurred in the commercial and military aircraft markets over the last few years. The cover of MDC's 1991 Annual Report shows a dramatic photograph of five of the Navy's F/A-18 Blue Angels miraculously pulling out of a steep dive with the caption "Turning the Corner."[5] Perhaps this prediction was a bit premature, but the question facing John McDonnell at this point was how to craft the firm's strategy in order to fulfill this prophecy in the long run.

History

In 1920, airplane designer Donald Wills Douglas opened the Douglas Aircraft Company (DAC) in the back room of a barbershop on Pico Boulevard in Los Angeles.[6] DAC manufactured a number of both military and commercial transport aircraft over the next five decades, from the Cloudster and the Dolphin to the DC-8 and the DC-9. DAC was very successful over this time period, as it was the premier transport aircraft producer until Boeing jumped ahead in the mid-1950s.

Also around 1920, an engineer named James Smith McDonnell, Jr., got an idea from Henry Ford, his former employer, to mass produce airplanes.[7] He formed a company in 1926 and built his first airplane, the Doodleburg. Neither company survived the great Depression, as families struggling to put food on the table could not afford to buy airplanes. In 1939, McDonnell then created the McDonnell Aircraft Company (MAC) to manufacture parts for other companies' airplanes. Partly because the big firms had all they could handle with the war production effort, in 1943 the Navy gave MAC a contract to build a jet fighter. This would mark the beginning of the production of a number of combat aircraft, including the F2H-2 Banshee, the F3H Demon, and the F-101A Voodoo.

By 1966, there was tremendous demand for DAC's DC-9, but the war in Vietnam reduced the labor pool and stressed the capacity of many parts suppliers. Skyrocketing costs forced DAC to seek a merger with a financially healthier company. Signal Oil, North American Aviation, and MAC all made presentations to the Douglas Board of Directors. James McDonnell, who had personally acquired 300,000 shares of DAC, offered to buy an additional 1.5 million shares of unissued stock, worth $68.7 million.[8] His offer was accepted almost immediately, and on May 1, 1967, McDonnell Douglas Corporation opened for business with 125,000 employees and billions of dollars in both government contracts and commercial aircraft orders. Since then, MDC has developed and manufactured an array of military and commercial aircraft, including the F-4 Phantom, the F-15 Eagle, the FA-18 Hornet, the AV-8B Harrier, the DC-10, the MD-80, and the MD-11.

James McDonnell, the founder and visionary leader of the company, died on August 22, 1980. His nephew, Sandy McDonnell, assumed the role of chairman until April 1988, when he stepped aside to allow the founder's son, John Finney McDonnell, to lead the firm. John McDonnell graduated from Princeton with a masters degree in finance in 1962.[9] When he took over MDC in 1988, he had three specific goals for the future: to be the leading aerospace company, to be a winner in information systems, and to be a creative innovator in complementary businesses.[10] In order to reach these goals, he felt that four critical issues should be addressed: (1) the need for continuous improvement, (2) the need for a better strategic focus, (3) the need for improved human resources development, and (4) the need to resolve a series of business line issues, primarily in commercial transports, information systems, and government aerospace.[11]

Organizing Structure

In 1992, the McDonnell Douglas Corporation is comprised of a number of distinct companies. The Douglas Aircraft Company (DAC), headquartered in Long Beach, CA, designs and manufactures large transport aircraft. Most of its products are targeted towards commercial aviation, although large military transport aircraft such as the C-17 are also produced there. The smaller military combat aircraft are designed and produced by the McDonnell Aircraft Company (McAir), headquartered in St. Louis, MO. McDonnell Douglas Missile Systems Company (MDMSC) produces missiles, space systems, sensors, and surveillance systems such as the Tomahawk cruise missile, the Advanced Cruise Missile, and the Delta space vehicle. Complementary businesses include the McDonnell Douglas Finance Corporation (MDFC), the McDonnell Douglas Systems Integration Company (MDSIC), the McDonnell Douglas Realty Company (MDRC), the McDonnell Douglas Travel Company (MDTC), and McDonnell Douglas Information Systems International (MDISI). Since nearly 80% of MDC's revenue come from either DAC or McAir, the most important strategic decisions revolve around the commercial and military aircraft business segments.

The Aerospace Industry

Aerospace is an important industry in the global marketplace. Most countries consider aerospace to be a catalyst for new technologies and a creator of high-paying, high-productivity jobs and business opportunities.[12] The U.S. has long maintained a leading position in the industry, but growing international competition has begun to close the gap. From 1985 to 1991, the U.S. share of free-world aerospace production declined from 73 to 60%, despite continuing growth in the total U.S. output.[13] Aerospace combines the characteristics of heavy equipment manufacturing and high-technology research. Operations typically include long development and production cycles and huge start-up costs. Firms sometimes derive designs from existing models, thereby mitigating the cost to some extent.[14] Major programs usually have long, steep "learning curves" where unit costs decrease as the total units produced increases due to improved labor productivity and other cost efficiencies.[14] Computer-aided design (CAD) and computer-aided manufacturing (CAM) are widely utilized in today's aerospace industry, allowing engineers to do many things that were impossible only a few years ago.[15]

Such industry characteristics have triggered intense global competition, which has in turn induced many firms to enter into international partnerships with other aerospace companies. For example, Boeing's next airliner, the 777, involves collaboration with Mitsubishi, Kawasaki, and Fuji.[13] Furthermore, Airbus Industrie, itself a consortium of British, German, French, and Spanish companies, is currently trying to enlist Asian help for a proposed 600 to 800-seat super-jumbo airliner.[13]

These cooperative ventures are displacing marketplace competition in the commercial aircraft sector, according to a U.S. university-sponsored study. This study maintains that U.S. dominance of the aircraft industry is severely threatened by the changing nature of competition coming from Europe and Japan.[16] Accordingly, U.S. aerospace firms are finding themselves at a disadvantage in 1992 because of the lack of a cohesive national strategy to ensure the profitability or even the survival of its two remaining major transport manufacturers, Boeing and MDC.[17]

Military Aerospace Segment

The most significant customer in the combat military transport aircraft and the missiles, space, and electronic systems segments is the U.S. government. The Department of Defense (DoD) rates prospective military contractors, awarding contracts to companies that are determined to be the most capable of meeting exacting specifications. Consequently, firms without strong track records are at a severe disadvantage.[14] Companies engaged in supplying military and space equipment to the U.S. government are subject to a number of extraordinary risks, including dependence on congressional appropriations and annual administrative allotment of funds, general reductions in the U.S. defense budget, and changes in government policies.[18] Furthermore, firms invest funds in programs that are both competitive and in the pre-development stage. There is no assurance that these investments will result in a contract or that a contract, if awarded, will be profitable.

The U.S. government may terminate its contracts for default or for convenience, wherever it believes that such termination would be in the best interest of the government.[19] In the latter case, the contractor is entitled to receive payments for the proportionate share of the fee for the work actually completed. Also, military contractors must be prepared to deal with periodic changes in DoD procurement rules. Contract terms can vary widely, depending on whether the agreement is based on cost-reimbursement or a fixed-price.[20] As an example of the dynamic nature of the procurement rules, in the late 1980s, the U.S.

government started to turn to second sourcing, a practice that creates competition in programs already in production by a single firm.[14]

The end of the Cold War and the emergence of the Commonwealth of Independent States (CIS) in early 1992 has shifted the focus away from the large-scale ground war that dominated U.S. military strategy in recent years. The DoD is now planning for conflicts such as Operation Desert Storm which require relatively small military forces capable of reacting quickly to crises in any part of the world.[21]

In the future, emphasis will be placed on making maximum use of advanced technology in preparing to fight "small wars" in remote locations and to provide a "shield" against the threat of attack from any one of a growing list of nations that could be capable of launching ballistic missiles with nuclear warheads.[22] Defense contractors face some particularly challenging times ahead given the drastic reductions and evolving nature of defense spending over the coming years. Current projects will experience "stretch-outs" when the time allotted for their completion will be increased and new projects will be under more scrutiny that ever. Beyond proven technology and cost-effectiveness, the risk of technical, projection, or operational difficulties will be minimized, and an "absolute need" for new weapons will have to be shown.[23] There will be a renewed emphasis on efficiency. The industry has already been forced to adopt strong cost-cutting measures, and this trend will most certainly continue. For example, aerospace employment fell by nearly 5% in 1990 and 9% in 1991. The DoD will stress research and development more than production to maintain a high-technology base, causing contractors to miss out on the more lucrative phase of full-scale production.[24] The U.S. government will increasingly consider "silver bullet" procurement programs, where relatively small quantities are produced as in the case of the F-117 stealth fighter.[25] Indeed, the challenge for U.S. defense firms in the 1990s will be figuring out how to keep skilled work forces and supplier bases intact while at the time sustaining adequate levels of return for shareholders as business pressures mount.[26]

Although these circumstances paint a gloomy picture for the defense industry over the next decade or so, the prospects are not universally bad for all defense contractors. The lack of new programs will create opportunities for those companies that already have systems in place to offer upgrades which are more cost-effective than entirely new projects.[24] Thus, large well-established firms which currently produce a number of weapons for the U.S. military may be in a better strategic position than before. For those companies with fully developed products, foreign markets will be more important than ever. Historically, arms exports have accounted for 12 to 15% of non-nuclear American arms production, but this amount could easily increase to 25% by the year 2000.[28]

Commercial Aerospace Segment

In stark contrast to the declining defense industry, the commercial aircraft industry appears to have a very bright future if it can solve some current problems. In general, industry forecasters predict annual growth in global passenger traffic, measured in revenue passenger-miles, of about 5%.[29] From 1990 to 2000, average annual growth is projected to be 4.4% for the U.S. domestic market, 5.7% for the intra-Europe market, 4.8% for the North Atlantic market, 8.5% for the trans-Pacific market, 9.98% for the intra-Orient market, and 14.2% for the Europe-Orient market.[30] Furthermore, growth trends favor larger aircraft, particularly after 1995, due to increasing congestion at airports and airways and changes in route patterns.[28] The increase in delivery share will be greatest in those aircraft with more than 300 seats, which are expected to go from a pre-1990 share of 7% to 31% over the next 15 years.[31] Such growth should provide aircraft makers with a wealth of investment and sales opportunities, but there are some very real concerns that they must first address. In the U.S., the domestic airline industry has had some disappointing years recently. Declining traffic, weak yields, and rising costs combined to produce record losses in 1990 and only slightly smaller deficits in 1991, forcing airlines to order far fewer aircraft.[32] There were only 402 orders in 1991, down from 1115 in 1990.[33] The declines in traffic caused by the Persian Gulf War and widespread recession significantly hurt the airlines and consequently the aircraft producers, but a healthier domestic and worldwide economy should induce traffic to resume rather steady growth.[34]

Unfortunately, 1992 brought about a new set of problems for the airline industry caused mainly by erratic pricing policies. In May 1992, American Airlines, led by CEO Robert Crandall, slashed summer advance-purchase fares by 50% in response to Northwest's 2-for-1 promotion.[35] The ultimate result has been huge second-quarter losses and more confusion. Executives of the larger airlines accuse bankrupt carriers of operating in the marketplace at an unfair advantage, while the smaller airlines accuse the larger ones of predatory pricing.[36] Obviously this oligopoly is still searching for some maturity and stability, and until it finds some, aircraft manufacturers will see weaker than normal demand for their products.

Concentration in the commercial aircraft sector is very high, resulting in a fierce battle for market share. Since 1981, Boeing and MDC have been the only U.S. firms to produce large jet transports, and they have only one major international competitor: Airbus Industrie, which is openly supported by the British, German, French, and Spanish governments and has made a dramatic impact on the industry. For example, after 14 years of purchasing only Boeing planes, United Airlines recently ordered up to 100 Airbus A320s, representing a $3 billion agreement.[37] Boeing's official statement after the deal read, in part, "We made a very attractive offer and went as far as prudence would dictate on the business terms. Obviously, Airbus could do more."[16] Government subsidies give Airbus an unfair competitive advantage (at least according to Boeing and MDC) which allows it to price its aircraft almost 10% below break-even cost levels.[38]

Not only does Airbus steal away market share from Boeing and MDC, but it also severely limits their ability to embark on new aircraft development projects. The cost of bringing a large commercial jet to market is about $4 billion, and sales of about 400 units are required to recover these launch costs.[25] Costs are so large that new product development becomes difficult in the wake of the declining market share that Boeing and MDC may experience in the future. Airbus has also been known to make "white-tails" (aircraft without a buyer) during production downcycles in order to reduce or eliminate the need for layoffs.[39] Such a strategy is basically unavailable to its U.S. competitors. Thus, the introduction of intense global competition into the oligopolistic commercial aircraft industry has created new threats for U.S. producers.

MCD's Strategic Position in the Military Aircraft Segment

McDonnell Douglas is in a relatively good position in the defense industry. In 1991, the company received approximately 5.9% of all DoD prime contract awards, making MDC once again the largest U.S. defense contractor.[40] Consequently, it has a number of weapon systems in place scheduled to be upgraded in the near future.

McDonnell Douglas is known for excellent quality in its fighter aircraft, and this reputation should help it to sell its products in the future, particularly to foreign customers. In the 1991 Annual Report, John McDonnell reminded shareholders that "our F-15s and F/A-18s accounted for all of the Iraqi fighter aircraft downed in aerial combat. Every single one." The Persian Gulf War was a sparkling tribute to the quality of MDC's aircraft, but financially it did more harm than good in the short run. The firm would have been better off financially had some of the airplanes and helicopters been destroyed. In that event, the Pentagon would have brought replacements instead of cutting production.[41]

MCD's Major Military Products

The F-15 Eagle is a dual-role Air Force fighter than can deliver more than 24,000 pounds of bombs with pinpoint accuracy. It can also defend itself with a full complement of advance air-to-air weapons and outstanding handling characteristics. MDC believes the F-15 to be the world's best long-range ground attack aircraft. Although the U.S. government would not purchase F-15s after 1993, MDC is in the process of trying to sell them to Saudi Arabia.[42] Approval of the sale by President Bush would keep the F-15 in production until 1997 and possibly lead to further export orders which could extend the line for several additional years.[43]

The AV-8B Harrier II is a Marine tactical jet capable of V/STOL (vertical and short take-off and landing). Four rotating nozzles allow it to take off vertically, without an airstrip. Although procurement of the AV-8B will not continue past 1992, there is a strong possibility that existing aircraft will be upgraded with the Hughes APG-65 radar system. The new configuration will remove a major obstacle to export sales of the AV-8B.[44] The F/A-18 Hornet is a naval fighter/attack jet that combines a top speed of 1.7 times the speed of sound with excellent maneuverability. The Hornet can carry 8.5 tons of ordinance including missiles, cannons, rockets, and bombs, and it is the safest jet in the Navy's inventory.[45]

The Air Force C-17 Airlifter is a large military transport designed to carry outside cargo in austere airfields. Its advanced features include short-field takeoff and landing capability, two-pilot and one-loadmaster operation, inflight refueling, loading systems, and an advanced supercritical wing design with winglets and advanced composite structures. The C-17 is in the development stage under a fixed-price contract. The program has been plagued with problems, including: (1) increased labor costs due to inefficiencies caused by the reassignment of workers resulting from layoffs at DAC, (2) additional engineering requirements, (3) increased supplier costs, and (4) investments to improve production quality.[46] Also a series of fuel leaks interrupted flight tests for 50 days in early 1992.[47] These unforeseen difficulties have resulted in a string of revised cost estimates well over $150 million in the last year.

MDC's Strategic Position in the Commercial Aircraft Segment

The most critical decisions facing management concern MDC's strategic position in the commercial aerospace industry. According to most experts, MDC is in serious trouble here. Even highly respected business professors are all but predicting the elimination of McDonnell Douglas as a commercial aircraft producer within the next decade.[48] Evidence of the company's decline in this arena is disturbing. MDC's market share has been gradually falling since 1988. Currently, Boeing has 55% of the market. Airbus has 31%, and MDC is fading with only 12%.[49] In 1991, MDC experienced a decrease in firm orders of 33 aircraft, while Boeing's orders increased by 222 and Airbus Industrie's by 70.[49] Simply looking at the number of different types of commercial airliners that the three companies produce, it is clear that MDC does not have a product line that can compete with Boeing and Airbus in all segments of the commercial aerospace market.

MDC's Major Commercial Products

The DC-9/MD-80 and the MD-90 (an advanced version of the MD-80 featuring fuel-efficient engines with reduced noise and exhaust emissions) compete directly with the Boeing 737 and the Airbus A320 in the short-to-medium range, 100- to 160-seat market.[50] Over the last 5 years, DAC has received 24% of the bookings in this aircraft class; however, the future may not be as bright, as MD-80 delivery forecasts have been steadily reduced over the last year.[51]

In 1991, the MD-11 tri-jet program completed the transition from development to full production. The MD-11 seats 293 passengers in a typical three-class configuration and has a range of nearly 7000 nautical miles.[2] It competes with the Boeing 747 and Airbus A340. There is currently a lot of concern about the flattening of the MD-11 learning curve. The program has incurred additional costs to reconfigure MD-11s for deliveries switched to different customers and to modify Delta's MD-11s so that they would meet guaranteed performance levels.[52] In short, recently stalled MD-11 sales and higher costs have stirred fears that Douglas could be added to the list of once-proud builders of commercial airliners that have fallen into oblivion.[53]

The most important decision facing MDC's top management at the current time centers around the fate of the MD-12. In October 1991, MDC's board of directors approved the offering of the MD-12 to commercial customers worldwide. As currently proposed, the MD-12 is a four-engine, wide-body aircraft that would carry more than 400 passengers on routes as long as 8000 nautical miles.[54] It would be the first direct competitor to the Boeing 747 in the high-capacity, long-distance segment of the market.[55] Over the past year, MDC has made some major design changes to the MD-12 proposal which, according to industry officials, have damaged the company's credibility.[56] There is further concern that once in production, the MD-12 would be "pencil-whipped" by Boeing as it would cut into its substantial 747 profit margin to win market share.

Looming above all of these questions is the matter of MDC's poor financial position. According to American Airlines Chairman Crandall, "The problem lies in the financial condition of McDonnell Douglas. It is not in any shape to start a new aircraft program. In order to support the launch of the MD-12, MDC is actively pursuing strategic alliances with various organizations, principally in the Asia/Pacific Region."[57] The company has spoken with prospects in Korea, Japan, Singapore, Malaysia, and Indonesia, but so far the most promising discussions have been with Taiwan.[58] In November 1991, MDC signed a memorandum of understanding (MOU) with the Taiwan Aerospace Corporation and began negotiations which may lead to investors in Taiwan acquiring up to a 40% interest in MDC's commercial transport business for up to $2 billion; however, the agreement has hit some major snags. The complex arrangement is taking longer than expected to evaluate, and Taiwan's news media and legislature are skeptical that the deal is financially sound from Taiwan's point of view. They believe that Taiwan deserves technology transfers for the amount of money it is offering, but the current agreement calls for only assembly to take place in Taiwan.[59] An assessment by a group of Chinese engineers and accountants in California claims that DAC has failed to make money for the past 25 years.[50]

Some analysts believe that the Taiwanese joint venture and the MD-12 are essential to MDC's continued presence in the commercial aircraft industry, but the Taiwanese agreement faces opposition in the U.S., as well. Some have expressed concern that, under the arrangement, it would be difficult if not impossible for MDC to protect proprietary information.[60] After all, how could MDC tell partners who own a substantial stake in the company that they cannot have access to all of the data? The U.S. government is also a bit wary of the deal.

Kevin L. Kearns, a fellow at the Economic Strategy Institute in Washington, D.C., stated, "We need to look at the costs of losing critical industries" such as aerospace.[61] Boeing Chairman and CEO Frank Shrontz believes that the Taiwan agreement would create yet another subsidized competitor:[60]

> "Taiwan's acquisition of part of McDonnell Douglas would be just the tip of the iceberg. It would be quite another thing for McDonnell Douglas to raise the additional billions that will certainly be needed to launch a new airplane program or programs. If that comes in the form of support from the government of Taiwan, they in fact will be creating an Asian 'Airbus' where, once again, deep government pockets eliminate the need for disciplined business decisions. We hope our government will insist that the Douglas/Taiwan Aerospace deal include a clear agreement that there will be no government subsidy and no bar to full market access."

In the 1991 Annual Report, John McDonnell explained top management's approach to the commercial market:[62]

> "We face a different set of challenges in our commercial jetliner business. Here we are in danger of being squeezed out of the market by larger, better financed competitors. With over 50% of the market, Boeing is the industry's low-cost producer. Backed by large subsidies from four European governments, Airbus Industrie is able to price its products below cost in order to gain market share. Both Boeing and Airbus are able to offer airlines a complete range of jetliners. MDC is not.
>
> "Strategically, MDC took a first important step in 1991 toward transforming our commercial airliner business into a new and different entity

— a truly international company, dedicated to becoming the commercial aircraft industry's low-cost, high-quality producer.

"We have the outlines of a global alliance involving investors in the Republic of China (Taiwan) and possible other participants in Asia/Pacific and elsewhere. A process of evaluation and definition has continued into 1992 with Taiwan investors, as have talks with other possible alliance participants."

Financial Position of MDC

McDonnell Douglas is currently experiencing some very serious cash flow problems caused in part by its tremendous amount of debt. MDC's overall debt-to-equity ratio is around three, while Boeing's is close to one. This figure does not include the $950 million of senior debt securities that MDC recently issued in April 1992.[63] Such a high degree of financial leverage created an interest expense of $264 million at MDC in 1991, in sharp contrast to Boeing's $250 million in interest revenue for the same time period. MDC cannot afford any major investments at this time that do not generate almost immediate cash flow.

On July 16, 1990, John McDonnell announced a corporate-wide plan to cut $700 million in costs. Since that time, the company has been continually down-sizing to adjust to declining work levels. Total employment has been reduced by more than 25% from 132,960 at June 30, 1990, to 99,096 at June 30, 1992, and further layoffs are expected to continue indefinitely.[64]

As if things were not bad enough, there are a few potential financial disasters in MDC's near future, as well. The Financial Accounting Standards Board has issued a pronouncement which will affect future periods and has not yet been adopted by MDC. SFAS No. 106, Employers' Accounting for Post-Retirement Benefits Other than Pensions, requires the projected future cost of retiree health care and life insurance to be recognized as an expense as employees render service rather than when benefits are paid.[65] MDC estimates the after-tax transition obligation to range between $1.2 and $1.8 billion in the first quarter of 1993, along with an annual after-tax expense of $120 to $180 million for every year thereafter.

Another potential financial setback lies with the resolution of legal proceedings concerning the A-12. On January 7, 1991, the Navy notified MDC and General Dynamics (the Team) that it was terminating for default the Team's fixed-price incentive type of contract for development and initial production of the A-12 contract. Should the Team lose in court, the cost would be about $1.2 billion plus accrued interest from January 1991 between the two firms.

Management

Since John McDonnell became Chairman of MDC, there have been a number of operating philosophies that have been officially endorsed by top management, including ethical decision-making and the "Five Keys to Self-Renewal". The most important of these has been the total quality management system (TQMS). Customer satisfaction, defined as achieving the highest possible quality at the lowest possible cost, is at the heart of this philosophy. Supporting tenets include teams and partnerships, disciplined systems and processes, and continuous improvement ("if it's not broken, make it better").[66] TQMS also calls for a supportive cultural environment where performance and improvement are quantitatively measured, workers are empowered to make important decisions, employment stability is maintained, communications are frank and open in both directions, education and training is stressed, and a foundation of trust is built throughout the organization. TQMS embraces and attempts to initiate change in the effort to improve continuously, with improvement ultimately determined by the customer. In order to explicitly measure this improvement, MDC has recently adopted the Malcom Baldrige National Quality Award criteria which include leadership, information and analysis, strategic quality planning, human resource development and management, management of process quality, quality and operational results, and customer focus and satisfaction. The company's goal is to reach "six-sigma" quality by 1996.

Employee Relations

The massive layoffs over the past 2 years have driven worker morale down to an all-time low. A strong distrust has developed among the employees toward management due to an intuitive suspicion of managerial hypocrisy.[67] For example, employees usually find out about layoffs throughout the local St. Louis newspaper and not from first-line or top managers. There is virtually no employment stability, and workers perceive that layoffs have been disproportionately small for management positions, resulting in an organization that has far too many managers. One of the things top management did was to redefine the term "manager" based on a minimum span of control. The end result was that the company claimed it significantly reduced the number of managers when, in fact, the jobs and the pay for those who were previously called managers did not change at all. Furthermore, it is well known even outside of MDC that the concept of "empowered" teams at the lowest levels of the company was abandoned relatively early, resulting in an increase in the number of executive and management levels.[68] All of these things directly contradict what management said it would do according to TQMS, thereby creating a wave of distrust within the rank and file.

In a recent copy of an MDC engineering newsletter, employees were asked to comment on the morale at MDC. Some of the responses were quite interesting and insightful:

> "Insecurity and instability of one's job and career contribute to lower morale. We all know there will be layoffs, as we are employed in the defense industry. Logic is thrown out the window with common sense during the layoffs, however, and most employees do not know the criteria for layoffs. Solution: Let people know where they stand. If a manager knows which personnel are likely to be hit, the manager needs to inform these people as soon as possible as an act of courtesy and decency. Many employees are the sole breadwinners in their households, and these families will be hard hit by the job loss. Give these people an opportunity to postpone major purchases and to search for another job while still employed. As it is now, employees don't have a clue as to who will be terminated and when. Therefore, all employees look over their shoulders and cower each time a manager's door is closed. ..."

> "We get no visible direction from corporate. Just exactly where are we headed? Is DAC going to fail, and if so, what will be the impact on MDC? ..."

> "Every three months there are announcements of layoffs or rumors of layoffs and they never seem to end. It would be nice to know once and for all when the layoffs will be, who they will affect, and when they will be over so people can quit worrying about whether or not they will have a job next week and concentrate on getting their work done. ..."

> "It appears that layoffs of non-management employees have disproportionately exceeded layoffs in the management ranks. It is a common perception at the engineer level that there are too many managers and levels of management. ..."

"Positive reinforcement for a job well done would be appreciated. Management tends to tell us we are lucky to have a job, not reward us for doing a good one. ..."

"Suggestion: Don't get taken hook, line, and sinker with every quality initiative and modern management technique that evolves. (If I sold philosophy to companies, I'd certainly knock on McDonnell Douglas' door first.) Malcom Baldrige and six sigma and TQMS all have some meaning, but we abandon all else to jump into these programs. If this company showed the commitment to employees that it does to Malcolm Baldrige, morale and quality would improve. But our company seems to care more for Malcom than it does the people that Malcolm critiques. ..."

"Suggestion: Set priorities. Let's not strive for six sigma on all facets of our business. If an airline concerns itself with loss of luggage and loss of human life with the same priority, we'd lose a lot less luggage and a lot more life. In the same way, our WALTS (Weekly Accounting Labor and Tracking System) percentage improves at the expense of cost, schedule, and quality. It appears that proper time charging is the most important grading technique we have."

In short, MDC is in a strong competitive positive in the declining defense industry and in a weak competitive position in the growing commercial aircraft industry. The company's newly announced strategy is to concentrate on business segments for which MDC is either the number one or number two supplier (in terms of market share), and if a particular business division cannot achieve that goal, the company will look to divest that operation.[4]

References

1. McDonnell Douglas Corporation, Second Quarter Report, 1992, p.2.
2. P.H. Nisbet, Company Report for Prudential Securities Inc., August 6, 1992, p. 2.
3. Anthony L. Velocci, Jr., "McDonnell Douglas' Earnings Plunge, Raising New Concerns About Future," *Aviation Week and Space Technology*, August 10, 1992, p. 26.
4. P.L. Aseritis, Company Report for The First Boston Corporation, August 20, 1992, p. 1.
5. McDonnell Douglas Corporation, Annual Report, 1991, cover page.
6. McDonnell Douglas Corporation, *Orientation Conference Workbook*, 1988, p. 5.
7. McDonnell Douglas Corporation, *Orientation Conference Workbook*, 1989, p. 12.
8. McDonnell Douglas Corporation, *Orientation Conference Workbook*, 1990, p. 17.
9. "The Corporate Elite," *Business Week*, October 12, 1992, p. 131.
10. John F. McDonnell, "Looking to the Future," *Spirit* (an MDC magazine), Spring 1992, p. 13

11. John F. McDonnell, "Looking to the Future," *Spirit* (an MDC magazine), Spring 1992, p. 14.
12. Michael Selwyn, "Global Ambitions: Aerospace Is Set To Be the World's First Truly Borderless Industry," *Asian Business*, June 1992, p. 23.
13. "U.S. Dominance Slipping," *Standard & Poor's Industry Surveys*, June 25, 1992, p. A16.
14. "U.S. Dominance Slipping," *Standard & Poor's Industry Surveys*, June 25, 1992, p. A17.
15. Breck W. Henderson, "CAD/CAM Systems Transform Aerospace Engineering," *Aviation Week and Space Technology*, June 22, 1992, p. 49.
16. Anthony L. Velocci, Jr., "Study Says Japan, Europe Threaten U.S. Leadership in Air Transports," *Aviation Week and Space Technology*, March 23, 1992, p. 33.
17. David W. Cravens, H. Kirk Downey, and Paul Lauritano, "Global Competition in the Commercial Aircraft Industry: Positioning for Advantage by the Triad Nations," *Columbia Journal of World Business*, Winter 1992, p. 58.
18. McDonnell Douglas Corporation, 10-Q form for the quarterly period ended June 30, 1992, p. 21.
19. McDonnell Douglas Corporation, Annual Report, 1991, p. 22
20. "New World Politics Dictate Lower Defense Profile," *Standard & Poor's Industry Surveys*, June 25, 1992, p. A26.
21. "Defense Spending Cuts Loom," *Standard and Poor's Industry Surveys*, June 20, 1991, p. A19.
22. McDonnell Douglas Corporation, Annual Report, 1991, p. 14.
23. David A. Bond, "U.S. Defense Budget Cuts to Curb Acquisition of New Weapon Systems," (McDonnell Douglas Corporation internal document).
24. "New World Politics Dictate Lower Defense Profile," *Standard & Poor's Industry Surveys*, June 25, 1992, p. A25.
25. Morton L. Siegel, "Aerospace/Defense Industry," *The Value Line Investment Survey*, October 9, 1991, p. 552.
26. "Defense Cuts Continue to Squeeze Market," (McDonnell Douglas Corporation internal document).
27. Amy Borrus, "Crying 'Jobs' to Sell Weapons Abroad," *Business Week*, March 16, 1992, p. 37.
28. "Order Boom Slows with Recession," *Standard & Poor's Industry Surveys*, June 20, 1991, p. A26–A27.
29. Richard G. O'Lane, "Airframe Makers Foresee Continuing Strong Markets," *Aviation Week and Space Technology*, March 18, 1991, p. 77.
30. "New Orders Take a Nose Dive," *Standard & Poor's Industry Surveys*, June 25, 1992, p. A21.
31. "Waiting for Economy To Give Airlines a Lift," *Standard & Poor's Industry Surveys*, February 20, 1992, p. A1.
32. "Orders Cool, But Backlogs Lend Support," *Standard & Poor's Industry Surveys*, June 20, 1991, p. A15.
33. Richard G. O'Lane, "U.S. Airframe Outlook Bright Despite Gloomy 1992 Results," *Aviation Week and Space Technology*, March 16, 1992, p. 53.
34. Andrea Rothman and Wendy Zellner, "The Airline Mess," *Business Week*, July 6, 1992, p 51.
35. James Ott, "Airline Fiscal Morass Erases Profits and Crimps Fleet Plans," *Aviation Week and Space Technology*, April 6, 1992, p. 36.

36. Jeff Cole, "Boeing's Dominance of Aircraft Industry Is Beginning To Erode," *Wall Street Journal*, July 10, 1992, p. A1.
37. James Ott, "Airbus Wins United A320 Order, Boosting U.S. Presence," *Aviation Week and Space Technology*, July 13, 1992, p. 22.
38. "U.S. Firms Lead This Global Market," *Standard & Poor's Industry Surveys*, June 21, 1991, p. A17.
39. McDonnell Douglas Corporation, 10-Q Form for the Quarterly Period Ended March 31, 1992, p. 18.
40. Thomas G. Donlan, "Riding for a Fall? Long-Term Prospects for McDonnell Douglas Are Cloudy," *Barron's*, October 21, 1991, p. 8.
41. McDonnell Douglas Corporation, Annual Report, 1991, p. 4.
42. McDonnell Douglas Corporation, Second Quarter Report, 1992, p. 1.
43. McDonnell Douglas Corporation, 10-K Form for the Year Ended December 31, 1991, p. 4.
44. McDonnell Douglas Corporation, *Orientation Conference Workbook*, 1990, p. 24.
45. McDonnell Douglas Corporation, 10-Q Form for the Quarterly Period Ended June 30, 1992, p. 23.
46. "First C-17 Returns to Flight Status After Fuel Tanks Resealed," *Aviation Week and Space Technology*, March 2, 1992, p. 62.
47. Lester Thurow, *Head to Head: The Coming Economic Battle Among Japan, Europe, and America*, William Morrow, New York, 1992, p. 36.
48. James E. Ellis, "Gone is My Co-Pilot?" *Business Week*, July 6, 1992, p. 72.
49. McDonnell Douglas Corporation, 10-K Form for the Year Ended December 31, 1992, pp. 7–8.
50. P. Friedman, Company Report for Morgan Stanley and Co., Inc., 18 March 1992, p. 2.
51. McDonnell Douglas Corporation, 10-K Form for the Year Ended December 31, 1991, p. 7.
52. James E. Ellis, "Douglas Is Struggling For Altitude," *Business Week*, November 9, 1992, p. 71.
53. McDonnell Douglas Corporation, 10-Q Form for the Quarterly Period Ended March 31, 1992, p. 30.
54. McDonnell Douglas Corporation, Annual Report, 1991, p. 5.
55. Bruce A. Smith, "Quick Changes in MD-12 Plans Damage Douglas' Credibility," *Aviation Week and Space Technology*, July 20, 1992, p. 27.
56. McDonnell Douglas Corporation, 10-Q Form for the Quarterly Period Ended March 31, 1992, p. 30.
57. Anthony L. Vocci, Jr., "Pace of Taiwan Venture Concern U.S. Partner," *Aviation Week and Space Technology*, February 3, 1992, p. 62.
58. James E. Ellis and Pete Engardio, "McDonnell Douglas' Far East Hopes Are Dimming," *Business Week*, March 9, 1992, p. 49.
59. Julian Baum, "A Deal of Trouble: Taiwan's McDonnell Venture Hits Snag," *Far Eastern Economic Review*, February 13, 1992, p. 43.
60. "Shrontz Explains Differing Roles of Foreign Partners," *Aviation Week and Space Technology*, February 3, 1992, p 62.
61. Chris Brown, James E. Ellis, and Dinah Lee, "An American Eagle Talks Turkey With the Taiwanese," *Business Week*, December 2, 1991, p. 55.
62. McDonnell Douglas Corporation, Annual Report, 1991, p. 3

63. McDonnell Douglas Corporation, 10-Q Form for the Quarterly Period Ending March 31, 1992, p. 14.
64. McDonnell Douglas Corporation, Second Quarter Report, 1992, p. 1.
65. McDonnell Douglas Corporation, 10-Q Form for the Quarterly Period Ended June 30, 1992, p. 49
66. McDonnell Douglas Corporation, 10-K Form for the Year Ended December 31, 1991, p. 19.
67. McDonnell Douglas Corporation, *The McAir TOMS Story* (an internal information booklet), August 1989, p. 8.
68. "Douglas Boosts Production Without Key TQM Provision," *Aviation Week and Space Technology*, Dec. 9, 1991, p. 61.

McDonnell-Douglas Corporation Consolidated Income Account
(Year Ended December 31)

	1995[a]	1994[a]	1993[a]	1992[a]	1991[a]
Revenues	14,332	13,176	14,487	17,365	18,061
Costs and expenses					
Cost of products, services and rentals	12,027	11,026	12,822	15,567	15,561
MD-11 account charge	1838	—	—	—	—
General and administrative expenses	681	684	720	825	1003
Research and development	311	297	341	509	429
Post-retirement benefit curtailment	—	—	(70)	(1090)	—
Interest expense					
Aerospace segments	116	131	89	309	232
Financial services and other segments	109	118	126	159	221
Total costs and expenses	15,082	12,256	14,028	16,279	17,446
Earnings from continuing operations before income taxes and cumulative effect of accounting change	(750)	920	459	1086	615
Income taxes	34	322	100	388	258
Earnings from continuing operations before cumulative effect of accounting change	(416)	598	359	689	357
Discontinued operations	—	—	—	20	(8)
Earnings from operations, net of income taxes					
Gain on disposal, net of income taxes	—	—	37	37	74
Earnings before cumulative effect of accounting change	(416)	598	359	689	357
Cumulative effect of initial application of new accounting standard for post-retirement benefits	—	—	—	(1536)	—

McDonnell-Douglas Corporation Consolidated Income Account (Year Ended December 31) (continued)

	1995[a]	1994[a]	1993[a]	1992[a]	1991[a]
Net income (loss)	(416)	598	396	(781)	423
Previous retained earnings	3576	3043	2702	3538	3168
Cash dividends declared	90	65	55	55	53
Shares purchased	123	—	—	—	—
Retained earnings	2947	3576	3043	2702	3538
Earnings per common share					
Primary					
Continued operations	($3.66)	$5.05	$3.06	$5.99	$3.11
Income from discounted operations	—	—	—	$.17	($.07)
Disposal of discounted operations	—	—	$.31	$.32	$.64
Accounting change	—	—	—	($13.18)	—
Earnings per common share	($3.66)	$5.05	$3.37	($6.70)	($3.68)
Common shares in millions					
Year-end:	112	117	118	118	115
Average:	112	117	118	118	115

[a] Millions of dollars, except share data.

Case 4. Ben & Jerry's*

Background

Ben & Jerry's Homemade, Inc., was founded in 1978 by childhood friends Ben Cohen and Jerry Greenfield, who opened a homemade ice cream scoop shop in an abandoned gas station in Burlington, VT. Their $12,000 investment, $4000 of which was borrowed from Ben's father, has grown into an over-$150 million, publicly held company that is nationally recognized as one of the most innovative, progressive, and socially responsible businesses in the world.

During their youth, Ben was more interested in extracurricular activities than academics, while Jerry was the scholar. Ben was an independent spirit who was motivated only by the things he wanted to do, while Jerry was more of a conservative who played by the rules.

With the exception of thinking about buying a big rig and becoming cross-country truck drivers, most of Ben & Jerry's ideas for a business involved food. Their original idea was United Bagel Service, which would deliver fresh bagels every Sunday morning, along with lox, cream cheese, and the *New York Times.* After some research, they decided the business was too capital intensive. They never actually priced out the equipment for making ice cream, their second business choice. They assumed it had to be cheaper than making bagels and decided not to find out if that was not the case.[1]

---

* This case was written by Elizabeth A. Sherod for discussion purposes only. Used by permission.

All renovations to the abandoned gas station built in the 1940s were done by Ben and Jerry and a few of their childhood friends who became members of the Ice Cream for Life Club in exchange for their services. Major equipment was purchased at auction, and Lyn Severance, another native of Burlington, handled the promotional and design work, including the now famous hand-lettered, pint-sized container. Word of "Vermont's Finest" was spreading, and sales in their first year were double the $90,000 they had projected in their original business plan, yet they made no profit and had no long-term strategy for ensuring the future of their business.

Ben and Jerry began wholesaling in January 1979, when Ben hit the open road delivering ice cream to restaurants and trying to sell new accounts. In May of 1979, they received a Small Business Administration loan of $30,800 and moved from the gas station to an old spool and bobbin mill five blocks away. Concerned that restaurant sales may not be enough to offset the increased overhead of the new plant and ice cream truck, the also set up four seasonal scoop stands around Burlington. The idea which transformed the business into a profit-making venture was switching from the two and one-half gallon tubs to the pint-sized container.[1]

Ben became a full-time salesman at the end of 1980, and another driver was hired. In 1981, they expanded their truck routes into Albany, NY, and took out an ad in the *Free Press* for franchised scoop shop owner/operators. Ten days after the first franchise opened in July of 1981, *Time* magazine ran an article claiming that Ben & Jerry's made the best ice cream in the world, and the article mentioned four other popular ice cream shops in the U.S.[1]

The impact of the article was immediate and served to make the original scoop shop a tourist attraction. However, burned out from working 16-hour days for the past 3 years, Ben & Jerry signed a listing agreement with Country Business Service (CBS) for $510,000 plus 3% royalty on sales over half a million dollars and the rights to continue operating under the trade name Ben & Jerry's. Their failure to honor the agreement later cost them $75,000 in an out-of-court settlement.[1]

Having decided not to sell after all, Ben embarked on redefining the business to align with his social consciousness. Jerry moved to Arizona with his wife, selling all but 10% of his shares to Fred "Chico" Lager, an MBA graduate turned local bar owner who was hired as general manager in December 1982 to implement the internal operating procedures and financial controls the company desperately lacked. Lager's unofficial contract would expire in 1989. Jerry remained active with the company as a consultant making quarterly promotional visits.

To raise additional capital for plant expansion, Ben & Jerry's made an in-state stock offering in 1984, selling one in every 100 Vermont families stock for a minimum of $120 per share and secured a $650,000 Urban Development Action Grant from the Department of Housing and Urban Development. In May of 1985, Ben & Jerry's was listed on NASDAQ at $17 per share and had found a site in Waterbury for their new facility.[1]

Lager was promoted to CEO in 1989, while Ben started a candy-making business as a result of a conversation he had with a non-profit organization working as an advocate for the world's native peoples. The foundation for the company's social mission was being laid. Meanwhile, the Waterbury project was bringing wastewater and plant engineering problems, zoning permit lawsuits, and delays in construction, adding to the conflict between management personnel and the company's direction.

Ben took back the title of CEO and responsibility for the company's marketing in December, 1990, when Fred Lager's unofficial contract expired. Chuck Lacey became Chief Operating Officer overseeing operations and sales, and Jerry returned from Arizona to become vice chairman, officially assuming a more active role in the management of the business.

Ben & Jerry's stock peaked in 1992 at $30 a share but began sliding under Ben's direction, due in part to the soaring cost of butter, a key ingredient. Bob Holland was hired as CEO in February, 1995, after a much publicized search conducted by Ben, who used an essay contest titled, "Yo! I want to be CEO." Holland, a management consultant, did not enter. He was found through a blue-chip search firm.[2]

Under Holland's direction, equipment capacity changes were made at the new plant in St. Albans, VT, the sorbet line was launched ahead of schedule, and the company began international expansion into Europe.[3] Holland resigned in September, 1996, stating that the company now needed someone with greater marketing skills. The company stock remained flat under this tenure. Perry Odak, a former executive of the firm that makes Winchester rifles, became new CEO in October, 1996. Odak signed a 3-year agreement and at this point plans to use his 25 years of marketing experience in consumer products to help Ben & Jerry's regain momentum and market share.[4]

Societal Values and Concerns

Ben & Jerry's is a company where you can be yourself. Employees are allowed to dress casually every day, personalize their workspace, and listen to music to make themselves more comfortable. Small group forums enable line-level employees to participate in the decision-making process and make suggestions for improvement.

The Joy Gang was started in 1987 in response to the increasing demands placed upon employees as a result of the company's growth. The Gang approaches fun at work in three ways: cash grants of up to $500 to accommodate an idea that will bring more joy to a particular department; planned activities that involve food, fun, and prizes; and secret activities that are not announced in advance and are intended to surprise employees.[5]

Ben & Jerry's has received several awards, including "Top Business of the Year" in 1988, *Personnel Journal*'s "Optima Award for Quality of Life" in 1992, and *Working Mother*'s "The 100 Best Companies for Working Mothers" for three consecutive years from 1994 to 1996.[5]

The company adopted the "linked prosperity" mission statement concept in 1988, which consists of three interrelated parts:

1. Product — To make, distribute, and sell the finest quality, all-natural ice cream and related products in a wide variety of innovative flavors made from Vermont dairy products.
2. Economic — To operate the Company on a sound financial basis of profitable growth, increasing value for our shareholders and creating career opportunities and financial rewards for our employees.
3. Social — To operate the Company in a way that actively recognizes the central role that business plays in the structure of society by initiating innovative ways to improve the quality of life of a broad community: local, national, and international.[5]

Underlying the mission of Ben & Jerry's is the determination to seek new and creative ways of addressing all three parts of the mission statement, while maintaining a deep respect for the individuals inside and outside the company and for the communities of which they are a part.

Ben & Jerry's gives away 7.5% of its pre-tax earnings through the Ben & Jerry's Foundation, employee Community Action Teams at five Vermont sites, and corporate grants made by the Director of Social

Mission Development. The Ben & Jerry's Foundation was established in 1985 through a company stock donation. The foundation offers competitive grants for not-for-profit organizations throughout the U.S. which facilitate progressive social change by addressing the underlying conditions of societal or environmental problems. The foundation seeks grassroots models that can demonstrate a plan for long-term viability while strengthening and supporting the self-empowerment efforts of those who have traditionally been disenfranchised in society.[5]

Ben & Jerry's continues to be a socially conscious company communicating awareness not only through their foundation, but also through print advertising, inscribing social messages on their pint containers, t-shirts, and promotional materials.

Marketing Strategy

Ben and Jerry set out to make an ice cream that was rich, creamy, smooth, dense, and chewy. That meant a low overrun and lots of butterfat, well above the 10% minimum required by law to be classified as ice cream. Their product was also going to be very heavily flavored, largely as a result of Ben's sinus problems. To compensate for Ben's inability to distinguish subtle flavor variations, they decided to put lots of chunks or add-ins in the ice cream.

Ben and Jerry came to describe their business as being "funky" which to them meant honest, no frills, handmade, homemade superpremium ice cream. In the early years, Ben decided the only way to increase their market penetration was by getting people to taste their product. The pint-sized containers carried the message:[1]

> "This carton contains some of the finest ice cream available anywhere. We know because we're the guys who make it. We start with lots of fresh Vermont cream and the finest flavorings available. We never use any fillers or artificial ingredients of any kind. With our specially modified equipment, we stir less air into the ice cream creating a denser, richer, creamier product of uncompromisingly high quality. It costs more and it's worth it."

They backed this sales pitch with a money-back guarantee intended to give customers the confidence that if they did fork out the money, at least they would be happy with the purchase. Once the customer had tried the product and discovered its unique large-sized chunky add-ins, they would be curious enough to try more than one flavor.

Ben & Jerry's ice cream was hand-filled in the 1980s, uncommon in the industry. They managed to gain competitive advantage by producing a product that was so difficult to make that no one else would put themselves through it. The company spent almost a decade modifying their equipment and production techniques so they could get huge chunks of add-ins such as Oreo cookies, candy bars, and fruit in their ice cream.

Another element of their strategy is their packaging, which delivers a real message to consumers from two guys who actually do exist and are not figments of advertising hype. The handwritten lettering, while originally a cost-saving necessity, inspires visions of honesty and truth. In addition to the packaging, they were creative in naming their flavors — Chunky Monkey, Heavenly Hash, and Cherry Garcia, named after the famous rock star, Jerry Garcia, of the Grateful Dead. This approach provided name recognition and piqued the curiosity of consumers, many of whom had not been drawn to the high-end ice creams.[1]

Ben & Jerry's image and marketing approach were exactly the opposite of everyone else's. The company was funky, unpretentious, down-home, and genuine compared to its more sophisticated competitors such as Haagen Dazs, Fr

üsen Gladje, and Alpen Zauber. Ben & Jerry's ice cream flavors set the company apart from the competition, who was producing straight flavors with traditional combinations and no chunky add-ins. They were able to capitalize on their product differentiation with retailers who were not going to carry more than three superpremium brands. Everyone was going to stock Haagen Dazs, the market leader, so Ben & Jerry's was competing with other industry clones to be second in the store. They successfully created a niche within a niche, methodically entering one large urban market after another based on the assumption that they could take away market share from Haagen Dazs and the clones.

Ben and Jerry were forced to abandon their existing marketing strategy when Richie Smith, creator of Früsen Gladje, acquired Steve's Homemade Ice Cream with plans to launch the product nationally into several markets which Ben & Jerry's had not yet entered. Ben was determined to take advantage of what little lead time they had over Smith and proposed entering a new market every month. Until this time, Ben & Jerry's had been without a sales manager for 6 months. The plan was to get a copy of the Yellow Pages and generate a list of all the grocery stores in each target city, send them a promotional kit outlining the advertising plan, and meet with them 2 weeks later. The plan was successful.

A key to Ben & Jerry's success in entering new markets was securing distribution with Dreyers, a leading premium ice cream manufacturer with its own system who was in the process of introducing its product on the East Coast under the name of Edy's. This allowed Ben & Jerry's to secure distribution in four major markets (Atlanta, Florida, Washington, D.C., and Philadelphia) and numerous smaller cities through the U.S.[1]

Competitors

While there are approximately 78 public and private ice cream manufacturers throughout the U.S., there are only a handful of companies producing the superpremium brands. Superpremium ice cream's main ingredient is cream, and its butterfat content is typically between 16 and 20%. Minimum overrun, the amount of air pumped into the mixture, cannot exceed 50% compared to regular ice cream, which can have an overrun of close to 100%.[6]

Haagen Dazs is the market leader, with a 58.4% market share in 1995, followed by Ben & Jerry's 36%. Other superpremium competitors include Baskin-Robbins, Double Rainbow, Reinhold's, and Carvel which have minimal market share.[7]

Haagen Dazs had already been in the market for almost two decades when Ben & Jerry's opened their first scoop shop. By 1980, Haagen Dazs was available in all but three states and had developed a cult following of well-educated, middle- and upper-income customers who were favorably disposed to a product with a foreign name. The superpremium ice cream market boomed in the 1980s, though, with virtually every ice cream manufacturer trying for a piece of the action. They were Haagen Dazs clones, with foreign names such as Très Chocolat, Perche No, Gelare, and Strasels, who tried to create slick and snobbish marketing images. These clones all but disappeared once the market became sluggish in the early 1990s as consumers became more health conscious.[1]

Haagen Dazs' ingredients are simple: fresh cream, skim milk, egg yolks (used as an emulsifier), and cane sugar. Ben & Jerry's starts with the same main ingredients, adding other natural emulsifiers and stabilizers such as guar gum and lecithin. Both Haagen Dazs and Ben & Jerry's have low overruns at 22% and virtually the same fat content at 19%. There is only a slight price difference: a pint of Haagen Dazs is $2.95, while a pint of Ben & Jerry's is $2.99 in the southeast and over $3.00 in other national markets. Ben & Jerry's began competing with Haagen Dazs in the sorbet market in 1996.

Threat of Substitutes

Substitutes for ice cream are ice milk, water ices, quiescently frozen dairy confections (sherbet), mellorine, frozen custards/yogurts, and tofu.[8] Ice milk contains between 2 and 7% butterfat, making it considerably less creamy and rich than superpremium ice cream. Water ices are a non-dairy substitute that provide the flavor and coolness of ice cream. Sherbet, a quiescently frozen dairy confection product, is made much like water ices except that they contain at least 13% by weight of milk solids. Mellorine is also made like ice cream except that the butterfat is partially or totally replaced with 6% vegetable fat and 3.5% protein. Frozen custards, also called French ice cream, contain 1.4% egg yolk solids with a minimum butterfat content of 10%. Frozen yogurt, a cultured dairy product produced using bacteria cultures such as *Streptococcus thermophilus* and *Lactobacillus bulgaricus*, contains 8.25% non-milk fat solids and 3.2% butterfat.

While these substitutes pose a threat as lower fat and calorie alternatives, the amount of stabilizers and commercial product agents used in the manufacturing process make them less appealing to the palate. While the world has had a love affair with homemade ice cream since the 1920s, the superpremium brand ice cream market has turned sluggish in the last few years as consumer preferences have shifted to these and other less-fat desserts. Wall Street continues to monitor the industry to see if this trend will continue. To remain competitive and keep their market leader positions, Haagen Dazs and Ben & Jerry's have both introduced lower fat products.

Bargaining Power of Buyers and Suppliers

Ben & Jerry's ice cream is sold to gourmet shops, mom-and-pop grocery stores, independent supermarkets, convenience stores, and larger grocery chains. Discounts on initial orders (referred to as "slotting fees" or "introductory allowances") were common in the 1980s when retailers were trying to offset the cost of "slotting" a product on their shelf. Today, introductory allowances are enjoyed mostly by the convenience stores and smaller grocery stores who can only carry one or two brands.

Ben & Jerry's enjoys bargaining power with their Vermont dairies. Sweetheart Paper Company handles their pint containers, and they have agreements with Nabisco for volume discounts on their add-ins such as Oreos and Heath Bars. They have a solid network of large independent distributors in each of their primary markets, such as Dari-Farms in Connecticut and Paul's Distributors of New York.

Global Implications

Ben & Jerry's entered the international market in 1988 with licensed scoop shops in Israel and Canada. They next entered the Republic of Karelia in Russia as part of a Vermont-Karelia sister state delegation. By 1992, they had formed a Russian-American joint venture — "Ben & Jerry's Ice Cream (ICEVERK)" —to make ice cream in Karelia and sell it in two scoop shops there. They entered the United Kingdom in 1994.[5]

In early 1995, under CEO Holland's direction, Ben & Jerry's set up an international department and started to explore the world's promising markets. Their most recent venture has been in France, with entry into other European and Asian markets expected soon.[5]

In keeping with their global social consciousness, Ben & Jerry's tries to buy ingredients for its ice cream that support a philosophy of "caring capitalism". For example, cashews and Brazil nuts are purchased from native forest people in Brazil who now earn three to ten times their previous income, and blueberries are grown by Maine's Passamaquoddy Indians to support economic development among Native Americans.[9]

Ben & Jerry's rival, Haagen Dazs, has a significant presence in over 100 European towns and cities. Haagen Dazs opened its first shop in Tokyo in 1984. Overwhelmed by the immediate success, the company set future development in the Far East as a key priority. By 1993, the number of shops in Japan had reached 100. Haagen Dazs now has shops in Germany, France, Scandinavia, Belgium, Italy, Spain, Greece, Switzerland, and the Netherlands.[5]

Laws and Regulations

Ben & Jerry's first experience with exclusive dealing came in March 1984, when Haagen Dazs threatened to cut off any distributor also carrying Ben & Jerry's. At the time, Haagen Dazs' market share was 70% and almost all the independent distributors in New England sold their ice cream. Ben & Jerry's was effectively barred from the market and sought to regain their rights by bringing a lawsuit against the Pillsbury Corporation, who acquired Haagen Dazs in 1983. In typical anti-establishment fashion, Ben & Jerry launched a media campaign, "What's the Doughboy Afraid Of?" that created brand awareness far in excess of anything they could have generated with paid advertising.[1]

Future Markets

Future trends in the ice cream business include low-calorie fat substitutes, bulking agents such as polydextrose, and cholesterol-free milk proteins. The potential threat of pathogens will continue to have a major impact on dairy operations. The application of hazard analysis and critical control growth (HACCG) will be essential to successful plant management.[8]

The mission of Ben & Jerry's new CEO, Odak, is to jump-start the company and find new customers. Odak believes the new sorbet and non-fat product lines will restore lagging sales as a result of high dairy costs, promotional spending, and the exit of small operators from the market. Ben & Jerry's will begin an aggressive marketing campaign, including product sampling to introduce its product to a wider customer group. It will also continue efforts to establish an international presence previously restrained by the company's founders, who gave weight to a country's social and nuclear policies before committing to enter the market.[7]

Financial

Historically, Ben & Jerry's has experienced phenomenal growth with sales of $19.7 million in 1986 expanding to $167.2 million in 1996. Sales are projected to be $180 million in 1997, despite a sluggish market.[7] Ben & Jerry's net profit margin dropped from a high of 5.1% in 1992 to 2.1%

in 1996. While investors are cautious, anticipating whether Odak will be able to jump-start the company, industry analysts project a net profit margin of 3.1% in 1997 and up to 4.3% by 1999.[7]

References

1. Fred "Chico" Lager, *Ben & Jerry's: The Inside Scoop,* Crown Publishers, New York, 1994.
2. Daniel Kadlec, "Can Ben & Jerry's Cool Its Meltdown?," *USA Today,* September 10, 1996, "Money" section.
3. "Ben & Jerry's Is Losing Chief, in Addition to Market Share," *New York Times,* September 28, 1996, p. C2.
4. "Ben & Jerry's Names Gun Consultant as New CEO," Reuters Release, Yahoo!, *On the Money,* January 2, 1997.
5. Ben & Jerry's Home Page on Internet, http://www.benjerry.com.
6. *Encyclopedia of Consumer Brands.* Vol. I. *Consumable Products,* St. James Press, New York, 1994, pp. 610–611.
7. *Value Line Investment Survey,* 10th ed., Part 3, *Ratings & Reports,* February 14, 1997, p. 1463.
8. Y.H. Hui, *Encyclopedia of Food Science and Technology,* Vol. 3, John Wiley & Sons, New York, 1992, pp. 1441–1447.
9. Jennifer J. Laabs, "Ben & Jerry's: Caring Capitalism," November 1992, http://deming.eng.clemson.edu.

Case 5. American Airlines, Inc.*

As of July 1, 1997, the only thing quiet at American Airlines (AA) has been its stage-three jet engines. The rest of the company has been hopping. In fact, in the 8 weeks since the pilots ratified a new labor agreement, American and its partner, American Eagle, have made more news than some airlines do in a year. "We definitely have momentum on our side," said American president, Donald Carty. "We said when the pilot contract was ratified that we'd be able to focus all our attention on running the best airline in the world, and its amazing how much we've accomplished."[1]

American Airlines is trying to recover from record losses realized in 1990. In the midst of a recession, their task has not been an easy one. Airlines, as an industry, lost more in 1995 than in any other year in their history. Bankruptcy has been widespread. Even the historically sound firms have failed to remain in the air.

AMR Corporation was incorporated in October 1982. American Airlines, Inc., the principal subsidiary, accounts for approximately 94% of its assets and expenses. AMR Corporation has seven other subsidiaries, including SABRE Computer Service Division, AA Decision Technologies, Inc., AMR Investment Services, Inc., AMR Services Corporation, and the SABRE Travel Information Network Division.

---

*   This case was prepared by Dr. M. Reza Vaghefi, assisted by Robin Capitain, for discussion purposes only.

SABRE Computer Services

Many of the other divisions of AMR Corporation receive development and technical support from SABRE Computer Services, an AA division whose more than 2400 professional information technology employees in locations across the world are responsible for telecommunications and computer services throughout the company. At SABRE Computer Services, they provide information technology services and solutions to give their clients a competitive advantage. SABRE Computer Services expertise has developed over 20 years of service for travel and transportation business and includes:

1. Superior ability to manage high-volume, on-line transaction systems
2. Expertise in applying information technology to achieve business results
3. Long-term recognition as a leader in successfully managing business critical applications, as well as computing and networking environments
4. Orderly and timely implementations through exceptional project management skills
5. Proven ability to expertly manage virtually any application, computing, and networking platform and desktop environment

SABRE Computer Services has a system reliability of 99.998% (includes scheduled downtime).[2] On June 18, 1997, The SABRE group announced the release of Planet SABRE in all the markets in the world. The product is now available in more than 65 countries and in six languages: English, Spanish, French, Portuguese, Italian, and German.[3]

SABRE 2000 prepares and tests large-scale computing facilities to prevent project delays if expansion is required beyond the limits of the existing machine. Testing an application portfolio containing millions of lines of code, validating compliance of software from third parties, and accomplishing the appropriate operating system upgrades call for careful planning and substantial resources. SABRE 2000 also performs tests on expanded existing machines that are at risk of contaminating production environments through improper system date manipulation. SABRE 2000 includes dedicated machines of up to 430 MIPS in processing capacity, terabytes of DASD, current operating systems, and transaction and database management software.[4]

AA Decision Technologies

AA's Decision Technologies, which developed American's industry-leading yield management and scheduling systems technology, applies its expertise in operations research, computer science, and industrial engineering to develop automated decision-support tools for airlines and for other corporations.

Major clients include the Federal Aviation Administration (FAA), Airbus Industrie, Federal Express, the French National Railroad, Amtrak, Consolidated Rail, Club Med, Lufthansa, and Britannia Airways. In 1991, AA's Decision Technologies won several awards from the Operations Research Society of America and the Institute of Management Science.

SABRE Decision Technologies (SDT) specializes in partnering with clients to develop solutions to their most complex problems. According to corporate literature, many companies, including those of AA, are in the midst of a struggle to gain a competitive edge. SABRE Decision Technologies works out solutions to its clients' most difficult business challenges, solutions that will give them a competitive advantage.[5]

AMR Investment Services

AMR Investment Services provides investment management and consulting services not only to American Airlines, but also to a growing list of mutual fund and institutional investors. AMR Investment Services, a wholly owned subsidiary of AMR Corporation, is an experienced provider of investment advisory services to institutional and retail markets. In 1991, assets under management grew by 27% to more than $9 billion. As of July 31, 1996, assets under management were approximately $14.2 billion.[6] The American AAdvantage Money Market Fund, Institutional Class, earned the #1 ranking in the country among the institutional money market funds during 1991, as ranked by Lipper Analytical Services and IBC/Donoghue's. In 1991, AMR Investment Services introduced the American AAdvantage International Equity Fund and the

American AAdvantage Money Market Fund, Mileage Class, which allows individuals investing in this fund to accumulate miles in American AAdvantage program.

In 1996, AMR Investments also managed the American AAdvantage Funds, a series of low-cost, no-load mutual funds open to institutional investors, retirement accounts such as IRAs, and individual investors. The American AAdvantage Funds family now includes the American AAdvantage Mileage Funds, PlanAhead Class; American AAdvantage Funds, Institutional Class; and the American AAdvantage Mileage Funds. Each fund family includes three money market funds, a balanced fund, growth and income fund, international equity fund, and short-term bond fund.[6]

AMR Information Services

In the 11 years since it was created, AMR Information Services has become a recognized leader in the field of information technology. They provide innovative approaches to automation through the use and management of data, as well as providing such services as telemarketing, software development, data processing, and reservations to a variety of industries.

One AMR Information Services venture is the implementation of a computer reservation system for hotel and car rental companies. The system has been developed through a partnership involving AMR Information Services, Marriott, Hilton, and Budget Rent-a-Car.

AMR Eagle

AMR Eagle, Inc., a wholly owned subsidiary of AMR Corporation, owns and operates four of the five regional airlines operating under the name "American Eagle", the service mark for the network of regional carriers associated with American. The American Eagle network provides passenger and cargo transportation to over 125 cities (from 143 in 1991) in the U.S., offering more than 1500 flights a day with connections via American's hubs and gateway cities. American Eagle is the world's largest regional airline system, operating throughout the U.S., Canada, the Bahamas, and the Caribbean. American Eagle's four affiliate airlines, all owned by AMR Eagle, Inc., are Executive Airlines, San Juan, Puerto Rico; Flagship Airlines, Nashville, TN; Simmons Airlines, Fort Worth,

TX; and Wings West Airlines, San Luis Obispo, CA.[8] In 1997, system traffic in May was 218.9 million revenue passenger miles on a capacity of 355.6 million available seat miles. The airline boarded 1.04 million passengers in April.[9]

Training of American Eagle employees is second to none. All are thoroughly trained professionals who have graduated from the industry's most intense training programs conducted at the world-class AA/American Eagle facilities. American Eagle's safety-based training program for pilots combines rigorous classroom study, systems training on computer workstations, and flight training on state-of-the-art flight simulators and cabin emergency evacuation trainers. American Eagle is the only regional airline system to make such an investment for every aircraft type they fly.[10]

The same training and investment standards apply to each of American Eagle fight attendants, mechanics, dispatchers, and ramp and customer service personnel to ensure passengers' safety and comfort every step of the way. In December 1995, the FAA issued new regulations establishing a single safety standard for regional and major airlines. American Eagle is a strong supporter of the stricter regulations for the entire regional airline industry. In fact, American Eagle was the first regional airline system to operate all of its aircraft using the same regulations as the major airlines.[10]

AMR Services

AMR Services provides ground services for airline and general aviation customers. When this subsidiary found that domestic growth of its Airline Services division was being hampered by the industry slowdown, it accelerated expansion overseas and is now aggressively pursuing ground handling opportunities around the globe from Eastern Europe to the Pacific.

AMR Combs

Another division, AMR Combs, remains the leader in the general aviation industry, earning recognition as the nation's best fixed-based operator for six consecutive years. It also became the world's largest provider of corporate aircraft charter services in 1991. AA Cargo received the 1995 International Community Award for Service presented by the

North Carolina World Trade Association. The award recognized AA Cargo's efforts to promote international trade to and from North Carolina. In 1995, for the second year in a row, American was named "Best Cargo Airline Servicing the Americas" by the LAX/Westchester Chamber of Commerce at the Los Angeles International Airport.[11]

AMR Distribution Systems

AMR Distribution Systems service offerings include: warehouse and distribution, transportation, freight brokerage and traffic management, and computer and electronics, all value-added services.[12]

SABRE Travel Information Network

SABRE Travel Information Network markets the capabilities of American's SABRE's computerized reservations system to the travel industry. Despite fierce competition in 1991, SABRE Travel Information Network sustained its industry leadership and increased its market share, operating margins, and profits. SABRE is now installed in more than 14,000 locations in the U.S. and provides the nation's travel professionals with the most sophisticated reservations technology available. SABRE Travel Information Network has expanded aggressively into international markets by providing travel agents, airlines, hotels, and other companies in 57 countries on five continents with SABRE automated reservation services:[13]

Americas		Caribbean	
Argentina	El Salvador	Antigua	Grenada
Belize	Guatemala	Aruba	Haiti
Bermuda	Honduras	Barbados	Jamaica
Bolivia	Mexico	Cayman Islands	St. Lucia
Brazil	Nicaragua	Caracas	St. Marten
Canada	Panama	Dominican	Trinidad/
Chile	Paraguay	Republic	Tobago
Columbia	Peru	French West	Turks &
Costa Rica	United States	Indies	Caicos
Ecuador	Venezuela		

Europe		Middle East	Asia
Belgium	Italy	Kuwait	China
Denmark	Netherlands		Hong Kong
England	Norway		India
France	Spain		Japan
Germany	Sweden		
Greece	Switzerland		
Ireland			

In 1996, for the third straight year, SABRE was voted as the world's leading computer reservation system in the World Travel Awards competition. The World Travel Awards are based on surveys of more that 150,000 readers of travel trade magazines published by the Miller-Freeman Group.[11] The SABRE computer reservations system was also named the best business travel system in the United Kingdom in voting by readers of *Business Travel World* magazine in 1995.

easySABRE and Travelocity

SABRE offers two Internet products through SABRE Interactive — easySABRE and Travelocity. easySABRE offers access to airline, car rental, and hotel information in a command-driven (ASCII) interface. The introduction of easySABRE was a result of consumer demand for an Internet version of the classic travel service that has been in operation for more than 10 years. Travelocity is designed for simple point and click navigation at www.travelocity.com. Travelocity lets travelers easily book and ticket travel or browse and plan their next getaway. easySABRE members are automatically members of Travelocity.[14]

SABRE Business Travel Solutions

SABRE Business Travel Solutions (BTS) promises powerful management tools, increased productivity, an open and flexible architecture, and bottom-line results. SABRE Business Travel Solutions is a comprehensive software suite that offers agencies the ability to help their corporate customers strategically manage their travel. SABRE BTS includes fully integrated applications that provide travel booking, travel policy management, expense reporting, and decision-making tools. SABRE

BTS integrates and manages data so travel agencies can help corporate customers analyze travel information.[15]

SABRE CruiseDirector

SABRE CruiseDirector is another Internet service that provides travel agencies with cruise information and reservations. It is an immediate access service provided to participating cruise-line systems for agency-specific fares, schedules, availability, pre/post packages, special services, and group bookings all on a single screen, all within a single format.[15] As of 1996, the following cruise lines could be found on-line at the SABRE CruiseDirector site: Princess Cruises, Carnival Cruise Lines, Windstar Cruises, Norwegian Cruise Line, and the Holland America Line. Lines to be added in 1997 include: Royal Caribbean International, Celebrity Cruises, Crystal Cruises, and Disney Cruise Line.

The Domestic System

Today, American's seven hubs — Dallas/Ft. Worth, Chicago, Miami, San Juan, Raleigh/Durham, Nashville, and San Jose — allow them to serve more markets than any other U.S. carrier. In 1996, for the third time, American won the Top North AA award at the third annual World Travel Awards.[11] In 1995, American was voted Best U.S. Domestic Airline for a record 13 years in a row by readers of *Executive Travel* magazine, one of Britain's leading magazines for frequent corporate travelers. American was runner up in three other areas as well: Best Trans-Atlantic Carrier, Best Carrier to the Caribbean and Central and South America, and Best Frequent Flyer Program.[11]

American Airlines made a major breakthrough at Chicago's O'Hare Airport, where they now occupy over 65% of the slots allocated to commuter operations. These slots have historically been limited to use by turboprop commuter aircraft, but in 1991 the FAA granted American permission to convert 70 of these slots for use by jet aircraft. With fewer than 110 jetliners, they used the converted slots to expand their jet service to small- and medium-sized cities.

The service offered to the more than 25,000 daily connecting passengers traveling through the Dallas/Ft.Worth hub was improved by the opening of the airport TRAAM. This innovative rails system makes it easier and faster for passengers to move between American's two terminals and the airport. The TRAAM is an important part of the $378 million expansion at Dallas/Ft. Worth, the largest of the seven hubs.

Miami, American's newest hub, has been a solid success since it was opened in 1989. Currently, American operates more than 200 flights per day to and from Miami, more service than any other airline has ever provided.

San Juan continues to grow and is the largest hub in the Caribbean, serving 35 destinations in the Caribbean and U.S. Traffic at the smaller hubs — Nashville, Raleigh/Durham, and San Jose — has been hit hard by the past recession. San Jose has been a particular problem because of the fierce pricing competition that characterizes many California markets.

Business JetSolutions and FlexJet

FlexJet is a new business jet ownership program for individuals and companies who need the flexibility and efficiency of a business jet, but who up to now thought the cost was out of reach. FlexJet is the flagship program of Business JetSolutions, a new business that combines the strengths of Bombardier's Learjet and Challenger programs with those of AMR Combs. FlexJet provides a fractional ownership program that allows the flexibility of selecting from a variety of share sizes and aircraft types, including the Learjet 31A, Learjet 60, and Challenger 601-3R.[16]

International Expansion

American Airlines launched a major expansion in 1991, highlighted by the inauguration of service to London's Heathrow Airport. Nonstop flights to Heathrow are offered from six major U.S. cities — New York, Newark, Chicago, Los Angeles, Miami, and Boston.

The Heathrow expansion, the result of American's purchase of Trans World Airline's route authorities, made American one of the largest U.S. carriers to the U.K., with nearly 90 flights a week to London, Manchester, and Glasgow. In 1996, 70,000 readers of the London-based *Caribbean World* magazine voted American as the Best Airline to the Caribbean.[11]

Service is also provided between Chicago and Milan (the first destination in Italy) and between Miami and Madrid. American is currently the largest carrier across the North Atlantic. In 1995, for the fourth year in a row, it was voted "Best Airline Across the North Atlantic" by readers of *Air Cargo News International*.[11]

Service to Japan has expanded with new flights to Tokyo from Seattle and San Jose. American began serving Tokyo from Dallas/Ft. Worth in 1987 and has been aggressively seeking expansion authority to Japan since that time.

Central and South American routes, most of which were acquired from Eastern Airlines in 1990, have been very successful, and AA is now the major airline in that market. More than 200 flights are offered every week to 22 Central and South American destinations, and American is currently expanding the services they offer.

Newer Fleet

American's aircraft fleet is the newest, quietest, and most efficient in the airline industry. The workhorses of American's long-range operations are its McDonnell-Douglas DC-10s and Boeing B767s. American has long believed that excessive use of paint detracts from the operating characteristics of the aircraft. Decals, rather than paint, are used for logos on many of their jets. The technologically advanced MD-11 recently went into service on American's long-range Pacific routes, and AMR Eagle took delivery of 79 new turboprop aircraft, which was the largest delivery of new planes ever accepted in one year by any carrier. American's newest jets incorporate the latest in computerized instrumentation systems.

Almost 75% of American's fleet are stage-three aircraft, a technical designation that simply means they meet the most stringent noise standards published by the FAA. Only about one half of the combined fleets of the other major U.S. airlines meets these standards. In 1995, 90% of the aircraft met the stage-three requirements. Thus, compliance with the federal law that mandates a phase-out of all non-stage-three aircraft by the year 1999 will result in less of a hardship on American Airlines than on its competitors. In fact, American's foresight in fleet planning should pay dividends for years to come.

From an operating standpoint, newer aircraft are much more efficient than older ones because they require less maintenance and are flown by a cockpit crew of two rather that three. These factors, together with the savings in fuel expenditures, will help American control its costs for years to come.

On June 10, 1997, in Fort Worth, TX, American Airlines ordered seven Boeing 777-200IGW (increased growth weight) aircraft, to be delivered in early 1999 and 2000, in addition to purchasing the rights for additional 777s in late 1999, 2000, and 2001. The 777 order builds on the long-term relationship with Boeing that was announced in November 1996, when American agreed to buy aircraft exclusively from Boeing in exchange for highly competitive prices and terms. American has not yet selected an engine manufacturer for the 777.[17]

Environmental Matters

Environmental awareness and responsibility have long been an integral part of the corporate culture at AMR, dating all the way back to the early 1930s when AA decided to fly its aircraft with polished, unpainted fuselages. Today, AMR's environmental program is as broad and wide-ranging as the corporation itself. AMR is committed to developing and implementing business practices that help safeguard the Earth's environment. A few of AMR's efforts include noise abatement, working with the Environmental Protection Agency, recycling, and effective maintenance.

Noise Abatement

The Secretary of Transportation and the Federal Aviation Administration started an Aviation Noise Abatement Policy in November 1976 and adopted regulations with respect to aircraft noise effective January 1, 1997. During 1990, regulations were issued by the Federal Aviation Administration which required the phased reduction in the number of stage-two aircraft. The use of any stage-two aircraft will be prohibited after 1999. American believes that because of its current fleet plan it will be in compliance with these regulations at all times. As the industry leader in stage-three aircraft, American is years ahead of the government mandate that 75% of an airline's fleet be stage-three by the end of 1998.[18]

The Aviation Noise Abatement Policy also recognizes the right for airport operators with special noise problems to implement local noise abatement programs as long as they do not interfere unreasonably with interstate or foreign commerce or the national air transportation system. Authorities in several cities have begun noise abatement programs, including the imposition of nighttime curfews. The Federal Aviation Administration itself imposed noise and capacity limits at Washington National Airport when it was the proprietor of this airport. These noise and capacity limits have been continued by the current owner. Other airport operators may attempt to impose additional noise reduction or capacity limitation requirements, and American cannot predict the nature of future requirements that may be imposed or the extent to which the Federal Aviation Administration or the courts will allow such requirements to be enforced. Although American has the highest percentage of stage-three aircraft (88.9%) and has the quietest and most fuel-efficient fleet[18] among the major U.S. carriers, adoption of noise regulations more stringent than federal requirements could adversely affect American.

Environment Protection Agency

Under the Clean Air Act, the Environmental Protection Agency (EPA) was authorized to issue regulations setting standards for aircraft emissions, and the Secretary of Transportation was charged with the responsibility of enforcing those standards. The Clean Air Act provides that state and local governments cannot adopt or enforce aircraft or emission standards unless those standards are identical to the federal standards. The engines on American's aircraft meet the turbine engine emission standards issued by the EPA.

American Airlines has been identified by the EPA as a potentially responsible party with respect to the Hardage disposal site, Criner, OK; Operating Industries, Inc., site in Monterey Park, CA; and Sand Springs site in San Springs, OK. All three sites have been identified by the EPA as Superfund Sites. At the Hardage disposal site, the EPA has brought suit against certain members of the potentially responsible party in order to recover expenditures associated with the remedial activities at the site. American has not been named as a party in that proceeding, but was named by the EPA as a small or *de minimis* party eligible to participate in a consent decree sponsored by the government. American participated in the government-sponsored consent decree for *de minimis* parties. American's participation protects it from any "re-openers" except for toxic torts and natural resource damage; however, there is no evidence of either of these contingencies at this site and therefore any future remediation should have no impact on American.

American is a member of the Operating Industries Steering Committee, an organization of potentially responsible parties whose primary purpose is to negotiate with the EPA regarding remedial activities at the site. In regard to the Operating Industries site, the EPA has brought suit against a number of potentially responsible parties, including American, and has simultaneously filed a partial consent decree which American has signed along with all the other potentially responsible party defendants and which has been entered by the court. The Steering Committee has successfully negotiated with the EPA as to the remedy for the portion of the site not covered by previous decrees. American has signed this decree, and it has been entered with the court. American will shortly make its final payment under the terms of the decree for its alleged contributions to this site. American's monetary contributions to the Operating Industries Steering Committee have been limited. Because of the limited nature of American's alleged volumetric contribution to the site, it is not believed that this proceeding will have substantial adverse effect upon American.

In regard to the Sand Springs site, American is a member of the Sand Springs Superfund Potentially Responsible Party Group Steering Committee, an organization of potentially responsible parties whose primary purpose is to negotiate with the EPA regarding remedial activities at this site. Atlantic Richfield Company has negotiated a comprehensive remedial agreement with the EPA without the involvement of the other potentially responsible parties or the Steering Committee. Atlantic Richfield had filed suit against all other potentially responsible parties, including American, to seek contributions toward the remedy. Because of American's limited alleged volumetric contribution to the site (approximately .97%), it is not believed this proceeding will have a significant adverse financial effect on American. American's monetary contributions to the Sand Springs Steering Committee have been limited.

Recycling

The in-flight recycling program was started at San Jose International Airport in 1989 by American's flight attendants. The program recycles more than 330 pounds of aluminum annually.[18] AMR began an "Anything that Tears" recycling program at its Ft. Worth, TX, headquarters facility, and 41 tons of magazines, newspapers, colored paper, and cardboard are recycled annually.[18] In addition, 701 tons of white paper and 15,295 pounds of aluminum cans are also recycled.[18] In addition to the recycling programs, the Chemical Product Control Program, initiated in 1994, has reduced the number of different types of chemicals at American from 15,000 to 2000.[18]

Maintenance

American's Tulsa maintenance base will invest more than $20 million by the end of 1997 in environmental systems and clean-up programs.[18] American's Ft. Worth Alliance Maintenance base features a sophisticated $14.3 million wastewater treatment plant. Another $5 million in environmental protection features were built into the facility in 1997.[18]

Employees

In 1983, American Airlines, headed by CEO Robert Crandall, decided to cut costs in an effort to gain market share. To do this, Crandall implemented a new pay level called the "B-scale". This cut in pay from the existing "A-scale" was accepted by the pilots as a method of securing much higher salaries in the future.

In 1990, American had purchased new planes and gotten new routes but had not yet given pilots their long-term pay increases. This caused an uproar in the Allied Pilots Association, a labor group that represents various employees at AA[19] and is the exclusive union for AA pilots. Talks between the union and American ensued, and, because no agreements could be reached, these talks evolved into rumors of a strike.

As politics would have it, Crandall tried to turn the Air Line Pilots Association (ALPA), the union for all airline pilots, against AA pilots. He said that they were calling in sick and being inefficient in an attempt to cost American money. (This was their bargaining chip.) Crandall also blamed the cancellations of numerous routes in January of 1991 on pilots. What he failed to mention, however, was that American cuts back routes in January every year to reflect the seasonally of the airline industry.

In the current agreement, American pilots can reach parity with the A-scale after 3 years. The APA has proposed that the years be cut down to 1 to 2 years. Although Crandall accepted this part of the negotiations, he and the APA could not agree on health benefits for active members and retirees. In January of 1991, a federal arbitrator stepped in to decide upon a plan and make a binding decision that both parties would have to live by. This type of binding arbitration is quite rare and exemplifies the way negotiations had been going. Since that time, though, American and its employees have settled their contracts; however, these contracts come up for review periodically.

AA currently employs over 97,000 people. Approximately 58.2% of these employees are represented by unions and covered by collective bargaining agreements. The airline business is labor intensive. American's wages, expenses, salaries, and benefits represented 33% of its total operating expenses in 1991. More recent information regarding operating expenses was unavailable.

Negotiations with the Association of Professional Flight Attendants resulted in an agreement in December 1987 that produced increased compensation for current flight attendants, continuation of current market rate pay scale for recently hired flight attendants, and changes to certain work rules designed to increase flight attendant productivity. American's collective bargaining agreement with its flight attendants became amenable on December 31, 1992.

In 1989, American negotiated new agreements with the Transportation Workers Union. The Transportation Workers Union agreements provided for market rate pay for current employees, flexible hiring rates of pay to reflect geographic differences in market rates, a flexible healthcare benefits program, and employee prefunding for critical fields. The collective bargaining agreements with the Transportation Workers Union employees, including maintenance, flight instructors, guards, dispatchers, assistants, and stores, was amended on March 1, 1995.

American's collective bargaining agreements with its pilots and flight engineers was amended in December 31, 1989. An agreement on new contracts was reached in February 1991, with the provision that certain outstanding items would be resolved in November 1991. American's collective bargaining agreement with its pilots and flight engineers became amended on August 31, 1994.

On June 16, 1997, AA announced that it planned to hire and begin training approximately 360 new flight attendants in 1997. AA expects to continue hiring flight attendants in 1998 and 1999. This marks the first time since early 1996 that American has hired flight attendants.[20] In the 2 weeks after announcing the openings, American received some 20,000 inquires.[21]

Employee Involvement

American actively recruits people over the age of 40 for flight attendant positions, rebutting conventional thinking that only younger people need apply. In fact, approximately 300 flight attendants over the age of 40 completed training in 1996. An important element of AMR Corporation's business philosophy is to encourage teamwork and communication among employees at all levels. Ideas generated by American employees in 1991 resulted in a savings of $58 million, which was more than enough to pay for a new Boeing B757 which employees aptly named "Pride of American". Improved de-icing procedures were the result of "breakthrough thinking", a concept designed to encourage employees to consider new ways to handle problems.

Leadership

"Committing to Leadership", a program dedicated to enhancing the leadership and communication skills of American's management team, was launched in 1989 and continues as the focal point of AMR's management philosophy. Committed to Leadership has expanded further within the ranks of the company, as almost 2000 more managers, supervisors crew chiefs, premium flight attendants, skycap captains, and Admiral's Club skippers have been trained in the leadership techniques intended to help generate more intensive employee involvement through coaching, counseling, and motivating. The leadership sought will be attained by:[2]

1. Setting the industry standards for safety and security
2. Providing world-class customer service
3. Creating an open and participative work environment which seeks positive change, rewards innovation, and provides growth, security, and opportunity to all employees
4. Producing consistently superior financial returns for shareholders

Safety

In 1995, the FAA presented a joint safety award to American and the Allied Pilots Association for their cooperative Airline Safety Action

Program, or ASAP.[11] As mentioned previously, in December 1995, the Federal Aviation Administration issued new regulations establishing a single safety standard for regional and major airlines. American Eagle, a strong supporter of the stricter regulations for the entire regional airline industry, was the first regional airline system to operate all of their aircraft using the same regulations as the major airlines. American says they have made safety their first priority.[22]

In May of 1991, Federal Aviation Administration Administrator, James Busey, wrote Chairman Crandall: "We feel an obligation not only to oversee and evaluate, but to compliment organizations which measure up well to world class safety standards. Yours has done that, and we appreciate your effort." Admiral Busey's letter was reprinted in the Congressional Record with favorable references to American's safety program.

Full motion simulators at American's Flight Academy are used to train pilots monthly to respond to unanticipated flight conditions. A sophisticated weather tracking system, monitored around the clock by a staff of 20 meteorologists, provides timely data to pilots around the world.

Engines are meticulously inspected, repaired, and overhauled at American's principle maintenance base in Tulsa, OK. The hanger at American's new Alliance Maintenance Base is more than a quarter mile long and can accommodate seven widebody jets, wingtip to wingtip, under one roof. Each of American's more than 600 aircraft undergo 11 man-hours of maintenance for every hour of flight. The maintenance program includes a daily check of every plane, a more detailed inspection every 3 days, a comprehensive field check every 6 days, and a detailed hanger check every 40 days; every 12 months, a base check is performed, during which the aircraft is literally taken apart, inspected, and re-assembled.

As of July 1, 1997, AA had equipped 247 of its aircraft with automatic external defibrillators (AEDs) to help treat sudden cardiac arrest and other heart problems, becoming the first U.S. airline to do so. American put the defibrillators on all of its aircraft that fly over water. The American Heart Association has estimated that 100,000 lives could be saved if AEDs were broadly deployed in areas where large groups of people gather, such as on aircraft. Although physicians or other medical personnel may be on board flights and can step forward to assist a passenger, flight attendants are already trained to be the first responder to an on-board medical emergency.[23]

Fuel Costs

American's reported fuel costs in 1996 were relatively the same as they were in 1991. Costs decreased by approximately 6.3%, primarily due to an 11% decrease in the average price per gallon of fuel. This decrease was partially offset by a 5.4% increase in consumption. Most of American's fuel is purchased under contracts that may be terminated upon short notice. While there is no reason to anticipate a significant reduction in fuel availability in the near future, the airline industry's dependency upon foreign imports of crude oil and the possibility of changes in government policy on jet fuel production, transportation, and marketing make it impossible to predict the future availability of jet fuel. If there were major reductions in the availability of jet fuel, American's business would be adversely affected.

AA customers may not have occasion to appreciate the fact that the aircraft in which they are riding are, on average, more fuel efficient than those of their competitors. This fuel efficiency, partially attributable to cleaner-burning engines that not only consume less fuel but reduce harmful emissions, is both economically and environmentally important. American has made an investment of more than $20 million to remove or upgrade underground storage tanks. The effort involves 150 tanks in 18 cities and was 95% complete in 1997.[18]

Marketing

American established its AAdvantage frequent flyer program to develop passenger loyalty by offering awards to travelers for their continued patronage. This program allows members to earn mileage credits for flights on American, American Eagle, certain flights on participating airlines, or by utilizing services of other program participants such as hotels, car rental firms, or bank credit card issuers. For example, American's AAdvantage program offers several ways for members to earn miles: by buying or leasing a new or used vehicle from one of hundreds of dealers participating in the AAdvantage Auto and Recreational Program, by staying at Best Western Hotels or New Otani Hotels, or by eating at AAdvantage dining participant restaurants in five cities: Salt Lake City, Cincinnati, Minneapolis/St. Paul, Grand Rapids, and Memphis.[23] In addition, American periodically offers special short-term promotions which allow members to earn additional free travel awards or mileage credits. American reserves the right to change the program rules, regulations, travel awards, and special offers at any time. This means that American may initiate changes impacting, for example, rules for participating affiliates as far as mileage credit, mileage levels and awards, blackout dates, and limited seating for travel awards. American also reserves the right to end this program with 6 months' notice.

Mileage credits can be redeemed for free, discounted, or upgraded travel on American, American Eagle, or participating airlines or for other travel industry and non-travel merchandise awards. Once a member accrues sufficient mileage for an award, the member may request an award certificate from American. Award certificates are subject to blackout dates and capacity-controlled seating. All miles earned after July 1989 must be redeemed within 3 years or they expire.

The number of travel awards used for travel on American for 1989, 1990, and 1991 were, respectively, approximately 920,000, 975,000, and 1,237,000. These awards represented approximately 4.8% of the total revenue passenger miles for each period. This displacement of revenue passenger miles is insignificant given American's load factors, its ability to manage frequent flyer seat inventory, and the relatively low ratio of free award usage to revenue passenger miles.

Summing Up

AA wants to maintain control, reduce costs, and continue to value add for the stakeholders. American is a moving target in the airline industry. "It's been exhilarating around this company the past couple of months," American's president Carty said, "and we don't plan to slow down. Our goal is to be tops in every conceivable category, and we won't rest until we get there."[23] AA faces increased government regulation, law suits, and employee contract renewal disputes in the future. The Environment Protection Agency continues to monitor noise and emission effects on society and continues to increase its restrictions. Most importantly, without economic recovery, American will fail to see an increase in passenger revenue, which is vital to their survival. As of 1997, their motto is "Full Speed Ahead at American Airlines."[23]

References

1. url://http://www.amrcorp.com/amr/Jul0197c (July 1, 1997).
2. url://http://www.amrcorp.com/amr/at_a_glance.html (June 9, 1997).
3. url://http://www.amrcorp.com/amr/June1897a.html (June 30, 1997).
4. url://http://www.sabre.com/scs/year2000.html (1997).
5. url://http://www.sabre.com/sdt/sat_home.html (June 19, 1997).
6. url://http://www.amrcorp.com:80/amr/mgmt/invest_ser.html (June 9, 1997).
7. url://http://www.amrcorp.com/amr/Jul0197c (July 1, 1997).
8. url://http://www.amrcorp.com/amr/May1997a.html (June 6, 1997).
9. url://http://www.amrcorp.com/amr/June0997a.html (June 9, 1997).
10. url://http://www.americanair.com:80/aa_home/eagle/train_sa.html (June 9, 1997).
11. url://http://www.amrcorp.com/amr/recog.html (June 9, 1997).
12. url://http://www.amercorp.com:80/amr_mgmt/amr_dist/service/offer.html (June 9, 1997).
13. url://http://www.amrcorp.com/amr/global.html (June 9, 1997).
14. url://http://www.easysabre.com/.html (June 9, 1997).
15. url://http://www.travel.sabre.com/btss/index.html (June 19, 1997).
16. url://http://www.amrcorp.com:80/amr_mgmt/bus_jet_sol.html (June 9, 1997).
17. url://http://www.amrcorp.com/amr/June1097b.html (June 30, 1997).
18. url://http://www.amrcorp.com/amr/environ.html (June 9, 1997).
19. url://http://www.amrcorp.com/amr/labor.html (June 19, 1997).
20. url://http://www.amrcorp.com/amr/June1697a.html (July 1, 1997).
21. url://http://www.amrcorp.com/amr/Jul0197c (July 1, 1997).
22. url://http://www.americanair.com:80/aa_home/aeagle/train_sa.html (June 9, 1997).
23. url://http://www.amrcorp.com/amr/Jul0197c (July 1, 1997).

AMR Corporation Consolidated Statement of Operations

	1996	1995
Operating revenues	8858	8277
Operating expenses	7871	7543
Operating income	987	734
Other income (expense)	(242)	(342)
Earnings before income taxes and extraordinary loss	745	392
Income tax provision	295	164
Earnings before extraordinary loss	450	228
Extraordinary loss, net of tax benefit	—	(13)
Net earnings	450	215

Note: Figures are expressed in millions and are unaudited.

Consolidated Highlights

	1991	1990	% Change	1993	1992	% Change	1995	1994	% change
Operating revenues	12,887	11,720	+10.0	15,816	14,396	9.9	16,910	16,131	4.8
Operating expenses	12,882	11,596	+11.1	15,126	14,421	4.9	15,895	15,131	5.0
Operating income	5	124	−96.0	690	(25)	a	1015	1006	0.9
Operating margin (%)	0	1.1	−1.1[b]	4.4	(0.2)	4.6	6.0	6.2	−0.2[b]
Earnings (loss) before extraordinary loss	(3.54)	(0.64)	a	(96)	(475)	(79.8)	196	228	(14.0)
Net earnings (loss)	(240.00)	(40.00)	a	(110)	(935)	(88.2)	167	228	(26.8)
Return on equity (%)	(6.40)	(1.00)	−5.4[b]	(3.4)	(26.2)	+1[b]	5.5[c]	5.3[c]	+0.2[b]
Ratio of current assets to current liabilities	0.59	0.55	+7.3	0.61	0.61	—			
Average equivalent no. of employees	102,400	92,900	+10.2	111,100	107,500	3.3	110,000	109,800	0.2
Approx. no. common shareholders of record at year end	19,600	20,500	−4.4	18,000	18,800	−4.3	16,200	17,200	(5.8)

[a] Greater than 100%.
[b] Points.
[c] Before extraordinary loss.

Note: Figures are expressed in millions of dollars, except per share amounts.

Case 6. The U.S. Automobile Industry: Will It Compete in the Future?*

Introduction

A banner year is expected in 1994 for the big three, General Motors (GM), Ford, and Chrysler. They forecast $15 billion profit in the current year and are optimistic for at least the next 2 years.[1] Having laid off over 100,000 employees in recent years and by employing new marketing strategies, they are poised to sustain the rivalry with the Japanese, at least for the near future. The automobile industry is such a massive sector that it has a major impact on the U.S. economy. The same holds true, more or less, for the economies of other countries. Global sales of cars are expected to reach 35.3 million in 1994 and 42.6 million by 1999.[30]

In recent years, one in every seven jobs in the U.S. was somehow related to the automobile. In 1987, U.S.-owned automobile manufacturers employed 711,000 people and paid $22.8 billion in wages. In addition, another 40,000 people were employed by transplants (mostly Japanese) which paid an additional $1.1 billion in wages. By 1991,

---

* Written by Dr. M. Reza Vaghefi and assisted by Brian L. Eddy.

domestic employment by automobile manufacturers was up to 776,000 workers. This translates to approximately 4.2% of total manufacturing employment in the U.S. In 1991, sales of new cars and light trucks to all consumers were $189 billion, or 3.3% of the gross domestic product (GDP). That same year, personal consumption of motor vehicles and related automotive equipment was $185 billion, or 4.4% of disposable personal income.[2] When automobile manufacturing jobs of the Big Three manufacturers (Ford, General Motors, and Chrysler) and their related parts suppliers are combined, total employment adds up to 1.4 million U.S. jobs. In relation to vehicle sales, 15,000 American jobs are supported for every 100,000 vehicles produced in the U.S.[3]

During the previous 10 years, the U.S. automobile industry had been buffeted by increasing competition and a deep recession which finally was showing signs of easing. During this time period, many of the automobile manufacturers had resorted to massive downsizing and restructuring of their manufacturing processes. These efforts, along with reduced sales, brought on by the recession and some required accounting policy changes, led the industry to record losses in 1991 of more than $7 billion.[4]

This chapter will try to analyze the automobile industry in the U.S., primarily using data related to the three largest manufacturers, also known as The Big Three. The Big Three sell automobiles, light trucks, and other utility vehicles to the American public and to foreign consumers around the world. From this point on, the term "automobiles" will include cars, light trucks, and sport utility vehicles. The individual categories will be specifically mentioned from time to time and will be addressed as such. Ford and GM also produce a variety of heavy vehicles and other industrial equipment, which will not be discussed in detail. Because The Big Three operate on a global scale, emphasis will be placed on how these U.S. industries compete and operate in a national, regional, and global environment.

Product Lines

Product lines in the automotive industry vary widely. The Big Three manufacturers produce cars which range from subcompacts priced at less than $8000 to large luxury vehicles priced in excess of $40,000. These cars can be arranged in classes which are as follows: subcompact,

compact, mid-size, full-size, and luxury. In addition to these classes, light pickup trucks and sport utility vehicles have become popular with modern consumers and therefore need to be included in the classification. All have various models that fit within these classes of vehicles, and all models come equipped with various standard and extra option packages used to differentiate the products from other products in that class and between classes. In addition to regular consumer automobiles, The Big Three also manufacture large trucks for over-the-highway use such as semi-tractor trailer units, large recreational vehicles such as campers, and large industrial machinery such as dump trucks, mining vehicles, and earth-hauling vehicles.

A secondary product related to the automobile industry is the parts. The Big Three maintain parts warehouses used to supply inventories at sales outlets, primarily independent dealerships and automobile manufacturing facilities throughout the world. The majority of these original equipment manufacturers' (OEM) parts are produced by independent suppliers and are manufactured to specifications set by the automobile manufacturers. These parts are used in production of new automobiles and for use in the secondary market as replacement parts.

Research and Development

Research and development (R&D) plays a large part in the success of the automobile industry. The Big Three automobile manufacturers employ approximately one of every 15 engineers and scientists working the U.S. Total expenditures for R&D by the Big Three represent more than 12% of the corporate research and development in the U.S.[3]

Industry sales hinge on new model introduction and improvements in existing models to keep the consuming public interested in buying new automobiles. In addition to model changes, R&D is constantly concerned with environmental improvement in automotive emissions and development of more fuel-efficient engines to power the various models. Research and development in recent years has led to the streamlining of most automobiles to improve aerodynamics. No longer are cars square and chunky looking. Lines are smooth to reduce wind noise and to decrease air resistance, which improves fuel efficiency. R&D also is ongoing in the area of safety. Every manufacturer does extensive crash testing to test new models for passenger safety. R&D led to the development of the air bag passive restraint system, which has saved many lives since its implementation. Chrysler is even researching a side-impact system using this technology to improve passenger safety in crashes other than head-on ones.[5] R&D is constantly improving the anti-rust features of automobiles and the exterior and interior coatings (paint primarily) that protect the automobile from the elements.

R&D plays an important role in the introduction of new models. In the past, new models have taken anywhere from 7 to 10 years to go from the beginning design stages to the production line. In the recent past, the design to production cycle has moved closer to the 4-year plan used by Japanese manufacturers. There has been some discussion within the Big Three about extending this aggressive policy back to a maximum of 5 or 6 years in order to slow the frequency at which new models are brought to market and changes made in existing models;[5] however, a lot depends on the behavior of Japanese manufacturers.

R&D in the past few years has led the Big Three to form several consortia to research projects jointly that may involve higher costs than the individual firms could afford.[6] These joint R&D projects are limited by the National Cooperative Research Act of 1984 to developing generic, fundamental technologies to bring automobiles to the market faster and at less cost to consumers. By law, joint R&D cannot pursue the design and production of specific vehicles.[7] Some of this joint research has been in the area of developing technology needed for electric vehicle manufacturing. The California Clean Air Act has mandated that starting with model year 1998, a specified percentage of vehicles will have to be "zero emission vehicles".[7] This is forcing the U.S. auto industry to develop new technology in order to meet these strict guidelines. Technology already exists that meets the rules, but the cost of production is too high for consumers to purchase electric automobiles at the present time. Also, current technology will only allow travel of a short distance before recharging must occur.

Marketing Strategy

For years, the automobile industry in the U.S. had only one marketing strategy: *If you make them the public will buy them.* This mentality is a carryover from the early days when automobiles were just starting to become part of everyday American life. Henry Ford was once quoted as saying "give the public any color automobile they want ... just as long as it is black." This concept prevailed until William Durant began purchasing many of the smaller automobile manufacturing companies and related parts manufacturers, starting what is now known as General Motors. The true breakthrough in marketing came when Alfred Sloan became CEO of GM. Sloan's idea of automobile marketing was to make the car a status symbol. He also was determined to make a car for every person no matter their status in life.[8] In designing automobiles, GM led the industry in styling. One of the major strategies used to boost customer demand was to change the style every year or two, which caused the public to want the newest model. Quality was very low, according to Tom and Ray Molitisie, hosts of a radio talk show named *Car Talk*.[8] Automobiles were updated based on new styles, and little attention was paid to what the public really wanted. While GM led the industry in styling, the other manufacturers were forced to follow this same strategy to keep pace with U.S. demand for model and styling changes. The public was rarely polled to find out what was important to them, and most decisions were made in the corporate offices located far from the reach of the ordinary buyer. The failure of the Ford Edsel is a classic example of corporate decision-making without consulting the consumer. This model failed miserably due to poor styling in the consumer's opinion. The public claimed the car looked as though it had just bit into a lemon.

In many ways, things have not yet changed as much as they need to. Chevrolet introduced the newly redesigned Caprice a few years ago, and the design was a flop. Had it not been for advance demand for the vehicle from police departments and fleet managers of municipalities, the Caprice would have been a total disaster for GM. One GM worker expressed his thoughts about the cars: "How can they [GM] expect to sell a car that is just plain ugly?"[8]

The general tendency to plan car design without consulting the public led all the major manufacturers to be more concerned about coming up with a new style than meeting customer demands. One of the first manufacturers to recognize the need to meet customer demand was Nash (later American Motors), which came out with a station wagon called the Rambler. This was a hit with the homemaker because she had room to haul the kids around, room to load groceries, and room to put everyday necessities. Nash even took the shift lever off the steering column for automatic transmission models and put push buttons on the dash to replace the awkward lever. (This proved to be very unpopular, even through it was practical. To this day, the Rambler is the only model ever to have tried this approach. American buyers just would not buy a car without a shift lever.)

Even though one company had some success, the major players continued to build cars without consumer input. As the American public became less and less satisfied with available models, a new player entered the market: Volkswagen with the Beetle. Thus far ignored by the Big Three, the small car market was wide open in the U.S. The American consumer was tired of having to buy a car every 3 or 4 years because the old one had become too expensive to maintain. The consumer was also tired of the cost of buying gasoline, the price of which had started to rise by the early 1970s. The Beetle was a hit with the American public, and millions were sold before the Big Three could mount any competition. When GM finally did get a small, economical car on the road, it was a disaster. The Corvair was deemed unsafe at any speed by Ralph Nader, a consumer safety advocate. The car was poorly designed, had shoddy workmanship, and was dangerous to drive. Ford's attempt was not much better with the Pinto. This car had serious design flaws which included a fuel tank that would explode upon rear impact.

About that time, the Japanese started exporting automobiles that had both quality and fuel economy. Market share was soon being lost to the Japanese at an alarming rate. It was not until the mid-1980s that the U.S. automobile industry finally woke up and decided to improve quality, design, and fuel economy to meet the consumer's needs. Ford was one of the first to provide a truly reliable automobile that had fuel efficiency and quality design. The Taurus was so well liked by the buying public that it propelled the car to number one in industry sales in 1992, replacing the Honda Accord as number one, according to J.D. Powers Associates.

Today, the emphasis is on quality production.[9] Stiff competition from the Japanese has caused the Big Three automakers to design and build cars that meet the buying public's desires. Manufacturers are highly conscious that market share is very important to success in the industry.[10] The Big Three have finally come back to the basic business principal: "The business really does start and end with the customer."[3] Customer focus has gained the spotlight in the automobile industry.

Marketing for the 1990s will be tougher than ever before. The price of new cars is taking an even larger portion of the buyer's disposable income.[11] One way the auto industry is coping with the high price of purchasing a new automobile is through leasing options. It is now possible to lease a car for a 3-year period for far less in monthly payments (about $300 on average) than by purchasing the same automobile. This is accomplished by setting very high residual values on the automobile at the end of the lease period and by requiring a sizable down payment. In addition to these requirements, a mileage fee is required for mileage in excess of the maximum set by the lease. In 1991, the percentage of new cars leased was 14% compared with 3% in 1982.[7] The lease aspect could also cause future car sales to diminish drastically as the lease cars are returned. The flood of cars being returned will cause the price of used autos to decline significantly, which will in turn allow buyers to purchase good, high-quality, used cars for prices far lower than new automobiles will cost. The financial arms of the automotive industry that initiated these leases with high residual values could find that used car prices will not support the high residual value and could be faced with huge losses in disposing of the inventory.[11] This is why, "within weeks of taking over GM, Smith cut fleet sales from 800,000 annually to 400,000 and saved $400 million."[12] A similar instance occurred in the 1980s when the automotive industry was pushing new car sales to the rental industry. The manufacturers promised to rebuy lease cars (called program cars) back from the rental companies after 3 months' use. When these program cars were released to dealers, the price of used cars declined drastically. Auto credit divisions of several banks were unable to survive the impact of losses incurred from having to sell stock at less than the residual value.[11]

Industry forecasts are also being taken into consideration by the marketing departments. Forecasts predict that U.S. automobile sales will peak in 1995 at approximately 14.5 million. This will fall short of the 1986 high of 16 million.[13] Auto sales will then fall back to about the 13 million level, which has been the rule for the early 1990s. Industry leaders feel that pent-up demand that exists as a result of the recession will be unleashed and consumers will initiate a buying frenzy.[14] As consumer confidence increases, this demand could cause auto sales to climb significantly in 1994 and 1995.[15] A secondary result of the recession was that the average age of the automobile on the highway had been increasing as owners held onto their automobiles and chose to maintain them rather than purchase new ones. The average automobile in the U.S. was around 7 years old in 1992. An estimated 37% of the cars on the road in 1992 were over 10 years old,[10] three times as many as in 1970.[11] Owners of these automobiles will also be looking to upgrade in the next few years as the economy begins to recover and consumer confidence increases.

Demographics are also affecting how the industry will market their product in the 1990s. Baby boomers are now in their forties and fifties and have adequate spending power to purchase new automobiles.[16] These older consumers are more likely to purchase larger and safer automobiles than are their younger counterparts. They are also less likely to be influenced by fuel efficiency as long as gasoline prices remain fairly inexpensive.[17] Many of the buyers in this older population are also moving toward light trucks and sport utility vehicles as a first or second family automobile. This classification includes the popular minivan market which has been dominated by Chrysler. The ownership of sport utility vehicles has become trendy, and many vehicles in this class have become quite luxurious in recent years, including Ford's Explorer, GM's Blazer, and Jeep's CJ-5. Some analysts see this segment as the fastest growing in the market in the next 5 years.[16,17]

International marketing will become more important as the U.S. market starts to decline in the late 1990s. The U.S. market is only expected to support a 1% growth rate over the remaining part of the decade. Europe's growth rate is expected to be slightly better at 1.5%. The fastest growing markets appear to be shaping up in Mexico, South America, Southeast Asia, and the Pacific Rim. Asia is expected to grow at least 3.3% annually, and Mexico and South America are expecting growth in the automotive area of 6.4%.[13] The Latin American market looks especially good since NAFTA has been accepted, and the border between the U.S. and Mexico is beginning to present no barrier. Car sales in Mexico are expected to increase at a tremendous rate of 15% from 1993 to 1995. The economy of Mexico will also begin to recover as more industries locate south of the border to get closer to cheaper labor. The increasing currency available will fuel more spending, some of which is sure to end at the local automobile dealerships.[6,18]

One of the biggest obstacles to marketing in the U.S. market will be to overcome the brand loyalty and fascination Americans have for Japanese automobiles.[14] Quality in manufacturing and increases in efficiency have helped the U.S. automotive industry to regain a competitive stance. Nearly all industry surveys now rank some U.S.-built automobiles in the upper listings. Ford's Taurus has won high praise nearly every year since 1988. Efficient manufacturing has also led to lower increases in automobile prices. GM is expecting to increase prices only 1.8% in 1994. The other manufacturers are expected to follow suit.[3] Also working in favor of the U.S. manufacturers is the strong position of the yen in the international currency markets. As the yen rises against the dollar, cars imported from Japan cost more in American dollars. As a result, the U.S. manufacturers have been regaining lost market share.[14]

Competitive Position of U.S. Automobile Manufacturers

Strengths

The automobile manufacturers in the U.S. are the major players in the domestic economy. They hold a large portion of the total market share, with approximately 70%. The rivalry between the individual domestic competitors is intense, and innovation and improved manufacturing processes have increased efficiency. Factory conditions in the U.S. also enhance the manufacturing strength of domestic automobile manufacturers. The U.S. has a large population which is highly skilled and educated. The educational institutions turn out qualified managers, engineers, and other specialists necessary to produce the sophisticated automobiles of today. The infrastructure within the U.S. is highly developed with excellent transportation systems and adequate electrical power and resource supplies. Demand within the U.S. is also very high, which allows the industry to sell its product successfully at home. There is a wide variety of suppliers willing and capable of meeting the manufacturer's needs and can produce parts and materials in an efficient and cost-effective manner. Many of these suppliers also compete globally, which allows the automobile manufacturers to use them in foreign operations as suppliers or sources of material. The government units within the U.S. back the automotive industry and support it in times of crisis. For instance, the federal government guaranteed loans to Chrysler when the firm was almost bankrupt. Local governments also support the industry because of its large impact on the local work forces. Many states and counties offer the manufacturers tax breaks on property and ad valorem assessments just to have the industry locate in their districts.

The industry is vertically integrated, although not as intensely as in the past. Manufacturers still have interests and maintain strong relations with many of the suppliers of parts and materials. The majority of the materials used in an automobile are not specialty items and can be obtained locally or nationally. Many of the materials have a commodity basis such as steel and aluminum.

The industry has an efficient distribution system using dealers located in virtually every medium and large city in America. This distribution system is also international, and the American automobile is sold worldwide.

In recent years the automobile industry has made remarkable progress in production efficiency. It is now believed the U.S. manufacturers can produce an automobile at a lower cost than the Japanese can produce one at home.[19] Among the U.S. manufacturers, Chrysler has recently been reported to be the lowest cost producer in the nation.[20] Productivity increases by workers have also improved the strong position of U.S. manufacturers. Ford, Chrysler, and GM had 1992 productivity levels of 2.99, 3.52, and 3.94 workdays per vehicle assembled, respectively, as compared to 3.25, 4.58, and 4.88 workdays per vehicle, respectively, in 1989. Toyota Motors (in Kentucky) and Nissan Motors (in Tennessee) had still higher 1992 productivity of 2.44 and 2.29 workdays per vehicle, respectively.[21]

The Big Three have also undergone massive restructuring to cut inefficient management layers and to downsize inefficient manufacturing operations. Some plants have even closed in high-cost manufacturing locations and moved to areas offering lower costs. All the manufacturers, and especially Ford, are building facilities in Mexico to capitalize on the lower cost labor across the border.[22]

NAFTA has also opened the border to other markets, primarily Canada and Mexico. The ability to trade freely in these areas opens up many opportunities in the marketing and distribution areas.

Weaknesses

One of the major weaknesses any large manufacturer faces is the ability to change. The inability of the U.S. manufacturers to change is easily demonstrated using GM as an example. All the domestic manufacturers had a difficult time adapting to Japanese competition, which used high-quality products, advanced manufacturing techniques such as *heijunka,*

and small model sizes as their main selling points. Each domestic manufacturer produced small, economical cars, but they were of poor quality
and fared poorly in the marketplace. When Chrysler came out with the
minivan, GM was not able to produce an acceptable model to compete.
Ten years after introduction of the minivan by Chrysler, GM still did not
have a model that could meet customer satisfaction tests.[8] It seemed that
GM had become so arrogant and complacent that the customer no
longer held any respect within the organization. Ross Perot, presidential
candidate in 1991 and director for GM, once responded to the question
to what he thought about GM: "GM doesn't like the customer, the
dealers, or the workers. Most of the directors don't even like each
other!"[8] Today, however, the ability to focus on the customer's needs
and make changes necessary to remain competitive is present within all
the manufacturers. The Big Three have made remarkable progress in
becoming customer focused, but there is still a long way to go.

Another weakness that relates to the inability to change is the failure
of the Big Three to mount an offense in tackling the upcoming environmental laws and regulations. California has passed a clean air act that
requires zero emission automobiles beginning in 1998. The major manufacturers seem to be procrastinating, hoping that most of these requirements will be relaxed or delayed into the next century. Professor Fredric
Vester has harshly criticized the automotive manufacturers for trying to
optimize existing products instead of working on new technology. He
blames nearsighted management for looking at short-term costs instead
of looking at long-term benefits that could be gained from developing
and introducing new technology. He also notes that current producers
are reluctant to move away from the internal combustion engine.[23]

A second weakness lies with the consumer's ability to buy an automobile. Cars are very expensive to own and operate. The average household real income has been declining in recent years in spite of the
reports of increases in per capita income. The average male worker
(approximately 67% of the male work force) has seen a 19% decline in
real wages in the past few years. Add to this the fact that family income
is no longer increasing at the rate it once did because the majority of the
women able to enter the work force have already done so. Many women
who have been in the work force are now choosing to stay at home
instead, so family income is actually declining in some circumstances.
This decline in disposable income will cause many consumers to move
away from purchasing new automobiles and toward purchasing used

automobiles.[11] Non-college graduates are also experiencing a drop in real wages. This group of "dynamic spenders" is slowly moving toward becoming a group that cannot afford to purchase new automobiles.[11]

Another weakness is the effect the economy has had on automotive sales. The automotive industry is much influenced by recessionary trends. One of the first large ticket items cut out at the beginning of a recession is the purchase of an automobile. Consumer confidence in the economy caused automobile sales in 1991 to decline so much that the Big Three suffered staggering financial losses.[14] The next recession expected to affect the automotive industry is predicted to come in 1997 or 1998, as sales once again are expected to begin to decline.[13]

Opportunities

Even though the automobile market in the U.S. is very well covered, opportunities do exist for domestic manufacturers. The development of "green" cars and light trucks is being seen as the wave of the future. Alternative fuels such as alcohols, methanol, and liquid natural gas are being tested as alternatives to gasoline-dependent cars. The move away from the internal combustion engine most likely will lead to electric cars.[6]

International opportunities will exist in foreign markets in the near future. The Chinese market may be opening up, and potential sales there could be staggering. Southeast Asia is also becoming more industrialized, with Thailand, Vietnam, and India as prospective markets. South America is also developing an infrastructure that will make the automobile more desirable. Trading zones have already been set up in South America which allow access to neighboring countries, and it is quite possible that these agreements will join NAFTA in the near future in uniting the entire Americas into one huge, free-trade zone.[18]

Threats

The largest threat to the domestic manufacturers is international competition. The Japanese offer substantial competition both in the U.S. and in the global markets. They are aggressively moving into the South America market and have already made inroads into China and Southeast Asia. They have a substantial presence in the European Union, mainly in Britain. Foreign manufacturers are not only competing by importing, but are also building plants and manufacturing facilities in the U.S. Domestic firms will have to maintain efficiency and increase productivity in order to compete.

The second and very real threat is the intervention in the auto industry by governmental agencies. The federal government has mandated that fuel economy and safety goals must be met. Also, the government has set goals for recycling of automotive wastes and obsolete parts. Today, mountains of tires exist in numerous locations that must somehow be put to beneficial reuse. Used motor oil must now be recycled, and old batteries must be turned in for recycling instead of being disposed of in landfills. Freon used in air conditioning systems must now be captured by technicians and disposed of properly.

State governments are increasingly getting involved in the environmental aspects of the automobile industry. As mentioned earlier, the California Clean Air Act requires that beginning in 1998 2% of the automobiles sold by any manufacturer must have zero emission. These requirements increase in the following years and become even more stringent later.[2] Other states in the northeast have followed California's example and have either passed or are considering similar legislation.

Competitive Rivalry

Competitive rivalry is fierce in the automotive industry. In the U.S., automobile manufacturers from all over the world compete to satisfy the buying public. The big three automobile manufacturing nations are the U.S., Japan, and Germany. Smaller competitors are the United Kingdom, South Korea, Italy, Mexico, Canada, France, and Spain.[6] South Korea is becoming a big player in the U.S. market as new Korean sport utility vehicles are becoming popular. As previously mentioned, the sport utility sector of the market is one of the fastest growing segments in the U.S. auto market. These products from Korea are popular with teenage drivers and those in their early twenties. Cost is a factor very important to this demographic group, and these vehicles offer good quality and style even though they are rather Spartan in the accessories department.

German manufacturers compete in the American market primarily in the luxury market. Mercedes, Porsche, and BMW are probably the best known of the German automakers. Volkswagen also competes in the small car market even though, in 1994, it is no longer selling the Beetle in the U.S. because it cannot meet federal safety requirements. Canadian manufacturers are primarily arms of the larger U.S. manufacturers. France and Spain offer product lines that target primarily the small and medium class of vehicle market.

The largest and most competitive foreign competitor is the Japanese. All the major Japanese manufacturers have a presence in the U.S., and most have moved some production to factories in the U.S. Part of this move has been to offset governmental regulation that requires foreign manufacturers to use American labor and parts and manufactured products in the U.S. The Big Three have continuously charged that even though the foreign manufacturers are assembling cars in the U.S., the majority of the parts are imported from abroad or are manufactured by foreign-owned manufacturers in the U.S.[8] As a matter of fact, Japanese manufacturers are creating their own *keiretsu*.

The Japanese entered the U.S. market and captured a whopping 32% of the total market share by offering quality-built cars that lasted years longer than U.S. manufacturers' models, fuel-efficient models that outpaced the domestic manufacturers for many years, and accessories in standard models that were offered only as add-ons in domestic models.[14] Japanese manufacturers produced some of the highest quality automobiles in the world and managed to do this in a very efficient manner. This allowed them to import automobiles at costs that undermined the Big Three automakers in the U.S. Chrysler nearly went bankrupt and had to be bailed out by federal loan guarantees in 1980.

Until the Japanese entered the U.S. market, domestic manufacturers were satisfied with manufacturing using the status quo, and improvements in efficiency and quality did not occur. After the entry of the Japanese, U.S. manufacturers finally moved to increase efficiency and improve quality in the 1980s. They also underwent drastic downsizing to get rid of inefficient assembly plants and to reduce overstaffing. Today, efficiency among domestic manufacturers has increased dramatically. In 1994, the Harbour Report stated that Chrysler had become the lowest cost producer in the auto industry. This claim was made when development costs were included with the manufacturing costs in determining cost per vehicle.[20] In the third quarter of 1994, Chrysler made $1000 on average on every vehicle, while GM lost $296.[31]

Foreign manufacturers did not remain idle while domestic manufacturers improved their product and efficiency. Mercedes has now developed a new assembly line which it calls the "rotogate". This line can clamp and hold four different body types at the same time while welding each body type to exact specifications. This line is expected to dramatically cut setup costs and reduce the need to have four separate assembly lines.[10]

Many foreign manufacturers are now offering warranties that extend beyond the 24,000 and 36,000 miles offered by the domestic manufacturers. A recent commercial seen on television offered a 100,000-mile warranty on the entire vehicle. It is also no longer unusual to see 50,000- and 75,000-mile warranties being offered.[24]

Foreign manufacturers are becoming even more price competitive since the yen has been growing stronger against the dollar. The Nissan Corporation is now offering the Maxima 94, a mid-size automobile costing about $22,000, at a price 10% lower than in 1993. Even with a 20% increase in the value of the yen, the total discount equaled approximately 30% off the prior year's price. The domestic manufacturers are crying "foul" and are asking the justice department to investigate this as illegal dumping into the U.S. car market. Nissan has commented that increases in efficiency have allowed it to discount the 1994 price by this much.[25] Manufacturers in other foreign countries are faced with the same or better advantages as the currency exchange rates fluctuate.

Entry Barriers

The automobile industry is very capital intensive. In addition, large expenditures must be spent up front in research and development and in design production. Once these steps have been accomplished, prototype vehicles must be built and tested to ensure that performance is as expected. If the new model is acceptable, the model must then be subjected to governmental testing for emission output and safety testing. If everything gets past the government, huge amounts of advertising must then be put into place to entice the consuming public to want to test drive and buy the new automobile. As previously mentioned, this process takes years to accomplish. To manufacture the large number of automobiles required to recover the initial costs, large assembly plants must be built. These facilities cost several hundred million dollars to build and put into production.[22]

The automobile industry is also characterized by a unionized workforce that has relatively high wage and benefit costs. Any new entrant would have to negotiate with the United Auto Workers union and get some type of agreement almost immediately upon hiring workers to work in the facilities.

Entry barriers to the U.S. market for import autos are not any less stringent. Any automobile brought into the U.S. must meet the same rigorous emissions and safety tests as domestic models. In addition, other regulations require that a certain percentage of parts used in construction of the automobile be made from domestic manufacturers.

Entry into the domestic manufacturing market is not very likely considering the huge costs involved in setting up a modern assembly line. One area that could experience a few entrants in the near future is the electric car market. The Big Three are posturing to keep environmental laws as lax as possible, in spite of California passing its clean air act and other states ready to follow in their footsteps. General Motors has already developed an electric automobile, the Impact, but claims that it would be too expensive for consumers to purchase. This automobile is capable of reaching speeds in excess of 75 miles per hour and meets the no-emission requirements. GM recently shelved the model in an effort to develop another technology.[8] GM appears to be passing up technology that exists and can be improved upon in the hopes that the regulations will be relaxed before actually going into effect. One GM engineer left the manufacturer and set up shop in his garage to develop the technology that GM is no longer seriously developing. He has modified a Honda body with the electronic components required to meet the California standards and is testing several prototypes that could be available sometime in the near future.[8] This small, do-it-yourself type approach could yield a new manufacturer in the market, should sufficient technology be developed to produce a vehicle that could be manufactured at a low enough cost to be affordable. The Japanese are not letting this opportunity get away, either. Toyota has dedicated 100 engineers to electric car production, and it is quite certain they will come up with a working model to meet emission standards.[8]

Entry into the U.S. market by importers is almost assured as many of the Asian countries become more developed. South Korea is already competing with its sports utility vehicles and other low-cost automobiles. While the low-cost Korean autos have not caught the attention of the U.S. consumer due to poor quality and workmanship, improvement is sure to come and quality is bound to improve. Thailand and India are two other Asian nations that are beginning to develop industrial bases, and it would not be surprising to find entrants from these countries, too. China, Eastern Europe, and the former Soviet Union states also have the potential to enter the market, but until the industrial bases can be built up sufficiently to allow efficient manufacturing, entry is not likely in the near future.[26]

Buyers' Power

The bargaining power of the end consumer is somewhat affected by having to deal with manufacturers' dealers that buy the automobiles directly from the manufacturer. The consumer always has the option to purchase a vehicle from another dealer at a better price or purchase a different model from another manufacturer's dealer. Value in the consumer's eye is often related to brand loyalty and trust in the personnel at any particular dealership. Many consumers have only owned one brand of automobile during their lifetime. Many of these brand loyalties result from family relationships or employment relationships. Brand loyalty in the future is likely to be created and influenced by customer and dealer relations more than by the product itself.[6] Detroit manufacturers are stressing the importance of dealer relations with the customer and are actually training dealership personnel on how to treat customers. The hard sell is no longer the approved method of trying to influence the customer. Saturn dealerships have been set up on this strategy and have been very successful in marketing their product this way. Customers have rated the purchasing of Saturn automobiles as one of the most enjoyable experiences encountered compared with their experiences with other dealerships.[8] Some dealerships such as Landmark Chevrolet in Huntsville, AL, have even developed the hard sell into an art.[27] Regardless of the success of some dealerships, the hard-sell approach is generally not seen as the correct approach to win customer brand loyalty.

The dealers have somewhat better negotiating power with the manufacturers. Most dealers are set up on volume discount plans that allow substantial discounts for volume sales. Manufacturers find it difficult to replace dealers when the dealer goes out of business or changes brands, but very few dealers have been able to change manufacturer brands successfully. Those that have, have done so gradually by slowly phasing in another manufacturer. Typically, these are small dealerships in small towns that have moved from U.S. manufacturers to foreign manufacturers. In larger towns and cities, the major players in the dealership game often open rival dealerships and gradually phase out the existing dealership. This, too, can represent a switch from a domestic manufacturer to a foreign manufacturer. Switching makers is extremely expensive, and dealerships are not easy to come by. Most dealers sign parts and inventory agreements with the manufacturers and cannot afford to break these commitments.

Power of Suppliers

Suppliers have become more important to manufacturing in recent years. Just-in-time inventory systems have made manufacturing firms very dependent on suppliers' products. Switching costs are expensive, especially when specialty suppliers are involved. Loss of a supplier could theoretically shut down an assembly line should a supplier decide not to supply product or be unable to supply product due to a strike in the supplier's manufacturing plant or transportation problems. In the past, the automobile manufacturers were vertically integrated and therefore were assured a supply of parts. This is no longer the case. Many of the parts supplied to the manufacturer are produced in specialty plants owned by unrelated parties. Manufacturers try to set up alternative suppliers, but with just-in-time processes it is sometimes necessary to depend on one supplier located near a given assembly plant. Single-source suppliers are also being used when they are able to provide the highest quality and are cost effective.[4]

Automobiles are becoming more and more dependent on electronic hardware to control the motors, transmissions, and electronic accessories. Many of these systems are developed by specialty manufacturers which also supply the product used in the assembly plants.[28] It is estimated that the electronics industry will also become more dependent on the automobile industry in the future and begin to suffer the same cyclical trends that automotive manufacturers face.[28]

Suppliers of steel will lose some of their power as manufacturing processes move toward plastic, aluminum, and magnesium in order to reduce weight in future models. Suppliers of the alternative materials will gain some power as the shift occurs. Steel is almost a commodity item; therefore, the power of existing steel manufacturers is somewhat limited. Manufacturers of alternative materials will suffer the same fate as the electronics industry by taking on a more cyclical nature based on the general economy and the automobile industry's economic pattern.[29]

One supplier not usually mentioned in this area is the supply of labor used in the manufacturing process. As production moves toward greater efficiency, less workers are required to man the assembly lines. Fewer workers perform a larger number of tasks and are therefore more important to the production process. With fewer workers, the likelihood that the assembly line can be successfully stopped during a strike is greatly enhanced. Even minor strikes by transportation resources or minor suppliers could result in lost production time. This is exactly what happened to the Saturn plant. A small strike in a relatively unimportant area resulted in shutting down the assembly line in less than 2 days.[2]

Substitutes

The automobile is very important to the lives of Americans. Without the auto, most people would have to live within the confines of the city where they work. Without the auto, many economic sectors would not exist. Tourism, for instance, would suffer immensely. The economy in general would suffer because shoppers would no longer be able to get in their cars and drive to the movies, mall, or park. The modern society in America would look much like that of a developing nation — population centers with huge masses of people crowded together within the city and vast rural areas occupied primarily by agricultural communities. A good example of this is China.

Should the price of the automobile become so high that the multitudes could not afford one, several alternatives exist. Bicycles, for example, are common in many parts of the world, such as in much of Asia, India, and less developed countries. Public transportation is also an alternative. Already in many of the larger cities, commuters take the transit system to work or to run errands. Most cities have bus systems in place, although many of them operate only with substantial governmental subsidies because commuters prefer to drive their cars.

Two factors that could result in a move away from so much dependency on the automobile are governmental regulations and the economic status of the average American. Governmental agencies are already limiting access to many large cities by placing restrictions on parking and age limitations on driving and by restricting the number of drivers driving alone in their car. In many cities, such as New York, Washington D.C., and Los Angeles, mandates have been enacted which require that large manufacturers restrict the number of automobiles parked at factories. Meeting these regulations can come through carpooling or use of public transportation. Many of the main transportation routes now have a "carpool lane" which is restricted to vehicles with two or more passengers. Orlando, Washington, D.C., New York, and most other large cities have adopted this practice to encourage drivers to carpool. In the future, more governmental regulation will likely occur as air pollution increases. Some municipalities have considered taxing drivers through permitting or licensing procedures that would substantially raise the cost of commuting in an automobile.

The second factor that could affect the number of automobiles on the road are the economic factors. Cars are very expensive to own and operate. The average worker now works 26 weeks to pay for an average new car.[11] In addition to buying the car, the owner must maintain the vehicle, buy fuel and insurance, license the vehicle, and provide parking for the vehicle. With the improvement in quality and workmanship, the cost of maintenance has actually decreased in recent years. Improvements in lubricants, such as better-manufactured parts that self-lubricate, have made maintenance a minor cost. Fuel and insurance expense are another story. Fuel costs today are relatively minor. The average cost of regular gasoline has remained at approximately $1.10 for several years and is expected to rise only slightly in the next few years based on availability of crude oil and the price of the crude.[17] Taxes on gasoline could raise the cost substantially, though. The federal government is constantly looking for ways to increase revenues, and one of the ways frequently mentioned is raising fuel taxes. States also add taxes to pay for road products and highway improvements.

All these costs could put the cost of ownership out of the reach of the ordinary consumer. Should this become reality, alternative methods of transportation will have to be sought, and the importance of the automobile will diminish in the lives of the average American. It does not appear that the U.S. public is going to give up its automobile willingly in the near future, no matter what the cost. Substitutes to the automobile will take over in an evolutionary manner rather than a revolutionary manner.

Conclusion

The automobile industry is truly a global industry. The Big Three auto manufacturers do a satisfactory job of competing in the U.S. and around the world. The following recommendations are intended to ensure that U.S. automakers continue to compete successfully on a global scale.

First, product design, style, and accessories should be determined by customer demand, not strictly by the corporate decision-makers. Customer focus must be a top priority in the future. The customer should be consulted at every stage of production, beginning with initial design and following all the way through production. Second, quality should be the absolute best. Without quality, other manufacturers will step in and satisfy the customer's desire for quality-made products. Third, production efficiency should be improved and result in less costly production. American automakers will have to keep pace, or costs will drive customers to less expensive cars. Fourth, overhead should be kept as low as possible. The industry has undergone a painful downsizing in the past few years, and the resulting hardships should not be forgotten. Costs should be kept as low as possible while still maintaining quality. Fifth, the American worker should not be abandoned for less-expensive labor abroad. American workers are some of the most skilled and productive workers in the world. Eliminating inefficiency to cut costs is a better alternative than simply cutting wages. Sixth, niche markets should be exploited. The sport utility market is really booming now, and there will be additional markets to move into.

Seventh, a close eye should be kept on international markets. New countries are becoming industrialized and will have a need for the automobile in the future. Competitors should not be allowed to gain the upper hand before U.S. manufacturers make a move into these territories. Eighth, short-term profits should not be allowed to ruin long-range returns. The electric car will almost certainly become a reality, so spending on R&D now will ensure availability of the necessary technology when it is required. Tied to this is the ninth recommendation: development of alternative fuels as potential sources of power in the future. Environmental laws will continue to get more strict in the future, and new technology will need to be available to meet the demand. The internal combustion engine can only be modified so many ways. Alternative technologies which are more environmentally "green" may pay high dividends to the innovator that develops the technology first.

References

1. Mike Jensen, *NBC News,* October 11, 1994.
2. Randal Miller, Heather West, and Charles Uthus, "Motor Vehicle Parts: Industry Overview," in *U.S. Industrial Outlook,* U.S. Department of Commerce, U.S. Government Printing Office, Washington, D.C., 1993.
3. John F. Smith, Jr., "Total Customer Satisfaction: Making a Vision a Reality," *Vital Speeches,* October 1 (Vol. 29, No. 8), 1993, p. 761.
4. "Auto Industry Forecast To Grow 50% by 2010," *Ward's Auto World,* July (Vol. 28, No. 7), 1992, p. 82.
5. Paul Rik, "Seeing into America's Future: New Automobiles for the U.S. Market During 1994–1998," *Motor Trend,* April (Vol. 46, No. 4), 1994, p. 68.
6. David Cole, "UM Auto Predications Are Predictable: University of Michigan Office for the Study of Automotive Transportation, Delphi VII, 1994 Forecast," *Ward's Auto World,* March (Vol. 30, No. 3), 1994, p. 31.
7. "Cars, Trucks — No Recovery Yet: DRI/McGraw-Hill Forecast," *European Rubber Journal.* January (Vol. 175, No. 1), 1993, p. 10.
8. "The Heartbeat of America," *Frontline,* Public Broadcast System, copyright 1993.
9. Jeff Karr, "U.S. vs. Them Revisited (editorial)," *Motor Trend,* March (Vol. 46, No. 3), 1994, p. 8.
10. Jim Dunne, "Detroit Spy Report: New Automobile News for 1994 and Beyond," *Popular Mechanics,* November (Vol. 170, No. 11), 1993, p. 120.
11. Bohon, C.D. "Still Uncertain: Hopes Are High that the Auto Industry Is on the Verge of a Huge Sales Boom," *Dealer Business,* February (Vol. 28, No. 6), 1994, p. 52.
12. Alex Taylor, III, "GM $14 Billion Turnaround," *Fortune,* October 17, 1994, p. 58.
13. Jon Lowell, "Forecast '94: Auto Industry Leads U.S. on the Winding Road to Recovery," *Ward's Auto World,* August (Vol. 29, No. 8), 1993, p. 24.
14. Jerry Cook, "Canadian Makers Pull Back on Track: Industry Overview," *Canadian Machinery and Metalworking,* January (Vol. 89, No. 1), 1994, p. 16.
15. "NADA Predicts $14.3 Million Sales Year, 1994 New Car and Light Truck Sales." *Ward's Auto World.* January (Vol. 30, No. 1), 1994, p. 9.
16. "Future Looks Bullish for Larger Vehicles, Bearish for Smaller Vehicles," *Ward's Auto World,* August (Vol. 29, No. 8), 1993, p. 18.
17. Barney Campbell, "It's a Big World After All: Large Automobiles Expected To Be a Fast Growing Market through 1998," *Ward's Auto World,* January (Vol. 29, No. 1), 1993, p. 15.
18. Drew Winter, "Only a Few '93 Bright Spots, Automobile Sales, Global Outlook: Latin America," *Ward's Auto World,* January (Vol. 29, No. 1), 1993, p. 35.
19. Jim McCraw, "Sneak Previews of U.S. Cars To Come," *Popular Science,* September (Vol. 241, No. 3), 1992, p. 68.
20. Douglas Lavin, "Chrysler Is Now the Lowest-Cost Producer in Auto Industry, Harbour Report Says," *Wall Street Journal,* June 23, 1994, p. B5.
21. Douglas Lavin, "GM Would Have To Cut 20,000 Workers to Match Ford Efficiency, Report Says," *Wall Street Journal,* June 24, 1994, p. C22.
22. Neal Templin, "Detroit South: Mexican Industrial Belt Is Beginning To Form as Car Makers Expand," *Wall Street Journal,* June 29, 1994, p. A1.

23. Stephan Schlote, "Germany's Harshest Critic: Professor Vestor Attacks the [Automotive] Industry for Trying To Optimize the Product Instead of Trying To Improve Transportation." *Automotive Industries*, December (Vol. 173, No. 12), 1993, p. 51.
24. Television commercials seen on cable television.
25. *CBS Evening News* (investigative report), July 22, copyright 1994.
26. "Car, Truck Data Printed: Eastern Europe," *European Rubber Journal*, May (Vol. 174, No. 5), 1992, p. 14.
27. Douglas Lavin, "Bucking Detroit Trend, Landmark Chevrolet Still Uses the Hard-Sell," *Wall Street Journal*, July 8, 1994, p. A1.
28. "Automotive Electronics Market To Rise to $15 Billion: Analysts See $15.5 Billion North American Market by 1996, Business Market Trends," *Electronic Business*, November (Vol. 18, No. 14), 1992, p. 32.
29. "'93 Will Be Tough Year, Industry Execs Predict," *Ward's Auto World*. November (Vol. 28, No. 11), 1992, p. 52.
30. *Financial Times*, October 4, 1994, p. 11.
31. *New York Times*, September 27, 1994, p. C12.

Case 7. Foreign Cars in the United States*

T he purpose of this section is to discuss the effects of Japanese auto imports on the American automobile industry, one of the most concentrated oligopolies in the U.S. economy. European imports will be discussed as and when necessary.

Japan had no serious automobile industry until the 1950s. The first car was built in Japan in 1902, but there was no significant auto manufacturing activity until the mid-1920s when Ford, Chevrolet, and Chrysler built small assembly plants there. A modest domestic industry was created in the 1930s as the economy mobilized for war, but it concentrated on the production of trucks and commercial vehicles. During this period of worldwide depression, patriotic zeal in Japan enhanced a rapid industrialization. The son of a small-town blacksmith, Soichiro Honda spent the 1930s as a wild amateur car racer and founder of a firm which intended to manufacture piston rings. Like the rest of his country, Honda's business was ravaged by the war.

In the 1950s, when the Japanese auto industry began, it was a source of amusement to Americans rather than a perceived threat, according to Glen Gardner, a Chrysler engineer. In 1953, Nissan began the production of the British Austin A-40 sedan under license; Hino made a similar arrangement with French Renault to manufacture the tiny 4-CV, and Isuzu contracted with the British Rootes Group to make the Hillman. This fit the Japanese stereotype: industry lore was that the Japanese were

---

* The note was prepared by Dr. M. Reza Vaghefi; A. Edara contributed to an earlier draft of this section.

simple innovators, copying everything they could. This smug dismissal of Japanese talent left Europe and America vulnerable. Even though the Japanese emerged from World War II with renewed vigor, they faced enormous handicaps. The label "Made in Japan" was synonymous with shoddy and tasteless products. But the significant advantages they enjoyed were that, despite the war, the Japanese remained a homogeneous society with powerful family loyalties and a strong tradition of working for the common good. Education, built around the work ethic, was and still is of uniformly high quality. The labor force was imbued with a sense of team play. Management seemed less inclined to distance itself from the workers, a phenomenon common in the West. Moreover, the major Japanese banks considered it their national mission to underwrite long-term Japanese industrial recovery.

In 1955, when Detroit pumped out a record 9.2 million cars and trucks, the entire Japanese auto industry produced 68,932 vehicles, of which only 20,000 were passenger cars:[14]

> "The mid-1950s was a golden age for the U.S. auto industry. Rising income levels ... made the United States an automobile society. And cars that Detroit produced and consumed became larger, and more powerful, and embellished with tailfins and great quantities of chrome. In fact, the emphasis on design represented the epitome of the strategy desired by Sloan back in the 1920s: that continual changes in styling and optional features would, despite rising price, induce consumers to buy new cars more often."

Gardner recalls that a lot of resources went into producing an acceptable skin, and little technology went under the hood. It was during 1958, that the Japanese import "miracle" began, but on a miniature scale. Datsun (now Nissan) and Toyota placed small allotments of their L-210 and Toyopet Crown four-door sedans on freighters to begin the slow, 10-day sea voyage to California. Their arrival was barely noticed. After all, over 50 brands of imported cars were fighting for less than 5% of the American market. The U.S. Big Three had, within the decade, driven Kaiser-Frazer into oblivion; forced Willys-Overland, Hudson, and Nash to merge; and had Studebaker-Packard propped for the final blow. No foreign manufacturer, much less the Japanese, seemed to pose a serious threat to the domestic industry.

But, 1958 brought the first serious postwar recession and with it a spurt in economical, small-car sales. Detroit had few of these to offer.

The Japanese were still non-players. In 1958, Datsun sold 83 cars in the U.S., and a similar number of Toyotas were sold. Most Americans remained loyal to the German and British brands that then dominated the import market. Except for Volkswagen and some of the higher priced British and German sports cars and sedans, the entire imported car boom of the late 1950s was a case of the wrong dealers selling the wrong cars to the wrong people.

The Japanese, though, meant business. Neither Toyota nor Nissan entered the U.S. lightly. Both studied the situation carefully before they committed themselves. They also had available to them the expertise of unique institutions, such as the Japanese trading corporations including Marubeini and Mitsubishi.[29] Getting established in the U.S. was still a long process; in fact, Toyota was virtually out of the passenger car market for a year or two in the early 1960s while it redesigned its models to meet American tastes and standards. The pickup trucks that Toyota and Datsun sold were of great help in attracting American buyers to Japanese vehicles, because a good many American servicemen had become familiar with them in Japan and Korea and knew them to be durable and economical. By the mid-1960s, the two companies' sales were growing rapidly, and in 1970 Toyota was second and Datsun third in sales of import cars in the U.S. — an advance that signaled a revolution in the automotive world.

By the early 1960s the bigger producers were finally bringing out their own small-car models, including "sporty" ones such as Ford's popular Mustang, which hit the streets in 1965. They did not, however, abandon their gas-guzzling "dinosaurs"; in fact, full-sized cars did end up more streamlined than before, but they tended to become larger and heavier each year. The American automobile companies were enjoying a rapidly rising market, to a high point of 12.6 million vehicles in 1973. Then, in October of that year, came the outbreak of the Yom Kippur War and the Arab oil embargo which lasted until the spring of 1974. The gas shortage, combined with a series of price increases by Detroit and a demand for small cars, brought about a drop of more than 20% in new car sales in 1974. Until the oil embargo of 1973-74, the U.S. market in passenger automobiles was divided into approximately 60% larger cars and 40% smaller.

The first foreign automaker to set up shop in the U.S. was West Germany's Volkswagen in 1978. During this time, Mercedes-Benz continued to dominate the heavy-duty imported trucks.

For the automobile industry the most important feature of the Energy Policy and Conservation Act of 1975 was its provisions for achieving fuel economy in motor vehicles. Under this law, all new automobiles in the U.S. were to reach a fuel consumption of not less than 27.5 miles per gallon by 1985, the goal to be attained in stages. These provisions of the Energy Act imposed on the automobile industry an extensive task of redesigning, but it was the gasoline crisis of 1979 and the Iranian Revolution that completely changed American buyer preferences in motor vehicles. In just about a month, the market for large cars almost vanished; customers were looking for vehicles with good fuel economy, and there was a stampede toward compacts. American motor vehicle manufacturers, though, were not able to provide compacts in anything approaching sufficient quantity because they had not anticipated any such drastic changes in demand. Large cars went unsold, and buyers turned in large numbers to the imports, which by this time were predominantly Japanese. Volvo's sales climbed 11.1% in 1978 from 45,790 units in 1977, they were being accepted among middle and upper-middle-price-range car buyers, and they were cited as a safe and emission-controlled car, but its relatively large cars were facing difficulty meeting the 1985 U.S. fuel economy goal of 27.5 miles per gallon. While sales of American-made passenger automobiles shrank, imports rose to 27% of the passenger car market; 99% of imported trucks were Japanese. The U.S. car market fell from 10.5 million units in 1979 to 8.9 million in 1980. While total industry car sales in the U.S. were down in 1980, Mercedes-Benz sold a record number of expensive luxury cars during this time.

With 38 automobile plants shutting down across the country and unemployment rising to alarming levels in the auto industry and its ancillary supplier firms, pressure mounted to impose restrictions on automobile imports (especially Japanese), to impose tariffs, or to require the larger Japanese companies to establish assembly plants in the U.S. In early 1981, to avoid a strong U.S. protectionist reaction, the Japanese government reluctantly moved on its own to limit exports of automobiles to the U.S. It self-imposed an annual ceiling of 1.68 million cars to be exported to America in late 1982. Announcement of plans for building Honda cars at the company's motorcycle plant in Marysville, OH, in 1982 and for the construction of a Nissan (Datsun) truck factory in Smyrna, TN, in 1983 helped relieve the tension. Toyota built its major assembly facilities in Georgetown, KY, at about the same time. Thus, the Japanese Big Three began to have a firm hold on the U.S. auto market by locating their plants on domestic soil; very soon, this changed the nature of the competitive game.

1981–1983

From selling 8.9 million units in 1980, the U.S. car market slid to 8.5 million in 1982 and dropped again to 8 million in 1982. While the American piece of the pie continued to shrink year after year, the sales of foreign cars had grown to nearly 30% of the market in 1991 from less than 15% in 1972. Attaining such market share, given the conditions, was a major achievement.

The domestic industry did not show strong signs of revival until some time after the 1981 "voluntary" export restraints by the Japanese. U.S. automakers used this period of protection to cut their costs and raise their productivity drastically. The quest was to reduce what was said to be a $1500 to $2000 differential in favor of the Japanese in the cost of producing a typical subcompact car. One third of the cost advantage was due to cheaper labor and greater efficiency, while the remainder could be attributed to the slide of the yen against the dollar and the Japanese tax system. Also, Japan was building the cars in 39 hours vs. 72 hours in the U.S. by utilizing high automation and fewer people. To the domestic automakers, this meant repeated efforts to get contract concessions from a sharply reduced labor force, radical changes in manufacturing techniques, and the adoption of Japanese methods such as "just-in-time" inventory and *kaizen* (continuous improvement) techniques.

Cost controls combined with an unexpected surge in large car sales and steadily increasing car prices allowed the industry to enjoy a dramatic comeback starting in 1983. The fruits of these policies were seen in Chrysler's breakeven point, which was reduced from 2.4 million units in 1979 to 1.1 million in 1983.

The urgency of the industry to become more cost and quality competitive on the small-car front led Detroit automakers to arrange joint car-building ventures with the Japanese in the U.S. in closed-up manufacturing facilities. GM got involved in a 50/50 joint venture with Toyota at Fremont, CA, in 1984, called New United Motor Manufacturing, Inc. (NUMMI). According to *Ward's Automotive Yearbook 1991*,[26] "NUMMI seems likely to become more 'Japanese'. Speculation abounds that Toyota would assume full ownership of the operation when the joint-venture agreements expires in 1996, if not before."

GM apparently applied some of what it hoped to learn from Toyota's methods and labor policies to the wholly owned Saturn subsidiary that the company announced in 1985. A 50/50 Chrysler-Mitsubishi joint venture called Diamond-Star Motors Corporation in Bloomington, IL, was launched in 1988. The GM-Toyota and Chrysler-Mitsubishi joint ventures are one indication that American producers used foreign investment as an opportunity to learn the "secrets" of the Japanese success in automaking.[14]

Gradually, more Japanese auto manufacturers started setting up operations in the U.S. Mazda launched its U.S. operations in 1987 in Flat Rock, MI. Toyota started its own production in 1988, in Georgetown, KY. Subaru launched a transplant in 1989 in Lafayette, IN, which was the first transplant co-owned by two Japanese automakers, Subaru and Isuzu.

Import Quota — Boon or Bane?

One of Detroit's biggest problems in holding off the Japanese has been its unwillingness to confront the threat from Japan. Instead, the industry has adopted a defensive mentality, fighting to keep Japanese automakers out. The process began with the voluntary import restraints of 1981 and is still going on — most recently with 1992's dispute over minivan imports:[12]

> "The complaint filed by the Big Three was that the wholesale prices of Japanese minivans — prices charged to dealers — are lower in the U.S. than in Japan, injuring U.S. industry, consumers and workers. The Big Three are also contemplating efforts to get the Clinton Administration to hike the tariff on imported minivans and four-door sport utilities from 2.5% to 25%."

Later the International Trade Commission (ITC) ruled against the complaint, citing that the Big Three enjoyed about 80% of the U.S. market for minivans. In 1993, Chrysler, Ford, GM, and all foreign makes had 45, 17.5, 17, and 20.5% U.S. market shares, respectively. A look at what happened thereafter should be sufficient warning against import restraints. The restraints helped Detroit pick up windfall profits — temporarily. Between 1984 and 1988, GM, Ford, and Chrysler together earned $25.5 billion. Instead of plowing the money back into their core business, however, they sought higher returns by investing their cash elsewhere. The import restraints, still in effect, never worked as intended. In their first years, they served only to limit supply, not depress demand. Dealers in Japanese cars found they could add yet another item to the sticker price: extra dealer's markup:[1]

> "By creating an artificial scarcity, the 'voluntary' quotas have dramatically driven up the prices of Japanese cars. The rise in Japanese price, in turn, has permitted domestic producers to push through sizable price boosts of their own. In 1983, new car prices (both foreign and domestic) rose $800 to $1000 as a direct consequence of import quotas; additional dealer markups on some Japanese models reportedly rose as much as $2600. In the aggregate, 'protection' from foreign competition is estimated to have cost American car buyers $15.7 million in artificially inflated new-car prices. Ironically, numerical restrictions impelled Japanese producers to upgrade their offerings and to invade the vast midsize region of the market, where they posed a much greater threat to domestic oligopoly."

The restraint agreements led to two other most significant developments. Apart from Honda, six other Japanese automakers joined in:[19] "Toyota's plant in Georgetown, KY, is a monument to automotive protectionists. Toyota would not have made anything like that $1-billion-plus investment without the agreements." Detroit has learned volumes from the Japanese, mostly about manufacturing and employee relations, but it still looks to the U.S. government for protection from all-out competition. The second significant development due to the restraint agreements was the upscale Japanese auto. Given the incentive to maximize the profit on each car shipped, the Japanese decided to export more expensive automobiles. Together, the Big Three Japanese automakers (Honda, Nissan, and Toyota) have skimmed gallons of cream off the U.S. market. Clearly, Detroit would have been much better off had it confronted the Japanese directly in 1981 rather than hiding behind import restraints. It would have been faster to adopt Japanese production methods and to rationalize its own factories. Instead, Detroit effectively conceded a permanent share of the U.S. market to the Japanese, who reinvested in more American plants.[19]

By 1990, the Japanese were building 1.2 million cars and trucks in the U.S. That additional production hit the market just as the economy started to weaken. Rather than cutting production, the Big Three (U.S.)

kept their factories running. To move the merchandise, they slashed retail prices and increased their scarcely profitable wholesale deliveries to fleet customers. GM had most of the overcapacity, so it took the lead in creating a buyer's market. It offered customers incentives of up to $2500 a car, which Ford and Chrysler were forced to match. By 1991, fleets accounted for nearly half the sales of such makes as Lincoln and Dodge. Much of this was money-losing business, but Detroit figured it was cheaper to keep the factories open than to shut them down and pay its workers for not working.[19] Despite these artificial life supports, car sales fell from 9.3 million 1990 to 8.2 million in 1991 — the worst performance since 1982. GM was the worst hit. Its North American operations lost $7 billion in 1991, Ford lost $2.2 billion, and Chrysler $795 million. It was left to Jack Smith, new GM CEO, to cut the fleet from 800,000 in 1993 to 400,000, saving the company $400 million.[31]

So the industry's attempt to use trade barriers to hold back the Japanese failed. Other decisions made during the 1980s had equally striking results — positive and negative. Among other things, those actions demonstrated that small ideas, if they are applied consistently — such as cutting costs and monitoring operations more closely — can produce better results than big ideas or broad strokes carried out erratically.[19]

Japanese Luxury Cars

The first Japanese luxury car was introduced in 1986 — the $20,000 Acura Legend, a four-passenger, mid-size auto powered by a V-6 engine. After a slow start, Acura developed a reputation for superior smoothness, refinement, and reliability — especially compared with the European cars that were its direct competitors. Less bound by tradition, the Japanese were compulsive about continuous improvement and bent on producing cars that would compete with any in the world. In late 1989, Toyota and Nissan both introduced a full line of luxury cars, realizing a long-cherished dream for both automobile corporations. The Japanese strategy was to offer higher quality cars at lower prices, just as it did over a decade ago in the compact car market. Toyota's Lexus and Nissan's Infiniti were designed to compete with Germany's Mercedes-Benz and BMW and the American Cadillac. Japanese marketing strategy was to produce automobiles equal in quality to European luxury models but selling at a price between the European model cost and the price of the U.S. luxury models. The Lexus LS400 has the proportions of a Mercedes-Benz 420 SEL but more up-to-date details; the Infiniti Q45 and J30 evoke a classic Jaguar sedan. These automobiles are roomier, loaded with electronics, and high on performance.[20] In 1990, Honda entered the sports-car market with its $55,000, 165-mph, NS-X, designed to compete with the Ferrari and Lamborghini.

Toyota's new high-performance sedan, the Lexus LS 400, raised to a new level the traditional Japanese virtues of high quality and superior engineering.[20] It is also faster, quieter, and more comfortable than its German competitors, in addition to being much less expensive. Toyota's manufacturing boss, Sekiya, aims to make Lexus the world quality champion, as measured in defects per 100 showroom cars (the industry's standard measurement).[20] When Lexus entered the U.S. car market, it carried a base sticker price of $35,000, nearly $30,000 less than the Mercedes 420 SEL. The inside tale of how Lexus came into being is rich in lessons for anyone who has years to develop up-market products. Toyota had to target its customer precisely, create all-new management organizations, rethink components down to the tiniest screw, and invest considerable time and money — 6 years and over $500 million. In 1983, chairman Toyoda challenged his engineers to "develop the best car in the world" using the Mercedes-Benz 420 SEL and BMW 735i as the engineering benchmarks.[20] Now Toyota is assuming the distinction of becoming a "benchmark" itself. In a recent study of Honda's plant in Marysville, OH, the author asked the assistant plant manager which product and company they used as a benchmark. His answer was "Toyota".

The entry of these two nameplates created unprecedented competition at a time when the luxury car segment was stagnant.[20] Lexus and Infiniti cite demographic trends as evidence that a major expansion in this market is imminent. For the next decade, Infiniti projects a 50% increase in $50,000 and up households, while Lexus expects a 90% increase in those households, which are the potential buyers of such luxury brands. The threat posed by Nissan's Infiniti and Toyota's Lexus is causing both European automobile importers and upscale domestic manufacturers to focus attention on the high-end market. Early success of this new strategy was exhibited in the market in 1992 where Mercedes' U.S. sales fell by 5%, while sales of Toyota's Lexus climbed 39%, and Nissan's Infiniti sales rose 7%. Daimler-Benz, maker of Mercedes, is feeling the Japanese onslaught the most in the U.S. and has been forced to restructure its operations and cut costs due to the success of the Japanese luxury sedans. It is attempting to close the 35% production cost advantage of the Japanese luxury makers. The current 1994 lineup is being refined by reduced noise and vibration, increased size and number of options, and improved safety. Acura, Lexus, and Nissan's Infiniti division have created a rich source of profits for themselves — and denied them to American automakers. While competition and fleet fuel-economy rules make small cars a breakeven business or worse, the luxury autos can return up to $11,000 each in gross profit.[19]

Overall Performance of the Japanese Automakers

The success story of the Japanese automobile industry must be interpreted in the context of the overall Japanese management system which can be best understood by the concept of oneness in the society. With a history of less than 100 years, the Japanese automobile industry has undergone several periods of change and progress, due to three forces: policies of the Japanese government, entrepreneurship of industry managers, and favorable environmental forces. The difference in efficiency between Japanese practices and in the plants of domestic producers is largely a difference in management. That difference involves the organization itself (*kanban*), human relations (quality circles, decision-making by consensus), means of production (few job classifications, little hierarchy, life-time employment, no gulf between line workers and engineers or managers), *kaizen* (managers encourage workers' proposals, ensuring continuous improvement in both quality and productivity), and psychology (no executive lunch rooms and offices). In the Honda plant cafeteria where the author had a simple lunch with the assistant plant manager, the shop floor workers were sitting on my right and the plant engineers on my left. A Spartan, but clean, cafeteria was symbolic of many features at the plant. The Japanese are concerned with long-time survival and success of a team of people rather than short-term returns from the company in which they invest.

Several of the Japanese automakers recently increased their plant capacity in U.S. and plan future expansions. Between the joint ventures and the independently produced vehicles, there is capacity in place today to produce more cars in the U.S. Total capacity could rise to about 3.0 million by 1995. Future additions are likely to be focused on the light truck market, which is still controlled mainly by the Big Three. Toyota is already seeking a U.S. site for production of a new pickup truck that it recently began to import to the U.S. Assembling the vehicle in the U.S. would allow Toyota to avoid a 25% tariff imposed on imported light trucks.

According to *Value Line*,[23] Toyota's balance sheet remains powerful in spite of weak auto markets. Nissan plunged into the red for the first time ever in the 6 months ended September 30, 1992, and remained troubled for at least the next 12 months mainly because of Japan's deepening recession. Honda's Acura Legend, the first Japanese luxury car, experienced a unit sales decline of 24% in 1992 — largely because of the success of Toyota's and Nissan's more expensive upscale models. The 1994 Accord was critical to Honda's fortunes and has done well.

Today, although Japanese imports are substantially below the revised 1.65 million cars a year allowed by the voluntary restraint agreement, total Japanese sales far exceed even the import limit. The substantial increase in market share combined with the economic weakness in the U.S. over the past 3 years has led to rising calls for protectionist policies by industry and union leaders. Meanwhile, imports may become somewhat less competitive.

To some extent, Japanese automakers' pricing policies also reflect political and market pressures in the U.S. Negative sentiment is mounting against the Japanese juggernaut that seemed intent on driving U.S. automakers out of business. After the Big Three filed a dumping complaint against Japanese automakers exporting minivans to the U.S., prices of Japanese minivan models were raised an average of 12%, making them less of a competitive three to the U.S. Big Three.

Conclusion

Starting in the 1970s, the U.S. auto industry suffered a serious setback to its comfortable position of guaranteed profits and a tight control over the domestic auto market. The U.S. Big Three has been losing market share for the past two decades, and now accounts for only about 60% of the U.S. auto market. The main reasons for this loss can be attributed to foreign competition (mainly Japanese), inability to meet market demand, and cost disadvantages. Chronic excess capacity and dumping by foreign producers have aggravated the cyclical swings of the industry and led to huge losses, negative cash flows, and continuous downsizing.

References

1. Walter Adams, *The Structure of American Industry*, Macmillan, New York, 1990.
2. Larry Armstrong, "The Luxury Mazda Just Couldn't Afford," *Business Week*, November 1992, p. 46.
3. Kristine Bruse, "Big Three Gain, but Japan Still Leads in Quality," *Automotive News*, June 1, 1992, p. 1.
4. *Business Week*, March 16, 1987, p. 110.
5. C.S. Chang, *The Japanese Auto Industry and the U.S. Market*, Praeger, New York, 1981.
6. Horton Cleveland and Raymond Serafin, "Recovery Is Good News for U.S. Auto Marketers," *Advertising Age*, June 22, 1992.
7. Mary Cornelly, "U.S. Claws Back: Big 3 Remaining 1–3 Points a Year from Japan," *Automotive News*, June 1, 1992, p. 1.
8. L. Thomas Friedman, "Automakers Ask Clinton To Limit Imports of Minivans from Japan," *The New York Times*, January 7, 1993, p. A9.
9. A. Melvyn Fuss and Leonard Waverman, *Costs and Productivity in Automobile Production*, Cambridge University Press, New York, 1992.
10. Subcommittee on Energy and Power Hearings, *What's Ailing the U.S. Auto Industry?*, U.S. Government Printing Office, Washington, D.C., 1992.
11. Yu Inaba, "The Final Battle: Japan Takes on the U.S. Luxury Car Market," *Tokyo Business Today*, February 1990, p. 26.
12. Rick Kranz and Rick Keebler, "Japanese Bash Dumping Claim," *Automotive News*, February 8, 1993, p. 8.
13. Mark Landler, "No Joyride for Japan: Nissan and Toyota Are Hitting Bumps in the U.S. Luxury Car Market," *Business Week*, January 15, 1990, p. 20.
14. Philip Mattera, *Inside U.S. Business: A Concise Encyclopedia of Leading Industries*, Dow Jones-Irwin, Homewood, IL, 1990.
15. John B. Rae, *The American Automobile Industry*, Twayne Publishers, MA, 1990.
16. Raymond Serafin, "Automotive Marketing: Upscale Stretching to Infiniti," *Advertising Age*, July 24, 1989, p. S8.
17. *Standard & Poor's Industry Surveys*, Standard & Poor's Corp., New York, February 25, 1993.
18. *Standard & Poor's Industry Surveys*, Standard & Poor's Corp., New York, October 8, 1992.
19. Alex Taylor, "U.S. Cars Come Back," *Fortune*, August 14, 1989, p. 62.
20. Alex Taylor, "Here Come Japan's New Luxury Cars," *Fortune*, August 14, 1989, p. 62.
21. John Templeman, "Downshift at Daimler," *Business Week*, November 16, 1992, p. 88.
22. Charles M. Thomas, "Futurists Place 7 Percent Solution," *Automobile News*, January 4, 1993, p. 26.
23. *Value Line Investment Survey*, Value Line Publishing, New York, December 18, 1992, p. 101.
24. *Value Line Investment Survey*, Value Line Publishing, New York, March 19, 1993, p. 101.
25. *Ward's 1984 Automotive Yearbook*, Ward's Communications, Detroit, MI, 1984.
26. *Ward's 1991 Automotive Yearbook*, Ward's Communications, Detroit, MI, 1991.

27. Peter Wickens, *The Road to Nissan: Flexibility, Quality, Teamwork*, Macmillan, London, 1987.
28. Charlotte Winter, "How Top 10 Fared," *Automotive News*, January 11, 1993, p. 1.
29. Brock Yates, *The Decline and Fall of the American Automobile Industry*, Vintage Books, New York, 1980.
30. David E. Zoia, "Japanese Teach Mercedes a Lesson: Get Lean or Lose," *Ward's Auto World*, July 1992, p. 80.
31. *Fortune*, October 17, 1994, p. 36.

Case 8. The New Chrysler Corporation*

The key figure associated with the beginnings of the auto industry was Henry Ford. The second major figure to move the industry was Waiter P. Chrysler. Chrysler was the head of the Buick Division of General Motors, but left the company in 1929 after a dispute with the chairman, William Durant. In 1923, Chrysler came out of retirement to reorganize the dying Maxwell and Chalmers Motor Car Companies. He was successful at this venture and later formed the Chrysler Corporation. In 1928, the Chrysler Corporation bought out Dodge and Plymouth, and by 1940 it had captured 25% of the domestic auto market. From the days of the innovations of Waiter Chrysler, the Chrysler Corporation has always had a dominating prowess in the field of engineering. Their engineers were the first to alleviate the vibrations in cars and to design electronic ignitions, modern electronic voltage regulators, hydraulic brakes, and under-the-hood computers. These past successful accomplishments convinced Lee Iacocca, during his tenure as chairman, that the Chrysler Corporation still had a chance for future success. Thus began Chrysler's fight for survival, driven by Iacocca, in the late 1970s and early 1980s.

* First published by *Journal of Management Case Studies* in 1987. This case was prepared by Richard E. Miller and M. Reza Vaghefi as a basis for classroom discussion.

351

The Situation in 1978

After beginning his career at Ford in August 1946, Lee Iacocca rose to the presidency of Ford, second only to Henry Ford himself. However, on July 13, 1978, Iacocca was fired by a "threatened" Henry Ford. During the summer of that year, Iacocca was offered top management positions at several corporations. The offer he finally accepted was the one made by the severely ailing Chrysler Corporation. When he accepted the position as Chrysler's president, Chrysler announced a third-quarter loss of almost $160 million, its worst deficit ever. At Chrysler, Iacocca found many seemingly insurmountable problems.

The first problem was the lack of a solid organization structure. There was no cooperation between individual departments, even for those departments that should have naturally formed a close relationship, such as engineering and manufacturing, and manufacturing and sales. Chrysler was a group of mini-empires, with no one paying attention to what anyone else was doing. One possible contributing factor was the fact that vice-presidents were often transferred from one division to another. If top management felt a vice-president had performed well in his particular field, they would not hesitate to move him to another area in the organization, the assumption being that if he could run one division efficiently, he must be able to manage another just as well.

The second problem at Chrysler was the lack of financial controls. There was no financial plan or projection of financial condition; consequently, top management was not aware that the company was running out of cash. John Ricardo, the chairman of Chrysler, and Bill McCagh, the treasurer, were spending the majority of their time dealing with the day-to-day concerns of keeping the outstanding Chrysler loans intact. Therefore, they were limited in their effectiveness to plan long-term strategy and manage the company's overall operations.

A third problem brought to Iacocca's attention was the fact that over 50,000 automobiles had been taken out of the production schedule for the first quarter of 1979 alone because there were no dealer orders for the cars rolling off the production line. Chrysler regularly amassed a huge inventory of cars, known as the sales bank. The company would then deplete the inventory by offering lower prices for the cars to the dealers at the end of each month. The lack of organizational plan and marketing strategy was stated succinctly by Lee Iacocca in his autobiography:[8]

"In the summer of 1979, when Chrysler first approached the government for help, the sales bank contained 80,000 unsold vehicles. At one point the number reached as high as a 100,000 units, representing about $600 million in finished inventory. At a time when our cash was dwindling anyway and interest rates were high, the costs of carrying this inventory were astronomical. But even worse, the cars were just sitting there in the great outdoors and slowly deteriorating."

Another situation that existed was the lack of attractive, innovative, and unique products among Chrysler offerings. Chrysler Corporation had lost the innovative image that it had enjoyed for many years. Chrysler's strategy was now one of playing catch-up to Ford and General Motors. In 1978, Chrysler's two divisions, Chrysler-Plymouth and Dodge, had a total of 15 models to offer and an 11.05% market share compared to Ford's 23.54% and GM's 47.70%.

Each of the three problems demanded Iacocca's attention, and their alleviation depended on Iacocca having a homogeneous, competent, and totally familiar team who could project confidence and a unique capability in the automotive industry. So the first step was put in effect: a survival strategy.

Survival

Over a 3-year period, Iacocca had to fire 33 of Chrysler's 35 vice-presidents. Iacocca was not daunted by their lack of ability to adapt to his system of management. With his Ford notebooks in hand, he began contacting competent executives with whom he was familiar and started to put together a new management team. Iacocca now felt confident that he and his new team could turn the ailing company around. One mistake they made, however, was not anticipating the Shah of Iran's departure or a lengthy recession. On January 16, 1979, the Shah left Iran. Within a few weeks, due to the shutdown of the Iranian oil industry and a chaotic world oil market, oil companies followed OPEC's lead and increased the price of oil from $12 a barrel to $36. The entire auto industry was shaken, and Chrysler, being the weakest auto company, was devastated. Just as Chrysler was taking expensive measures to retool and begin producing more small cars, the economy plunged into the worst recession in 50 years. Annual sales of cars sold were cut almost in half. Chrysler had to close plants and fire and lay off both salaried and hourly workers. In April 1980 alone, Chrysler cut their white-collar ranks by 7000 people. In an interview with Tom Brokaw, Iacocca said,[9] "The ultimate price (for Chrysler's success) was paid by the 20,000 white-collar people we laid off, probably forever, and the 40,000 blue-collar workers in the cutbacks and closing of plants and the thousand or so dealers. They paid the ultimate price." However, all the cutting and slashing could not counter what the government and economy were doing to Chrysler.

Consolidation

The Loan Guarantee Act was passed at the end of 1979, and it gave Chrysler a possible chance to hold their ground. The loan by itself was not enough to save Chrysler; other measures had to be taken. Iacocca began by taking a self-imposed cut in salary from $360,000 annually down to $1 a year. Then he started in on the executives by tossing out their stock-incentive plan and cutting salaries by 10%, which had never before been done in the auto industry. The third cut was suffered by the unions and their members. In Iacocca's own words:[8]

> "I had to lay it on the line. I talked tough to them. 'Hey boys,' I said, 'I've got a shotgun at your head. I've got thousands of jobs available at seventeen bucks an hour. I've got none at twenty so you better come to your senses.' A year later when things got even worse, I had to go back to them a second time. One bitter winter night at ten o'clock I spoke to the union negotiating committee. It was one of the shortest speeches I've ever given; "You've got until morning to make a decision. If you don't help me out, I'm going to blow your brains out. I'll declare bankruptcy in the morning and you'll all be out of work. You've got eight hours to make up your minds. It's up to you."

Concessions had to be made by all the people from executives to suppliers all the way down to the workers in order for Chrysler to survive:[8] "And that's how Chrysler pulled through. It wasn't the loans that saved us, although we needed them badly. It was the hundreds of millions of dollars that were given up by everybody involved. I called this equality of sacrifice."

In addition to across-the-board cuts from unions, employees, and executives, the New Chrysler Corporation embarked on a massive rebate campaign that was controversial to say the least. Chrysler had to resort to drastic measures to clear the lots of thousands of cars sitting there and rusting. The rebate campaign has now become an integral part of pricing policy not only of the automotive industry, but of whomever has a commodity to sell, from a bottle of Italian wine to an expensive car.

The most extraordinary feature of this period was the election of Douglas Fraser, President of the United Auto Workers of America, to the Board of Chrysler. This was yet another unconventional way in which Iacocca dealt with the issue of consolidation of the car company.

Counterattack

"Net income for 1984 was $2.38 billion, $240 million better than our previous profit record, set just last year. This produced earnings of $18.88 per common share in 1984, compared with $5.79 per common share in 1983. At the end of the year, total debt was 19.7% of the total debt plus equity — down from 52.7% in 1983 and 69.8% in 1982, and our best ratio in 17 years."[6] These words were from Iacocca to the stockholders, as reported in Chrysler's 1984 Report to the Shareholders. From 1980, when Chrysler received loans backed by U.S. government guarantees, to 1984, Chrysler Corporation had traveled a long road, with many highlights. In 1980, Chrysler launched its most successful line of products led by the K-cars, Dodge Aries, and Plymouth Reliant. Aries and Reliant both received the *Motor Trend* Car of the Year award, and Chrysler products achieved the best corporate average fuel economy in the industry.

In 1981, Chrysler was the only U.S. automobile company to increase both its unit sales and its market share, and once again it had the best corporate fuel economy in the industry — 28.4 miles per gallon, up from 25.5 in 1980. With the success of the Dodge Aries and Plymouth Reliant, the highest mileage six-passenger cars on the market, Chrysler sales accounted for 22% of the compact-car market segment. In 1981, Chrysler introduced the Dodge Power Ram 50 from Mitsubishi, a four-wheel-drive pickup that was named "Four Wheeler of the Year" by *Four Wheeler* magazine.

In 1982, Chrysler recorded its first third-quarter profit in 5 years; this was aided by two important developments. Chrysler sold its defense subsidiary, Chrysler Defense Incorporated, which increased their cash flow. And, most importantly, between 1980 and 1982, Chrysler had reduced its fixed costs by $1 billion and cut its breakeven point in half. Chrysler introduced the first U.S.-built convertible in 6 years, which proved very popular with the car-buying public. During 1982, Chrysler launched a record $6.6 billion program to develop and design products capable of capturing special segments of the market. This program has enabled Chrysler to establish itself as a company that produces innovative and attractive products — exactly the opposite of the image they had projected for years.

The year 1983 was a banner one for Chrysler, highlighted by their excellent financial position. This position was attributed to four factors. The first factor was the repayment of $1.2 billion in government-guaranteed loans, 7 years early, which save $392 million in interest and government fees. The second factor was the classifying of $1.1 billion of preferred stock into common stock. The third factor was the placing of the winning bid of $311 million for the 14.4 million Chrysler warrants held by the U.S. government. These warrants were retired, and the danger of their potential dilution and stock-price effect was alleviated. Fourth, Chrysler resumed dividend payments on 10 million shares of preferred stock. This year also saw Chrysler launch the first American-built, front-wheel-drive sport cars — the Dodge Daytona and Chrysler Laser. Once again, Chrysler received a prestigious commendation for the Dodge Daytona Turbo Z from *Car and Driver* as one of the ten best cars of the year. The company boosted its product-investment plan from $6.6 million to $8 billion. Chrysler's commitment to quality was reflected in the facts: 7403 Chrysler cars were recalled because of defects compared to 1.6 million Fords, 1.2 million GM cars, and 1.2 million Japanese imports.

During 1984, Chrysler opened the first new auto plant in 20 years, the Sterling Heights Assembly Plant in Missouri. It is one of the most advanced and automated assembly plants in the world, with 57 welding robots, 32 material-handling robots, and 162 lasers and cameras that inspected more than 350 points on the car body. Chrysler renewed their financial strength even further by retiring their preferred stock and buying back close to 20% of their outstanding common stock. The two minivans, Plymouth Voyager and Dodge Caravan, received the *Consumer's Digest* Consumer Hall of Fame award and were listed by *Car and Driver* as the best minivans of 1984. In October 1984, Chrysler Corporation announced its plan to increase capital spending to $9.5 billion over the next 5 years, including an accelerated new-car program that called for introducing a new car every 6 months. This attitude has helped Chrysler reach new heights of success and will help continue the growth and prosperity begun by Iacocca.

Globalization

During the summer of 1978, while Iacocca was semi-retired, he entertained the concept of a venture called Global Motors, based on his product-market mix. According to this vision, a combination of German engineering, Japanese production, and American marketing could be most efficient in this global industry. His idea called for an international arrangement between car companies of Europe, Japan, and the U.S.:[8] "The partners I had in mind for Global Motors were Volkswagen, Mitsubishi, and Chrysler, although the plan could also work with a different partner such as Fiat, Renault, Nissan, or Honda. But Chrysler was the logical American choice." Iacocca dismissed the idea after he was advised that the plan would run counter to American antitrust laws. Since that time, a new attitude has prevailed that might possibly have allowed such an arrangement. Evidence that gives support to this notion is provided by the joint-venture agreement between two of the largest automakers in the world, General Motors and Toyota, which was signed in February 1983. The formal dedication of the New United Motor Manufacturing Incorporated (NUMMI) plant occurred at Fremont, CA, in March 1985:[1] "'I believe what we're doing in this plant will help the balance of trade,' Smith [GM Chairman] said, noting that the cars are 'being produced here rather than being imported.'" The Toyota chairman said NUMMI "will continue to better relationships between Japan and the U.S. and will help the automotive industry prosper in both countries."[1] Japan's ambassador to the U.S., Nobuo Matsunage, said the joint venture "demonstrates that Japan and the U.S. are their largest trading partners and confident investors in each other's economic growth and strength."[1] At the same ceremonies, Smith also said that GM will continue to pursue joint-venture activities aggressively around the world wherever it is in the interest of the corporation. This attitude seems to be quite prevalent at other U.S. auto manufacturers. At first mention of the agreement between GM and Toyota, Chrysler filed a lawsuit to block the joint venture; however, in April 1985, Chrysler dropped the lawsuit after a settlement was reached between the companies. The agreement called for an 8-year active cooperation between GM and Toyota instead of the original 12 years. "Active cooperation" refers to the GM employees who are a part of the venture. The agreement also restricts GM to buying no more than 250,000 units annually from either Toyota or NUMMI for sale or distribution in the U.S. and Canada. Chrysler had alleged the joint venture would have a devastating effect on competition because GM and Toyota are the price leaders in their respective markets. The increased realization of the interdependence between countries of the world has sent other automobile manufacturers scurrying for partners, as seen by the joint-venture agreement between Chrysler and Mitsubishi. The dropping of the lawsuit was viewed by many as a prelude to Chrysler's announcement of the Mitsubishi joint venture. However, Baron Bates, Chrysler's vice-president for public relations, said,[2] "It has nothing to do with it. Our basic argument had to do with the size of the venture. Chrysler and Mitsubishi are smaller companies. If GM were to do something with Isuzu or Suzuki, we would have no objection. Bigness was the issue." Shortly thereafter, GM began importing Isuzu-built Spectrums and Suzuki-built Sprints for sale through their Chevrolet dealers. General Manager Robert D. Burger said,[2] "The nine states where Sprint was launched account for 19% of total U.S. small car sales. The 16 Eastern states where Spectrum is being launched account for 43%."

In 1983, before the GM-Toyota plan was given the go-ahead by the Federal Trade Commission, Iacocca said,[7] "If GM carries out its Japanese strategy, car imports from Japan will climb to 4 million because Chrysler and Ford will import them, too, instead of making them here, and the U.S. will be out of the small car business." How prophetic! Chrysler and Mitsubishi began their relationship in 1971 when Chrysler purchased 15% of Mitsubishi Motors Corporation (MMC) and began selling its products through Chrysler dealerships. In the mid-1980s, Chrysler was selling three Mitsubishi cars: the Conquest, Vista Horizon, and Colt, as well as a Mitsubishi truck, the Ram 50. In April 1985, amid many rumors, Chrysler finally announced a joint-venture agreement between Mitsubishi and Chrysler. The new car would, in effect, be the replacement for the existing Dodge Colt and Plymouth Horizon. Chrysler also increased its ownership share of MMC from 15% to 24%. The joint venture, called Diamond Star, would begin production in 1988 and be located in Bloomington, IL. Production was expected to reach 180,000 cars a year, with half being sold by Chrysler and half by Mitsubishi

Motors Sales of America, the Mitsubishi independent distribution arm in the U.S. Iacocca hailed the deal as good for the U.S.:[3] "The new plant will directly employ 2500 people, and another 9000 jobs will be created for suppliers." Further, Chrysler in May 1985 revised its contract with Mitsubishi to import a 3-liter, V-6 engine that to be used in 1987 minivans, a C-car in 1987 or 1988, a new A-car in 1988, and the Imperial in 1988.[1] Because of Chrysler's healthy cash reserves and marketable securities of nearly $3 billion, they began looking to diversify even further. Chrysler entered into an agreement with Lotus Cars, Ltd., concerning the development of a new engine and use of Lotus' electronically controlled suspension. A Chrysler executive stated the company would soon announce the purchase of 5 to 10% of Lotus as part of Chrysler's new global business strategy.[4] Chrysler also contracted with the Italian automaker Maserati S.P.A. to develop and build a two-seater sports car for the U.S. market, the production of which would amount to 5000 to 10,000 cars annually. The car would sell for at least $25,000 and be introduced in the spring of 1987. Chrysler, in turn, paid $2.3 million for a 5% stake in Maserati. Chrysler also signed a deal with the Korean electronics firm, Samsung Group, for parts and components. Chrysler also held 14% of French automaker Peugot, and was looking at the possibility of a joint venture in the labor-rich People's Republic of China. Chrysler diversified further by purchasing Gulfstream, which makes corporate jets, for $641 million, and E.F. Hutton Credit Corporation for $125 million:[5] "We're not going out on an acquisition binge, but Chrysler and its management represent attractive partners today to a lot of companies in a lot of businesses around the world." However, Chrysler then announced that it had agreed to buy Regie Nationale de Usines Renault's controlling interest in ailing American Motors Corporation, thus paving the way for Chrysler to acquire AMC.[18] The acquisition would combine the third and fourth largest American car manufacturer's capabilities (see tables).

General Motors and Chrysler were not alone in their efforts to globalize. Although talks between Ford of Europe and Fiat concerning a possible merger broke off, the two companies emerged from the discussions with a stronger relationship. Ford of Europe and Fiat are partners in the development of the CVT automatic transmission, and the two companies are still looking at a truck venture between Fiat's Iveco and Ford in Great Britain. Back in the U.S., Ford and Mazda were coming close to signing an agreement whereby Mazda would sell part of its Flat Rock, MI, passenger-car output to Ford, according to Louis Ross, former Ford executive vice-president for North American Automotive.

Operations, said Ford, would probably buy between 40 and 60% of Mazda's 140,000 production capacity. After Ford lost out to GM in the bidding for Hughes Aircraft, it announced in August 1985 it would buy First Nationwide Financial, parent company of the nation's ninth largest savings and loan, for $493 million. Ford also purchased in 1985 the New Holland farm equipment division of Sperry for $463 million.

Other global movements include the Japanese shifting into European assembly and manufacturing with alliances between Honda and Austin Rover and Nissan and Alfa Romeo. The shifting patterns of globalization and diversification by major auto manufacturers show not only a closer interdependence between countries of the world, but also a desire by manufacturers to strengthen their defense against the volatile auto industry. Joint ventures help ensure against one company's suffering huge losses, and diversification helps a company to "ride out" lags in the number of automobiles purchased. General Motors also stated one reason for the GM-Toyota joint venture was to gain technologic knowledge from the Japanese. So it appears for the time being and the near future that the globalization that Iacocca envisioned will continue to prosper.

The Man Behind the Turnaround

"It seemed as if the company might join Studebaker and Hudson — out of automaking. Now look what's happening."[19] The miraculous turnaround of the falling and failing Chrysler Corporation surprised everybody. One person who was not surprised, however, was the man who engineered the amazing feat, Lee Iacocca.

> "In an age of media heroes drawn largely from the ephemeral world of sports and entertainment, Iacocca became a real-world Rocky. The son of Italian immigrants, he swiftly climbed the corporate ladder at Ford Motor Company, built one of the best-selling cars in U.S. history — the Mustang — got thrown out by Henry Ford II himself, then went on to save the failing Chrysler Corporation and 600,000 American jobs."[10]

> "He's become the nation's foremost symbol for 'hanging tough', for 'toughing it out' under high-pressure nerve-wearing situations. He came out of nowhere to become the executive-apparent of Ford Motor Company — he was named to the key vice presidency at the age of 36. He became the

'industry genius' who conceived the Ford Mustang which had the highest first-year sales in automobile history — and who later led Ford Motor Company to net profits of $1.8 billion in each of two successive years. It hadn't been done before. It hasn't been done since. So he was fired."[11]

"He is a hard-nosed, direct man who demands the absolute most from his underlings and who has virtually no patience for their delinquencies, however minor: When one of his senior vice-presidents was two minutes late for the takeoff of a company plane on one occasion, Iacocca ordered the plane to leave without him. His underlings at Chrysler reacted to the change from 'easy rider' to 'snap-to' leadership in the expected way: Some of them began calling him 'Lee Ayatollah'."[11]

"Mr. Iacocca also is a product man supreme and marketing man genius. When he puts all that together with his people skills from decency to a tremendous computer-type mind, he's just a helluva fun guy to work under if you can take the beating."[9]

Indeed, Iacocca was the type of leader that Chrysler needed in order to survive. Further comments on the turnaround included: "Iacocca is absolutely the worst loser in the world. There's no way the guy can lose because he simply will not let it happen."[9] This image of Iacocca has helped him not only to provide leadership for Chrysler Corporation, but also to provide leadership for the country:[12]

"After saving and then rebuilding Chrysler Corporation against all odds, Lido Anthony Iacocca, 60, is now achieving another, more ephemeral sort of American miracle: he has become an industrial folk hero in a supposedly post-industrial age, and more improbably still, a corporate capitalist with populist appeal, an eminence terrible admired by working class and ruling class alike."

"'I owe it all to Iacocca,' says Sarah Haynes, a Chrysler assembly-line worker now back at work after a 5-year layoff. 'If the workers are saying he's great, it ain't no jive.'"

"'He went out and did exactly what he said he was going to do,' says Gordon North of Rochester, Minnesota. 'He's probably the most honest man in America.'"

"Economist Robert Lekachman wrote, 'Above all, the juices of humanity course through his veins.'"

"'He's real,' says attorney Joseph Califano, formerly a member of the Carter Administration Cabinet and now of Chrysler's board. 'And he cares — I think that comes through. He takes on fights he doesn't have to. He's like the hero of *Raiders of the Lost Ark*: He's been down, on the edge, picked himself up, came to the top again.' "

"'He tapped into America's frustrations,' says Ron DeLuca, the Kenyon and Eckhardt advertising agency executive in charge of Chrysler's ads. He said, 'It doesn't have to be this way. You can create your own destiny,' says Leo Arthur Kelmerson, president of Kenyon and Eckhardt. 'The country was starved for leadership and charisma. Lee talked directly to the American people.' "

"Gil MacDougald of Atlanta thinks Iacocca is great, and has a plausible sociological explanation to boot. 'In America, people pull for underdogs and they just love a winner. Iacocca was both.' "

Certainly these few comments made by those infatuated with him did not show the complete Iacocca, but they at least gave one a glance at the super businessman. Iacocca became very involved with the Statue of Liberty-Ellis Island Centennial Commission, and the fact that his father and mother both passed through Ellis Island might explain his preoccupation with the project. "The Statue of Liberty is just that — a beautiful symbol of what it means to be free. The reality is Ellis Island," Iacocca writes.[9] "Freedom is just the ticket of admission, but if you want to survive and prosper, there's a price to pay ... What the last 50 years taught us was the difference between right and wrong, that only hard work succeeds, that there are no free lunches, that you've got to be productive. Those are the values that made this country great."

John Morrissey of Kenyon and Eckhardt Advertising said,[9] "I don't know anybody else in Detroit who could have done what he did. I don't know anybody else who has the same kind of feeling for cars, toughness in doing what has to be done, as far as people, situations, and products are concerned. There may be somebody else who could have gotten it done, but I'll be damned if I know who it is."

With a 13.2% market share and massive personal promotion to widen his home base, it would remain to be seen if Iacocca's charismatic leadership could increase Chrysler's market share at home and abroad in view of unrestrained Japanese imports and the entry of Hyundai (from South Korea), and a close to $1 billion investment by Honda, Toyota, and Suzuki to produce over 200,000 units of small cars in U.S. assembly plants. Iacocca passed the first test with an A+. There would be many unknowns and determined players in the second contest yet to be faced by Iacocca.

Today Chrysler stands as strong as ever, bringing to the automotive industry a diversified Chrysler that is more confident then ever. Chrysler

Chairman and CEO Robert Eaton is steaming into cities worldwide, concentrating on global growth. No auto manufacturer has suffered more than Chrysler's equivalent of a manic depression; however, Chrysler today can be described as Detroit's new profitability champion.

Automotive Operations

Chrysler manufactures, assembles, and sells cars and trucks under the brand names Chrysler, Dodge, Plymouth, Eagle, and Jeep and related automotive parts and accessories, primarily in the U.S., Canada, and Mexico. Passenger cars are offered in various size classes and models. Chrysler produces trucks in pickup, sport utility, and van/wagon models, which constitute the largest segments of the truck market. Chrysler also purchases and distributes certain passenger cars manufactured in the U.S. by the Mitsubishi Motors Corporation's (MMC) subsidiary, Mitsubishi Motors Manufacturing of America (MMMA).

Although Chrysler currently sells most of its vehicles in North America, Chrysler also participates in other international markets through its wholly owned subsidiaries in Argentina, Brazil, Taiwan, Korea, Italy, France, and Venezuela; a majority-owned distributor in Japan; a joint venture in Austria; and through minority-owned affiliates located in China, Egypt, and Thailand. Chrysler sells vehicles and parts and provides related services to independent distributors and dealers in various other markets throughout the world.

Chrysler's strategy is to focus on its core automotive business. As part of this strategy, in 1996, Chrysler sold Electrospace Systems, Inc., and Chrysler Technologies Airborne Systems, Inc., which were principally engaged in the manufacture of defense electronics and aircraft modification, respectively, and represented substantially all of the operations of Chrysler Technologies Corporation (CTC), a wholly owned subsidiary of Chrysler. Also in 1996, Chrysler entered into an agreement to sell Pentastar Electronics, Inc. (PEI), which produces automatic test equipment for military applications and represented the remaining operations of CTC. The sale of PEI was completed on January 10, 1997. During the past several years, Chrysler has sold other such assets and businesses which were not related to its core automotive business and is exploring the sale of other non-core assets and businesses in the near term.

North American Operations

The automotive industry in North America is highly competitive with respect to a number of factors, including vehicle quality, pricing, development and introduction time, appearance, size, special options, distribution organization, warranties, reliability, safety, fuel economy, dealer service, and financing terms. As a result, Chrysler's ability to increase vehicle prices and to use retail sales incentives effectively is significantly affected by the pricing actions and sales programs of its principal competitors. Moreover, the introduction of new products by other manufacturers may adversely affect the market shares of competing products made by Chrysler. Recently, Chrysler has been very successful in bringing new products to market in greatly reduced vehicle development time. However, several of Chrysler's competitors have larger worldwide sales volumes and greater financial resources, which may, over time, place Chrysler at a competitive disadvantage in responding to its competitors' offerings, substantial changes in consumer preferences, governmental regulations, or adverse economic conditions in North America.

Chrysler's long-term profitability will depend significantly on its ability to continue its capital expenditure and vehicle development programs and to market its products successfully in an increasingly competitive environment. The success of Chrysler's new vehicles will depend on a number of factors, including general economic conditions, competition, consumer acceptance, product quality, new product development, the effect of governmental regulation, and the strength of Chrysler's marketing and dealer networks. As both Chrysler and its competitors plan to introduce new products, Chrysler cannot predict the market shares its new products will achieve. Moreover, Chrysler is substantially committed to its product plans and would be adversely affected by events requiring a major shift in product development.

Chrysler's principal competitors in North America are General Motors and Ford. In addition, a number of foreign automotive companies, principally Toyota, Honda, and Nissan, own and operate manufacturing and/or assembly facilities in North America ("transplants"), and there are a number of other foreign manufacturers that distribute automobiles and light-duty trucks in North America.

Chrysler de Mexico S.A.

Chrysler's consolidated subsidiary, Chrysler de Mexico S.A. (Chrysler Mexico), operates manufacturing and assembly facilities in Mexico, producing vehicles and components for both Mexican and export markets. In addition, Chrysler Mexico provides certain major automobile components to Chrysler, including engines, transmissions, and air conditioning condensers. Chrysler Mexico shipped 359,444 vehicles in 1996 and 207,004 vehicles in 1995. Of these totals, 36,283 vehicles and 26,503 vehicles were sold in Mexico in 1996 and 1995, respectively. Sales of vehicles exported to Mexico were 17,221 vehicles and 6565 vehicles in 1996 and 1995, respectively.

Chrysler Mexico's retail vehicle sales accounted for 14.4% of the Mexican car market and 20.1% of the Mexican truck market in 1996, compared with 14.5 and 17.7%, respectively, in 1995. Within the Mexican industry, Chrysler Mexico's retail unit sales ranked fifth in cars and third in trucks in 1996. Retail industry sales in Mexico are estimated to have been approximately 330,500 units in 1996, 232,600 units in 1995, and 618,900 units in 1994. The decrease in retail industry sales in 1996 and 1995, compared with 1994, was primarily attributable to unfavorable economic conditions in Mexico, commencing with the devaluation of the Mexican peso in December 1994. Although Chrysler expected the economic conditions in Mexico to continue to improve in 1997, Chrysler cannot predict when Mexican automotive industry sales will return to predevaluation levels. Chrysler's operating results, when compared to operating results prior to the devaluation of the peso, will continue to be adversely affected to the extent that the unfavorable economic conditions in Mexico continue.

International Operations

Outside of North America, the automotive industry consists of numerous manufacturers, with no single dominant producer. However, certain manufacturers account for a majority of total vehicle sales within specific countries. Many of the factors that impact sales volumes and profitability in the North American automotive market are also prevalent outside of North America.

Chrysler shipments to markets outside of North America in 1996 were 187,057 units, an increase of 19,677 units or 12% from 1995. Retail sales in European markets in 1996 were 102,139 units, compared to 84,585 units in 1995. Retail sales in 1996 in other world markets, primarily Japan, Taiwan, and the Middle East, were 119,896 units compared to 101,349 units in 1995. In addition, Chrysler exported 36,600 kits to worldwide affiliates for assembly in 1996, compared to 40,892 kits in 1995. The majority of the kits were Jeep products shipped to China, Indonesia, and Venezuela. Chrysler's international operations are divided primarily into three regions: Europe, Asia/Pacific, and Latin America/Middle East/Africa.

Europe

Outside of North America, Europe is the largest market for the sale of Chrysler vehicles. Chrysler's automotive operations in Europe consist primarily of manufacturing operations in Austria, where Jeep Grand Cherokees are assembled under an assembly contract with Steyr-Daimler-Puch Fahrzeugtechnik (Steyr), and Chrysler Voyagers are assembled by Eurostar Automobilwerk Ges.mb.H & Co. KG (Eurostar), a joint venture between Chrysler and Steyr. Chrysler vehicles assembled in Austria are both sold in Europe and exported to other markets. Chrysler also exports finished vehicles produced in North America to independent distributors and to wholly owned distribution companies in Italy and France. During 1996, Chrysler established its wholly owned distribution companies in Italy and France and a European Headquarters Office in Brussels, Belgium.

Asia/Pacific

Chrysler's automotive operations in the Asia/Pacific region include the assembly in China of Jeep Cherokees for distribution in China by Beijing Jeep Corporation, Ltd., a minority-owned joint venture. In addition, Chrysler has agreements for the assembly of righthand-drive Jeep vehicles in Malaysia, Indonesia, and Thailand. Chrysler sells vehicles in this region through wholly owned distributors in Taiwan and Korea, a majority-owned distributor in Japan, a joint-venture in Thailand, and independent distributors and dealers.

International Strategy

Chrysler's international expansion strategy is based primarily on the integration of international and North American product development which enables Chrysler to satisfy market demands for righthand-drive versions shortly after lefthand-drive versions debut in the U.S. At the end of 1996, five righthand-drive models (Chrysler Neon and Voyager and Jeep Cherokee, Grand Cherokee, and Wrangler) were available for sale in certain international markets. Also as part of its international expansion strategy, Chrysler expects to continue to focus on growth opportunities in major markets in Western Europe, Japan, and China and explore developing markets in South America, Eastern Europe, and the Asia-Pacific region. New manufacturing and joint venture operations could be established if market conditions, sales levels, and profitability opportunities are consistent with Chrysler's corporate objectives.

Although it sells products and sources components internationally, Chrysler presently does not have significant risks related to changes in currency exchange rates because its business is primarily conducted in the U.S. When Chrysler sells vehicles or purchases components outside the U.S., transactions are frequently denominated in currencies other than U.S. dollars. The primary foreign currencies in which Chrysler conducts such transactions are the German mark, French franc, Japanese yen, Canadian dollar, Mexican peso, Taiwan dollar, Austrian schilling, British pound, Spanish peseta, Italian lira, Swiss franc, Dutch guilder, and Belgian franc. To the extent possible, sales and purchases in specific currencies are offset against each other. In addition, Chrysler periodically initiates hedging activities by entering into currency exchange agreements, consisting primarily of currency forward contracts and purchased currency options, to minimize revenue and cost variations which could result from fluctuations in currency exchange rates. Chrysler also utilizes written currency options to close out existing purchased currency options.

At December 31, 1996, Chrysler had currency exchange agreements for the following primary foreign currencies: German mark, French franc, Japanese yen, British pound, Swiss franc, Dutch guilder, and Belgian franc. Chrysler's operating results are affected by changes in currency exchange rates during the period in which transactions are executed, to the extent that hedge coverage does not exist. However, the impact of any changes in currency exchange rates on unhedged transactions is not expected to be material to Chrysler's operating results or financial position.

Chrysler does not use derivative financial instruments for trading purposes. Chrysler's hedging activities are based upon purchases and sales which are exposed to foreign currency risk. The currency exchange agreements which provide hedge coverage typically mature within 3 years of origination, consistent with the underlying purchase or sales commitment. These hedging instruments are periodically modified as existing commitments are fulfilled and new commitments are made. Chrysler's management believes that its hedging activities have been effective in reducing Chrysler's limited risks related to currency exchange fluctuations.

Automotive Marketing

New passenger cars and trucks are sold at retail by dealers who have sales and service agreements with Chrysler. The dealers purchase cars, trucks, parts, and accessories from Chrysler for sale to retail customers. In the U.S., Chrysler had 4612 dealers as of December 31, 1996, compared with 4652 at the end of 1995. Chrysler Canada had 598 dealers at December 31, 1996, compared with 609 dealers at December 31, 1995.

The quality and strength of Chrysler's dealer organization will have an important impact on future sales. Chrysler maintains programs to provide dealership operating capital through equity investments where sufficient private capital is not available. The programs anticipate that the dealer receiving such assistance will eventually use its share of the dealership profits to purchase Chrysler's equity investment. Chrysler's equity interest in U.S. and Canadian dealerships totaled $17 million in 43 dealerships as of December 31, 1996, compared with $22 million in 51 dealerships as of December 31, 1995.

Chrysler continues to focus on quality customer service. A customer satisfaction survey process provides Chrysler and its franchised dealers continuous customer feedback regarding dealer sales, service, and parts operations. In addition, the Chrysler Customer Center is designed to promote customer satisfaction and communicate customer concerns to dealers and internally to vehicle platform teams.

Manufactured and Purchased Products, Components, and Materials

Chrysler continues to focus on its core automotive business. Chrysler manufactures most of its requirements for engines, transmissions, and transaxles; certain body stampings; electronic components; and fabricated glass parts. Chrysler purchases materials, parts, and other components from numerous unaffiliated suppliers. Chrysler used approximately 1050 suppliers of productive materials in 1996, compared to approximately 1150 in 1995. Interruptions in production or delivery of these productive materials could adversely affect Chrysler. Chrysler purchases a larger portion of its productive materials from unaffiliated suppliers than do its principal competitors and expects to continue purchasing its requirements for these items rather than manufacturing them.

Mitsubishi Motors Corporation

As a result of relatively low sales volumes in recent years, Chrysler and Mitsubishi Motors Corporation (MMC) agreed in 1996 to terminate the U.S. Distribution Agreement (USDA) under which Chrysler imported and distributed selected models of passenger cars manufactured by MMC in Japan. A similar distribution agreement covering the Canadian market was also terminated in 1996. During 1996 and 1995, Chrysler sold 4692 and 14,823 MMC-manufactured vehicles in the U.S., respectively, representing less than 1% of Chrysler's U.S. retail vehicle sales in each year. Chrysler will continue to purchase 2.5-liter and 3.0-liter V-6 engines from MMC for use in certain minivans and other vehicles through the 1999 model year. Chrysler purchased approximately 308,000 such engines during 1996, compared to 372,000 engines in 1995.

Mitsubishi Motors Manufacturing of America (MMMA) produces small sporty cars in the U.S. for Chrysler and Mitsubishi Motor Sales of America. Pursuant to a distribution agreement that terminates in July 1999, Chrysler retains the right to purchase vehicles up to a specific maximum allocation that has been agreed to by the parties for each model year. In addition, Chrysler will provide engines and transmissions for use in certain MMMA vehicles. Chrysler's sales of MMMA-manufactured vehicles in 1996 and 1995 represented 3.3 and 3.7%, respectively, of Chrysler's U.S. retail vehicle sales volume in each period.

Chrysler previously owned an equity interest in both MMC and MMMA. Chrysler sold its 50% interest in MMMA to MMC, its partner in the joint venture, in October 1991. Chrysler subsequently sold its equity interest in MMC in 1992 and 1993.

Research and Development

For the years ended December 31, 1996, 1995, and 1994, Chrysler spent $1.6 billion, $1.4 billion, and $1.3 billion, respectively, for company-sponsored research and development activities. These activities relate to the development of new products and services and the improvement of existing products and services, as well as compliance with standards that have been and are being promulgated by the government.

Employees

At December 31, 1996, Chrysler had approximately 126,000 employees worldwide. Of this total, approximately 74,000 hourly workers and 26,000 salaried workers were employed in the U.S., and 13,000 hourly workers and 2000 salaried workers were employed in Canada. In the U.S. and Canada, approximately 97% of Chrysler's hourly employees and 24% of its salaried employees are represented by unions. Of these represented employees, 97% of hourly and 90% of salaried employees are represented by the United Automotive, Aerospace, and Agricultural Implement Workers of America (UAW) or the National Automobile, Aerospace, and Agricultural Implement Workers of Canada (CAW).

In 1996, Chrysler negotiated 3-year national agreements with both the UAW and CAW, without an interruption of production. The UAW and CAW contracts provide for essentially the same level of wages and benefits as Chrysler's major domestic competitors. In addition, the local plant agreements at all of Chrysler's major production facilities have been settled.

Chrysler's pension plans, group life, and health-care benefits for active and retired employees generally follow the structure of benefits common to the automotive industry.

Financial

Earnings for the year ended December 31, 1996, include a charge of $97 million ($61 million after taxes) for costs associated with a voluntary early retirement program for certain salaried employees, a charge of $77 million ($51 million after taxes) related to a write-down of Pentastar Electronics, Inc., a charge of $65 million ($100 million after taxes) related to a write-down of Thrifty Rent-A-Car System, Inc., a charge of

$50 million ($31 million after taxes) for lump-sum retiree pension costs related to the new UAW collective bargaining agreement, and a gain of $101 million ($87 million after taxes) from the sale of Electrospace Systems, Inc. and Chrysler Technologies Airborne Systems, Inc.

Earnings for the year ended December 31, 1995, were reduced by a $263 million charge ($162 million after taxes) for costs associated with production changes at Chrysler's Newark assembly plant and a $115 million charge ($71 million after taxes) for a voluntary minivan owner service action. Net earnings in 1995 also include an after-tax charge of $96 million for the cumulative effect of a change in accounting principle related to the consensus reached on Emerging Issues Task Force (EITF) Issue 95-1, "Revenue Recognition on Sales with a Guaranteed Minimum Resale Value."

The increase in sales of manufactured products in 1996 as compared with 1995 primarily reflects an 11% increase in vehicle shipments and an increase in average revenue per unit, net of sales incentives, from $18,305 to $19,442. The increase in average revenue per unit in 1996 as compared with 1995 was principally due to pricing actions and an increased proportion of truck shipments to total vehicle shipments. The increase in sales of manufactured products in 1995 as compared with 1994 primarily reflects an increase in average revenue per unit, net of sales incentives, from $17,663 to $18,305, largely offset by a 3% decrease in vehicle shipments. The increase in average revenue per unit in 1995 as compared with 1994 was principally due to pricing actions, partially offset by higher sales incentives.

The increase in finance and insurance revenues in 1996 as compared with 1995 was primarily attributable to higher average automotive finance receivables outstanding and vehicles leased. The increase in finance and insurance revenues in 1995 as compared with 1994 was primarily attributable to higher average automotive finance receivables outstanding.

References

1. *Automotive News*, April 8, 1985, p. 2.
2. *Automotive News*, April 15, 1985.
3. *Automotive News*, April 22, 1985, p. 49.
4. *Automotive News*, May 13, 1985, p. 8.
5. *Automotive News*, May 27, 1985, p. 2.
6. Chrysler Corporation, *Annual Report*, 1984.
7. *Forbes*, November 7, 1983, p. 43.
8. Lee Iacocca, *Iacocca, An Autobiography*, Bantam Books, New York, 1984.

9. NBC News Special Report with Tom Brokaw, *Iacocca: An American Profile*, 1984.
10. "Behind the Wheels," *Newsweek*, October 8, 1984, p. 50.
11. "The Chrysler Deal," *Saturday Evening Post*, March 1982, p. 72.
12. "A Spunky Tycoon Turned Superstar," *Time*, April 1, 1985.
13. "Chrysler's Back," *U.S. News and World Report*, February 14, 1983.
14. "Danger Rough Road Ahead," *Fortune*, March 17, 1997.
15. "Can Chrysler Keep it Up?," *Business Week*, November 25, 1996.
16. Chrysler Corporation, Annual Report, 1996.
17. "Chrysler's Great Expectations," *Fortune*, December 9, 1996.
18. *Wall Street Journal*, March 11, 1987, p. 24.
19. *U.S. News and World Report*, February 14, 1982, p. 68.

Chrysler and American Motors Corporation Compared (1986 Data)

	Chrysler	American Motors Corporation
Number of assembly plants	7	4
Capacity (vehicles per year)	1,854,764	796,000
Employees	120,900	19,500
Car market share	11.9%	0.7%
Share of total U.S. light-truck market (incl. utility vehicles)	12.8%	4.5%
Net income (loss)	$1.40 billion	($81.3 million)
Number of dealers	4026	1300

Source: Data from *Wall Street Journal*, March 11, 1987.

5-Year Supplementary Data

	1995	1994	1993	1992	1991
Total revenues	$53,195	$52,235	$43,600	$36,897	$29,370
Earnings (loss)	2121	3713	2415	505	−538
Primary earnings per common share	5.55	10.11	6.77	1.47	−2.22
Net earnings	2025	3713	(2551)	723	−795
Dividends declared per common share	2.00	1.10	0.65	0.60	0.6
Total assets	53,756	49,539	43,679	40,690	43,076
Total debt	14,193	13,106	11,451	15,551	19,438
Convertible preferred stock (in shares)	0.1	1.7	1.7	1.7	—

Note: Dollars and shares are expressed in millions.

Industry Segment Data

	Car and Truck	Financial Services	Consolidated
December 31, 1995			
Revenues	50,979	2439	53,195
Operating earnings	3191	522	3539
Interest expense	275	—	101
Depreciation/amortization	2139	81	2220
Capital expenditures	3774	335	4109
Identifiable assets	38,358	17,835	53,756
Liabilities	30,701	14,533	42,797
December 31, 1994			
Revenues	50,388	1995	52,235
Operating earnings	5829	1995	6023
Interest expense	311	—	190
Depreciation/amortization	1880	75	1955
Capital expenditures	3796	228	4024
Identifiable assets	36001	16,648	49,539
Liabilities	28,580	13,375	38,845
December 31, 1993			
Revenues	41,715	2039	43,600
Operating earnings	4050	267	4200
Interest expense	445	—	328
Depreciation/amortization	1530	110	1640
Capital expenditures	2977	18	2995
Identifiable assets	32,492	14,251	43,679
Liabilities	28,787	11,120	36,843

Note: Figures expressed in millions of dollars.

Financial Position, Year End

	1995	*1994*	*1993*	*1992*	*1991*
Current assets	$12,414	$11,991	$8485	$6777	$5763
Current liabilities	14,583	13,063	10,995	8948	8694
Working capital	−2169	−1073	−2510	−2171	−2931
Current ratio	0.85	0.92	0.77	0.76	0.66
Total assets	40,475	38,077	34,020	27,644	25,544
Long-term debt	1763	2097	2281	3643	3672
Shareholders equity	10,959	10,694	6836	7538	6109
Shares of common stock outstanding	378.3	355.1	353.7	295.5	292

Note: Dollars and shares are expressed in millions.

Case 9. Toyota Motor Corporation*

Pre-World War II

In 1926, Sakichi Toyoda established the Toyoda Automatic Loom Works in central Japan to produce a loom that he had invented. In 1930, just before his death, Toyoda sold the rights to his invention and gave the proceeds to his son Kiichiro to start an auto business. Three years later, in 1933, Kiichiro Toyoda established an automobile division within the loom factory copying U.S. engine designs he had seen on earlier visits to American automobile plants. Finally, in 1935, Toyoda's infant plant produced its first prototype vehicle. Japanese protectionist legislation provided Toyoda the necessary leverage to try to compete with GM and Ford, who were the preeminent forces in worldwide automotive industry, even having plants in Japan. In 1937, Toyoda split off the automobile department from the loom factory and took the car facility public, changing the name to Toyota (to ensure its clarity in spoken Japanese).[1]

Due to the country's inherent shortage of natural resources, such as oil, the company's instinctive direction for production was towards highly fuel-efficient engines. Toward this end, the company also established a research center in 1939 to explore battery-powered vehicles. By 1940, the company was expanding in all areas at a furious pace with the

* This case was written by Dr. M. Reza Vaghefi and Jay Coleman and assisted by Keely Mitts for classroom discussion only.

establishment of the Toyoda Science Research Center (which is the heart of today's Toyota Central R&D Laboratories, Inc.), Toyoda Works (currently Achi Steel Works, Ltd.), and Toyoda Machine Works, Ltd.[2]

Unfortunately, the Japanese government had forbidden the company to build passenger cars because the emperor needed production centered around the country's war efforts of World War II, so the company was unable to exploit that lucrative market.

After World War II

After the war, Toyoda realized that the government could not provide protection for the industry in the form of high import duties or other barriers, especially since the country was controlled by the U.S. government. The company consequently redirected its efforts and so elected to stay away from the market for medium and large vehicles dominated by the American manufacturers. As a result, the company focused its efforts on what it knew best — production of small, efficient cars.

In 1949, the country and its business industries were in great turmoil with union demands and national fiscal and monetary problems. Toyoda had placed such strong emphasis on production that it neglected to balance it with the proper sales. The resulting liquidity quandary required the company to restructure to meet the demands of the tumultuous economy. Subsequently, Toyota Motor Sales, the company's marketing arm, was created as a separate company, responsible for domestic and worldwide sales.

As part of the restructuring program, representatives of the company visited Ford plants in the U.S. to seek new ideas. One of those adopted was the formulation of suggestion systems which encourage every employee to make suggestions for any and every kind of improvements. More importantly, the company developed its *kanban* system of synchronized parts delivery for more efficient production control. In conjunction with these changes, the company renewed its commitment to R&D modernization and intense quality production.[2] These long-term policies saw the company grow very efficiently and successfully. Also, in an effort to push domestic market consumption and boost sales, the company developed driving schools across the country, taking advantage of the country's increasing prosperity, ballooning desires for new products, and growing motorization.[1]

The Golden Years and Beyond

After Japan became a member of GATT in 1955, Toyota saw great opportunities for increased international trade and was able to establish its presence in the U.S. market in 1957.[2] Unfortunately, its first production launch of the small-engine Toyopet Crown was a failure. After better market studies of the American consumer needs, the company introduced the successful Corona model in 1965 and the best-selling car of all time, the Corolla, in 1968, 2 years after it was successfully introduced in Japan. Toyota's success was a direct result of the investments made in production control and quality management in the 1950s. The positive outcome of its efforts saw the company being awarded the coveted Deming prize for quality control achievement in 1965. By 1970, Toyota was the fourth largest auto manufacturer in the world.[1]

The '70s, '80s, and '90s

Toyota continued to expand rapidly through the oil crisis of the 1970s, as the company's chairman, Eiji Toyoda, was convinced that the automobile was increasingly becoming a necessity and not a luxury. To provide for the changing environment as he saw it, Toyoda quickly eliminated facilities designed exclusively for the production of specific models. Instead, flexible production systems were adopted that easily responded to changes in market demand. This philosophy of general-purpose plants that could be quickly re-tooled to produce different models was one of the key to success during this period. By 1975, Toyota displaced Volkswagen as the number one importer of vehicles into the U.S., and the company continued to blossom.[1]

By 1980, the U.S. had fallen behind Japan with respect to its aggregate automobile production. In fact, Toyota was now ranked second only to the mighty General Motors in total number of cars produced. Toyota's rapid success actually resulted in the company becoming the target of criticism because of its aggressive stance with parts procurement and subcontractor dealings. To try to combat that predicament, intense public relations became an increasingly important part of operations for the company. Automobile production in the U.S. began in 1984 as a joint venture with GM which was one way to help ease tensions between the two countries. This event though was the precursor for the company opening its Georgetown, KY, plant in 1988 as a means of taking advantage of the growing American market.[2] The company was again evaluating its market position and marched into the luxury line with the launch of its successful Lexus model in 1989. Production of the Lexus line was kept in Japan, where experience was necessary, quality controls were better with more efficient output, and growing pains of new facilities would not hamper efficiencies. At that point in time, the company had 12 different models under the Toyota label and three under Lexus, providing a car for every possible consumer taste.

Profile

Toyota is totally dedicated to quality and performance with the goal of absolute customer satisfaction. Everyone within the company is committed to achieving performance efficiencies. The company has very little top-down management because of empowerment policies where team workers are responsible for production quality, a critical element of Toyota's philosophy.

Corporate Culture

The corporate culture is based on traditional unquestioning loyalty and discipline exemplified by Samurai warriors; however, management style is very cooperative, more on the side of Douglas McGregor's "Theory Y" type of participative management. With decisions being made by consensus, everyone plays a part in the decision-making process, with decisions percolating from the bottom up. A decision with everyone behind it is far better than a decision imposed form the top. Because everyone already knows what is to be done, such a process makes immediate implementation of a decision easy and effective.[3]

Management

This management style lends itself well to the quality circles, where workers manage their own section of the production line, do their own production planning, and control their own quality. Management then simply brings all the parts together. A system of synergy quickly evolves.

In spite of the participative management style, the company's organizational structure is typically hierarchical, but the positions involve less of a financial responsibility and authority and more of earned respect. The role of each manager is that of mediator for those lower in the organizational structure and not as a boss who imposes his own will on his employees. Also, the positions have less functionality and greater overall company orientation.

Market Coverage

The company's competitive scope is divided into two frontiers. The first contains the Toyota name tag and all its products. The other is the Lexus line of cars designed to meet the needs of a different market. Each functions separately with different goals and objectives. Toyota's main line of products are for the general consumer market which is typically quite price sensitive or more value conscious. A broad range of products is necessary to serve a wide customer base. The Lexus line is more differentiated. It also brings higher margins with that exclusivity. Status and style are the overwhelming concerns for the consumers willing and able to pay for the fewer product selections in this line.

As a global player in the automobile industry, Toyota possibly touches every conceivable market in the world. The reach of its markets is unparalleled by any other car company in the world. Larger market needs are accommodated with domestic production and a more localized marketing approach. Smaller markets feel the strength of globalized marketing strategies of standardized products. In either event, the company is attempting to maximize its production efficiencies as it covers the world.

Current Environment

Japan

Japan's 1993 vehicle production was expected to fall to levels last seen a decade ago, according to an Japan Automobile Manufacturers Association (JAMA) official. JAMA also announced that vehicle production in the first 6 months of 1993 was down 7.2% from a year earlier, to 5,877,626, the third straight year decline for the period. This represented the second biggest year decline for a first half of the fiscal year period. The worst was a 9.4% fall in the first 6 months of 1974. Although the weak economy hurt sales, a lack of inventory also kept sales thin.

Japan's vehicle output in 1992 totaled 12,499,284, down 5.6% from the year before, a second straight year decline. Toyota cut its forecast of overseas vehicle output to 880,000 or 890,000 (16%) in 1993 from a December forecast of 940,000, against an actual 764,292 in 1992.[4]

Following is the production of five major manufacturers, as of July 1992, and how it compared with the previous year:

Toyota	322,528	down 15.2%
Nissan	169,489	down 11.3%
Mitsubishi	123,927	down 2.4%
Honda	105,555	down 2.7%
Mazda	80,530	down 29.4%

JAMA also expected vehicle exports to be down 14% for July of 1992 compared to a year earlier.[5]

Overseas

Meanwhile, in Europe, car sales declined as recession persisted in Western Europe. In 1992, sales hit a record 13.5 million after accelerating smoothly through the 1980s from just over 10 million in 1984. Now the European car market is down by 20% at the half-year point in terms of new car sales. Sales are predicted to dive to 11.3 million in 1993, before struggling back slightly to 11.7 million in 1994, and 12.5 million in 1995.[6]

Regardless of the gloomy economic news there are signs of hope. Detroit's Big Three and the seven Japanese companies that build cars and trucks in the U.S. sold a total of 280,778 vehicles in the period of September 11–20, 1993, up 20.9% from the same time last year. Among Japanese automakers that build cars in the U.S., Toyota's sales jumped 59% during that period. The reviving U.S. economy has proved very beneficial for the industry in general.[7]

Value-Added Marketing

The automobile market is definitely a buyer's one. Companies have to work hard to get the customer's dollar. In an effort to lure customers, there has been a return to the basics, particularly to attract the under-35 generation of people who have no brand preference. Product content enhancement plus better engineering, new technology, and added value are necessary to develop a more sophisticated message that provides more information and very specific customer benefits. Identifying specific benefits in dramatic ways and answering the customer's question of "Why should I buy this car?" are the strategic objectives of marketing startegies.[8] Consumers are less likely to be moved to a purchase by flashy, glittery promises and impassioned company war cries such as Chevrolet's "The Heartbeat of America" theme. In other words, consumers are looking for quality at a reasonable price, value-added features, and safety.

To address these consumers wants, Toyota has spent more on R&D than any other Japanese automaker. Toyota puts great emphasis on the safety of the consumer and the environment. They believe safety should not be compromised, and consumers on any budget should have access to safety features. This concept is illustrated by the Starlet. The Starlet is a small, affordable vehicle with a reinforced cabin structure, airbags, and an antilock brake system.

Another safety feature Toyota has introduced is the vehicle safety control (VSC) system. This system senses the direction of the car and the turning angle of the steering wheel to avoid sideways skidding. The direction of the car is interpreted to determine deviation as with sideways skidding. If deviation exists, the system actuates the brakes and engine control throttle to achieve stability.

Toyota has also won the Japan Society of Mechanical Engineers award for advances in lean-burning technology. This technology provides a leaner air/fuel ratio which allows the production of more fuel-efficient vehicles. These lean-burn engines are especially important in economies where the price of gasoline is a major determinant in the decision of a consumer to buy. These engines are currently available in Japan and the U.K. in vehicles such as the Carina, Corona, Premio, Caldina station wagon, and the Carina E.

Looking toward the future, Toyota has established the Intelligent Transport Systems Planning Division to develop and commercialize highway developments. Currently, Toyota has a driverless car in operation on the proving grounds in Japan. It operates by use of magnetic markers embedded in the road.[9]

Price

The company increased its U.S. prices of 1994-model cars and trucks by an average of 3.9%, or $601, over comparably equipped 1993 models.

The Lexus division's 1994 U.S. car prices increased an average of 5.9%, or $2209, compared with comparable 1993 models.

The relatively large Toyota price increase on the 1994 models was driven primarily by the appreciation of the Japanese yen (which had risen almost 20% against the dollar) and the cost of new government safety and emissions control equipment.[10] The consumer obviously would be expected to respond by buying the lower priced American alternatives. In an effort to stem the exodus of customers from their products, Toyota has pushed for more efficiency and productivity and has held its price increases to moderate levels by dipping into its profit margins in an effort to maintain market share.

Rivals

In spite of Toyota and other Japanese car makers' price hikes, U.S. automakers have continually threatened that they may file dumping charges against their Japanese counterparts if they fail to raise prices even more to compensate for a higher yen. On the other hand, Toyota believes that the effect of the yen has been somewhat moderated by the flat or falling cost of certain key raw materials that are bought with dollars, by stringent cost-cutting steps by Toyota and its suppliers, and by the growing production of Toyota vehicles and components in North America. Toyota's cost-cutting programs have offset some of the increase in the value of the yen, but there is only so much that can be done without an appropriate increase in car prices.[10]

To demonstrate dumping, the U.S. automakers must prove two things: that importers are selling cars in the U.S. for less than in their own country and that the pricing has hurt their own ability to sell cars and make profits. The Big Three for years have kept close track of importer pricing. Two years ago, they filed a formal dumping case accusing Toyota and Mazda of underpricing minivans. They also considered, but decided against, filing a case over pickup trucks. As long as U.S. automakers continue fighting competitive battles with lobbyists rather than engineers, consumers end up the losers.[11]

The battle continues on other fronts as Toyota will experience strong competition in its commanding small-car category from Chrysler, which is hoping to attract a younger generation of buyers with cars such as the "fun to drive" and affordable Neon. Designed at a cost of $1.3 billion, Chrysler's new Neon started production in November 1994 and went on sale in the U.S. in January 1995. It will go head to head with Toyota's Corolla.[12]

In the meantime, Toyota is expected to announce plans to sell the Lexus GS300 in Europe for the first time to compete at the high end of the executive car class, dominated now by the BMW "5" series.[6]

Symbiosis

A good, affordable car cannot be made without good, affordable parts. As a result, automakers are heavily dependent upon their suppliers as they vie to outdo the ever-improving competition. That means an increasingly competitive environment for parts makers as pressure from automakers for high-quality, low-cost parts has also meant lean, mean production capabilities for these businesses. Parts makers must do far more than simply fill orders. Suppliers are expected to play critical roles in the design of new cars, make top-quality parts, deliver them just before the auto plants need them, and do it all with extreme efficiency as a means of putting the customer first.

Demands on Suppliers

Lean manufacturing endorses a method of production that uses fewer resources and is more flexible. Workers become multi-faceted, doing more than one job. Work teams must be able to change setups quickly to accommodate a different product as needed. The zero defect goal must be the work cry for all employees while workers are continually expected to produce more in less time. Those companies that improve production processes and quality to meet these standards of excellence which are demanded from Toyota will be phenomenally successful.

Toyota does not tell parts makers how to run their business but sets rigid standards for quality, cost, and delivery that must be met. If the supplier has a problem, Toyota will lend its expertise. The relationship is long-term, based on mutual trust and respect, with suppliers being merely an extension of the company, a Toyota *keiretsu*. Suppliers are also learning how to hold costs down with the help of Toyota by emulating its efficient manufacturing techniques. The company recently opened the Toyota Suppliers Support Center in Lexington, KY, to do just that.[13]

The power of suppliers in the end can be pretty substantial if they ship on time and produce reliable products. If, however, that is not the case then they naturally lose that bargaining edge. Also, many suppliers produce unique components and such companies would be difficult to replace. This is why Toyota goes to such extents to help its suppliers. Though Toyota demands a great deal from its suppliers, the benefits are mutual profits.

Production

Kentucky

Toyota Motor recently laid down a plan with GM to buy engine blocks to use in its Camry sedans built in Georgetown, KY. The engine blocks will come from the GM's powertrain division in Defiance, OH. The order for 180,000 units annually will be worth $30 million.[14]

Toyota Motor Manufacturing USA undertook an $800 million expansion at its Georgetown, KY, plant. The current size of 4.45 million square feet is designed to produce 240,000 vehicles. The expansion plan has added 200,000 square feet to the powertrain area and 3.2 million square feet to the assembly plant. Production began in March 1994. When the expansion is completed, the entire plant will have an annual stated capacity of 400,000 vehicles. Also, the number of employees is expected to rise from 4700 to 6000.[15] To keep stride with expansion at its plant, Toyota has hired the help of Cincinnati Milacron of Ohio to make seven manufacturing cells of a plastics machinery plant.[16]

California

One of Toyota's greatest successes came not just for itself but in the joint venture with General Motors when together they created the New United Motor Manufacturing, Inc. (NUMMI) to use the production facility of the car factory in Fremont, CA. That plant is currently enjoying phenomenal success due to the widespread application of an adaptation of Frederick Winslow Taylor's "scientific management" whereby the stopwatches and clipboards for the time-and-motion regimen have been placed in the hands of workers, not managers. The reason Taylor's method has produced such startling results is that Toyota has persuaded the workers that they are the key element in the factory's success. The same philosophy is used in their Japanese plants. The GM factory at

Fremont had been one of the company's worst since it opened in 1963 with extremely low quality, a depressed level of general productivity, and high absenteeism. In 1986, 2 years after GM restarted the Fremont assembly line with Toyota as its partner, the new plant under NUMMI saw its productivity soar higher than any other GM factory and more than twice as high as the level achieved at the same factory under GM management, while absenteeism dropped from between 20 and 25% at the old plant to a steady 3 to 4% at NUMMI.[17,18]

Committed to R&D in the U.S.

In April of 1993, Toyota opened a vehicle-testing site larger than Manhatten island in the Arizona desert near Whitman. The test site, one of the biggest in the world, was developed at a cost of $110 million. Part of this 12,000-acre proving ground, includes a 10-mile, high-speed oval track; a 40,000-square-foot garage; and a 15,000-square-foot office building. In acreage, the Toyota proving ground eclipses the 5000-acre General Motors proving grounds in the southeast valley, formerly the biggest test facility in the state. Other carmakers with test facilities in Arizona are Chrysler (with a 3800-acre site north of Sun City), Ford, Jaguar, Nissan, Volvo, and Volkswagen, all with much smaller facilities.[13]

Toyota made great efforts to maintain its social responsibility by being as environmentally sensitive as possible to the desert plants and animals. For instance, large culverts allow animals to pass underneath the oval track while only about 4% of the site was disturbed to build such test features as a 1.5-mile ride-and-handling course, a 1.5-mile dirt track, and a 1.75-mile brake-test lane. This testing center will help Toyota remain competitive in the crowded American market.

Back in late 1957, upon entering the U.S. market, Toyota did not offer what Americans wanted or needed so they spent the next 35 years trying to do a better job of earning the satisfaction of American car buyers. This facility will help realize that goal.

In general, the company has complete commitment to the U.S. market and even its economy. Not only is Toyota's presence felt on the roads, but it also significantly impacts U.S. employment with over 50 facilities of various types each providing over 1000 jobs and thousands more small facilities. Needless to say, Toyota is in this market for the long haul.

As part of its efforts to sell foreign-made vehicles in Japan, Toyota has been marketing Volkswagen and Audi cars since April 1992 through its DUO outlets. In August of that year, import and sales of a new station wagon manufactured by Toyota in Georgetown, KY, commenced. The car, called the Scepter, was the first U.S.-built vehicle Toyota will import for sale in Japan. It is a righthand-drive version of the Camry wagon, which was introduced to the U.S. in April 1992.[19] Toyota is also promoting exports of U.S.-built vehicles such as the Camry wagons to Europe and Canada. Toyota's plan to double the capacity of its Georgetown, KY, plant is concurrent with its policy of using its U.S. operations as export bases.[20]

For fiscal year 1992, Toyota's share of the Japanese new vehicle market was 32%, while the new car market share was 43%. At the same time, revenues from North America contributed only 24% to the total consolidated income statement, while 58% came from the Japanese market. It is easy to see that the U.S. market, with lots of room to grow, plays a major role in Toyota's economic wellbeing. In that same year, 37% of Toyota's North American sales were from vehicles produced in North America. With the expansion plans in Kentucky and expansion of truck output at NUMMI, 47% of sales in North America would be from vehicles produced in North America, a figure expected to increase to over 50% in 1995 and beyond.[21] Changes in unit volume coupled with changes in global geographic mix will position Toyota as a leader in the automotive industry worldwide. It is building or expanding six assembly plants around the world with a total capacity of 1 million vehicles.[22]

North American Market

Toyota Motor Corporate Services of North America, Inc., announced that in February 1997 American-produced cars rose 63.2% for the month, illustrating Toyota's commitment to localization. Total North American production has increased 5.4% as of March 1997 as compared with the same period the previous year. Much of this success is attributed to the Georgetown, KY, plant which produces the Camry, the Avalon, and the Sienna minivan. The production of Camrys at Georgetown has increased 19.1% compared with March of 1996. The production of the Camry amounted to over 30,000 units for 4 consecutive months. Overall, North American production increased over 5% as compared to the same period the previous year.

In June 1997, Toyota announced that U.S. production since 1986 has surpassed the 4 million mark. As of March 1997, Camry alone made up over 2 million of Toyota's U.S.-produced cars. Toyota had provided U.S. employment of more than 20,000 by the end of 1996, up 4000 from 3 years previous. Toyota's U.S. investment was expected to total $7.23 billion by 1996.[23]

Toyota's place in the U.S. market is illustrated by 1996 sales figures (expressed in millions of dollars):

	Sales	Debt/Capital Ratio
Toyota	$94,505	26.5
Honda	$42,108	31.7
Ford	$142,705	72.1
General Motors	$164,472	61.5
Chrysler	$60,208	42.7

Median sales for all companies surveyed was 56,727. Toyota operates on a lower debt/capital ratio than the four other companies listed above. Their debt/capital ratio is also lower than the median for all companies surveyed, which was 44.4.[24]

Toyota is making plans to globalize "everything". Starting with North America, Toyota will localize management. Americans buy more than one million Toyotas a year; for demand like that, Toyota believes that it is necessary to localize production. In 1996, North American Toyota production reached 782,962, a 7.3% increase from the year before, and more than six of ten Toyotas sold in America that year were also made in America.[23] To respond to American demand efficiently, Toyota broke ground in May 1996 for a $700 million plant in Indiana, which is expected to make T100 pickup trucks by 1998. A West Virginia plant to produce engines for the Corolla and another vehicle assembly line are in the works.[9] Toyota Motor Manufacturing Canada in Ontario produced 97,344 Corollas in 1996. This was an 8% increase from the year before. The production capacity is expected to increase to 200,000 units by fiscal year 1998.[23]

European Market

By 1992, Toyota had positioned itself in Europe to respond to the predicted upswing that the Continent was expected to experience over the next few years. The company took advantage of greatly improved industrial relations and rising productivity in the U.K. by establishing an automobile factory in Derby, England, in 1992. Most of the output from that plant was to be exported to mainland Europe.[25] Undoubtedly, sales gain would come at the expense of other producers, as Vauxhall, Rover, and Ford — the largest manufacturers in the U.K. — had all been going through crises that threatened their survival in the late 1980s and early 1990s. All of them were still far less competitive than Toyota. Fortunately for them, they had some time to recover still, as under an agreement between Japan and the European Community in 1991 imports of vehicles from Japan would be frozen at current levels until 1998. If Japanese production in the U.K. is not similarly limited, their share of the West European market is expected to increase from 12% in 1991 to 20% by 2000, of which Toyota will have a significant share.[26] In 1992, only England was experiencing any economic recovery, and Toyota saw volume sales there increase 42.7%, even though the new car market recorded an improvement of 9.1%. Toyota was definitely making its presence felt.

Today, Toyota is expanding in the U.K. In 1995, the U.K. vehicle plant produced 88,500 Carina E's. Toyota is building a second assembly line to include the Corolla which is expected to increase total production to 200,000 vehicles. They are also expanding the engine plant, which is expected to double production. Furthermore, Toyota opened an accessory and service center which serves as a service center and training facility for European repair technicians. Toyota is also planning to build a giant plant in northern France or possibly Poland in efforts to increase European production from 715,000 to 1.2 million by the year 2000. The company is hoping that expansion will help in the European market, which seems to be Toyota's biggest problem. Toyota holds merely a 2.5% market share in Europe, as compared with 8% in the American market.[9]

Asian Market

Japanese manufacturers are focusing their overseas direct investment primarily on Asia, particularly on China. China is attractive not only because of its cheap labor, but also because of rapidly rising demand from its 1.2 billion consumers. If China continues to import at the current rate, and its gross national product (GNP) continues to grow at over 10% per year, by 2010 China will be importing as much as the U.S. does today.[27]

The Asian markets as a whole are growing at a head-spinning rate. In 1992, Toyota owned almost 25% of the ASEAN market — Philippines, Singapore, Malaysia, Indonesia, and Thailand — and planned for 30% in 1993. With the region's sustainable long-term growth expected to be over 6%, Toyota needs a substantial strategy for corporate restructuring to support that area.[28]

In 1996, Toyota implemented such a strategy to help support the area. They have decided to expand plants in their East and Southeast Asian markets to achieve production of 600,000 vehicles by 1998. The East and Southeast Asian markets are expected to account for most of the growth in vehicle demand. Over the past 5 years, new automobile sales have increased 50% (this does not include sales in China or Japan). The East and Southeast Asian market, excluding Japan, is expected to be a 7.8-million-vehicle market. To take advantage of this market, Toyota is building on its existing market leadership in Brunei, Indonesia, Singapore, Thailand, and the Philippines. They began by opening a second plant in Thailand and working on a second plant in the Philippines. In China, Toyota has set up a joint venture with Tianjin Automobile Industrial Co., Ltd., to produce engines. Toyota also opened a technical center in Tianjin in 1995.[9]

Comparative Outlook

The long-term outlook for Toyota looks fairly sound. The major expansion at the Kentucky plant has cost the company a considerable amount, but compared to the other major automobile makers in Japan, Toyota is in very good shape. During 1991, the industry (in Japan) actually looked very healthy with a debt/equity ratio of only 55.1%; however, when Toyota is removed from the picture, the financial totals change, showing a debt/equity ratio of over 100%, indicating that Toyota was propping up the industry figures with its superior balance sheet. The same was true in 1993.

Honda, because of its greater dependence on the U.S. market for its sales, posted better 1993 figures as a result of the upswing of the U.S. car industry resulting from a slowing growing economy. At the time, Honda, for example, earned 61% if its revenue from exports, while Toyota earned only 37%.

Nonetheless, given the liquidity of Toyota's fiscal year 1991 balance of Y4850 B in current assets, it puts the company head and shoulder above the rest of the field. Honda and Nissan, in comparison, had current assets for fiscal year 1991 of Y2953 B and Y3156 B, respectively.[29]

Toyota, again compared with its Japanese competitors, stood ahead of the bunch with fiscal year 1991 operating profit margins of 5.07%. Next was Suzuki with 4.39% and Honda with 4.42%, followed by Mazda at 2.72%. Nissan was down the list with a 2.11% operating profit margin.[30] In spite of comparatively better situation with respect to its competitors, Toyota's balance sheet has deteriorated due to high capital spending and increased working capital needs in North America (NUMMI and Georgetown) in conjunction with falling sales profits.

Company Performance Outlook

Even though sales have steadily increased over the last 10 years, the cost of sales has also been escalating which has helped chew into profit margins (see tables). Selling, general, and administrative (SGA) costs have been increasing every year, and again this is eating right into the profit margins. Toyota by necessity needs to take the necessary steps to curtail these "easily" manageable costs in an expedient manner. Between 1987 and 1991, SGA costs increased over 61.21%, while sales increased only 52.25% for the same period. Earnings per share (EPS) showed increases over the same period, as assets increased almost 105%. However a delayed drop in the EPS was reflected in the increased liability of 115% over the same period for 1991 and 1992 (see tables).

Operating margins were expected to be very small for fiscal years 1993 and 1994, with a pickup expected for the following year. Even with the increase in prices, North American sales volume was expected to increase more than 1%, as Continental demand for cars was expected to increase over 5%. This increase in sales volume for Toyota would add approximately Y65 billion to the operating income of the company.[21]

Toyota's SGA costs declined from 1992 to 1995; however, 1996 surpassed 1992 SGA costs, which declined from Y1,173,345 million to Y1,074,600 million from 1992 to 1994, then rose to Y1,355,631 in fiscal year 1996. From 1992 to 1996, SGA costs increased 15.53%, while sales for the same period rose only 5.46%. Earnings per share for the period from 1992 to 1996 rose 7.51% from 61.90 to 66.55. The equity-to-asset ratio for 1996 was 66.4%, an increase of 2.4% from 1992.[9,31]

In the late 1980s and early 1990s, there had been a definite profit depreciation as a result of the appreciating yen. This currency effect resulted in dollars being translated into fewer yen as the exchange rates increased from US$1 to Y220 to Y110 between the 1980s and 1990s. However, within Japan, Toyota experienced benefits of a high yen in lower variable manufacturing costs because of the conversion of the cost of U.S. parts into fewer yen. The same cost savings can be accomplished from the rising yen against the currencies in Europe, where Toyota has parts manufacturing facilities. In addition, Toyota has cut costs by standardizing parts, cutting temporary workers, and reducing the number of its models, while extending their product life cycles.

Today, Toyota is the world's third largest automobile maker and is under the leadership of Hiroshi Okuda, Toyota's president as of 1995 and the man responsible for cutting production time, production costs, and introducing new engines with 30% fewer moving parts. Another factor contributing to the improved conditions at Toyota is the depreciation of the yen. The yen has fallen 36% against the dollar in the past 2 years. This means that additional yen bought by the dollar contributes about Y10 billion to Toyota's net profit. Y140 billion was added to Toyota's operating profit for 6 months to September 1996 due to the favorable exchange rate. It is expected that the fiscal year 1997 will top Y600 billion on sales of Y11.5 trillion. Most of this additional profit has come from the U.S. when the yen went to Y120 to the dollar, causing American car sales to increase 36%.[32]

Strategy

Toyota has implemented four policies: to give vehicle designers power to exercise a feel of what is right for the market, supplement sedan strength with new products, to allocate major resources to provide a wide range of varying products, and to get products off the drawing board and out into the market quicker. Toyota wants to be the first to introduce a generation of vehicles. They have an advantage, as they are one of only a few who have the capability to take on more than one development plan at a time. In fiscal year 1996, Toyota introduced 12 new or completely remodeled vehicles in Japan. These innovations have worked mainly to strengthen the utilitarian, urban-oriented vehicles. They also strengthened the minivan and sport utility vehicle segments.

Toyota is now reaching the market faster than ever. They have been able to bring a product to the market within 18 months of approving the design. A couple of years ago, this process took 27 months. This cut in lead-time is attributed to advances in computerization, simplified clay models, and increased pressure on designers. Clay models are no longer used to determine angle or contours, only shape and concept. It used to take 4 months to translate and measure these models accurately for diagrams and specifications for parts suppliers. Now, with the aid of a system which translates the clay form into digital computer data, Toyota can provide specifications and drawings to suppliers twice as fast. Designers are feeling the pressure of Toyota's agenda to speed up production time. Designers are put under pressure to be less perfectionist. Toyota has cut much time by fully developing and endorsing the first prototype; the second prototype is reserved for minor adjustments.[9]

Diversification

Toyota recognizes that no single industry has remained profitable for more than 40 to 60 years; therefore, Okuda announced plans to expand its non-vehicle manufacturing businesses. Okuda plans to focus primarily on telecommunications. The objective is to produce 10% of sales through products ranging from prefabricated houses to cellular phones to sales financing by the year 2000. The 10% goal is not farfetched, as non-vehicle businesses already make up 6.6% of Toyota's consolidated sales, and the telecommunications business can be incorporated into vehicles which are expected to drive vehicles sometime in the future. Telecommunications could become another means of value-added marketing. These systems are already in use in Japan, where 20% of drivers purchase voice navigation systems. The company has set up a $500 million fund for venture investments. This comes at a time when Toyota's share of the Japanese market has fallen below 40% for the first time in 14 years. Traditionally, Toyota has maintained 40% of the Japanese market, but their share fell as low as 31% between 1994 and 1995.[33,34]

Toyota is also exploring the aircraft market. In December 1996, Toyota received permission from the Federal Aviation Administration to make a small-aircraft engine. This engine is based on the 4-liter V8 engine found in Toyota's Lexus. Toyota has also been discussing building a four-seat aircraft. They intend to set up a $1 billion U.S. subsidiary to undertake the project.[35]

For fiscal year 1996, the net sales by business segments where as follows (in billions):[9]

Automotive	Y9842.0
Finance	387.2
Miscellaneous	571.5

The Final Word

The combined impact of weak Japanese markets and the high value of the yen could force a restructuring of the industry over the medium term. Companies may be forced to pull out of the market — as Isuzu has done by exiting the U.S. car market and concentrating on its jeep segment — or look for bigger partners to protect them or renegotiate strategic alliances. The winners will be those that have strong balance sheets and are strategically well positioned within international markets, particularly in the U.S. for the short term and the European and Asian markets for the longer term.

One of the key ways in which Toyota has responded to the high yen and low domestic sales is through the export of cars from its U.S. factories to Japan. Toyota can take advantage of the lower cost of these Japanese transplants and the high buying power of the yen for U.S. goods in Japan which make purchasing an American-made Toyota car in Japan less expensive than buying the identical Japanese-built car. In fact, Toyota has less exposure to currency swings than it did in the 1980s because it builds more cars and buys more parts in North America than ever before.[36]

Toyota's earning potential is realized as the yen continues to stabilize and the demand in the North America car market takes off. As Toyota's rate of increase in capital spending slows down with the completion of the major projects in Kentucky and with NUMMI, the balance sheet will recover considerably in the long run, and the income statement will also rejuvenate as interest rates begin to climb slowly.

Toyota is doing all that is necessary to maintain its flagship orientation in the automobile industry. The company is functioning within the industry from a position of strength as it tries to cut costs across the board. R&D is constantly being conducted, and technologies are being integrated with market application being delivered. Leveraging of global R&D facilities along with marketing locally is typical of Toyota and its "trans-national" approach to business. In conjunction with all of this, the company is set to reap the rewards of its capital investments with lean and flexible manufacturing. No wonder that Toyota is the benchmark of the automotive industry, worldwide.

References

1. *Hoover's Handbook of World Business*, Hoover Institution, Palo Alto, CA, 1992. p. 302.
2. T. Derdak, "Toyota," *International Directory of Business*, 1989, pp. 203–205.
3. *Japan, Inc.*, Barrs Films, 1989.
4. "Vehicle Output May Fall To 10-Year Low," *Reuter Business Report*, July 23, 1993.
5. Sebastian Moffett, "Toyota's Profits Suffer from Weak Car Market," *Reuter Business Report*, Aug. 26, 1993.
6. Neil Winton, "Outlook Dire For Europe's Car Makers," *Reuter Business Report*, Sept. 5, 1993.
7. Jerry Dubrowski, "Automotive Launch of New Models With Flurry of Commercials," *Reuter Business Report*, Sept. 23, 1993.
8. Jerry Dubrowski, "Toyota 1994 U.S. Prices Rise: Automakers Report Strong Earnings," *Reuter Business Report*, Sept. 23, 1993.
9. Toyota Motor Corporation, Annual Report, 1996.
10. David Lawder, "1994 Prices To Rise," *Reuter Business Report*, Sept. 2, 1993.
11. "Detroit Tries to Lobby Prices Up," *Consumer Report*, Oct. 10, 1992.
12. "Chrysler Unveils New Neon," *Reuter Business Report*, Sept. 7, 1993.
13. Bob Golfen, *The Arizona Republic*, April 23, 1993, p. 3.
14. *Detroit Free Press*, July 13, 1993, p. 13.
15. *Lexington (KY) Herald-Leader*, June 14, 1993, p. 5.
16. *Cincinnati Business Record*, July 5, 1993, p. 18.
17. Anon., "Manufacturing Management: Return of the Stopwatch," *The Economist*, Jan. 23, 1993, p. 69.
18. Paul S. Adler, "Time-And-Motion Regained," *Harvard Business Review*, January-Feb. 1993, pp. 97–108.
19. "Business Trends: Toyota Motor Corp.," *Lexington (KY) Herald-Leader*, 1992, pp. 25–26.
20. Douglas Lavin, "A New Export Power in the Auto Industry? It's North America," *Wall Street Journal*, Oct. 18, 1993, p. A1.
21. B. Moyer, "Toyota Motor-Company Report," *Merrill Lynch Capital Markets*, June 16, 1993, pp. 4–5.

22. Alex Taylor, III, "How Toyota Copes with Hard Times," *Fortune*, Jan. 25, 1993, pp. 78–81.
23. http://www.toyota.com/newswire/local/loc text/.
24. Steve Kichen, "Consumer Durables," *Forbes*, Jan. 13, 1997, p. 130.
25. Neasa MacErlean, "Car Markers' Fortunes Turn on Souped-Up Production," *Accountancy*, June 1993, pp. 30–33.
26. "Britain's Car Industry: Hai Swindon," *The Economist*, Oct. 3, 1992, pp. 70, 72.
27. Shibata Yoko, "Japan's New Target for Investment Is China," *Global Finance*, June 1993, pp. 54–56.
28. *The Economist*, April 24, 1993, p. 33.
29. *Moody's International*, Moody Investment Services, New York, 1992, pp. 3054, 3087, 3125.
30. K.C. Donaldson, "Toyota Motors Company, Ltd.," *Salomon Brothers, Inc.,* Dec. 29, 1991, p. 7.
31. Toyota Motor Corporation, Annual Report, 1994.
32. "Toyota on the March," *The Economist*, March 22, 1997, pp. 83–84.
33. Emily Thornton, "Seeking Immortality: Why Toyota Is Turning to Telecommunication?," *Far Eastern Economic Review*, Jan. 30, 1997, p. 50.
34. "Changing Gear at Toyota," *The Economist*, Oct. 5, 1996, p. 68.
35. "Sprouting Wings," *Forbes*, Jan. 13, 1997.
36. *Fortune*, May 17, 1993, p. 12.

Sales (1987–1992)

	Sales	Cost of Sales	Cost as % of Sales
1987	$6675.4	$5600.7	83.90
1988	7215.8	5989.3	83.00
1989	8021.0	6704.9	83.59
1990	9192.8	7479.0	81.36
1991	9855.1	8226.9	83.48
1992	10,163.4	8,771.5	86.30
Increase from 1987 to 1992	52.25%	56.61%	

Source: Data from "Toyota Motor Corporation Company Report," *Dasfa,* June 1, 1992.

Assets and Liabilities (1987–1996)

	Current Assets	Current Liabilities	Current Ratio (Assets/Liabilities)
1987	$2,530,168	$1,380,921	1.83
1988	2,807,201	1,596,290	1.76
1989	4,343,971	1,958,583	2.22
1990	5,167,190	2,691,260	1.92
1991	4,849,394	2,625,877	1.85
1992	5,180,391	2,980,864	1.74
1993	4,529,754	2,592,597	1.75
1994	4,697,879	2,822,522	1.66
1995	5,019,961	3,075,440	1.63
1996	4,998,831	3,659,565	1.37

Source: Data from "Toyota Motor Corporation Company Report," *Dasfa,* June 1, 1992.

Case 10.
Mercedes-Benz*

Background

In 1985, Daimler-Benz (a German corporation headquartered in Stuttgart) decided to implement a new course of action and established a future-oriented corporate structure, thereby becoming an integrated high-technology organization. This enabled the company to participate in a global market. Primarily known for automobile manufacturing, Daimler-Benz began purchasing shares in Motoren-and-Turbinen-Union GmbH (MTU), a widely acclaimed manufacturer of turbines, aero-engines, and high-speed diesel engines. This act was followed by the acquisition of a majority of the stock in Dornier GmbH of Friedrichshafen, a company with a long tradition in the aerospace sector of the market. Finally, Daimler-Benz acquired a 56% share of Aktiengesellschaft (AEG), whose activities include energy systems, industrial and rail systems, communication systems, and domestic appliances.

By 1989, Daimler-Benz began restructuring its assorted group of highly technical groups within the business. The company became the executive holding company, whose task was to ensure the optimal use of each group's resources. First, the vehicle sector of the business was transferred to the newly formed Mercedes-Benz. Second, aerospace

---

* The case was prepared by Dr. M. Reza Vaghefi, assisted by Raejean Echegaray, for discussion purposes only.

activities were grouped together in Deutsche Aerospace (Dasa), which consisted initially of Dornier, MTU, and Telefunken Systemtechnik (TST) and later was followed by Messerschmitt-Bolkow-Blohm GmbH (MBB). Third, the business of AEG continued to be carried on within an unchanged corporate structure. Finally, Daimler-Benz created a fourth corporate unit, Daimler-Benz InterServices. This new entity offers customers both inside and outside the company a range of services including software products, computer communication services, financial services, insurance brokerage, and marketing services. Each of these four subsidiaries has its own individual logo to mirror the fact that each is a separate entity accountable for its own destiny.

Of the four Daimler-Benz subsidiaries, this chapter will focus primarily on the automobile sector, Mercedes-Benz. The company has a long, rich history dating back to 1883. The motor car was developed by two inventors working independent of one another. Both exhibited a strong fascination for technology — specifically, engines. Karl Benz, one of the founders of Benz & Cie, developed one of the first motor cars that took to the road in 1886. Under the Benz patent, the motor car make its first public trip through the streets of Mannheim, Germany. Around that same time, Gottlieb Daimler, founder of Daimler-Motoren-Gesellschaft (DMG), began developing the first motor carriage. Together, these inventions launched the beginnings of a tradition in the automobile manufacturing sector of the global marketplace.

In 1924, the Daimler and Benz companies formed an association that marketed their cars under the trade name Mercedes-Benz. The name "Mercedes" was selected by Emil Jellinek, a valued customer of Daimler products, whose passion for racing Daimler cars led him to use the name "Mercedes". When Jellinek took part in the Nice-Magagnon rally, he entered the car under the pseudonym "Mercedes", his daughter's name. As the company became more involved with racing and touring cars, it entered the cars under the name Mercedes, and thus began the Mercedes era. The idea to use the star as a trademark came from Daimler's sons. Its three points symbolize the three branches of motorization: on land, on water, and in the air.

Finally, two years later, in June 1926, the companies merged to form Daimler-Benz. This was to be the beginning of a long and prosperous alliance that continues to be successful today. In 1936, the company entered the international trade arena. It began this process by delivering trucks on consignment to China, which resulted in a contract for the construction of an assembly plant located in Shanghai. In 1950, exports soared from 6 million Deutsche marks (DM) to 66 million DM. During that time, Daimler-Benz extended its manufacturing capabilities to South America by opening a plant in Argentina. Three years later, a Mercedes-Benz commercial vehicle manufacturing plant was established in Brazil. In 1955, the company formed Daimler-Benz of North America, based in Delaware.

In the early 1970s, Daimler-Benz made a significant investment in the Tabriz Engine Factory in Iran which catapulted sales of commercial vehicles to countries in the Middle and Far East. At this time, all Mercedes-Benz products carried the Mercedes star.

By the early 1980s, Daimler-Benz began investing heavily in the U.S. in companies such as Freightliner Corporation, a leading American manufacturer of heavy-duty trucks, located in Portland, OR. Also, during this time frame, the new compact series (Mercedes 190) was introduced to the public and became instantly successful.

Mercedes-Benz's Divisions

Since July 1989, Mercedes-Benz has been responsible for the entire motor vehicle business within the Daimler-Benz group. This segment of the business is divided into two groups: passenger car division and commercial vehicle division. The passenger car division incorporates a modern production system with mutual supplies of assemblies and components. The headquarters and development center are located in Stuttgart, Germany. This is where all passenger car engines, transmissions, and axles are produced. The passenger car division views itself as an exclusive manufacturer of premium cars in the automotive sector. The commercial division is a diversified range of vehicles which includes vans, trucks, buses, touring coaches, and industrial engines such as the Unimog. The target of this division in their capacity as a full-line manufacturer and world market leader is to further develop the international production network.

The company employs approximately 150,457 people at its 12 domestic vehicle plants (passenger and commercial divisions) and 43 company-owned sales and service outlets and the Mercedes-Benz headquarters. Regarding global expansion, the company has more than 50 production and assembly plants and approximately 6200 sales and service outlets throughout the world. It employs about 197,500 people in its production and sales companies outside of Germany. Both the passenger and commercial vehicles are sold in more than 170 countries throughout the world.

Competitors

Mercedes-Benz operates in the automotive industry as a major exporter of Germany and as one of the world's leading manufacturer of passenger and commercial vehicles. The company's competitors are both domestic and foreign. The U.S. and international automotive markets are highly competitive. The company's major competitors generally have a substantial amount of financial and marketing resources available. The company's principal competitors include BMW, Volvo, Renault, Porsche, Lexus, Ford, Infiniti, and General Motors.

In 1994, Mercedes-Benz sold over 590,000 cars. This was the second highest volume of sales in the company's history. Above-average growth was achieved in many key markets, accompanied by a healthy market share gain. In 1995, revenues from passenger cars grew slightly over the previous year's outstanding level, and in the commercial vehicle division they grew by 13%. One way Mercedes-Benz has found to compete with its rivals is by actively investing in production and assembly facilities, importing supplies from foreign countries, and developing new technologies.

As mentioned above, Mercedes-Benz owns 12 domestic and 50 production and assembly plants worldwide, with plans to purchase more. Mercedes-Benz has increased its investments in property, plant, and equipment by over six billion DM and has concentrated on product innovations and the introduction of new production technologies. The main emphasis has been on capital expenditures, predominantly for new products and successor modes, but also for the continued internationalization of business.

Entry Barriers

The threat of new entrants is minimal due to the maturity of this industry. The start-up costs require great amounts of capital and also skilled workers. This is an industry that must reinvest much of its resources for continuous research and development. Because Mercedes-Benz operates globally, it must be aware of the politics and stringent government regulations that exist in different countries. Also, the constant fluctuations in foreign currency can impede upon the success of a company. These factors act as major deterrents to entry for future companies. Because of so few competitors, this commerce is desirable for entry, but, as mentioned previously, there are some constraints.

Power of the Buyers

Consumers represent a crucial element to the success of a company. Mercedes-Benz has made it a point to watch for economic changes and to pay close attention to the concerns and needs of its clientele. Taking the concerns of potential buyers into account, Mercedes-Benz has lowered its prices and offered more services so that more people are able to purchase its products. Currently, the company has introduced the new E Class automobile. The introduction of this new series demonstrates the fact that Mercedes-Benz has completely overhauled its entire passenger car product range in only 5 years. More new products are in store, such as the C Class and E Class station wagons, the SLK Roadster, and the Viano, which will be manufactured in Vitoria, Spain. In 1997, the company launched an independent mid-range coupe (the A Class) and an all-activity vehicle, manufactured in the U.S. Mercedes-Benz is currently developing the Smart Car, which will assist in driving functions. The commercial division will launch the new Sprinter van. Also planned is a new generation of heavy trucks in the U.S.

On the whole, Mercedes-Benz continues the positive trend reflected by the 3% increase in revenues over the first half of 1994 to 35.6 billion DM. There was significant growth in Western Europe outside of Germany (+10%), in South America (+40%), South Africa (+55%), and the Far East (+12%). Domestically, revenues increased by only 1% to 14.6 billion DM. Total sales of 156,300 units (+16%) of the commercial vehicle sector sold more vehicles than ever before. The record result in 1994 predominantly reflected the recovering economies in important commercial vehicle markets, particularly in the European Union, since the late summer of 1994. Moreover, the market success of the Sprinter contributed to 15% higher sales of vans, which reached 55,000 units. An even greater expansion was in the truck sector, where sales were up 17%

to 88,100 units. The buses and Unimogs also achieved noticeable growth as compared to previous years. Mercedes-Benz expected these growths to expand over the next 5 years.

Power of Suppliers

In an attempt to become more immune to exchange-rate fluctuations, Mercedes-Benz has adjusted the structure of its value added. The company currently imports 20% of its supplies. This figure is expected to increase to at least 30% in the long term. By importing from suppliers, Mercedes-Benz avoids possible problems with the fluctuations of currency in different countries by establishing a relationship with these suppliers.

Regarding the passenger car division, Mercedes-Benz can manufacture the car, car engines, transmissions, and axles all in one plant located in Stuttgart, Germany. The company's largest factory is the bodywork and assembly plant in Sindelfingen, Germany. By tradition, Mercedes-Benz passenger cars are manufactured in Germany. Nonetheless, assembly plants have for many years been in existence in the Far East and South Africa. The company plans to expand its production activities to develop an assembly plant located in Mexico. A milestone in the internationalization strategy of Mercedes-Benz is the new U.S. passenger car plant constructed in Tuscaloosa, AL, expected to produce some 60,000 units annually of the new four-wheel drive sport utility vehicle from 1997 onwards.

The company owns all of its facilities worldwide and manufactures a majority of the parts associated with the vehicles. The company develops a strong bond with the suppliers in order to establish loyalty. The one concern the company must constantly pay attention to is the diverse cultures involved. Before Mercedes-Benz establishes a supplier base or develops a plant, it must first evaluate that country's culture to be sure that it has the resources available to perform the tasks required to produce the product.

Internal Environment

Mercedes-Benz continues to strive to become a global organization and acquire a greater market share by investing in foreign countries and developing innovative technologies that enhance its products. The company is constantly evaluating opportunities to improve current models in the passenger car division. Recently, Mercedes-Benz has reintroduced a revised version of the E Class model. In addition, the company is offering the C Class and E Class station wagons, the SLK Roadster, and the Viano. The company has future plans to work with a Swiss company by the name of Schweizerische Gesellschaft fur Mikroelektronik und Unhrenindustrie (SMH) to produce a two-seater sports car. The commercial vehicle division constantly strives to develop models that fit the needs of a diverse clientele.

Mercedes-Benz, being conscious of the environment, has made major improvements to its facilities and its automobiles. Right from the beginning of the design process, Mercedes-Benz's engineers take into account the possibility of saving resources, minimizing pollutant emissions, and ensuring the lowest possible environmental impact the car might have. Some of these changes include the fact that all plastic components weighing more than 100 grams are marked to enable segregated recycling. The aim of designers is to increase the use of recyclable materials which can be reused for the production of secondary products. Approximately 95% of the lead, sulfuric acid, and plastics used in production are reused. The floor mats, glove compartments, and many other components are composed of recycled materials. To address the environmental impact of the painting process, the company has reverted to water-based paints. Finally, to reduce the volume of waste materials to be dumped and to save valuable raw materials, the company has reused old catalytic converters.

Mercedes-Benz employs over 197,164 worldwide. The principle job groupings include production and assembly workers, engineering and technical positions, general office employees, and professional positions. The company prefers to promote qualified specialist candidates from within the ranks, as companies with well-educated employees are more competitive. Professional training remains an important element of the company's long-term personnel strategy and is a necessary investment in the future.

Along with renewing the entire product, Mercedes-Benz is currently reorganizing its internal structure and procedures. By creating product and regional sections carrying a high degree of responsibility, market proximity and flexibility will be improved. Mercedes-Benz is devising and implementing measures that aim to optimize processes, reduce costs, and increase productivity. This involves further decentralization and promoting an entrepreneurial business environment, as well as utilizing the group work concept in the production process and revising its performance and reward system. The range of parts has been reduced, new purchasing sources have been located, and a new standard of cooperation among both employees and suppliers has resulted.

External Environment

Mercedes-Benz's ability to provide both passenger and commercial vehicles to the consumer can be hampered by economic and/or government regulations and policies worldwide. Such issues as exchange rates present a major threat to the potential earnings of the company. Given the present exchange rates, it is extremely difficult to sell German products profitably on many foreign markets.

In addition, political climates can be extremely unfavorable, thus restricting market share in new growth markets. This is very much evident in the huge markets for communications, energy, and transportation. Such practices as those exercised by the U.S. administration contradict the principles of the World Trade Organization (WTO), which was founded at the beginning of 1995 to succeed the General Agreement on Tariffs and Trade; the intent of the WTO was to promote liberalization of world trade. These measures could pose a major concern for Mercedes-Benz, because it may distort the parameters of competition and could easily lead to escalating trade conflicts.

Evaluation

In today's constantly changing environment (both economically and politically), Mercedes-Benz must strive to maintain strong market share positions by continuously improving its products, offering superior customer service, and developing innovation technologies. To maintain its international presence, it must invest in foreign countries, which not only helps that country economically but also leads to a larger portion of the market place for the company.

To stay ahead of the competition, Mercedes-Benz must constantly be aware of economic changes that affect the purchase of its vehicles and government regulations imposed by foreign countries. It must strive to maintain good relationships with its foreign counterparts. In addition,

Mercedes-Benz must take a proactive stance in the development of new technologies if it is to survive in the future. The Vario is one such innovative technology that will eventually offer the consumer a versatile car. The Vario will aid in the development of cars of the future by combining Mercedes-Benz's expert knowledge of cars with the desires and input of the consumer.

New and Redesigned Products

Over the past several years, Mercedes-Benz has been redesigning their cars and expanding their product lines. Its traditional model series is still comprised of the C Class, E Class, and S Class. The C Class was the first series for which the models were offered in four different design and equipment versions. Reasonably priced, this compact Mercedes has been a huge success, with worldwide sales of 303,000 in 1995. The E class has also been completely redeveloped. The most successful Mercedes-Benz car of all time, it has sold more than 2.7 million models in 167 countries. The S Class is still among the best-selling models in the luxury car market, not just in Germany and Europe, but also in the U.S. and Japan.[1]

In 1996, the company expanded its product range by adding the V Class and the SLK roadster. With the V Class, Mercedes is establishing a foothold in the strongly growing market for multi-purpose vehicles (MVPs). This new model series satisfies the demand of customers who want a spacious and versatile vehicle. The new SLK roadster is the latest sports car from Mercedes. A two-seater, its name is an acronym for sporty, light, and comfort. Soon after its introduction, the SLK was named North American Car of the Year.

The CLK coupe, the A Class, and the M Class (all-activity vehicle) are all new products for 1997. The CLK coupe is being positioned between the successful C and E classes. The model is original and sporty, while adhering to the basic Mercedes-Benz style. Mercedes' new product line in Europe includes the new A Class, a mini-car nearly three feet shorter than any other Mercedes. The A Class is designed to protect Mercedes' classical car image yet appeal to younger buyers. It will not compete with small, inexpensive cars made by mass marketers such as Volkswagen or Fiat, but should create its own niche in the market.

Mercedes-Benz in Alabama

In 1993, Daimler-Benz announced its decision to locate the M Class (AAV) plant in Tuscaloosa, AL, following a comprehensive selection process which included more than 150 sites and existing facilities in 30 states. The decisive criteria for Tuscaloosa included the quality of the workforce, a good infrastructure, the presence of a major university, a positive business climate, and a strong sense of commitment and support from state and local officials. The manufacturing site in Alabama also offers significantly lower manufacturing and labor costs and a more flexible production systems than is true for a traditional German facility. In addition, Alabama provided a package of land, infrastructure, and financial incentives worth $250 million. Including development costs, the project represented an investment of about $1 billion for the company.[2]

This one-million-square-foot production facility sits on about one third of its 1000-acre site. The plant includes a body shop where the metal stampings are assembled, an environmentally safe paint shop, and an assembly shop. The facility also has a training institute and a visitors' center. At full capacity, the plant will produce some 65,000 vehicles annually, with half scheduled to be shipped throughout North America and the remainder in Europe and other parts of the world. The Tuscaloosa plant will be the single production source for the M Class.

Actual construction began in October 1994, and the plant was completed 18 months later. Mercedes-Benz U.S. International (MBUSI) — the company formed with responsibility for M Class development, production, and worldwide strategic marketing — launched an extensive hiring campaign in August of 1994. Within a matter of weeks, some 60,000 people requested applications for approximately 1000 jobs. When the plant is operating at full capacity in 1998, it will employ about 1500 people.

Mercedes also recruited the best talent to run and design the plant. Managers and engineers from Ford, General Motors, Chrysler, Mitsubishi, Honda, Nissan, Toyota, Saturn, Subaru, and Isuzu were hired. This brought together many different skills and experiences from different cultures that was invaluable to Mercedes.[3]

In spring of 1995, the first production team members from Alabama were hired and sent to Germany, where they spent the next 6 months training on the line at the company's Sindelfingen plant. Production of all-activity vehicles began in February 1997. To ensure the launch of a quality product, Mercedes began with a very slow production pace of just 10 vehicles per day. German trainers double checked production as it flowed out of every work station from the body shop to the assembly line.

For this Alabama plant, company executives abandoned the strict hierarchy of the typical Mercedes production line in Germany. Instead, they borrowed heavily from the Japanese, stressing teamwork and continuous improvement. Employees are empowered to stop the assembly line at any time to correct manufacturing problems. The plant also deploys a system called visual management which encourages managing by walking around, observing, and talking to team members. Management has worked very hard to create a casual, cooperative atmosphere. Uniforms, even for executives, include polo shirts with the employee's name embroidered on the pocket.

The administrative offices run through the heart of the manufacturing area. All vehicles that are delivered from the paint shop to the assembly shop cross right through the middle of the offices. The area is glassed in, but there is easy access to the team members. This arrangement is unique and keeps everyone focused on building Mercedes-Benz automobiles.

This plant design is a catalyst to communication and employee participation, aids process and material flow, and enables the pull system of manufacturing (build to customer demand) to function efficiently. The company's just-in-time and just-in-sequence delivery requirements have reduced the need for warehousing materials, thereby reducing costs. Unlike a typical European operation, this plant has less than 2 hours' worth of working inventory available at workstations and on the assembly line.

In addition, the management team has taken a relatively low-tech approach to building the all-activity vehicle. Plant automation will be kept simple. Initially, about 25% of the body shop tasks will be performed using robots so that production team members can learn hands-on welding skills.

MBUSI has partnered with some 65 systems suppliers in the development and production of the M Class. These suppliers play a significant role in that they have participated in the development of the vehicle from the early stages and provide complete modules or systems, as opposed to individual parts or components. Mercedes will use the next generation of modular construction techniques to manufacture the all-activity vehicle. For example, the entire cockpit or dash assembly will be delivered as one unit by just one major supplier. About a dozen of these suppliers will be connected by file transfer protocol, a faster version of electronic data interchange, to the plant. Approximately 65% of the content of the M Class is sourced from with North America. Engines and transmissions come from the plants in Bad Cannstatt and Unter-türkheim, both in Stuttgart.

Sales and Financial Data

Sales in the passenger car division have increased worldwide to 645,000 cars, setting a new record in the company's history (sales in 1995 were 590,200 units). Mercedes achieved double-digit growth rates in numerous important markets and improved their position worldwide in the market for luxury cars. The E Class contributed the majority of this growth; its sales increased by 46% to 291,500 vehicles.

In 1996, sales of passenger cars in Germany, at 264,000 units, were 10% higher than in 1995. Market share in the luxury car segment rose to 26%. Mercedes-Benz had an 8% share of the overall market, which was higher than in the previous year (7.5%). Outside of Germany, the company sold nearly 381,000 Mercedes-Benz passenger cars in 1996, surpassing the previous year's record by 9%. Business remained successful in the Western European markets outside of Germany where sales increased by 10% to 174,000 vehicles, and Mercedes continues to expand their market position.

In the U.S., 90,800 passenger cars were sold, representing an 18% increase over the previous year. The company's share in the luxury car market segment climbed to 10.1% (compared to 8.7% in 1995).

In Japan, new car sales increased by 17%, reaching a new high of 41,000 units. In the process, market share in the luxury class rose to approximately 10%. In Eastern and Southern Europe, Latin America, the Middle East, Australia, South Africa, and Canada, sales also surpassed the previous year's level.

The Commercial Vehicle Division sold a total of 348,100 vans, trucks, buses, and Unimogs in 1996, surpassing the record level in 1995 by 9%. The Vans Europe unit increased its sales by 32% to a total of 151,100 units. This success was primarily related to the new Sprinter and Vito vans. Due to tremendous demand for these vehicles, market share in the Western European van market jumped from 12.7 to 15.5%.

Because of the difficult market conditions in Western Europe and buyer resistance in anticipation of model changes in the heavy-duty truck class, sales of the Trucks Europe division dropped to 64,400 units in 1996 (compared to 70,000 in 1995). However, the new heavy-duty truck Actros (named Truck of the Year for 1997) was recently launched, and the company expects to see unit and DM sales increase again in this sector. Mercedes has continued to maintain its position as the market leader for trucks over 6 tons in Western Europe.

Freightliner Corporation reported a record sales level by selling nearly 75,000 vehicles in North America. It was also able to extend its market share in Classes 6 to 8 (over 8.8 tons) to 22% (compared to 19% in 1995). Due to the success of the new Century Class, which was launched in October 1995, Freightliner was able to expand its market position significantly in the heavy-duty Class 8 (over 15 tons) to a 29% share (compared to 26% in 1995). With the acquisition of Ford's heavy-duty truck business, Mercedes plans to further strengthen its position in the North American Commercial vehicle market.

References

1. http://www.mercedes-benz.com.
2. http://www.daimler-benz.com.
3. Brian Moskal, "Not the Same Old Mercedes," *Industry Week,* 245 (Oct. 7), 1996, pp. 12–21.

Overview of Mercedes-Benz 1993–1995

	1995	*1994*	*1993*
Sales (DM)[a]	72,030	70,715	64,696
EU market	42,287	39,730	37.394
Germany	28,188	26.906	25,998
EU without Germany	14,099	12,284	11,396
Other markets	29,743	30,985	27,302
Sales (units)			
Passenger cars	583,432	592,356	508,078
Germany	237,638	251,048	218,739
Foreign	345,794	341,308	289,339
Commercial vehicles	320,089	290,354	253,939
Germany	85,307	77,666	78,982
Foreign	234,782	212,688	174,957
Employees (at year end)	197,164	197,568	209,933
Germany	150,475	148,194	160,175
Foreign	46,707	49,374	49,758

[a] Figures in millions of DM.

Source: **http://www.mercedes-benz.com.**

Mercedes-Benz 1996 and 1995

	1996[a]	*1995[a]*
Total		
Operating profit[b]	2942	2349
Revenues[b]	77,624	72,100
Investments in property, plant, and equipment	4451	3331
Research and development	3996	3728
Employees	199,099	197,164
Passenger cars		
Revenues[b]	45,949	40,467
Unit sales	644,957	590,180
Research and development	2906	2503
Employees	83,732	80,733
Commercial vehicles		
Revenues[b]	31,675	31,633
Unit sales	348,087	320,089
Research and development	1090	1225
Employees	80,483	82,041

[a] Figures in millions of DM, except unit sales and number of employees.
[b] Unconsolidated figures of the business.

Source: **http://www.daimler-benz.com.**

Passenger Cars

	First Quarter 1997	First Quarter 1996
Revenues (DM)[a]	11,426	10,313
Production (units)	161,696	163,326
Sales (units)	154,011	147,994
Employees	85,492	82,508

[a] Figures in millions of DM.

Source: **http://www.daimler-benz.com.**

Commercial Vehicles

	First Quarter 1997	First Quarter 1996
Revenues (DM)[a]	8157	7438
Production (units)	93,100	88,499
Sales (units)	84,927	80,841
Employees	80,732	79,852

[a] Figures in millions of DM.

Source: **http://www.daimler-benz.com.**

Logos Enhancing Recognition of the Brands They Represent

1. Borden
2. IBM
3. Mercedes-Benz
4. Nabisco
5. Nestle
6. Oscar Mayer
7. Kraft, Inc.

Source: Adapted from *American Demographics,* April, 1994, p. 22.

Case 11. Anheuser-Busch Companies*

A nheuser-Busch Company, Inc. is a diversified corporation with major operations in numerous industries ranging from beer to baseball, with operations located all over the world, including Japan, Mexico, and Europe. This case will focus on the beer industry, that is, Anheuser-Busch, Inc., and the international aspects of this industry.

History of U.S. Brewing Industry

The ancient Egyptians are generally credited with the invention of beer, the oldest alcoholic beverage. Records indicate that the most ancient cultures — the Babylonians, Assyrians, Egyptians, Hebrews, Africans, Chinese, Incas, and others — enjoyed their beer, at all levels of society.

Although native Americans had developed their own form of beer, Europeans brought their own beer with them to America. The beer of the colonial period was quite different from the beer of today. Ale, porter, and stout were the predominant types of beer enjoyed during this time, and they were lusty, fairly dark, and high in alcohol content. These beers did not enjoy widespread popularity in the late eighteenth and early nineteenth centuries, as Americans were consuming much more whiskey than beer.

---

* The case was prepared by Dr. M. Reza Vaghefi, assisted by Elise Englert, for discussion purposes only.

Modern lager beer was introduced by German immigrants in the 1840s and changed the nature and importance of the U.S. brewing industry. Lager beer is aged, and the fermentation process utilizes a special yeast that settles at the bottom of the fermentation tanks. This process produces a lighter, more effervescent, and more highly hopped beer than the English beers.

Prior to 1880, it was necessary to produce beer locally because of its perishability. Pasteurization and refrigerated transport opened the way for wide-scale bottling and the off-premise consumption of beer. This shift in beer marketing away from the delivery of kegs of beer for on-premise consumption toward the delivery of packaged beer for off-premise consumption has led to concentration in the beer industry. When beer sales were primarily by the keg for on-premise consumption, the small brewer could survive by selling to taverns in its immediate area, but packaged beer sales are primarily for off-premise consumption. The wider distribution of packaged beer increased the importance of product differentiation and brand emphasis. The small brewer had neither the capital for massive advertising campaigns nor the capacity for the needed volume to expose itself in the market.

In 1919, Prohibition nearly destroyed the brewing industry. Many brewers went out of business, but a number of the larger brewers remained open by diversifying in other markets. For example, Anheuser-Busch diversified into markets such as carbonated soft drinks, corn products, baker's yeast, ice cream, and truck bodies. Prohibition lasted until April 1933, and by June of that year, 31 brewers had resumed operations. The number grew to 750 in 1935, but the trend toward concentration was apparent. By the late 1970s, just over 40 firms remained in operation, and today, there are 65 U.S. breweries in operation.

Prior to Prohibition, the U.S. brewing industry was very competitive. Entry was easy, and there were many producers; however, increasing concentration and increased barriers to entry for new firms pose a threat to the future level of competition in the beer industry. With increased concentration, there is the potential for the remaining firms to engage in collusion to establish a joint profit-maximizing price and output; however, at this time, there is a great deal of excess capacity within the industry which encourages the larger brewers to battle even more amongst themselves.

History of Anheuser-Busch

Eberhard Anheuser, owner of a successful soap-manufacturing business, became the brewer owner in 1860, after it had financially faltered. In 1864, Adolphus Busch, a brewery supplier whom Eberhard Anheuser's daughter had married, joined the brewery as a salesman. He eventually became president of the company and is credited for transforming the company into an industry giant. He pioneered the pasteurization process, created the Budweiser and Michelob brands, and was extremely gifted in merchandising the beers. As a matter of fact, the original beer that Anheuser produced was said to be terrible, but Adolphus Busch was Anheuser's "secret weapon" — he was a very good salesman!

August A. Busch, upon his father's death, became president of Anheuser-Busch in 1913. He directed the company through the tough times of the First World War, Prohibition, and the Great Depression. Adolphus Busch, III, and August A. Busch, Jr., directed the company between 1934 and 1975.

August A. Busch, III, chief executive officer since 1975, represents the fourth generation of the family to lead the company. Under his leadership, the company has expanded to 13 breweries with a combined shipping capacity of approximately 98.4 million barrels. They increased vertical integration with the addition of new can manufacturing and malt production facilities. They also diversified into container recovery, metalized label printing, snack foods, international marketing, and creative services. Today, Anheuser-Busch Companies, Inc., is a diversified corporation with many subsidiaries. These subsidiaries are grouped into three sections: beer and beer-related operations, food products operations, and entertainment operations.

The beer and beer-related operations include Anheuser-Busch, Inc., the world's largest brewer and U.S. industry leader since 1957; Busch Agricultural Resources, Inc., which has responsibility for the quality of incoming raw materials for Anheuser-Busch, Inc.; Anheuser-Busch Recycling Corporation, in 1991 the world's largest aluminum beverage container recycler; Metal Container Corporation, which produces cans and lids for Anheuser-Busch, Inc., and U.S. soft drink companies; Busch Media Group, Inc., which is responsible for purchasing all the company's national broadcast media time and local advertising schedules; Busch Creative Services Corporation, the company's business communications subsidiary; St. Louis

Refrigerator Car Company, which provides repair and maintenance of railroad cars; and Manufacturers Railway Company, which provides terminal rail-switching services to St. Louis industries.

The food products operations includes Campbell Taggart, Inc., the diversified food producer of baked goods, refrigerated dough products, and frozen foods for retail and food service customers. Also, Eagles Snacks, Inc., is the company's snack food subsidiary which produces quality snack and nut products, including potato chips, nacho chips, dips, and honey-roasted peanuts.

The entertainment operations includes Busch Entertainment Corporation, one of the largest theme park operations in the U.S., which includes Busch Gardens, Cypress Gardens, and Sea World parks. Also, the Civic Center Corporation subsidiary owns various downtown St. Louis properties, including Busch Stadium.

The St. Louis Baseball Club, Inc., is the company's major league baseball subsidiary, known as the St. Louis Cardinals. This team plays in Busch Stadium and is in the National League baseball division.

Beer Industry Structure

Concentration in the U.S. beer industry has led to a tightly knit oligopoly. Their were 369 independent brewing companies in the U.S. in 1950. Today, that number has been reduced to 65.5 The size of most of the remaining companies has increased dramatically, causing a great deal of overcapacity.

There are five main causes of the increased concentration. First, mergers have been numerous and ultimately led to the demise of inefficient firms. Antitrust action prevented the leading brewers from expanding by merger; Anheuser-Busch's growth was created by reinvestment, not merger.

The second cause of concentration includes economies of scale and minimum efficient size. There has been a steady decline in breweries with capacities less than one million barrels. Faster packaging equipment and plant automation have caused scale economies to rise.

Third, price competition has contributed to the exit of many small brewers and, in turn, to increased concentration in the beer industry. Small brewers could not compete with Anheuser-Busch and Miller in the 1970s, when Philip Morris dumped almost $3 million into Miller.

Fourth, product differentiation has contributed to the increased concentration in the beer industry. Product differentiation is the extent to which customers are convinced that the product of one firm is superior to that of others. Considerable resources are devoted to publicizing these real or imagined differences in beers with the hope of producing product differentiation.

Finally, the barriers to entry in the U.S. brewing industry are enormous and are the result of the huge amount of capital required. The initial capital required to build the facility and purchase the necessary equipment is obviously high, but the extensive amount of advertising and marketing efforts to introduce a new brand against already established brands would be enormous. This is why most new competition comes in the way of mergers between already established firms.

The brewing industry is confronted with a variety of laws and regulations concerning labeling, advertising, credit, container characteristics, alcohol content, tax rates, and litter assessments that affect the marketing of their products. There is little forward integration by brewing firms into the retail distribution of beer. This is mainly because, in the U.S., brewers are prohibited by law from owning any retail outlets. Therefore, the wholesale distribution of their products is the only way forward integration is available. Most brewers rely on independent distributors to channel their products to retail outlets. For the major brewers, agreements with brewer-authorized distributors usually include provisions that require the distributor to carry only one major national brand and several regional, imported, or secondary brands.

Anheuser-Busch Structure

The Anheuser-Busch plant is described as a machine type of organization. The basic structure of such an organization is a machine type of bureaucracy, with highly specialized, routine operating tasks; large size operating tasks units; and an elaborate administrative structure with a sharp distinction between line and staff. This type of organization is developed primarily for maintaining control; it exists in simple and stable environments. It is most common in mass production organizations, where control is achieved through standardization of work processes and repetition.

August A. Busch, III, Chief Executive Officer, states "It's team management, it's creativity and ingenuity, it's the application of management science, it's people, common sense, and hard work...," but how creative or ingenious can a workforce become when the processes are so very standardized? The application of management science removes the "brain work" from the shop floor and also removes the initiative from the people who work there. The result of these problems is high absenteeism, high worker turnover, sloppy workmanship, and low worker morale. All these problems lead to even more tightening of controls; however, the company is striving to increase worker participation to improve the quality of work life and to make the worker feel important to the operation. This is a difficult task, as the operations are so standardized. Besides, they have not changed the way they make beer since the 1800s!

The Brewing and Packaging Operations

The brewing process is very standardized, as is apparent from the following description. The process begins as barley malt and rice (or corn) are ground in huge mills. Rice is used in Budweiser and Michelob brands for lightness and crispness, while corn is used in Busch brands, King Cobra, and Natural Light to produce a milder flavor. The ground malt and rice (or corn) are mixed with water in separate tanks, then combined in the mash tanks. During mashing, enzymes in the malt break down starch into fermentable sugars. The grains are then strained, leaving a clear, amber liquid called wort. The wort is then transferred through the plant and into the brew kettle where it is brought to a boil and the natural hops are added. The hops are the spice of beer, providing the aroma, flavor, and character. The hops are then strained, the wort is cooled, and then it is transferred to primary fermentation tanks, where yeast is added to convert the fermentable sugars to carbon dioxide and alcohol, and the wort becomes beer.

At the set time, the beer is transferred to larger tanks where kraeusening takes place. This is where flavor is matured and natural carbonation is developed. Also, during this phase, a layer of beechwood chips is manually spread on the bottom of the tank to age and naturally carbonate the beer. The beer is then transferred to a chillproofing tank to keep the beer from becoming hazy when cooled to drinking temperature. Finally, the beer is filtered and sent to the packaging department.

The packaging department operates within a mass production structure. The canning and bottling operation is highly automated, with machines washing, filling, capping, and packing the cans and bottles at a rate of 7 million barrels per year. The work is routine, unskilled, and very formalized. Little supervision is necessary due to the automation, resulting in a wide span of control for the first line supervisors.

As can be determined from the above, the brewing and packaging operations at Anheuser-Busch are very standardized and can be described as a machine-type organization. The basic structure of this type of organization is a centralized bureaucracy, with highly specialized, routine operating tasks, large operating units, and an elaborate administrative structure with a sharp distinction between line and staff.

Financial Review

On July 26, 1995, the Board of Directors of Anheuser-Busch Companies, Inc., approved a planned spinoff of 100% of the company's Campbell Taggart, Inc., subsidiary to shareholders during the first half of 1996. Under the spinoff, each AB shareholder would receive a prorated share of the voting common stock of Campbell Taggart in a special dividend. Campbell Taggart would then become a separately traded, publicly held company. In connection with the spin-off, Campbell Taggart would pay a dividend amount of $140 million to Anheuser-Busch.

On October 25, 1995, Anheuser Busch announced that it would be selling its snack food and baseball subsidiaries, including Eagle Snacks. The company would also close its high-cost Tampa, FL, brewery. The company has also been seeking to enhance its system profitability by reducing wholesaler inventory levels throughout the U.S.

These efforts at corporate restructuring have greatly improved the financial standing of the Anheuser-Busch companies, which had record gross sales during 1996 of $12.62 billion, an increase of $6.17 billion over 1995. Sales for the first three months in 1997 exceeded sales for the first three months of 1996 by $91.1 million. Net income of Anheuser-Busch Companies for the year ended December 31, 1996, was $1.2 billion compared to a much lower income for the year ended December 31, 1995, of $642 million. Earnings per share for 1996 were $2.28 following a 2-for-1 stock split on July 25, 1996. Net income per share was $2.27. The company has led in volume sales and market share since 1957.

The Demand for Beer

The consumer leaders within the alcoholic beverage industry are in the under-25 age group and those with annual incomes under $10,000. The beer market is fragmented into different segments. There are taste segments (light, dry, draft, and nonalcoholic) and price segments (premium-priced beers, popular-priced beers, and imports). Anheuser-Busch has products in each of these segments. For example, Bud Light and Michelob Light are premium-priced light beers, while Busch and Natural Light are examples of popular-priced beers. Carlsberg is Anheuser-Busch's import label, while O'Doul's is their nonalcoholic brand. Anheuser-Busch had five labels in 1980 — Budweiser, Michelob, Michelob Light, Busch, and Natural Light. It now has 16.

The volume of Budweiser, Anheuser-Busch's classic consumer brand, fell 5.2% in 1991, to 47.2 million barrels. Between 1987 and 1991, the beer industry grew by 3%, while Budweiser sales fell 5%. With 24% of the market, Budweiser's closest rival, Miller Lite, has less than 12%.

Anheuser-Busch blamed the sales decline on temporary factors such as a doubling of the federal excise tax and the switch to less expensive beers as a result of the recession between 1990 and 1991. In order to attack this decline, the company increased its advertising budget by $100 million and is portraying the Budweiser brand as the one brand for everyone.

Using another strategy for maintaining market share in a recessionary market, Anheuser-Busch has discounted heavily; however, this is an expensive way to stay on top. For example, in 1991, an average 5% discount could have meant a 15 to 20% drop in the brand's operating profit for the year, unless there were offsetting cost cuts. Through efforts such as these, Anheuser-Busch hoped to ride through the economic recession of the early 1990s. The company did, in fact, show a declining net income from 1992 to 1995, but, as previously mentioned, income for 1996 was greatly improved.

Globalization of the Beer Industry

With U.S. beer consumption growing less than 1% annually throughout the 1980s, most U.S. beer producers are tapping overseas markets. According to the Washington-based Beer Institute, U.S. beer exports rose to 32.6 million cases in 1991, up more than 19% from 1990 shipments.

In 1991, Japan was the leading importer of U.S.-brewed beer, accounting for 17 million gallons in imports. Canada, Hong Kong, and Mexico were second, third, and fourth, respectively. Despite the rise in exports over the last several years, those shipments comprise less than 1% of sales by U.S. brewers.

International competition differs greatly from industry to industry. International competition is said to take the form of multi-domestic when competition in each nation is essentially independent. The industry is present in many nations, but competition takes place on a country-by-country basis. The industry is merely a collection of domestic industries.

International competition takes the form of global industries when a firm's competitive position in one nation greatly affects its position in other nations. Firms compete against each other on a worldwide basis and use their competitive advantages that they have obtained in their entire network of activities. There are three types of international transactions — merchandise trade, licensing agreements, and foreign direct investment. Also, certain economic factors, such as economies of scale and trade barriers, affect the internationalization of an industry.

Merchandise Trade

The increase in beer trade — and world trade in general — can be attributed to lower trade barriers, more efficient communication and transportation technology, and growth in real personal incomes. World trade in beer has nearly tripled since 1965, growing at an average annual rate of 6.5% between 1965 and 1987. The largest exporters of beer in this growing market are the Netherlands, West Germany, Czechoslovakia, Belgium, and Canada. The largest importers are the U.S., the U.K., France, Italy, and West Germany. Most of the countries that export beer also import some beer and vice versa. This is known as intra-industry trade.

Licensing Agreements

A typical licensing agreement allows a brewer in one country to brew and market the beer of a foreign brewer. The licenser is selling its expertise in brewing a specific beer, the right to use a trademark, and the name recognition it has built in exchange for royalty payments from the licensee. For example, Anheuser-Busch has a licensing agreement with

John Labatt, Ltd., which allows Labatt to brew and market some Anheuser-Busch beers, such as Budweiser and Michelob, in Canada. Labatt, in return, pays a royalty fee to Anheuser-Busch. Several factors promote the use of licensing agreements. First, they can be used to circumvent trade barriers. Second, the physical qualities of beer promote the use of licensing agreements, as beer is 90% water. Third, it sometimes proves more profitable to license existing plants and distribution systems to handle their products rather than build their own plants and establish their own distribution systems.

Foreign Direct Investment

Foreign direct investment includes the purchase of an existing firm by another brewer or the investment of new or existing facilities in a foreign country. Lower labor and energy costs and fewer government regulations are reasons for using foreign direct investment.

Demand for Foreign Beer

People consume foreign beer for several reasons. First, the quantity of beer demanded at the price of foreign beer is larger than the quantity of beer supplied domestically. Secondly, some consumers prefer the attributes, or characteristics, of the foreign beer over the domestic brands. These attributes include taste, caloric content, alcohol content, and packaging. The consumer will choose the brand that has the attributes they want, depending on price and income limitations.

Growth in the demand for foreign beer has several characteristics. The demand for foreign beer can expand if its price falls relative to the price of domestic beer. Also, an increase in consumer incomes can increase the demand for foreign products. As a matter of fact, the market for imported beers grew at a much higher rate than most domestic beer markets during the late 1970s and early 1980s, a period of income growth for most countries. This is evidence that per capita income growth has contributed to the internationalization of the beer industry.

A brewery's total cost of supplying a foreign market is equal to the beer's cost of production plus transportation and distribution costs, marketing costs, and overhead. The production cost is a function of existing production technology and the cost of its inputs, such as labor, agricultural ingredients, and packaging materials. Economies of scale exist in the brewing industry and encourage direct exporting when the quantity demanded of foreign beer is relatively low and encourages foreign production through licensing or direct investment when the quantity demanded is relatively high.

Transportation costs and trade barriers can offset production cost advantages. If a target country has high tariffs or distribution systems for imported goods that are relatively costly, production cost advantages in the home country may not be feasible, and licensing or direct investment may be the only feasible methods of entering the market.

Barriers to Beer Trade

In Japan, two types of barriers exist. The most significant is the Japanese distribution system, which is a complex, multi-tiered system, where beer moves from producer to wholesaler to consumer. Also, Japan has little warehouse space, which means smaller, more frequent shipments are required. Japan also charges a small customs duty on imported beer.

Canada's trade barriers include discriminatory markups at provincial liquor outlets and different marketing techniques for foreign beer, such as smaller packages and warm foreign beer sales at the governmental outlets.

The main trade barrier in the U.K. is the distribution system, as it is in Japan. Most beer consumed here is draft beer, most of which is sold in pubs. Most of these pubs are owned and managed by breweries or are leased by the breweries to individuals who enter into exclusive supply agreements with them. Therefore, foreign label breweries have found it difficult to get local breweries to carry their products in British pubs. The only way to enter this market is through licensing agreements with the domestic firms.

Anheuser-Busch's share of the very concentrated American beer market grew from 6.5% in 1950 to 44.1% in 1991. However, with stricter drunk-driving laws and more emphasis on health, this growth has become stagnant. As a matter of fact, the average beer consumption was 7% less in 1988 than in 1980. In order to continue to grow, Anheuser-Busch realizes it must aggressively pursue the international markets; however, there are many obstacles to entering the international beer market, and Anheuser-Busch has had its own difficult time trying to penetrate overseas markets.

Anheuser-Busch has had particular problems in Europe. Europeans have been switching from dark and draft beers to lighter lager beers, but Anheuser-Busch has had trouble overcoming European drinkers' view of American lagers as weak, gassy, and tasteless. Also, licensing agreements with European companies to brew and distribute Budweiser locally have created more problems than profit. Therefore, Anheuser-Busch is looking at possibly buying breweries in Europe, but they are not interested in paying inflated prices for these properties. They are also pursuing the possibility of building their own breweries in Europe.

Specifically, Anheuser-Busch is targeting the U.K. They increased spending by 50% to $18 million for 1992, compared to U.K. brewers' total advertising spending of $180 million in 1991. Also, Anheuser-Busch launched its first national television campaign for Budweiser brewed in the U.K.

Anheuser-Busch considers the U.K. a test for its international expansion efforts and an opportunity to learn more about international markets. Their desire to expand abroad is their number two goal behind their number one goal of obtaining a 50% share in the domestic market.

The lifting of restrictions to its European marketing will help Anheuser-Busch's efforts. These restrictions involved trademark rights related to the Czechoslovakian brewer Bud, which prevented Anheuser-Busch from selling Budweiser in Germany and Austria (two of Europe's largest beer markets). Anheuser-Busch expects to acquire a 30% share in Bud that will give them the rights to market Budweiser all over Europe in return for taking over some marketing of the Czech beer outside its home areas.

The U.K. is Anheuser-Busch's first strong opportunity to manage its brands overseas. Many of their overseas marketing programs have been by licensees that give the company less control of their brands. Anheuser-Busch already has extensive distribution in Spain and Ireland, where Budweiser is brewed and supported by Guinness.

Due to Japan becoming the third largest beer-consuming country and its high price of beer ($45 per case), that country is a definite priority for Anheuser-Busch. They are renegotiating their agreement with Suntory International to play more of a direct role in the brand's marketing. Suntory has already given Anheuser-Busch a 60% share of the international beer market in Japan.

Objectives for Future Growth

Anheuser-Busch believes that, despite the industry volume decline in 1991, there is additional growth available in the domestic market. Their growth will come primarily from existing brands and will be supported by increasing their marketing investment, primarily for their premium brands.

Anheuser-Busch will continue to maintain the image of its Busch and Natural products as quality beers for the price-sensitive consumer. Also, the company will continue their price promotion policy of matching competitive discounts. The company will continue its dedication to plant modernization and productivity improvement programs to support profit growth.

The international market also represents additional growth opportunities for Anheuser-Busch; however, there are many obstacles and challenges, as discussed in this case, which are impacting its ability to penetrate the overseas markets effectively.

Anheuser-Busch's corporate mission statement states that, "Beer is and always will be Anheuser-Busch's core business." The goals were to "extend its position as the world's leading brewer of quality products, increase its share of the domestic beer market to 50% by the mid-1990s, and increase its presence in the international beer market."

Anheuser-Busch set four specific strategic objectives for 1997: (1) to pursue growth of its premium brands by focusing on the Budweiser family of brands, (2) to improve the profitability of their sub-premium-priced brands, (3) to increase productivity, and (4) to continue to adapt to the changing business environment.

Summary

Anheuser-Busch Companies, Inc., is a very successful diversified corporation that is still run by the Busch family. The company has prospered, even through the tough times of Prohibition, and continues to lead the industry. Anheuser-Busch, Inc., the company's massive beer brewing subsidiary, continues to lead its competitors with 44.1% of the U.S. market.

Although Anheuser-Busch, Inc., continues to dominate the U.S. domestic market, they have had trouble marketing internationally. As discussed in the preceding pages, Anheuser-Busch has just recently begun aggressive pursuit of the U.K. market and to use this experience to propel them into other European markets. With the problems abroad, Anheuser-Busch is determined to increase its share of the American market continually throughout the 1990s.

Japan, with its large beer-consuming market and high beer prices, is also a prime target for Anheuser-Busch to pursue aggressively. Canada is also a very strong beer market, along with Mexico and other international markets. However, there are many constraints that have impacted Anheuser-Busch's ability to penetrate these foreign markets successfully.

Anheuser-Busch continues pursuit of its goal of obtaining 50% of the U.S. market; however, their second goal of becoming more internationally distributed is proving more difficult. How can Anheuser-Busch overcome these challenges? What resources are needed to help Anheuser-Busch penetrate the international markets? How can Anheuser-Busch utilize its knowledge and expertise to market its products successfully in the U.S. market while still trying to market its products in foreign countries? These serious questions, along with many more, must be answered if Anheuser-Busch expects to be a successful worldwide leader in the beer industry.

Reading List

1. William L. Downward, *Dictionary of the History of the American Brewing and Distilling Industries*, Greenwood Press, Westport, CN, 1980.
2. *Ward's Business Directory of U.S. Private and Public Companies*, Gale Research, Detroit, MI, 1992, p. 105.
3. Peter Hernon and Terry Ganey, *Under the Influence*, Simon & Schuster, New York, 1991, p. 29.
4. *Anheuser-Busch Companies Fact Book*, Anheuser-Busch Companies, Inc., St. Louis, MO, 1992.
5. Douglas F. Greer, "The Causes of Concentration in the U.S. Brewing Industry," *Quarterly Review of Economics and Business*, Winter 1981, pp. 87–106.
6. Kenneth G. Elzinga and Thomas F. Hogarty, "The Demand for Beer," *Review of Economics and Statistics*, May 1972, pp. 197–206.
7. Henry Mintzberg, *Mintzberg on Management*, The Free Press, New York, 1989, pp. 131–152.
8. Margaret K. Ambry, *Consumer Power — How Americans Spend Their Money*, New Strategy Publications, Ithaca, NY, 1991.
9. James R. Norman, "Beer Barrel Blues," *Forbes*, June 22, 1992, p. 98.
10. Pei-Tse Wu, "U.S. Beer Companies Tap Export Markets To Spur Growth," *Journal of Commerce and Commercial*, March 20, 1992, p. 9B.

11. Michael E. Porter, *The Competitive Advantage of Nations,* The Free Press, New York, 1990, p. 53.

12. Jeffrey D. Karrenbrock, "The Internationalization of the Beer Brewing Industry," *Federal Reserve Bank of St. Louis Review,* November/December 1990, pp. 3–19.

13. "Innocent Abroad," *The Economist,* March 17, 1990, p. 72.

14. Ira Teinowitz, "A-B Turns Up Heat Under U.K. Marketing," *Advertising Age,* July 20, 1992, p. 38.

15. Anheuser-Busch Companies, Annual Report, 1991.

16. Anheuser-Busch Companies, Annual Report, 1995.

17. Anheuser-Busch Companies, Annual Report, 1996.

18. *Moody's Investor Service,* Vol. 1, Moody's Investor's Services, New York, p. a-1.

19. *Moody's Investor Service,* Vol. 68, Moody's Investor's Services, New York, pp. 37, 44.

Consolidated Balance Sheet: Anheuser-Busch Companies, Inc., and Subsidiaries (in millions; year ended December 31)

	1996	1995
Assets		
Current assets		
Cash and marketable securities	93.6	93.6
Accounts and notes receivable, less allowance for doubtful accounts of $3.1 and $1.9 in 1996 and 1995	632.7	544.3
Inventories		
Raw materials and supplies	319.5	382.2
Work in process	80.6	58.6
Finished goods	131.0	141.9
Total inventories	531.1	582.7
Other current assets	208.4	290.0
Total current assets	1465.8	1510.6
Investments and other assets	1789.6	1553.3
Investment in discontinued operations	—	764.0
Plant and equipment, net	7208.2	6763.0
Total assets	10,463.6	10,590.9
Liabilities and shareholders equity		
Current liabilities		
Accounts payable	726.8	682.8
Accrued salaries, wages, and benefits	227.6	247.0
Accrued taxes	233.0	86.3
Other current liabilities	243.5	225.9
Total current liabilities	1430.9	1242.0
Post-retirement benefits	524.6	512.1
Long-term debt	3270.9	3270.1
Deferred income taxes	1208.1	1132.8
Common stock and other shareholders equity		
Common stock, $1.00 par value, authorized 800,000,000 shares	705.8	347.3
Capital in excess of par value	929.2	1012.2
Retained earnings	6924.5	6869.6
Foreign currency translation adjustment	(8.8)	(12.1)
	8550.7	8217.0
Treasury stock, at cost	(4206.2)	(3436.0)
ESOP debt guarantee offset	(315.4)	(347.1)
	4029.1	4433.9
Commitments and contingencies	—	—
Total liabilities and equity	$10,463.6	$10,590.9

Consolidated Balance Sheet: Anheuser-Busch Companies, Inc., and Subsidiaries (in millions; year ended December 31)

	1996	1995	1994
Cash flow from operating activities			
Net income	1189.9	642.3	1032.1
Discontinued operations	(33.8)	244.3	(17.6)
Income from continuing operations	1156.1	886.6	1014.5
Adjustments to reconcile net income to net cash provided by operating activities			
Depreciation and amortization	593.9	565.6	517.0
Deferred income taxes	93.8	51.3	68.5
After-tax gain on sale of St. Louis Cardinals	(33.4)	—	—
Shutdown of Tampa brewery	—	112.3	—
Decrease/(increase) in noncash working capital	233.7	(262.0)	(57.0)
Other, net	(75.2)	72.1	120.0
Cash provided by continuing operations	1968.9	1425.9	1663.0
Net cash provided by/(provided to) discontinued operations	52.0	(11.0)	(93.5)
Total cash provided by operating activities	2020.9	1414.9	1569.5
Cash flow from investing activities			
Proceeds from sale of St. Louis Cardinals	116.6	—	—
Capital expenditures	(1084.6)	(952.5)	(662.8)
New business acquisitions	(135.7)	(82.9)	(28.8)
Cash used for investing activities	(1103.7)	(1035.4)	(691.6)
Cash flow from financing activities			
Increase in long-term debt	773.6	567.6	182.2
Decrease in long-term debt	(575.1)	(296.4)	(102.5)
Dividends paid to shareholders	(458.9)	(429.5)	(398.8)
Acquisition of treasury stock	(770.2)	(393.4)	(563.0)
Shares issued under stock plans	113.4	91.8	45.5
Cash used for financing activities	(917.2)	(429.9)	(836.6)
Net increase/(decrease) in cash and marketable securities during the year	—	(50.4)	41.3
Cash and marketable securities, beginning of year	93.6	144.0	102.7
Cash and marketable securities, end of year	93.6	93.6	144.0

Consolidated Summary of Operations: Anheuser-Busch Companies, Inc., and Subsidiaries (in millions, except per share data)

	1996	1995	1994
Beer sold (barrels)	91.1	87.5	88.5
Sales	12,621.5	12,004.5	11,705.0
Federal and state excise taxes	1737.8	1664.0	1679.7
Net sales	10,340.5	10,025.3	10,883.7
Cost of products and services	6964.6	6791.0	6492.1
Gross profit	3919.1	3549.5	3533.1
Marketing, distribution and administrative expenses	1890.0	1756.6	1679.9
Gain on sales of St. Louis Cardinals	54.7	—	—
Shutdown of Tampa brewery	—	160.0	—
Restructuring charge	—	—	—
Operating income	2083.8[a]	1632.9[b]	1853.3
Interest expense	(232.8)	(225.9)	(219.3)
Interest capitalized	35.5	24.3	21.8
Interest income	9.4	9.9	2.6
Other income/(expense), net	(3.0)	20.5	17.6
Income before income taxes	1892.9[a]	1461.7[b]	1676.0
Income taxes (current and deferred)	736.8	575.1	661.5
Revaluation of deferred tax liability	—	—	—
Income from continuing operations	1156.1[a]	886.6[b]	1014.5
Income/(loss) from discontinued operations	33.8	(244.3)	17.6
Income before cumulative effect of accounting changes	1189.9	642.3	1032.1
Cumulative effective of changes in the method of accounting for post-retirement benefits (FAS 106) and income taxes (FAS 109), net of tax benefit of $186.4 million	—	—	—
Net income	1189.9	642.3	1032.1
Primary earnings per share			
Continuing operations	2.28	1.72	1.92
Discontinued operations	.07	(.48)	.04
Income before cumulative effect	2.35	1.24	1.96
Cumulative effect of accounting changes	—	—	—
Net income	2.35	1.24	1.96

Consolidated Summary of Operations: Anheuser-Busch Companies, Inc., and Subsidiaries (in millions, except per share data) (continued)

	1996	1995	1994
Fully diluted earnings per share			
Continuing operations	2.27[a]	1.71[b]	1.90
Discontinued operations	.07	(.47)	.04
Income before cumulative effect	2.34	1.24	1.94
Cumulative effect of accounting changes	—	—	—
Net income	2.34	1.24	1.94
Cash dividends paid			
Common stock	458.9	429.5	398.8
Per share	.92	.84	.76
Preferred stock	—	—	—
Per share	—	—	—
Number of common shares (wtd. avg.)			
Primary	505.8	515.7	528.2
Fully diluted	510.6	524.4	538.0

[a] 1996 results include the impact of the gain on the sale of the St. Louis Cardinals. Excluding the Cardinal gain, operating income, pretax income, income from continuing operations, and fully diluted earnings per share would have been $2029.1 million, $1838.3 million, $1122.7 million, and $2.21, respectively.

[b] 1995 results include the impact of the one-time pretax charge of $160 million for the closure of the Tampa brewery and the $74.5 million pretax impact of the beer wholesaler inventory reduction. Excluding these nonrecurring special items, operating income, pretax income, income from continuing operations, and fully diluted earnings per share would have been $1867.3 million, $1696.2 million, $1032.3 million, and $1.99, respectively.

Note: All per share information and average number of common shares data reflect the September 12, 1996, 2-for-1 stock split. All financial information has been restated to recognize the 1995 divestiture of the food products segment. All amounts include the acquisition of Sea World as of December 1, 1989. Financial information prior to 1988 has been restated to reflect the 1988 adoption of Financial Accounting Standards No. 94, "Consolidation of Majority-Owned Subsidiaries."

Balance Sheet and Other Information: Anheuser-Busch Companies, Inc., and Subsidiaries
(in millions, except per share and statistical data)

	1996	1995	1994
Balance sheet information			
Working capital (deficit)	34.9	268.6	57.0
Current ratio	1.0	1.2	1.0
Plant and equipment, net	7208.2	6763.0	6494.6
Long-term debt	3270.9	3270.1	3066.4
Total debt to total capitalization ratio	44.8%	47.1%	47.3%
Deferred income taxes	1208.1	1132.8	1081.5
Convertible redeemable preferred stock	—	—	—
Shareholders equity	4029.1	4433.9	4415.5
Return on shareholders equity	30.0%[a]	25.0%[b]	29.9%
Book value per share	8.10	7.22	6.64
Total assets	10,463.6	10,590.9	10,547.4
Other information			
Capital expenditures	1084.6	952.5	662.8
Depreciation and amortization	593.9	565.6	517.0
Effective tax rate	38.9%	28.2%	39.5%
Price/earnings ratio	17.6[a]	19.6[b]	13.1
Percentage of pretax profit on net sales	17.4%	14.1%	16.7%
Market price range of common stock (high-low)	42-7/8–32-1/2	34–25-3/8	27-5/8–23-1/2

[a] These ratios have been calculated based on reported income from continuing operations, which includes the $54.7 million pretax gain on the sale of the St. Louis Cardinals. Excluding the Cardinal gain, return on shareholders equity would have been 29.2% and the price/earnings ratio would have been 18.1.

[b] These ratios have been calculated based on reported income from continuing operations. Excluding the two non-recurring 1995 items ($160 million pretax charge for closure of the Tampa brewery and $74.5 million impact of the beer wholesaler inventory reduction), return on shareholders equity would have been 29.1% and the price/earnings ratio would have been 16.8.

Note: All share and per share information reflects the September 12, 1996, 2-for-1 stock split. All financial information has been restated to recognize the 1995 divestiture of the foods products segment. All amounts include the acquisition of Sea World as of December 1, 1989. Financial information prior to 1988 has been restated to reflect the adoption in 1988 of Financial Accounting Standards No. 94, "Consolidation of Majority-Owned Subsidiaries."

Case 12. Union Camp Corporation*

Background

Union Camp Corporation is the result of the 1956 merger of Union Bag and Paper Corporation and Camp Manufacturing Company. Union Bag and Paper Corporation was the outgrowth of several companies, the oldest of which was Union Paper Bag Machine Company. This was a patent-holding company formed in 1861 by Francis Wolle, a Moravian teacher and minister who, in 1852, invented the first paper bag machine.

Camp Manufacturing Company dates back to 1887 with the purchase of a lumber manufacturing operation that began production in Franklin, VA, in the 1850s. Camp entered paper manufacturing in 1938. The two merged companies operated under the name of Union Bag-Camp Paper Manufacturing Corporation until 1966 when the company changed its name to Union Camp Corporation.

Corporate Overview

Union Camp Corporation, headquartered in Wayne, NJ, is a leading manufacturer of paper, packaging, chemicals, and building products.

---

* The case was prepared by Dr. M. Reza Vaghefi, who was assisted by R.E. Holewinski and E. Kempey, for discussion purposes only.

433

The company ranks among the top 200 U.S. industrial companies in sales and employs about 21,000 people worldwide. Domestic operations extend from Florida to Maine and west to California. Outside the U.S., Union Camp has operations in 27 countries.

The paper manufacturing segment consists of four pulp and paper mills. Two produce white paper for business forms, printing, direct mail, and other communication uses. The other two mills produce unbleached kraft paper and linerboard, primarily packaging material.

Within a network of 58 packaging plants, Union Camp converts more than half of its unbleached kraft production into boxes and bags for consumer and industrial products. Four packaging plants produce plastic bags and films. Three others produce folding cartons. Three additional paper products plants manufacture school supplies and stationery. In December 1990, Union Camp acquired Chase Packaging, a company with $180 million in sales.

The company's other domestic manufacturing plants include nine building products operations, four chemical plants, and three flavor and fragrance facilities. Other domestic activities involve residential activities and commercial land development. Overseas, the company has corrugated container plants, chemical plants, and flavor and fragrance facilities.

Research and development are centralized at the Company's Corporate Technology Center in Princeton, NJ. Chemical development laboratories are located at the company's Savannah, GA, manufacturing complex and Jacksonville, FL, chemical plant. Flavor and fragrance development laboratories are in Montvale, NJ; the U.K.; and Singapore. A woodlands research facility is located in Rincon, GA.

Southeastern U.S. woodlands provide the raw material base for most of Union Camp's product. Union Camp's woodlands, which currently furnish 50% of the company's pulp mill and saw mill requirements, total approximately 1.65 million acres in six states. Compared with other major producers in the industry, Union Camp has relatively few pulp and paper mills, but they are all large-scale facilities. Two of them are the largest of their kind in the world. This concentration of high production capabilities at a few highly efficient sites is a major factor contributing to Union Camp's performance as one of the lowest cost producers in the industry.

The company continually invests to upgrade and modernize its facilities to produce high-quality products as efficiently as possible. For the 4-year period from 1989 to 1992, it spent about $2.4 billion on capital projects.

Operating Segments

Paper and Paperboard

Paper and paperboard are produced at the company's four major mill locations: Eastover, SC; Franklin, VA; Savannah, GA; and Prattville, AL. White uncoated fine papers are produced at Eastover. Coated and uncoated bristols are also manufactured at Franklin. Various grades of kraft paper and linerboard are produced at the Savannah mill, while the Prattville operations produce strictly kraft linerboard.

The Paper and Paperboard division is now classified as the Fine Paper Division. It accounted for 23.8% of 1996 sales for the company. The division is continuing to penetrate the small business and home office markets with expanded product lines and increased advertising. Great White is a recycled content business paper that has been very successful for the company, causing them to expand its product line. The division's Express System was able to penetrate the corporate market because of its design for high productivity demanded by the business market.[1]

Packaging

The Packaging Group integrates the Paper and Paperboard division and its packaging and converting business. The keystone of the group, Paper and Paperboard, supplies the bulk of the raw materials from which the company's packaging plants produce containers and bags. These plants, located in every region of the U.S., are aligned in four packaging divisions: Container, Bag, Folding Carton, and School Supplies and Stationery.

The Container division operates 34 plants that produce corrugated boxes. The Bag division manufactures paper and plastic packaging, plastic films, and specialty packaging at 21 facilities. The Folding Carton division's three facilities produce consumer packaging products. The School Supplies and Stationery division manufactures for schools, homes, and offices at three locations.

The Packaging group represented 42.9% of the company's 1996 sales. The group acquired O'Grady Containers, a leading producer of point-of-purchase displays and containers, of Fort Worth, TX. A new container plant in Hanford, CA, began producing heavy-duty corrugated products, such as laminated boxes. The group also began marketing UNIPAL, a corrugated pallet that is a recyclable and disposable alternative to wood and is being used by the Nabisco Company.[1]

Chemicals

By-products from the pulping process make up the core raw material supply for Union Camp's chemical products. The Chemical group is comprised of the Chemical Products division and the Bush Boake Allen division. The Chemical Products division (whose major raw material is tall oil, a by-product from the paper mills) has plants in Savannah, GA; Dover, OH; and Valdosta, GA, and overseas operations in the U.K. The division's products are sold into a wide range of applications including cosmetics, plastics, lubricants, detergents, inks, coatings, adhesives, and oil drilling.[2]

The Bush Boake Allen division was acquired by Union Camp in 1983. It is based in the U.K., with division headquarters located in London. The Bush Boake Allen division is divided into two major sectors: Chemicals and Flavor and Fragrances.

The Chemical sector processes turpentine, a by-product of the kraft pulping process, into a wide range of chemicals. The resulting chemicals are sold to large-scale consumer products and industrial companies such as Proctor and Gamble, Clorox, Monsanto, Unilever, Colgate Palmolive, CIBA-Geigy, and IFF.[3] The range of applications includes aroma products used in soaps, toothpastes, detergents, perfumes, dryer sheets, among others, and terpene products used in tackifier resins, industrial solvents, household cleaners, lubricants, and agricultural chemicals. The Chemical sector has manufacturing sites in Jacksonville, FL, and Widnes, U.K.[4]

The Flavor and Fragrances sector of the Bush Boake Allen division produces a wide range of natural and synthetic seasonings and fragrances for the food industry and uses aroma chemicals produced at the division's chemical plants for its fragrances. The Flavor and Fragrances business has operations in 27 countries around the world.

The Chemical group sales were 17.5% of total 1996 sales as the division continued to move into growth markets in Mexico, Latin America, Asia, Eastern Europe, and India, part of the company's strategy to expand internationally. The segment also developed new products, such as a line of ink resins for the lithographic industry and environmentally friendly polyamide adhesives that are non-solvent based.

Wood Products

Union Camp's wood products include a broad range of lumber, plywood, and particleboard products. Dimension lumber is produced at six locations in Alabama, Georgia, North Carolina, and Virginia. Particleboard is manufactured at the Virginia facility. Plywood products and veneer are produced at two facilities in Alabama.

Woodlands and Land Resources

Union Camp owns or controls approximately 1.65 million acres of woodlands in six southeastern states: Alabama, Florida, Georgia, North Carolina, South Carolina, and Virginia. Support for these operations is provided by a forestry research center in Rincon, GA, and seedling nurseries in Belleville, GA; Capron, VA; and Union Springs, AL.

Advanced forest management practices bring the trees in Union Camp lands to full growth in constantly replenishing cycles. These practices, aimed at generating maximum wood fiber from each tree, include techniques in genetics, reforestation, cultivation, and harvesting. The company's woodlands are among the most productive in the nation. Union Camp plants more than three trees for every one it cuts. These superior seedlings grow to marketable size in about 25 years.

The emphasis on achieving maximum yield continues after harvesting. Timber, woodchips, sawdust, shavings, and bark are all channeled according to their most profitable end use in the company's pulp mills and wood products facilities. As an example, depending on supply, demand, and current prices, bark is either burned as fuel in mill paper boilers or bagged at plants in Alabama, Georgia, and North Carolina. The bagged bark is distributed through retail garden centers as mulch and decorative chips.

The Forest Resources division, including woodlands and wood products, represented 8.9% of annual sales in 1996. The division acquired 46,000 acres of timberland in South Carolina and has an option to purchase 69,000 more. The sawmill in Folkston, GA, was modernized, increasing capacity at the site by 33%. The segment also announced its plan to move into the fast growing market for engineered wood products.[1]

Paper Distribution

Union Camp entered the paper distribution business during 1996 by acquiring the Alling & Cory Company, a leading distributer of business communications and printing papers, industrial packaging, and business products. The segment accounted for 6.9% of total 1996 sales. The company opened a large distribution center in Cleveland, OH, to support the growing market.[1]

The Industry

The forest products, paper, and packaging industry is highly cyclical. In good times, record profits are achieved, but during recessions this industry is one of the most affected. The biggest reason is that the industry's two largest customers, construction and publishing, are two of the most significant recession victims. The packaging side of the business is less sensitive to economic swings.

The economic growth experienced from 1985 to 1989 boosted profits of paper manufacturers tremendously. In 1988, industry returns on equity averaged 19% and topped the market as a whole for the first time since 1975. This in turn led to huge capacity increases. The U.S. industry added an estimated 2.5 million tons of additional production capacity for paper and board in 1991, marking the highest annual volume increase in history. Another 2.0 million tons of new capacity are scheduled to be brought online. This enormous capacity growth has upset the balance between supply and demand in a number of markets and has resulted in significant price declines for market pulp, newsprint, coated papers, and uncoated free-sheet papers. Most of the price and earnings deterioration for these grades has already occurred. A number of efforts have been made recently to raise product prices, particularly for uncoated papers and market pulp, but any meaningful recovery will depend on boosting demand by a substantial amount each year.

The growth of the U.S. economy in the near term is subject to different interpretations. Some analysts feel as though we have entered a period of slow growth, while others see continued moderate growth, and still others see greater growth just around the corner. Most analysts believe the paper industry will enjoy a recovery similar to past industry cycles but timing is a critical variable. As a result of the huge capacity increases, it may take longer to increase the operating rates of the mills and subsequently implement price increases. A muted economic recovery combined with a capacity surplus in many grades will result in a sustained period of 89 to 91% operating rates for paper grades, a pattern not seen since the 1960s when price hikes were sporadic. Historically, upward price hikes have not been supported until operating capacity rates reached 93%.

Continued weakness in advertising, finance, real estate, and white collar employment in general has sharply reduced demand for communications grades of paper. The manufacturing sector of the economy has fared somewhat better, which explains the favorable demand for linerboard and corrugated boxes. In addition, market pulp prices have shown recent evidence of improvement, but prices remain deeply discounted.

The paper industry is a highly competitive industry. In the U.S. it is comprised of 25 major companies ranging from $500 million to $13 billion in sales. Few major companies have the financial resources to undertake major acquisitions in the U.S. paper industry as long as credit is in tight supply, and it is unlikely that non-industry firms will make a hostile bid.

The major scene of merger and acquisition activity will be in Europe, because the transformation to a single market in 1992 creates the need for larger companies to create economies of scale and greater pricing power. U.S. companies that have already expanded in Europe include Stone Container Corporation, James River Corporation, International Paper Company, and Kimberly Clark Corporation.

As always, there will be transactions involving the purchase and sale of individual mills as well as converting and distribution operations. Some companies are selling assets to improve their operating results, while others are attempting to restructure operations to focus on core businesses. As industry earnings and net free cash flow increase, the climate for larger transactions will be more favorable.

A recent trend in the industry is environmental improvements replacing capacity additions as the driving force behind capital spending plans. Most of this dramatically increased spending will go toward reducing dioxin formation, installing secondary treatment facilities, and controlling odor at kraft pulp mills. A long-term effect of the environmental trend may be to "weed out" the smaller, less committed players in the paper industry.

Corporate Strategy

Union Camp's main strategic focus is to expand and strengthen the company's already low-cost systems for production of uncoated free-sheet and linerboard, two grades that have shown faster than average industry growth. A $2.4 billion, 4-year capital investment program was completed in 1992 to bring paper and board production capacity up 26% and reduce labor energy, and chemical costs 5 to 10%. To provide an outlet for this expansion, the company has been fairly aggressive in developing export markets for its products.

Vertical Integration

A significant focus of Union Camp's strategy is vertical integration. The company has its own woodlands, harvests its own wood, produces pulp and paper, processes the chemical by-products, and manufactures packaging and building products. The idea is to add value to all of its products and capture the profits that would otherwise be lost to other entities.

Environment

Like all U.S. paper companies, Union Camp is under pressure to meet tougher environmental regulations. But CEO Raymond E. Cartledge used the forced plant upgrades to make things more efficient. Union Camp recently developed a process to bleach pulp using ozone instead of chlorine. The process reduces bleaching costs, at least 30%.

Nearly 100 full-time environmental experts help ensure that Union Camp plants operate in full compliance with environmental regulations. And the company backs up that commitment with its vast technological resources and capital, which allow the implementation of control equipment. In 1990 alone, the company spent more than $46 million on environmental improvements. Most of the company's paper, and packaging products are recyclable. The company also has a history of recycling waste paper at its mills and is focusing capital spending on increasing recycle capacity in the future.

Union Camp has led the U.S. paper industry in drafting and adopting voluntary environmental health, safety, and forestry principles. The company has improved its environmental performance by dedicating significant research, engineering, and financial resources to minimize the impact on the environment. They continue to sustain forest management that helps preserve endangered species and places of special historical or ecological significance, environmentally improved and updated manufacturing processes and technologies, and a responsible corporate behavior to the environment. The company has grown over 1.2 billion seedlings and maintains a Forest Resources Group (FRG) comprised of field experts and scientists in order to help protect the environment.[5]

Acquisitions

As opposed to its competitors, Union Camp has primarily grown through internal investment. In the last cyclical peak, many of the major players in the paper industry, notably Stone Container and Jefferson Smurfit, have grown through acquisition. Union Camp did, however, purchase Chase Bag in 1990. With a strong balance sheet, Union Camp may be poised for future acquisitions — says Cartledge, "I'm ready and able to compete and win anywhere in the world."

During 1996, Union Camp has divested four smaller business units to allow them to engage in investments yielding higher returns. The company has also invested in expanding internationally by moving into fast-growing overseas markets. Union Camp acquired two corrugated packaging additions in Spain and Turkey and broke ground for a new packaging plant in China and another packaging acquisition in Argentina. The company moved into the paper distribution business with the acquisition in 1996 of the Alling & Cory Company, a market leader serving the printing and business paper markets.[1]

Fixed Costs

Due to the cash squeeze created by the extensive capital investment program, coupled with the unfavorable pricing environment, Union Camp instituted a hiring freeze. As opposed to across-the-board personnel reductions imposed by other large corporations, the company has chosen to reduce fixed costs by attrition and spending cuts. This move produced shock among the management ranks of Union Camp because such measures in the past were unheard of.

The company has also sought to improve the capital-intensive production processes by investing in research and development to keep manufacturing costs minimal. The fixed cost structure of the industry makes cash flows essential to Union Camp's survival: "The disciplined use of cash flow is a core philosophy for us in order to manage the company," observed Chief Operating Officer Craig McClelland.[1]

Union Camp is a very conservative company. The company, up until recently, carried very little debt on its balance sheet. Funds required for capital investment are typically generated through operations. The current situation has forced the Company to borrow about $900 million, which is an all-time record for Union Camp.

The annual operating budget is part of the culture of Union Camp. The company pays a lot of attention to deviations from budget. The operations managers are rewarded based on their performance vs. budget. The target return on assets for all divisions is 10%. In addition to budgets, forecasts have become increasingly emphasized. All operating sites are required to submit a current month plus a 3-month rolling forecast. Surprises from forecasts are given heavy scrutiny from corporate.

The company had a record year in 1995, with net sales of $4.2 billion and earnings per share of $6.45, and was able to outperform its peer group. The company attributed this record to the success and expansion of the growing economy. However, 1996 represented the other extreme for the company. Sales fell to $4.0 billion, and earnings per share decreased to $1.23. The 1996 financial year is representative of the volatile and cyclical paper industry.[1]

Employee Involvement

The company has recently placed a lot of emphasis on participative management/employee involvement. Managers have been sent to facilitation training courses in order to learn participative management skills. Union Camp has begun gain-sharing programs at many of its operating sites for all employees to encourage their participation and involvement in managing the Company.

During 1996, training and safety became the focus for developing and operating an effective corporate culture. Union Camp's employee safety is a top priority, and company safety records are set for the year. Employee training is a critical investment for the corporation in order to improve business performance and employee competence.[1]

Company Management

Union Camp has a reputation of being conservative. The decision-making process can be quite cumbersome and frustrating to entrepreneurial types. All decisions requiring capital outlays over $50,000 require approval from the CEC (Capital Expenditure Committee), a committee comprised of corporate senior management. Upon approval from the CEC, these jobs are then submitted to the Board of Directors. Many of the more creative types have left the company and sought opportunities where more risk taking is accepted.

In December 1989, W. Craig McClelland was elected President and Chief Operating Officer of the Company. He had been an Executive Vice President of Union Camp since November 1988. From September 1986 to November 1988, McClelland was a Director and Executive Vice President of International Paper Company and President and Chief Executive Officer of Hammermill Paper Company (a subsidiary of International Paper Company). He has extensive marketing and general management experience in the paper industry and is the heir apparent to CEO Raymond Cartledge, who is now 62 years old.

Outlook for the Future

When the company began the third quarter of 1992, prices for fine paper and linerboard had not firmed up. Earnings for the year appeared to be well below security analysts estimates. The increased depreciation from the capital investments and interest changes from the newly acquired debt also would impact earnings. The company had to borrow money to pay the quarterly dividends in the last two quarters.

The company's focus of being the low-cost, high-quality producer in fine paper and certain grades of linerboard has put a burden on the finances of Union Camp. Also, increasing government regulations require capital spending on environmental measures. Certainly an economic rebound, creating increased demand for paper, can be expected to return prices to 1988 levels and beyond. When this occurs, the company could be in an enviable position. Timing is a critical issue. If a further recession is imminent, the company will face rough times. Deep discounting of Union Camp stock could make it a prime takeover target.

Meanwhile, an increasing emphasis on reducing working capital is taking shape at Union Camp, and the hiring freeze is still in effect. Will these measures be enough until the paper industry emerges from this cyclical trough, or will the company look at divesting some of its noncore businesses and selling some of its extensive assets? At the present, it looks like business as usual at Union Camp.

The company's 1995 financial results proved that the paper industry can have very profitable years; however, the cyclical nature of the industry and the volatile conditions in the worldwide paper markets present an ongoing challenge for the business. According to McClelland,[1] "Looking ahead, the global trends for the paper and forest products are very positive: rising population growth, improving standards of living, increasing worldwide trade, and the growing information age that will on balance continue to generate favorable growth rates for the paper and packaging products. However, the capital-intensive nature of the paper business, operating in a climate of slowing economic growth and inflation, will mean that only the strong, smart and dedicated paper companies will succeed through both the current downside and pending upside of the cycle."

In order to respond to changing market conditions and still be able to maximize shareholder wealth, Union Camp must improve the results. The company must be able to meet the challenge of the as-yet-unrealized possibility of a "paperless" society that could be created by the information age. To be successful, the company must become more flexible and dynamic, allowing it to lead the paper industry and to determine what direction the industry takes to drastically reduce and improve its cost structure and financial returns.

References

1. Union Camp Corporation, Annual Report, 1996.
2. Linda Killan, *Forbes*, Jan. 6, 1992.
3. George McLaren, *Pulp and Paper*, January 1992.
4. Steven Weiner, *Forbes*, Jan. 9, 1989.

Union Camp Corporation Financial Data (in thousands)

	1996	*1995*	*1994*	*1993*	*1992*
Operating results					
Net sales	4,013,197	4,211,709	3,395,825	3,120,421	3,064,358
Costs and other charges	3,772,691	3,381,607	3,121,325	2,908,797	2,883,782
Net income	85,308	451,073	113,510	50,043	76,233
Earnings per share	1.23	6.45	1.62	0.72	1.10
Financial position					
Current assets	1,134,110	1,033,817	951,133	910,718	1,016,117
Current liabilities	779,869	620,113	883,924	909,372	892,115
Working capital	354,241	413,704	67,209	1346	124,002
Total assets	5,096,307	4,838,343	4,776,578	4,685,033	4,745,197
Long-term debt	1,252,475	1,151,536	1,252,249	1,244,907	1,289,706
Deferred income taxes	723,431	709,850	605,643	583,155	553,871
Stockholders' equity	2,093,594	2,121,692	1,836,321	1,815,848	1,881,878
Percent of long-term debt to total capital	30.8%	28.9%	33.9%	34.2%	34.6%

Case 13. Note on the Pharmaceutical Industry*

Today, the U.S. pharmaceutical industry remains the leader in world industry sector competitiveness and innovation and is undergoing adjustments to changing market conditions. Changes are largely due to demands for medical cost containment, mergers, and acquisitions among the leading drug makers.[1] Change is also constant within the regulatory environments, and drug manufacturers' anticipation of the impacts is becoming essential. Given the current climate, minimizing the risk of non-compliance remains paramount.[1]

Research and development (R&D) investment has doubled every 5 years since 1970. In 1993, the industry invested more than $12.6 billion in R&D, a 14.5% increase over 1992. In 1994, R&D expenditures represented 16.7% of total sales.[2] In 1994, U.S. manufacturers accounted for nearly half of the major pharmaceuticals worldwide.[2] The U.S. pharmaceutical industry, historically one of the nation's most profitable and fastest growing segments of the economy, is faced with an increasingly difficult operating environment in the years ahead. Mounting competitive pressures, such as changes in customers, relative slowing of new drug launches, managed health care, mergers, new regulations, and over-the-counter (OTC) markets, have been shifting and slowing the industry's phenomenal growth rate.

---

* The note was prepared by Dr. M. Reza Vaghefi, who was assisted by Carol Beasley and Tatia Binecoff-Mickelwright, for discussion purposes only.

Changes in the drug industry have led to an environment in which drug companies can no longer count on favorable pricing to lead to profit growth. Instead, they have to emphasize new strategy developments. These include the discovery and development of new types of products and finding ways to increase sales of existing products. Joint ventures and strategic alliances in the industry are proving to be profitable.[3] Reflecting increasingly competitive global pharmaceutical markets and more restrictive pricing environments, drug companies are expected to move toward fortifying their operations through product development, market alliances, and outright mergers and acquisitions in the years ahead.[4] In fact, in 1995 there were more than 50 drug companies, but the industry was dominated by just a dozen firms. While there is little competition in prescription drugs, generic drugs are the big challenge.[5]

Another way for companies to avoid the pricing problems has been to follow the increasing market trend by switching from prescription to OTC drugs. Although OTC drugs tend to be much cheaper because of escalated competition, the disadvantages are more than offset by higher volumes.[2] Generic substitutions are also increasing in popularity due to cost-conscious consumers. The generic market was expected to increase to more than $21 billion by 1995, and 51 of 1994's prescription drugs expired.[2] The industry also faces increased consumer interest in natural products and the growing demand for medicinals and botanicals. Producers of these products make bulk organic and inorganic medicinal chemicals and their derivatives, and they process bulk botanical drugs and herbs.[6] The environment in the drug industry is changing even more dramatically under the Clinton Administration.

The Clinton Administration, however, has brought about one of the first international agreements to make changes to regulations that corporations say hinder international commerce. Under the accord, the FDA agreed to allow European regulators and third-party inspectors to certify safety and production standards for items made in Europe and sold in the U.S.[5] In contrast, the biological products industry, including vaccines, serums, plasmas, and other blood derivatives, will continue to face stringent regulations. In response, large pharmaceutical companies are pressing for federal permission to sell some of their most important drugs without a doctor's prescription. Such a move is the result of being able to offer milder doses, the expiration of patents, and implementation of heavy consumer advertising.[7] Products of such a strategy include Tagamet from Smith-Kline and Pepcid from Merck & Company.[7] However, the

Food and Drug Administration plans to issue regulations requiring the makers of OTC drugs to report cases of adverse reactions, which is already a requirement for prescriptions.[2]

The pharmaceutical industry is also concerned with areas of environmental policy, specifically the Clean Air Act regulations, pollution prevention, guidelines and limitations for wastewater discharges, and environmental assessments. In 1997, new air emission standards were implemented, but the industry worked with the Environmental Protection Agency (EPA) to develop standards and to seek flexibility in monitoring. The EPA adopted new pharmaceutical industry requirements for toxic pollution in 1996,[4] and the pharmaceutical industry also has the highest rate of participation in the EPA's voluntary 33/50 program to reduce toxic waste.

The pharmaceutical stocks have been off by about 35% from their fourth-quarter 1991 peak as the industry has absorbed the impacts of heightened cost-containment pressures, growing popularity of low-cost managed care, and apprehension associated with Clinton's efforts to reform health care. The stocks were especially hard hit by threats of government price controls.[4] More intense pressure from the government has already begun to restrict industry pricing. In an effort to stave off new and potentially restrictive federal price controls, nearly all the U.S. drugmakers have voluntarily agreed to hold price increases on their products to the general inflation rate as measured by the Consumer's Price Index.

Entry Barriers

The pharmaceutical market is competitive. There are 22 major drug firms, and none of them has a market share greater than 7.5% as of the mid 1990s.[8] New entrants face barriers that include huge investments in R&D and marketing, large capital investments, government policy interventions, and new types of health care groups such as managed care. In addition, all new entrants face stiff competition from established firms, such as Merck, Pfizer, Lilly, and Upjohn, to name just a few.

One of the most difficult barriers to overcome is the expenditure in R&D. In 1994, the Pharmaceutical Manufacturers' Association (PMA) projected an increase in R&D expenditures of approximately 13% for more than 100 PMA member companies.[9] This was a 9.3% gain over 1993. R&D is expensive, and the risks are enormous. The industry's profits are largely channeled into research. In 1996, as a percentage of sales, the industry R&D approached 23%, nearly twice that for the rest of the health care industry. Although this seems to be a large budget, it is decreasing each year in relationship to sales.

New entrants can little afford the enormous financial burden or the time needed to see the profits. The average drug requires 12 years to go from concept to market, and because the pharmaceutical companies find more dry holes than gushers, some 70% of the new drugs that reach the market are expected to lose money.

Most drugs never get beyond the research phase. In a given year, 30,000 to 45,000 medical articles are published on drug therapies. Of these, the government grants patents for 2000 to 4000 a year. Companies list about half of those with the federal Drug Administration for approval. The manufacturer must submit a New Drug Application (NDA), which is the compilation of research completed during the three phases of testing. Usual applications sometimes exceed 50,000 pages. On an average, 3 years may lapse between submission of the NDA and final approval. Another half fall out by the third phase — drug trials. Actual filing applications barely number 8 to 250; of these, the FDA approves between 20 and 60 per year. In all, firms market only 1 in 100 products for which patents have been developed.[8]

New entrants who have made the large investment in time and money for R&D now face marketing and distributing their products. Drug firms often equal or exceed the R&D spending with spending on promoting their products. In 1996, Merck spent over $3.8 billion in marketing and administrative costs.[10] Previously, the industry was known for spending lavishly, wining and dining physicians. Industry analysts estimate 22% of drug revenues are spent on advertising and marketing.[11] Most marketing dollars are used to persuade physicians and pharmacy directors to prescribe or buy their product; after all, very few patients go to their doctor and request a specific medication by brand name. Access to distribution channels can be difficult. Hospitals and managed care facilities are turning to formularies which limit the number of me-too drugs used by physicians. Larger established drug companies are better able to contract to these established channels.

Newcomers can also find difficulty funding their technology. Drug projects are inherently uncertain and provide little collateral. Securities offer unlikely sources of capital. Many funds are internally generated, a significant advantage of larger established firms. Even for firms with access to capital markets, internally generated funds may be preferred, as confidentiality is enhanced. Large established firms have a significant advantage by defraying the high fixed costs associated with specialized laboratory equipment.[12]

Buyer Power

Pharmaceutical companies have long had the best deal among American businesses. The industry followed its own set of rules: raising prices at will with almost complete freedom from the market forces of supply and demand. Today, as part of a plan to transform the cost of health care, an attack has been launched on America's drugmakers. Although the industry has improved patients' health, it has also contributed to the rising health care cost. From 1985 to 1996, drug prices rose over 86%, more than twice the inflation rate.[13]

These price increases are extremely painful for the elderly, the largest demographic segment of pharmaceutical consumers. Compounding the challenges faced by the elderly on fixed incomes is the fact that Medicare does not cover prescription drugs. Market forces have begun bringing in lower drug costs. The free-market system of discounts has worked for HMOs, hospitals, managed care groups, mail-order pharmacies, and other purchasing organizations. The growing power of group purchasing organizations is revolutionizing the prescription drug market.[14] To position themselves better, managed care groups use a variety of techniques to reduce drug costs, including aggressive negotiations, restrictive drug utilization (formularies), and the sometimes required use of generic drugs.

While these group purchasing agents can significantly affect the industry, there are many buyers not represented by these organizations. Medicare patients are still depending on their physicians to prescribe the least expensive drug and can do little else than look for the least costly pharmacy at which to purchase their medicine.

Independent retail pharmacies are another segment of buyers who are challenged by growing drug costs. Drugmakers grant them few discounts for one simple reason; pharmacies have little power to shift market share. They must sell what the physicians prescribe. Since they cannot lure manufacturers with larger orders, they pay much more than mail-order houses.[15]

Supplier Power

Obviously, bulk chemical compounds play a role in the drug industry. The power wielded by these bulk compounds, however, is minor. Generic drugmakers within the U.S. must obtain almost all their raw materials from independent bulk pharmaceutical suppliers in Europe. American suppliers are not a viable option for them because the brandname manufacturers have the U.S. production market depleted.[16]

A more important aspect of supplier power is the intellectual talent. Highly educated, innovative researchers in major scientific fields alter the course of the industry. Therefore, colleges and medical schools are a major source of suppliers of these researchers to the industry.

Technology

Searching for innovative products is a difficult task for all pharmaceutical companies. The products involve the highly complex fields of molecular biology, biochemistry, and the intricate workings of human physiology. The quest for new pharmaceuticals combines the understanding of multiple disciplines and intuitive acumen to theorize and devise new therapeutic modalities.

Advances in biotechnology, genetic engineering, monoclonal antibodies, cellular biotechnology, and immunology are expected to produce revolutionary therapies.[17] These advances will help drug manufacturers improve the lives of millions of people, although they continue to challenge even the advanced technology of drug researchers and developers.

Substitutes

Generic drugs offer the toughest competition for off-patent drugs. Generic drugs have become more sophisticated, and name-brand companies are looking into joint ventures and mergers to protect some of their sales. The outlook for products coming off patent is very good. Generic drugs provide off-patent copies at one fifth to one half the price of the competitive brand name — and they are getting less expensive each year.[18] By 2001, $21 billion worth of brand products will lose patent protection. Without a sound strategy, the effects on the industry will be phenomenal.

Marketing and product revival are part of generic strategies to increase profitability. Larger generic companies can emphasize quality products, but the doors are open to smaller companies for specific market niches. Manufacturers of generic drugs focus on market distribution and cost. There is no product differentiation. The generic industry is receiving a push from the FDA by elevating generic drug reviews to an office-level operation review. This has eliminated bureaucracy and allows for tentative approvals of drugs not off patents.[19]

A growing number of private managed care and public programs require the use of generic drugs. Generic drugs are also moving into hospital formularies to help curtail health care costs.

A major force has been in the explosion of similar or identical me-too drugs. These drugs are newly patented rivals that are chemically different but have the same medical effect. These drugs are crowding the market to compete with name-brand drugs. Presently, there are eight patented "ace" inhibitor drugs for hypertension and four copycat ulcer drugs.[20] This is an area that the industry needs to reevaluate. How many ulcer drugs are needed? Perhaps research money should be allocated to providing relief or cures for other illnesses.

Global Forces

The global effects on the pharmaceutical industry are now influencing health care reform. The U.S. is the world's single largest market, accounting for an estimated two thirds of all drug sales. Other markets include Japan (13%), Germany (6%), France (5%), Italy (5%), and the U.K. (3%).[21] These figures have been fairly stable throughout the 1990s.

Many critics in the industry have observed the disparity between prices charged for drugs in the U.S. and the prices charged for the same drugs in other countries. In a Mexican study, pharmacies offered drugs at a fifth of the cost of their U.S. counterparts. Of 800 impoverished Texas border residents interviewed, one quarter crossed the river for their medicine.[22] The effects of NAFTA are still being researched, but it appears that it may make it easier to purchase medically prescribed drugs legally across the border. It would also remove tariffs and save U.S. drug and medical device firms an estimated $400 million per year.[21]

Germany has initiated tough measures to drive down drug prices. A 5% cut in pharmaceutical prices combined with a 2-year freeze was reinforced by imposing a ceiling on drug expenditures within the country's health care system in 1993. Doctors were held liable and could have had as much as DM 240 million deducted from their incomes if fixed drug budgets were exceeded.[23] The ceiling was lifted in 1995 and the implications are still being identified.

In the U.K., the government extended a scheme for restricting drugs available under the country's National Health Service from 17 to seven therapeutic categories. Some product markets could be completely destroyed as a result.

In France, the average number of drugs per prescription is four times higher than the average number in the U.S., and the government has resorted to restricting physicians' abilities to prescribe in an effort to curb expenditures. In return, physicians are offered an increase in remuneration.

Italy is also making tentative moves at the government level to limit prescribing budgets for physicians. At the present time, many inexpensive drugs have been removed from the reimbursement list because they can now be obtained over the counter.

Scandinavian governments are using a reference-price system. There is a single, fixed, reimbursable price for a class of drugs or therapeutic groups, with the patient paying the difference.

One of the largest global forces is the Economic Unification of European markets. Several key issues will be beneficial to the industry. The centralized product registration system will enlist a single approval process for all of the European community member nations. There will be free market pricing, instead of individual countries dictating prices. A unified patent protection agency will be enforced throughout the community.

Japan's involvement in pharmaceuticals is a serious threat. The Japanese have analyzed the world market and decided to forge ahead with research on new drugs. The cost of trying to treat the top eight currently incurable diseases is approaching $500 billion. Innovative technology holds the key to solving some of the great mysteries of science and treatments of debilitating diseases. New pharmaceuticals reduce the reliance on more expensive therapies such as surgery. These considerations have compelled the Japanese to invest heavily in pharmaceutical opportunities for their potential value.[24]

Government Regulations

The drug industry has been encumbered with government regulations. The primary regulatory agency is the Food and Drug Administration. Until recently, new drugs could be delayed for 12 years before being released to the market. One FDA goal is to cut processing time for new drug applications in half. With a new users' fee established in 1992, the FDA has been able to make strides in attaining its goals. The new fee has been used to provide more staff and equipment aimed at accelerating drug approvals.[25]

Generic drugs have had some reprieve in filing since 1984 with the passing of the Waxman Hatch Act. This allowed companies to file Abbreviated New Drug Applications (ANDA) for imitations. The process became quicker and more economical.

Medicaid, the government's health insurance program for low income Americans, had a policy of full reimbursement for both high-priced name brands and the cheaper generic version of the same drug. Under the Medicaid program, most states require pharmacists to sell patients generic drugs, but some allow a doctor to sign the statement "brand medically needed". When asked, most doctors have a difficult time justifying the prescription of a brand name drug rather than a generic equivalent.

In the late 1980s, Medicaid began to flex their muscle to push the price down. They established formularies and used red tape to discourage physicians from prescribing costly drugs. Pharmaceutical companies feared their biggest customer would shut out their new expensive products. In 1990, a bargain was reached — Medicaid would receive a flat 15.7% rebate in exchange for dropping formularies and reducing red tape for physicians.[15] The bargain proved very effective for Johnson & Johnson. In 1996, 35% of their total sales were made up of products that had been introduced within the last 5 years.[26]

In 1993, Senator Pryor's amendment to restrict tax breaks enjoyed by U.S. pharmaceutical makers with factories in Puerto Rico was vetoed by a two-to-one margin. This bill would have reduced or eliminated Section 936 tax credits for companies "gouging" consumers on prescription drugs.[27]

President Clinton's government involvement in health care reform has been the largest threat to date for the pharmaceutical industry. The impact of his proposed plan would have been devastating to the pharmaceutical industry had the measure been passed. The industry was largely targeted for runaway profits and there was an apparent willingness to spend more on marketing and promotion than R&D. As noted previously, to wave off government regulations, the major players in the industry have agreed to hold price increases to the general inflation rate as measured by the Consumer's Price Index.[28]

Societal Values and Concerns

Many of the high expenditures of health care are due to societal factors. They include poverty, lack of education, homelessness, drug abuse, alcoholism, smoking, poor diet, lack of exercise, stress, lifestyles, trauma, violence, and abuse.[29]

A second set of factors also drives the costs of health care up. As a society we expect the best health care available, and we want it on demand. We abuse the use of emergency rooms and expect pharmacies to be open 24 hours per day, plus we want those pharmacies to carry the latest drugs at the lowest cost. We do not want to travel too far, and we expect the best in our community.

We expect all drugs to be perfectly safe. A drug that saves millions but may kill 100 people is kept off the market. We monitor the pain medication given to a dying patient who is suffering excruciating pain because we fear they may become addicted. Lifesaving treatments for our elderly are withheld because the FDA is not certain whether the same drug may be safe for a young pregnant woman.[30] One would think that perhaps the government should simply restrict the use of such drugs rather than withhold them from those who may benefit. Although these issues are valid, the pharmaceutical industry has a difficult road to follow when a society takes so little responsibility for its own welfare and health.

Marketing, Distribution, and Administration

The area of marketing, promotion, and advertising is a more complex issue. Previous marketing programs have targeted physicians. There is a sprawling network of salespeople, called detail men, hawking products door to door. With the number of managed-care providers increasing, cost-conscious purchasing agents and committees will be delegated the responsibility of choosing a few cost-effective drugs for their provider.

Because the traditional sales approach may not fit into the future stream, drugmakers are building managed-care teams schooled in finance as well as science.[31] Because all physicians do not belong to managed-care teams, drugmakers will have to strive for a new marketing mix. With this in mind, marketing, distribution, and administrative costs will continue to rise as the industry makes proper adjustments in order to survive. In essence, once the new marketing structure has been implemented, the large number of marketing and salespeople (detail men) will no longer be necessary.

Research and Development

Like marketing, research and development are also important issues. Much of the industry's research and development effort is being taken outside of the U.S., in areas where the tax laws and the political climates are known. The industry argues that restricting price increases stifles research and development and causes a reduction in new drug discoveries. Australia, for example, has developed very few drugs due to stringent government regulations.

It should be noted here that the federal government does quite a bit of R&D of its own for many drugs. Pharmaceutical companies may then come in and obtain exclusive rights to commercialize the drug, the cost of which taxpayers have funded about 85%.[32]

Strategies

In analyzing the industry, we have seen the way the industry has progressed. In light of pending health care reform, many changes are being initiated. Large industry leaders are merging, and joint ventures are being pursued to capture market shares companies do not currently have.

Pharmaceutical companies are getting away from the me-too mentality and are discovering novel drugs. Individual corporations are defining the type of business they are in. Eli Lilly has chosen five fields of research to pursue: diseases related to the central nervous system, endocrine diseases (including diabetes and osteoporosis), infectious diseases, cancer, and cardiovascular diseases.[33] This has been quite controversial, because AIDS research was taken off their development scheme.

Shortened FDA approval should help in the long run if the new users' fees are used to accelerate the approval process. Obtaining more exclusive rights from the government will save some of the R&D expenditures. Managed care is now a way of life, and the large sales forces will not be needed to see to the individual needs of the physicians.

Conclusions

The pharmaceutical industry is one of the most successful industries in the U.S. They are forced to focus on financial strategies that include government regulation, changing market structures, and international economic issues. The Clinton Administration's continued effort to create a managed-care national health care system casts much uncertainty upon the pharmaceutical industry. Health care reform and payer controlled medicine are changing the way the industry must do business. In turn, the voluntary price increase restraints may become regulated and incorporated into this legislation.

Similarly, the trends toward generic drugs and over-the-counter distribution are also creating marketing and economic challenges to industry participants. International economic condition concerns have replaced previously limited domestic views. Moreover, the overall competitive marketplace has been expanded to include an area that does not always comply with patent and other competitive legal protection.

In essence, the drug industry's future is subject to active debate. International economic conditions and market structures are changing. Restructuring and new mergers are becoming common. R&D programs are being downsized, and companies are allowing the federal government to foot the research bill to alleviate major public health concerns. Although the environment is worrisome, drugmakers will have to adjust to lower prices while they continue to battle the proposed health care reforms. With many of the top brands nearing the end of their patent-protected era, the ball seems to be in the drugmakers' court to introduce new drugs, and only the future can tell what they will be.

References

1. Allison Spiller, *Consilium Hosts Pharmaceutical Industry Executive Summit on Issues Facing Drug Makers in the New Millenium*, Consilium Inc., Mountain View, CA, 1996.

2. Ronald H. Brown, Secretary, and Jeffrey E. Garten, *U.S. Industrial Outlook 1994: Forecasts for Selected Manufacturing and Service Industries*, U.S. Department of Commerce, Washington, D.C., January 1994, pp. 43-1–43-4.

3. Thomas P. Au, "The Drug Industry," *Value Line Investment Survey*, Aug. 7, 1992, p. 1257.

4. *Standard & Poor's Industry Surveys*, 160(34), Aug. 20, 1992, p. H18.

5. Daniel Green, "Takeover Fever: The Wave of Acquisitions and Mergers in the Drugs Sector Is Set to Continue," *Financial Times*, August 22, 1995, p. 10.

6. *Washington Times*, from dialogue via Individual, Inc., **http://ches2.acs.amedd. army.mil/lstbin/read_story/FIRST/970629/8/8/82i**.

7. Milt Freudenhiem, "Rearranging Drugstore Shelves: More Products Ship to Nonprescription," *The New York Times*, September 27, 1994, pp. C1, C9.

8. *Business and Society Review*, July 1989, pp. 51–54.

9. "Growth of R&D Spending to Slow in '94," *Chemical and Engineering News*, Jan. 17, 1994, p. 7.

10. Merck, Annual Report, 1996.

11. Andre Rock, "Cut Your Spiraling Drug Costs 70%," *Money*, June 1993, p. 132.

12. Samuel B. Graves and Nan S. Langowitz, "Innovative Productivity and Returns to Scale in the Pharmaceutical Industry," *Strategic Management Journal*, November 1993, p. 593.

13. Shawn Tully, "Why Drug Prices Will Go Lower," *Fortune*, Nov. 3, 1993, pp. 56–66.

14. Michael J. Dillion, "Drug Pricing: One Size Fits None," *The Journal of Commerce and Commercial*, Aug. 3, 1995, p. 6A.

15. *Fortune*, December 27, 1993, p. 16.

16. Ira Breskin, "EC Laws Pinch U.S. Generic Drug Manufacturers," *Journal of Commerce and Commercial*, November 15, 1993.

17. "Drug Industry," *Standard & Poor's Industry Surveys*, September 1993, pp. H18–H30.

18. Alice Naude, "Into the Mainstream," *Pharmaceutical '92*, October 1992, p. 131.

19. "Drugmakers Contend with Inevitable Change," *Chemical Week*, March 31, 1993, p. 23.

20. Shawn Tully, "The Plots To Keep Drug Prices High," *Fortune*, Dec. 27, 1993, pp. 120–124.

21. *Standard & Poor's*, 1993.

22. "Blaming High Prices in the U.S., Americans Buy Medicine in Mexico," *Wall Street Journal*, June 29, 1993, p. B10.

23. Sean Milmo, "Tightening the Screws," *Pharmaceutical '93*, July 1993, p. 47.

24. "Price Controls: Rx for Failure," *Journal of Commerce and Commercial*, Feb. 9, 1995, p. 7A.

25. "Pharmaceuticals Under Pressure," *Chemical Week*, Jan. 6–13, 1993, pp. 29–30.

26. Johnson & Johnson, Annual Report, 1996.

27. "Drug Firms May Lose Tax Break for 'Gouging'," *Journal of Commerce and Commercial*, Feb. 9, 1994, p. 7A.

28. *Standard & Poor's*, 1993.

29. James D. Barber, "Telling the Public the Real Health Cost Story," *Hospitals*, June 20, 1992, p. 68.

30. George Newman, "Now Take This," *Across the Board*, July/August 1993, pp. 9–10.

31. "Drugmakers Get a Taste of Their Own Medicine," *Business Week*, Apr. 26, 1993, p. 104.

32. *Money*, June 1993, p. 66.
33. Eli Lilly, Annual Report, 1996.

Case 14. Schering-Plough Corporation*

Introduction

Pharmaceuticals are synonymous with big business — big money coupled with big risks. In 1991, the pharmaceutical industry brought in $40.7 billion.[1] Internationally, the industry is said to be estimated at approximately $180 billion with an average annual growth of 10%.[2] Such revenues are paid for dearly. The successful launch of a pharmaceutical product anywhere is based on years of meticulous research and planning.

Schering-Plough (SP), an international pharmaceutical company based in Kenilworth, NJ, has consistently made significant medical advancements while earning a sizable profit. In 1993, sales rose 7% to $4.34 billion.[3] More than half of sales are generated domestically. Foreign operations, however, are gaining in financial importance: 40, 41, and 47%, respectively, for 1990, 1991, and 1992. Like many companies in the industry, Schering-Plough's success has been built on their strong commitment to research and development.

As a company, SP has made a name for itself in the ethical pharmaceutical industry by excelling in the production of medicines for respiratory ailments such as asthma and allergies, cardiovascular diseases, and cancer. SP is also well entrenched in the over-the-counter (OTC)

---

* The case was written by Marie S. Hartman for classroom discussion. Used by permission.

market, selling such well-known household brands as the Coppertone skin-care line, Dr. Scholl foot-care products, and Drixorol, to name a few. Until 1991, Maybelline was also part of the SP family of products.

The changing political and economic environment in America for health care, however, has forced SP and others in the industry to brace themselves for some significant adjustments. Ethical pharmaceutical sales have traditionally been seen as recession resistant. Double-digit returns were considered the norm within this industry. The advent of the Clinton health care reform, however, has had a negative impact on those returns. The cost of many drugs are under careful scrutiny.

Due to its type of products, the ethical pharmaceutical industry has a differentiation strategy, with a focus on promoting particular medications to specific physician specialties. While cost does play a role in choosing a product, physicians usually pick the product that they perceive best fits the particular patient for his/her specific ailment. In the doctor's mind, the most expensive medicine is the one that does not work. As a result, the doctor will choose a medication that is effective, safe, and the most convenient to take for the patient, most of the time regardless of cost. When people are sick, they want relief as quickly as possible; the cost of the medication is often secondary.

Society's Values

Americans have always taken pride in having the freedom to make their own choices. Medical care is no exception. The U.S. truly maintains a superpower status in the pharmaceutical research and development arena. As a result, patients in the U.S. have access to state-of-the-art medical technology and the care that this technology can provide. Unfortunately, the costs associated with obtaining the world's best medical care have skyrocketed.

The medical community at large, and the pharmaceutical industry in particular, are now under close examination. Pharmaceutical companies can no longer demand top dollar for their products. A case in point is that for the last 3 years, SP has kept its price increases on par with the consumer price index.[3]

Generics, chemical equivalents of their brandname drugs, have been able to capitalize on this trend. In an effort to control their mounting costs, many hospitals, health maintenance organizations (HMOs), and other health care provider plans are choosing generics whenever possible.

Many companies are looking to HMOs and PPOs (preferred provider organizations) to help contain the rising expenses associated with providing health care benefits. The downside is that many Americans are losing the freedom to choose their own physicians. By their very nature, these organizations also deny them the access to certain medications which may have more benefits but as a result are also more expensive.

Government Laws and Regulations

Several alternative health care bills are in the making. One bill that received a lot of attention several years ago was sponsored primarily by Representative Jim Cooper (D-TN) and was entitled "The Managed Competition Act of 1992."[4] Like the President's plan, the Cooper bill also promoted managed competition and put HMOs and PPOs at the heart of its proposal. The main difference was in the fact that the Cooper bill would not affect Medicare, Veterans Administration hospitals, or prescription drug pricing. As can be seen, these policy-related issues will have an instrumental impact on the future of the pharmaceutical industry.

The Food and Drug Administration (FDA) also plays a pivotal role in the success of a drug company's product. The successful launch of a pharmaceutical product anywhere is based on years of meticulous research and planning. The role the FDA plays actually can be constituted as a barrier to entry and therefore will be discussed later.

Entrants

The barriers to entry are extremely high within this industry. They can be primarily attributed to three factors: the FDA approval process, the staggering costs associated with researching and developing a drug, and the high cost of marketing the product once it is approved.

During the initial stages, a drug company's research and development department first nominates a new compound. It is then submitted for FDA approval by completing a New Drug Application (NDA).[5] It is at this point that a new drug's time clock starts ticking. Only 17 short years pass from the birth of a new compound, to the completion of successful clinical trials, sales promotion, and patent expiration.[5] Adding to this race against time is the statistic that only three out of ten drugs actually make it to the marketing stage.[1]

In the area of spending, while the National Institutes of Health (NIH) does considerable research, most of the burden of research and development (R&D) falls on the shoulders of the pharmaceutical companies. In 1991 alone, pharmaceutical companies spent $7.5 billion on research and development.[6] It is estimated that the cost of bringing a new drug to market is $231 million.[1] This price tag, furthermore, does not include actual promotional activities. It is estimated that an additional $100 to $300 million is spent on marketing the product.

By researching and developing life-improving (and in many instances life-saving) drugs, the pharmaceutical companies have been able to make significant contributions to humanity. These contributions are possible primarily because the industry has been lucrative. As these profits become threatened, it remains to be seen if many of the companies within this industry will be able to cope with the astronomical costs of bringing a medication to market.

Rivalry Among Competitors

Because the risks as well as the rewards are so high, competition within the ethical pharmaceutical industry is extremely strong. SP alone spent $1.747 billion on marketing expenses in 1993. This constituted 40.3% of sales for that year.[3] Companies with similar products in the same therapeutic class are competing for the same market share. The goal is always the same: prescriptions. In order to have prescriptions written for their products, each company must convince the doctors that their particular drug best fits their patient profiles as well as matches his/her prescribing habits.

There are several ways in which the pharmaceutical companies achieve prescriptions. The first and most effective tool is their sales forces. Each company markets their pharmaceutical products through a well-trained sales force. Backed with the knowledge of their particular product and the ailment it is to treat, the sales force has a distinct message that is targeted at specific physician specialties. Each "detail representative" has a territory to cover. They are then given targeting data that enable them to know which zip codes carry the highest potential. In addition, often times they may have information showing which doctors are the most prolific prescribers of drugs within their product's therapeutic class. Armed with this data, the detail representatives visit the doctors on a monthly, sometimes bi-monthly, basis to win over the doctor's prescriptions.

Another tool used to garner prescriptions is the use of educational speaker programs. This involves the participation of physicians who are considered thought leaders in a particular field. These doctors most often are involved in the clinical trials prior to the drug's FDA approval. They are asked to educate the physicians at these educational conferences as to the cutting edge knowledge of the specific disease entity and the drugs they see as best to treat it. With the advent of various forms of communication technology, conferences no longer only take the form of dinner programs but are also conducted via telephone or video conferences to the particular doctor's office itself. In this way, the meeting can be more personalized and does not infringe too much on the doctor's free time.

Finally, other marketing campaigns include television and journal ads in specific medical forums, as well as mailings and coupons sometimes even aimed at the patients themselves. SP's successful marketing efforts for the product Claritin, a once-a-day, non-sedating antihistamine for seasonal allergies, is one such example. SP has used all of the above-mentioned tools, in addition to aggressively marketing the product in *Ladies Home Journal,* as well as in newspapers and pharmacies, in order to increase patients' awareness of this new product. Claritin was launched in the U.S. in April 1993 and by December of that year already had sales totaling $130 million. To date, Claritin is considered SP's most successful product launch.

Substitutes

Depending on the type of ailment, the threat of substitutes can vary. For example, people with chronic back pain have the choice of using medication or physical therapy. Some choose to have massage therapy. Others use a combination of the three. For the most part, however, medication is almost always a part of the treatment regimen.

Proven treatments for patients with cancer, AIDS, or Alzheimer's disease, for example, are few. For many advanced diseases such as these, the threat of substitutes is very low. The choice is to use one of the few medications available or to go without any medical treatment at all. Switching costs are extremely high: it could mean the life or death of a patient.

Global Economic Trends

Profit levels in the pharmaceutical industry are threatened by the high cost of research and development which recently has yielded fewer innovations.[7] In addition, there is increasing pressure to contain costs not only in the U.S. but in Japan and Europe as well. The growing strain resulting from aging populations, cost containment, and the increasing burden of providing medical care through their national budgets have all contributed to an environment where lower drug prices internationally are expected in the near future.

For U.S. pharmaceutical companies, health care reform will reduce after-tax margins to 13%, down 6% since 1991.[8] As a result of these mounting pressures, growth in the pharmaceutical industry is slowing down as firms cut costs and price competition increases.[9] In order to maintain higher profit margins, pharmaceutical companies in the U.S. are repositioning and looking to expand their markets by manufacturing generic drugs and by expanding their activity abroad.

The growth of the generic drug industry is due primarily to pressures from cost containment. Many pharmaceutical firms are positioning themselves for the not so distant future when a large number of drugs will expire between now and the year 2000. National health care contracts, as a result of health care reforms, will lower pharmaceutical costs by encouraging the use of generics.[10] The impact of health care reform in the U.S. is expected to increase the demand for generic drugs from 25 to 40%.[11]

The growth in generic drug manufacturing in the U.S. has been slow. Historically, U.S. pharmaceutical companies export 10% of their pharmaceutical production, with the European Community currently being the principal foreign market.[12] However, in 1993, the European Community instituted stringent regulations curtailing the shipment of raw materials to generic drug makers in the U.S. By curtailing these shipments, the introduction of certain generic drugs from the U.S. into Europe has been delayed by 3 to 5 years, which has been timed in such a way as to coincide with the expiration of many European drug patents.[13] As a result, U.S. pharmaceutical companies are expanding their activities in Europe as opposed to expanding in the U.S.

As the European market moves toward unification, there is growing uncertainty as to whether external trade barriers will develop. Because of this uncertainty, some companies are collaborating with existing European manufacturers for relatively quicker entry into the $1.6 billion European pharmaceutical market. Several U.S. and Japanese pharmaceutical firms have established operations in Ireland for this purpose. Schering-Plough, for instance, has expanded their manufacturing facilities to include a new plant in Brinny, Ireland, in an effort to meet anticipated worldwide needs. In addition, SP has enlarged its Rathdrum, Ireland, manufacturing plant to meet the growing demand for bulk chemicals. The unification of Europe is expected to bring in more income as well as lower the cost of sales for those U.S. pharmaceutical companies located in the European Community.[14]

Another growing trend that has come about as a result of mounting R&D costs is the development of joint ventures between pharmaceutical firms. Companies are consolidating their resources. Many smaller firms have the capability to create new compounds. What they lack, however, is the capital to complete successful clinical trials, a large sales force, and the corporate clout to win over the big revenues needed to turn research and development expenditures into profits. A case in point is the small Swedish firm, Astra Pharmaceuticals, which has developed numerous compounds. Merck entered into a joint venture with Astra to further develop and market their anti-ulcerant drug, Proscar. Another dual effort by Merck and DuPont is also in the works. They have jointly developed a new anti-hypertensive drug, Losartan, which is the first in its class. Since DuPont is not as familiar with the anti-hypertensive market, they have turned the marketing and promotional reins over to Merck. In addition, Schering and Glaxo have co-developed and co-marketed several drug entities. The oral corticosteroid used to prevent asthma attacks is called Vanceril under the Schering brand and Beclovent under the Glaxo brand. Even though both sales forces compete for the same market share, they benefit from lower capital expenditures and increased detailing time in front of the physicians. It is up to the better sales representatives to convince doctors to choose their brand.

The Buyer

Unlike any other industry, ethical pharmaceuticals are not marketed directly to the consumers; rather, they are promoted to physicians who prescribe them for their patients. Unfortunately, the end-users or the patients usually wield the least power. Traditionally, the doctors constituted the primary market and carried control because of their prescribing power. However, due to rising medical costs, many pharmaceutical companies today must not only sell to the doctors but also to the retail pharmacists and to the pharmacy and therapeutics (P&T) committees of hospitals, HMOs, PPOs, and government institutions.

Retail pharmacists wield a certain degree of power because they can switch prescriptions from a brandname product to its generic equivalent, when legally appropriate, unless the doctor writes "dispense as written" (D.A.W.) on the prescription. They also may switch among brands, as in the case of Vanceril and Beclovent, which are identical drugs except for their names. The latter action is considered unethical but still happens. Pharmacists carry out such activities because their profit margins are greater with generics than with brandname products. Although identical drugs with different brand names cost exactly the same on a wholesale basis, pharmacists may often sell one at a lower price due to the fact that it may have more market share than the other. This market leader status attracts patients to their pharmacy because of the less expensive price.

Pharmacy and therapeutics committees also hold a great deal of clout. Unless a product is on their formulary (a list of drugs that the physicians can prescribe) a doctor cannot prescribe it. As a result, the pharmaceutical sales representatives must convince the P&T committee member of their product's advantages and cost effectiveness before the committee will allow it on their formulary. This task is often a difficult one, as the names of most P&T committee members are kept secret. In an effort to keep their institution's costs down, more often than not the price of a drug is the primary concern for many of these committees, especially in those therapeutic classes where many drugs have the same indications and have similar therapeutic characteristics regarding their efficacy and safety. Even though a certain medication may be more convenient for a patient to take, P&T committees may choose an older, more cumbersome product due to its lower price.

Finally, the government, through the Medicare and Medicaid programs, often designates how much it is willing to pay for drugs within the same therapeutic category. If the medication costs more, the patient will often pay the difference. In the case of certain HMOs and PPOs, the cost difference may come out of the doctor's salary. Doctors who work for these health care providers are often given a cost range to stay within. If they perform too many expensive procedures or prescribe too many drugs not on the institution's formulary, the cost difference comes out of their pocket. This usually motivates the doctor to prescribe only what is on the formulary.

The Supplier

Pharmaceutical companies, in increasingly rare instances, have the greatest control over the price of their product when it is the only drug in a therapeutic class. In this case, there are no me-too drugs. The pharmaceutical companies do not have to compete on the basis of price alone in this scenario.

It is also important to remember that although cost is an important factor when prescribing a drug, for most doctors it is not the overwhelming reason. When patients are sick, they want relief now. Physicians choose a product primarily based on its scientific efficacy, safety profile (lack of side effects), and convenience. The latter is an important concept, because patients can have difficulty remembering to take a drug more than twice a day. As a result, drugs with a once-a-day dosing regimen are most preferred by physicians.

Financial Data

Given the fact that ethical pharmaceutical sales have traditionally been seen as recession resistant, double-digit returns were considered the norm within this industry. Today, however, as noted previously, the costs of many drugs are under careful scrutiny. As a result, for the last three years and into the near future, SP has and will keep its price increases on par with the Consumer's Price Index.[3]

Like other major companies within this industry, SP is keeping a close eye on all its expenditures. Ways in which the company is doing so are: (1) joint ventures in R&D and selling efforts, (2) efficient management of their receivables and inventory, and (3) using financial leverage to their advantage. In addition, Schering has continued to meet its most critical challenge: producing successful, innovative products.

Sales historically have increased on average by 9.3% annually for Schering. Gross profit, as a percentage of sales, increased slightly during the period 1990–1992. A recently reported gross profit percentage of 77.8 is well over the 42.4% for the industry average.

Historically, operating expenses such as selling, general and administrative costs, and costs attributed to R&D have been at least half of sales: 52.74, 53.62, and 54.28%, respectively, for 1990, 1991, and 1992. This trend is well above the industry average of 32.9%. One of the reasons for this is SP's high commitment to research and development. In 1993, they completed a $300 million Drug Discovery Facility.[3] The building houses many of the top names in research as well as the latest in state-of-the-art technology. This, according to their annual report, is designed to keep the company's product pipeline filled well into the next century.

The largest contributing factor to high operating expenses points to Schering's selling, general, and administrative costs, which have been historically high but are on a declining trend. This trend reflects lower promotional spending following the launch of the over-the-counter product, Gyne-Lotrimin, and the divestiture of Maybelline.

Overall, Schering performed well during 1993, topping $4 billion in sales, although, compared to the industry median, Schering is less liquid. In fact, SP's current ratio over the last 3 years is below the industry average of two. The higher the ratio, the greater the "cushion" between current obligations and a firm's ability to pay them. In 1992, the company seemed to have serious liquidity problems. When looking at the balance sheet, total current assets as a percentage of total assets decreased from 1991 to 1992, but total current liabilities increased from 38.07% in 1991 to 47.38% in 1992, mostly due to short-term borrowings. This is well above the industry average of 29.4%, indicating that SP is financing more of its investment using debt than the average firm in the industry.

Additionally, although SP's total asset turnover ratio increased from .81 in 1990 to .98 in 1992, it was still well below the industry average of 1.5. This shows that Schering was not using it resources to generate sales as effectively as it could have. Each of Schering's major asset investment programs — accounts receivables, inventory, property, plant and equipment — was found somewhat lacking, and this ratio reflects this.

A look at SP's debt ratio shows that for all 3 years it was well below the industry average of .45. This means that SP's creditors were financing only 0.18 of the firm's total assets during 1990, 0.28 in 1991, and 0.14 in 1992. These low ratios indicate more protection against liquidation or any other financial problems. This is especially beneficial during recessionary periods when sales may falter or during times of inflation when interest costs may increase. Looking at the balance sheet, total debt from 1990 to 1991 increased almost twice as much due to an increase in capital expenditures, then decreased in half in 1992 as a result of paying much of it off that year. The cash flow statement also shows this large reduction of long-term debt.

Finally, SP's return on investment increased from 14% in 1990 to 16% in 1991 and to 17% in 1992. Although no RMA figure was available, these figures reflect SP management's ability to utilize the company's assets effectively to generate returns. Because Schering's total asset and fixed asset turnover ratios are well below the industry median, an assumption can be made that their current return on investment is also below the industry average.

Conclusion

On the one hand, Schering-Plough's strengths are numerous. The company has a strong presence internationally. Almost half of its pharmaceutical sales are generated overseas. International sales increased significantly in 1992, from 40% in 1990 to 47% in 1992. As a result, Schering not only experienced its highest total sales figures ever (over $4 billion), but also better positioned itself for health care reform in the U.S.

Another SP advantage is its relatively stable line of non-prescription products, including over-the-counter drugs and foot and sun care products, which account for one quarter of its aggregate revenues. With two new prescription products recently approved by the FDA and others waiting in the wings, Schering stands ready for future sales generation. The completion of their state-of-the-art Drug Discovery Facility enhanced their R&D efforts.

Schering's management appears to be very effective in making decisions regarding pricing and the control of production costs. This is supported by the gross profit margin, which is well above the industry average of 0.43. The profitability ratios also show an increasing trend, further corroborating their management's effectiveness on pricing and cost control.

Historically, SP has had low long-term debt and plans to remain equity financed in the near future. Their low debt ratios indicate more protection against liquidation or any other financial problems. The other financial leverage ratios tell a similar reassuring story to counterbalance the weakness in liquidity that will be discussed later.

Another SP strength may be reflected in the other (income) expense item on their income statement. In 1990, they showed an unusually large amount of other income. It is revealed that this was due to a management decision to offset the cost of the restructuring resulting from the sale of the Maybelline cosmetic line.

Furthermore, Schering continues to grow earnings at an impressive rate. The company grew share earnings by more than 20% over a 6-year period. These strong bottom-line performances reflect impressive volume growth and wider margins due to a more profitable product mix.

As for Schering's weaknesses, their primary weak point is their liquidity position. The company is less liquid than the average firm in the industry. Both its current and quick ratios are well below the industry standard and the trend is decreasing. Although the low liquidity in 1992 could have been attributed to increased transportation costs and currency problems related to international sales, further investigation is necessary. Also, additional examination of their credit terms and policies is warranted.

Another indication of liquidity problems, or perhaps a cash management problem, is the increasing trend in days payable. Schering has historically been above the industry norm. The difference, however, is growing. Additionally, cash and cash equivalents decreased greatly due to the increase in accounts receivables. SP also invested in fixed assets to a greater degree than their sales growth and lowered long-term debt by buying back much of their stock.

Another area of concern is the rapid expansion in the company's levels. Both inventory turnover and days inventory ratios have historically been below average, although further research on these ratios revealed SP adopted currency option contracts to hedge future inventory purchases that are deferred and ultimately reduced the cost of inventory.

In summation, Schering's first priority should be to improve their liquidity position. Lacking in cash and cash equivalents in relation to current obligations could cause major cash flow problems. One way of improving their position would be to decrease the percentage of total assets going to fixed asset items such as property, plant, and equipment. Now that they have positioned themselves well for the future by building the Drug Discovery Facility and manufacturing plants in Ireland, it may be time to put some of that money into cash and cash equivalents. In this way, their total asset turnover ratio may also improve. If this option is unacceptable, management may want to consider supplementing cash and cash equivalents with some money from their net profits. In addition, although Schering has traditionally been equity financed, they may want to consider better utilizing their leveraging ability. The use of long-term debt may enhance shareholder wealth.

In order to improve their inventory ratios, closer scrutiny of their credit policy is necessary, especially if it is too stringent. If this is the case, Schering may want to loosen it and/or offer price discounts to enhance account receivables, while at the same time improving inventory turnover. One thing Schering is definitely doing right is bringing in the profits. Additionally, they are taking a proactive stance regarding health care reform, and this should position them well for what the future may offer.

References

1. "The Value of Pharmaceuticals," in *Business Health Annual*, Vol. 10, Medical Economic Publishing, 1991, pp. 28, 29.
2. Robert Cawthorn, "Internationalize and Be Innovative," *Directors and Boards*, Fall, 1991.
3. Schering-Plough International, Annual Report, 1993, pp. 2, 4–6, 20.
4. "Interview with U.S. Representative Jim Cooper," *Managed Care Update*, Vol. 14, Schering Laboratories, 1992, p. 10.
5. Telephone interview with Chris O'Toole, European Marketing Director of Anti-Infections, Schering-Plough International.
6. Telephone interview with Wyn van Denhouweele, Director of European Market Coordination of New Products, Merck, Sharpe, and Dohme.
7. "World Drug Industry Less Hot in 1990s," *Economic Review*, August 1990, p. 28.
8. Jane Cutaia, "Swallowing a Bitter Pill: Curbing Health Care Costs May Squeeze Profits," *Business Week*, Jan. 11, 1993, p. 82.
9. Joseph Weber, "Withdrawal Symptoms: Drug Makers Are Waking Up to a Nightmare," *Business Week*, Aug. 2, 1993, p. 20.
10. Valentine Cardinale, "Generics, Where Now?" *Drug Topics*, July 19, 1993, p. 3S.
11. Charles Wagner, "Drug Firms Wary of Health Bill," *Modern Healthcare*, April 29, 1988, p. 42.
12. "What To Export Now," *Business America*, March 28, 1988, p. 23.
13. Carol Ukens, "Europe Moves to Restrict Pipeline for U.S. Generics," *Drug Topics*, May 17, 1993, p. 22.
14. Deborah Denaro, "Global Markets Await: Upcoming Economic Transition May Provide the Opening U.S. Health Care Merchants Need," *Modern Healthcare*, June 9, 1989, p. 20.

Consolidated Income Account: Schering-Plough Corporation
(year ended December 31)

	1995[a]	1994[a]	1993[a]	1992[a]	1991[a]
Assets					
Sales	5104.4	4536.6	4229.1	4055.7	3615.6
Cost of sales	1004.8	906.8	862.4	900.6	816.4
Selling, general, and administrative expense	1990.4	1755.5	1698.5	1503.5	
Research and development	656.9	610.1	567.3	521.5	425.9
Other income (expense), net	57.6	37.5	27.8	49.9	9.0
Total costs and expenses	3709.7	3309.9	3156.0	3101.8	2754.8
Income before income tax	1394.7	1226.7	1073.1	953.9	860.8
Income tax	341.7	300.5	257.5	233.9	215.2
Income before extraordinary item	886.6	922.0	825.0	720.0	645.6
Income from continued operations	1053.0	926.2	815.6	—	—
Income (loss) from discontinued operations	(10.2)	(4.2)	9.4	—	—
Income (loss) from disposal of discontinued operations	(156.2)	—	—	—	—
Discontinued operations	(166.4)	—	—	—	—
Extraordinary item	—	—	—	(26.7)	—
Cumulative effect of accounting change	—	—	(94.2)	27.1	—
Net income	886.6	922.0	730.8	720.4	645.6
Previous retained earnings	3978.2	3435.6	3044.4	2624.2	2817.8
Cash dividend on common shares	416.4	379.4	339.6	300.2	273.6

**Consolidated Income Account: Schering-Plough Corporation
(year ended December 31) (continued)**

	1995[a]	1994[a]	1993[a]	1992[a]	1991[a]
Common shares retired	—	—	—	—	565.6
Retained earnings	4341.8	3978.2	3435.6	3044.4	2624.2
Earnings per common share (primary)					
Continuing operations	2.85	2.42	2.09	1.80	1.51
Extraordinary item	—	—	—	(.07)	—
Discontinued operations	(.45)	(.01)	.02	—	—
Accounting change	—	—	.24	.07	—
Earnings per common share	2.40	2.41	1.88	1.80	1.51
Common shares					
Year-end	364.2	372.0	387.1	399.0	403.6
Average	369.7	382.5	390.2	400	429

[a] Millions of dollars, except share data.

Case 15. Merck, Inc.*

About 15 years ago, P. Roy Vagelos, Research Chief for Merck, was part of a major breakthrough for a drug that helped patients with prostate difficulties. Today, Merck has 17 research centers and 4500 research and development employees scattered across several countries in Europe, Japan, and North America. In the 1980s, Merck introduced a wide array of new products, including the anti-hypertensive Vasotec and the cholesterol-lowering Mevacor. Blockbuster drugs such as these have more than tripled Merck's earnings over a 5-year period. This growth has not been as evident in the 1990s primarily due to the fact that Merck's laboratories are not producing as many blockbuster products as they did in the 1980s. Analysts estimate that Merck's annual sales will rise only 8 to 10% per year during the 1990s, a rate which still would position Merck as being above average when compared with the average large pharmaceutical drug company. Merck continues to enhance its position as one of the top pharmaceutical companies in the world. Merck accomplishes this through the introduction of new products, sales volume gains of established products, growth outside of the U.S., continued success of strategic alliances, and heavily involving themselves in managed health care.

Mission Statement

The mission of Merck is to provide society with superior products and services — innovations and solutions that improve the quality of life and

---

* The case was prepared by Dr. M. Reza Vaghefi, who was assisted by Tatia Binecoff-Mickelwright and Scott Beecher, for discussion only.

satisfy customer needs — to provide employees with meaningful work and advancement opportunities and investors with a superior rate of return.

Values

1.   Preservation and improvement of human life. All actions must be measured by success in achieving this goal. Merck values their ability to serve everyone who can benefit from the appropriate use of their products and services, thereby providing lasting customer satisfaction.
2.   Commitment to the highest standards of ethics and integrity. Merck claims responsibility to customers, to employees and their families, to the environments, and to the societies served worldwide.
3.   Dedication to the highest level of scientific excellence and a commitment of research to improve human and animal health and quality of life. Merck strives to identify the most critical needs of customers and to devote resources to meeting those needs.
4,   Expectation of profits, but only from work that satisfies customer needs and benefits humanity. Merck's ability to meet responsibilities depends on their financial position, which invites investment in research and makes delivery of research results possible.
5.   Recognizing the ability to excel — to most competitively meet society's and customers' needs — depends on the integrity, knowledge, imagination, skill, diversity, and teamwork of employees, and Merck values these qualities most highly. Merck strives to create an environment of mutual respect, encouragement, and teamwork.

Business Core

Merck is a worldwide organization, a leading research-driven pharmaceutical products and services company, and one of the largest pharmaceutical companies in the U.S. Merck discovers, develops, manufactures, and markets a broad range of innovative products for humans, animals, and plants. The Merck-Medco Managed Care Division manages pharmacy benefits for more than 40 million Americans, encouraging the appropriate use of medicines and providing disease management programs. Human health products include therapeutic and preventive agents, generally sold by prescription, for the treatment of human disorders. Among these are cardiovasculars, anti-ulcerants, and antibiotics. Animal health protection products include medicinals used for the control of disease in livestock, small animals, and poultry. Insecticides and miticides are its largest-selling crop protection products.

Background

Merck was founded in 1891 with public ownership and is currently headquartered in Whitehouse Station, NJ. In the early 1980s, the company demonstrated its continuous commitment to research and development by redirecting basic research activities from chemistry to applied life sciences and to new product development. By the mid 1980s, it had 65 new compounds under some form of testing (clinical or human). Despite Merck's 1991 $1.1 billion investment in research, there was a research and development (R&D) shortfall as 27% of annual earnings growth from the 1980s slowed. The company felt that its 1993 earnings were depressed by health care cost containment, unfavorable currency rates, and high startup costs. However, defectors from Merck say that the company's slow-moving bureaucracy has driven its scientific talent to competitors over the years. Another problem identified by former Merck scientists was that, by the time prospective projects made it through the reviews, more flexible and lean rivals were passing the company by.

Research and development and capital expenditures increased to $2 billion in 1993 and included a re-evaluation of their Research Planning Model. With a more current and sophisticated model, payoffs included better decisions, considerations of uncertainty, considerations of the context of the whole business against scientific problems, and a broader financial perspective.

As of 1996, Merck employed 49,100 people, and provided products and services to millions. R&D for 1996 was estimated at $1.487 billion and continues to be refined through improved processes. The company's major business areas include (1) research, with eight major centers in the U.S, Europe, and Japan; (2) manufacturing, carried out in 30 plants in the U.S., Europe, Central and South American, the Far East, and the

Pacific Rim; (3) product marketing, which includes sales in the same countries as manufacturing; and (4) services marketing, which covers the Merck-Medco Managed Care Division.

The Products

The company's business is divided into two industry segments: human and animal health products and specialty chemical products. In 1992, Merck expanded markets for its human health, animal health, and crop protection products, and specialty chemicals.

Human health products include antihypertensive and cardiovascular medications, which are marketed as Proscar, Vasotec, Mevacor, Zocor, Cozaar, Prinivil, and Vaservetic. Of the antibiotics, Primaxin, Mefoxin, and Noroxin are the largest. Merck also manufactures and markets anti-ulcerants, anti-inflammatory/analgesic products, vaccines, ophthalmological products, and other human health products.

In 1995, Merck introduced six major products, which is a record number for Merck in one year. Merck's new products included Fosamax, Cozaar, Hyzaar, Trusopt, Varivax, and Pepcid AC. Fosamax is a breakthrough in the treatment for osteoporosis in postmenopausal women. Osteoporosis is a disease characterized by loss of bone mass that leads to reduced bone strength, poor bone quality, and increased risk of fractures. It is estimated that osteoporosis costs the U.S. about $5 billion a year to take care of patients. Fosamax is the first in a new call of drugs called aminobisphosphonates used to treat the disease in postmenopausal women. It has been shown to build healthy bone, reduce risk of spinal fractures by nearly half, and decrease the resulting loss of height. Fosamax has been introduced in 21 countries, including the U.S., and has been cleared for marketing in more than 10 other countries.

Cozaar and Hyzaar are the first in a new class of drugs to treat high blood pressure. They block a potent hormone called angiotensin II, resulting in a gradual, smooth, 24-hour blood pressure reduction. Cozaar is in the late stage of development for treating heart failure and is also being studied for effectiveness in slowing or preventing kidney disease in diabetic patients. Hyzaar was launched with Cozaar in the U.S. as a second product to which appropriate patients requiring additional blood pressure reduction could be switched. It produces an additional 50% reduction in blood pressure beyond that obtained by Cozaar alone.

Trusopt represents an innovation for reducing intraocular pressure in glaucoma. Merck is already the leader in treating glaucoma, and the launch of this drug in the U.S. and European countries strengthens that position. Glaucoma is a common eye disease affecting 2 to 3 million Americans. It produces an increase in the normal pressure within the eye, the intraocular pressure, which rises too high for the continued health of the eye. Trusopt is applied topically and lacks many of the side effects of the oral formulations. For these reasons, it has found wide acceptance among prescribing physicians and patients.

Varivax is a vaccine against chickenpox. Chickenpox infects about 4 million Americans each year, most of whom are children 5 to 9 years of age. The disease still results in about 100 deaths and 10,000 hospitalizations per year. Varivax is recommended by the American Academy of Pediatrics and the Advisory Committee on Immunization Practices to the Centers for Disease Control and Prevention for universal use in early childhood and for immunization in susceptible older children and adolescents. By the end of 1995, more than 1.5 million children and adults received Varivax.

Pepcid Acid Controller (Pepcid AC) represents a new consumer advancement for heartburn and acid indigestion. Four weeks after its introduction in the U.S., it achieved the top-selling position and has maintained that position. It is a non-prescription formulation and first in its class to be cleared by the Food and Drug Administration (FDA) for over-the-counter (OTC) use for both treatment and prevention of heartburn and acid indigestion. Pepcid AC is also the first outcome of Merck's strategy to develop and market OTC formulations of certain prescription medicines through a joint venture with Johnson & Johnson.

Of Merck's more current product developments, Singulair is an investigational asthma medicine which is a result of two decades of research in Canada. Clinical studies show positive and promising results in seeking a new way to treat the disease. The company has also been working on a new painkiller which involves research in a more active field in which drugs would prevent sensitization while patients retain normal feelings and avoid severe pain. Another major area to which Merck is contributing includes "miracle" drugs for HIV. Merck's protease inhibitors include Crixivan, Hoffman-LaRoche's Invierase, Abbott's Novir, and Agouron's Viracept. Concern over these types of drugs includes the possible side effects of diabetes and blood-sugar control problems in some patients.

Animal health and agricultural products include medicinals used for control and alleviation of disease in livestock, small animals, and poultry. These products are primarily antiparasitics, of which Ivomec and Heartgard-30 are the largest selling. Other products include coccidiostats for the treatment of poultry disease, agricultural chemicals, and poultry breeding stock.

Merck's specialty chemical products have a wide variety of applications. These include use in water treatment, manufacturing of paper, oil-field drilling, food processing, cleaning, disinfecting and skin care. The company acquired BritCair Limited, a British firm which developed an innovative wound dressing from algin. Other divisions include Kelco, Calgon Vestal Laboratories, and Calgon Water Management. Kelco is the world's largest manufacturer of alginates and biogums used in various food, dairy, pharmaceutical, and industrial products and for oil-drilling operations. New product introductions and growth of existing market share reflect the performance of Calgon Vestal Laboratories. The Calgon Water Management Division is involved in the development of products for industrial cooling systems.

The company also publishes materials which provide a wealth of information on drugs, medical issues, animal health, and elderly care. These materials are called *The Merck Index, The Merck Manual, The Merck Veterinary Manual,* and *The Merck Manual of Geriatrics,* respectively. Any of these continually updated publications can be ordered by telephone, fax, or mail through the Merck publishing group.

Manufacturing Strategies

In order to bring new products to market as quickly and cost effectively as possible, modeling technology has become a valuable tool. It defines the best manufacturing process early in the development cycle which optimizes the total cost to manufacture products over its life cycle. Modeling technology is also used to identify new ways to recycle costly solvents and reduce the amount of waste generated from operations.

Through the use of robotics, automated facilities, and devices that monitor quality, Merck maximizes productivity and limits worker exposure to solvents and products. Flexibility for the future is being promoted through construction and renovation of manufacturing facilities. This is being done through modular designs that can be adapted to the production of different bulk chemicals for medicines. In other words, high-volume plants are created to accommodate seasonality so that they can be easily converted for other product uses.

Merck has successfully integrated chemical, pharmaceutical, and biological manufacturing, as well as corporate engineering, environmental, and safety operations, into one Merck Manufacturing Division (MMD). MMD manages more than $2.7 billion in assets and has 11,600 employees at 31 manufacturing facilities in 16 countries. To increase manufacturing flexibility, Merck invests in facilities, advanced technology, and equipment at key manufacturing sites and capitalizes on opportunities to eliminate redundant costs and capacity at other facilities. MMD is seeking new operating efficiencies by lowering inventories, developing new manufacturing and packaging techniques, and streamlining distribution systems. As a single manufacturer, MMD is able to implement supply-chain management from the raw materials to the delivery of finished goods. These actions also help reduce inventory and optimize customer service levels.

To leverage Merck's global purchasing power, a management team reviews worldwide purchasing to develop a more effective and efficient procurement system. Since 1993, procurement reengineering has generated $250 million in savings. By creating partnerships through long-term contracts with major supplies, Merck has been able not only to leverage purchasing power, but also to reduce cycle times, improve quality and customer service, and lower costs. They work continuously to improve synchronized production and optimize inventory levels. Merck has consolidated production planning for plants in Europe and North America into two regional planning hubs. In Europe, where the plan has been working for a year, manufacturing cycle times have been reduced for key products, inventory levels have been lowered along with costs, and customer service is still improving.

Distribution and warehouse operations also offer significant opportunities for productivity improvements. Merck performed studies on selected manufacturing sites through 1996. For example, an analysis technique known as activity-based management was used for a plant in France. It improved productivity by reducing material movement, which increased production capacity and minimized warehouse and distribution costs.

Merck's environmental leadership has won worldwide recognition. In the U.S., the company was awarded the National Medal of Technology and received the National Wildlife Federation Corporate Conservation Council's 1992 Environmental Achievement Award. It was also named to the National Environmental Development Association's Honor Roll. MMD's plant in Ireland was awarded the 1992 Good Environmental Management Award by the Minister of Environment. Merck is committed to conducting its business globally in a manner that protects the environment, as well as the health and safety of its employees and the public.

Sales and Marketing

Sales of the company's human and animal health products are generally made by professional representatives. The targeted customers for health products include drug wholesalers and retailers, hospitals, clinics, governmental agencies, and other institutions. The customers for the animal health and agricultural products segment include veterinarians, distributors, wholesalers, retailers, feed manufacturers, veterinary suppliers, and laboratories. Sales of specialty chemical products are made to channels of trade including industrial users, health care providers, distributors, wholesalers, municipalities, and utilities.

Merck is competing to maintain its global leadership in the industry by redefining its role in the worldwide health care market as the market undergoes dramatic changes. The company plays a leadership role in pricing principles and is precedent-setting in its efforts to achieve cost-containment through cost-effective medicines. In 1990, Merck introduced the Equal Access to Medicines Program in a number of states, wherein it voluntarily granted its best price to those state Medicaid programs that have open access to all the medicines made by Merck. This innovative program was used as a model for national legislation applicable to all prescription drug manufacturers. Merck believed that this law would improve the availability of quality health care and alleviate some of the budget problems under which the Medicaid program operates. Outside the U.S., governments have been forcing the company to limit selling prices in order to be competitive. Expiration of patents and the rise of generic drug sales have slowed the sales growth of certain products. Governmental efforts and competitive pressures are limiting the company's ability to balance the effect of inflation on costs and expenses through price increases.

Merck responds to competition by developing innovative sales, marketing, and education techniques; developing strategic health care alliances with large pharmaceutical buyers; and becoming more productive throughout the entire organization. Other strategies include using every means possible to reduce the months necessary for drug discovery, development, and application processes. Merck believes biomedical research is a key to improving the quality and value of health care. Also, the company has concentrated on adopting managed health care and utilizing Medco's resources.

Many of the company's marketing initiatives that seek to drive revenue growth are about promoting existing products, maximizing the success of new product launches, and continuing commitments to research. Merck sees potential for growth by expanding prescriptions, reaching untreated patients, and keeping people on chronic medications. The company also designs clinical trials to provide outcomes that can be transferred directly into health economic studies and disease management programs.

Strategic Alliances

Astra Merck

The Astra Merck group was established in 1992 to help implement the terms of the 1982 agreement between Merck and AB Astra, a Swedish pharmaceutical company. Under this agreement, Merck currently markets three Astra products in the U.S. The 1982 agreement stipulates that if U.S. sales reach a predetermined level prior to December 31, 1993, measures will be taken from a separate entity for the operations related to Astra products, in which Astra can have a 50% share. The separate entity will have U.S. rights to Astra products and most future Astra research discoveries. This company hopes to be flexible and rapid in its response to changing health care environment.

The DuPont-Merck Pharmaceutical Company

DuPont-Merck markets pharmaceutical and imaging agent products in 80 countries. Under the licensing arrangements with Merck, the joint venture has marketing rights to five products in France, Germany, Italy, Spain, and the U.K. The company reached sales of $975 million by the end of 1992, strengthening its position in Europe, and was listed among the Fortune 500 companies. The joint venture is currently reinvesting almost 30% of its sales in its research pipeline. The research will be focused on developing medicine to treat heart disease, cancer, neurological disease, and AIDS. In 1994, important organization changes were made to reduce costs and better meet customer needs. DuPont-Merck also established a generics subsidiary, Endo Laboratories, LLC.

Johnson & Johnson-Merck Consumer Pharmaceuticals Company

This joint venture was formed in 1989 and aims to become one of the leading self-medication companies by year 2000. This alliance has gained strong entry into the OTC market in the U.S. with the acquisition in 1990 of the Mylanta product line from ICI Americas, Inc. In 1992, the joint venture extended its product line in Europe with the introduction of a new analgesic in Germany. In early 1993, the joint venture consolidated production operations for manufacturing antacids in the U.S. to increase efficiencies. In 1994, they launched Pepcid AC OTC, which proved to be extremely successful.

Merck-Medco Managed Care, Inc. (Medco)

The 1993 acquisition of Medco brought important new capabilities to improve patient care and reduce total health care costs to a rapidly expanding client base. Medco managed drug benefits for about 47 million people, as of 1995, which was about 1 out of every 6 Americans. Medco, with about 4400 employees, also manages a retail pharmacy and mail-order prescription service to provide fully integrated drug benefit services. Medco Health Management Programs include the treatment of asthma, allergic rhinitis, congestive heart failure, chronic obstructive pulmonary disease, peptic ulcer disease, diabetes, gastroesophageal reflux disease, and high cholesterol; an integrated cardiovascular program; Partners for Healthy Aging (largest enrollment included 14 million in 1995); smoking cessation; and women's health programs. In 1995, the number of prescriptions managed by Medco grew about 30% during the year, representing drug expenditures of more than $6.6 billion. New employers choosing Medco as their pharmaceutical benefits manager in 1995 included United Technologies and Dow Chemical, while existing customers such as AT&T and GE added new groups of covered individuals. Medco is also strengthening its relationships with Blue Cross/Blue Shield plans and is winning major accounts in the U.S. As managed care continues to grow, Medco's success in winning contracts with leading health maintenance organizations and other providers becomes vital. This customer segment is Medco's fastest growing.

International Competition

The U.S., Japan, and Western Europe are the major markets in Merck's business. Over the next 15 years, Merck will also concentrate in other international markets such as Eastern Europe, China, Russia, Poland, and Hungary.

Japan

The Japanese take in about twice as many pills as the Americans or Europeans. Physicians in Japan dispense drugs instead of pharmacists. The government reimburses the physician for these prescriptions. This demanding market has prompted Japanese firms to expand within their own market. Most of these firms have shown a remarkable apprehension to expanding globally, especially when one compares this behavior to the global competition in the automobile industry.

Foreign companies in Japan, such as Merck, have taken about 21% of the Japanese drug market, which is the second largest and the highest priced in the world. The only way the Japanese can strike back is to try to gain market share in Europe and America. The Japanese will have a tough time pursuing this because companies such as Merck are forging alliances in order to stay competitive in today's market. The Japanese will have to try to follow a similar suit if they want to compete successfully in this market.

Europe

The pharmaceutical sales were hurt in the first quarter of 1993 due mainly to the strength in the dollar of European currencies. The strong dollar means that pharmaceutical companies receive fewer dollars for sales made with international currencies. Merck is one of four American companies with the highest international exposure. This volatile shift in the strength of the dollar is a reason that Merck strives to structure its forces to a changing market. Even though Merck's profits will decline during these times, it will be able to endure better than its competitors.

Health Care Reform

Merck has acknowledged the need for health care reform and is actively involved with it for two main reasons, the first being for the betterment of society and the second for Merck's shareholders. Merck is committed to working with government officials and health care providers regarding health care reform in order to improve the efficiencies of the health care system while maintaining quality care.

Merck feels that the managed competition model represents the most promising structure for health care reform. This system is designed to reduce costs of the current system by making current administrative barriers more simple and accessible. If this reform system is managed properly, it will not impair Merck's desire to innovate because the competitors will be challenged with the same guidelines. Merck's major concern is whether our government can set provisions without constraining the research and development process that is innovated by the private sector. Merck's commitment to innovation is their process for finding ways to reduce costs.

Merck has already been progressive in this managed care environment. Merck has acquired 75% of its targeted managed care market in the U.S.; however, this is prior to any major reform by a government plagued by many problems including an aging population, increasing number of AIDS cases, and advanced medical technology that is causing the price of health care to soar. Sacrifices are going to have to be made by all parties to implement these reforms. Policymakers are aware that any type of reform will be painful to all involved. The continuing move toward managed care in the U.S. creates an opportunity for Merck to increase their leadership in this industry. In the 1990s, close to 75% of the population is enrolled in a managed care program, and Merck-Medco is aggressively working to grow along with this industry. Their growth is based on winning new accounts and expanding services to existing customers. Partners for Healthy Aging, an example of a successful Merck-Medco health management program, covers over 14 million retirees in the U.S. This program creates a link between physicians and pharmacists to provide a comprehensive view of a patient's use of prescription drugs and can identify potential problems, such as inappropriate drugs for elders or dangerous drug interactions. From an economic standpoint, such inappropriate use costs the U.S. $20 billion per year in health care costs that could have been avoided.

Research and Development

Merck's growth is attributed to its heavy investment in R&D. Since 1983, Merck has invested between 11 and 12% of its annual sales in R&D. For 1992, this amounted to $1.1 billion. Merck's researchers are focused on designing medicines that prevent or mitigate the cycle of a disease.

Merck's Manufacturing Division is always studying new ways to reduce costs in their inventory and distribution system. MMD works to reduce its inventory while maintaining its customer base, and the MMD packaging process itself has a significant effect on sales and distribution. MMD is committed to continued innovations in its packaging process.

Merck is committed to Total Quality Management (TQM), and MMD has shifted the quality process from the laboratories into the manufacturing division in order to encourage participation from all employees. Statistical quality control is also used in the manufacturing process.

Merck's reputation for heavy R&D investment has paid off tremendously. When a Merck product is brought before the FDA for approval, it is typically approved faster than those of its competitors. When Merck sales representatives seek to make sales calls to physicians, the physicians usually make a good effort to schedule appointments because there is a good probability that a novel product will be presented, offering an opportunity for the physician to get in on the ground floor of new products.

New Leadership

Roy Vagelos retired as Merck's Chairman on November 1, 1994, following almost two decades of achievements. Dr. Vagelos joined Merck in 1975 and led the laboratories into the most productive period in their history. He also led the industry in developing strategic responses to cost-containment pressures and headed the acquisition of Medco. Under his direction, corporate citizenship became a hallmark of Merck through the funding of education, health, and social programs as well as emergency relief. He also made the decision to donate supplies of Mectizan, a medication that prevents river blindness, a disease found in Africa and South America.

Raymond V. Gilmartin became Vagelos' successor as CEO and president. Gilmartin was considered well suited to guide Merck and its $6.6 billion acquisition of Medco. Gilmartin is known for his deft touch with people, for being a decent executive, for his demonstrated strategic thinking and cost-cutting techniques, and for his successful track record.

Gilmartin believes that shareholder value is a combined function of growth and profitability, that growth will come based on responses to external markets and the needs of health-care systems worldwide, and that profitability will be driven by internal management of productivity and cost structure. As his first objective, he met with people throughout the company to assess strategies and establish a management team. The team established goals and made fundamental decisions. Gilmartin is also seeking to focus on Merck's core competencies as a research-based ethical pharmaceutical company specializing in human and animal health. To reach the main goal of remaining a top-tier growth company, the management team agreed to focus on making the Medco acquisition pay off, preserving the profitability of Merck's core business, and driving revenue growth.

Reading List

1. Reed Abelson, "Health Care Companies Are Scrambling To Control the Costs of their Products and Services Before Washington Does It for Them," *Forbes*, Jan. 4, 1993, pp. 162–163.
2. Merck, Annual Report, various issues.
3. Susan Caminiti, "The Pay Off From a Good Reputation." *Fortune*, Feb. 2, 1992, pp. 74–79.
4. "Cost of Capital, The Managerial Perspective," *California Management Review*, Summer 1991, pp. 16–18.
5. Paula Dwyer, "We'll Need Hillary Clinton in Holland," *Business Week*, Nov. 8, 1993, pp. 72–73.
6. Joan Hamilton, "Sure the Drug Works, But Is It Worth It?," *Business Week*, Aug. 26, 1991, p. 62.
7. "Japan's Medicine Men Take Aim," *The Economist*, March 2, 1991, pp. 61–62.

8. Phillip Kotler, "Designing Marketing Strategies," *Marketing Management*, 7th ed., 1991, p. 300.
9. Michael Porter and Cynthia Montgomery, "Strategy," *Harvard Business Review*, 1991, pp. 301–303.
10. James Brian Quinn, Jordan Baruch, and Penny Paquette, "Exploiting Manufacturing Services Interface," *Sloan Management Review*, Summer 1988, p. 45.
11. Jennifer Reese, "Americans' Most Admired Corporations," *Fortune*, Feb. 10, 1992, pp. 74–79.
12. *Standard & Poors Industry Surveys*, 161(36), Sept. 9, 1993, p. H–21.
13. "Strategic Is the Word," *Institutional Investor*, January 1991, pp. 74–77.
14. Elyse Tanouye, "Drug Concerns Expect Earning To Grow Slowly," *Wall Street Journal*, April 9, 1993, p. A-7.
15. "The Big Pill," *The Economist*, March 1993, p. 67.
16. Joseph Weber, "Merck Needs More Gold from the White Coats," *Business Week*, March 18, 1991, pp. 102–104.
17. Shaker Zahara and Diane Eller, "Accelerating New Product Development and Successful Market Introduction," *Sam Advanced Management Journal*, Winter, 1993, pp. 9–11.

Merck Financial Summary

	1996[a]	1995[a]	1994[a]	1993[a]	1992[a]
Sales					
Materials and production costs	19,828.70	16,681.10	14.969.80	10,498.20	9662.50
Marketing/ administrative expenses	3841.30	3297.80	3177.50	2913.90	2963.30
Research/ development expenses	1487.30	1331.40	1230.60	1172.80	1111.60
Equity loss from affiliates	(600.70)	(346.30)	(56.60)	26.10	(25.80)
Gains on sale of specialty chemical businesses	—	(682.90)	—	—	—
Restructuring charge	—	—	—	775.00	—
Gain on joint venture formation	—	—	(492.00)	—	—
Provision for joint venture formation	—	—	499.60	—	—
Other (income) expense, net	240.80	827.60	232.80	10.10	(46.30)
Income before taxes	5540.80	4797.20	4415.20	3102.70	3563.60
Taxes on income	1659.50	1462.00	1418.20	936.5	1117.00
Net income	3881.30	3335.20	2997.00	2166.20	2446.60
Earnings per common share	3.20	2.70	2.30	1.87	2.12
Dividends declared	1793.40	1578.00	1463.10	1239.00	1106.90
Dividends paid per common share	1.42	1.24	1.14	1.03	0.92
Capital expenditures	1196.70	1005.50	1009.30	1012.70	1066.60
Depreciation	521.70	463.30	475.60	348.40	290.30

Merck Financial Summary (continued)

	1996[a]	1995[a]	1994[a]	1993[a]	1992[a]
Year-end position					
Working capital	2897.40	3870.20	2291.40	541.60	1241.10
Property, plant, and equipment	5926.70	5269.10	5296.30	4864.60	4271.10
Total assets	24,293.10	23,831.80	21,856.60	19,927.50	11,086.00
Long-term debt	1155.90	1372.80	1145.90	1120.80	495.70
Stockholders equity	11,970.50	11,735.70	11,139.00	10,021.70	5002.90
Financial ratios — net income as a percentage (%) of					
Sales	19.60	20.00	20.00	20.60	25.30
Average total assets	16.10	14.60	14.30	14.00	24.10
Year-end statistics					
Average common shares outstanding	1213.60	1236.10	1257.20	1156.50	1153.50
Number of stockholders	247,300	243,000	244,700	231,300	161,200
Number of employees	49,100	45,200	47,500	47,100	38,400

[a] In millions of dollars, except per share amounts.

Case 16.
Boeing Company*

Introduction

The Boeing Company began manufacturing airplanes in 1916 with production of a small seaplane, and it has been producing quality aircraft ever since. Boeing airplanes carry people and products all over the world. They have a superior reputation for designing and building high-quality commercial jet airplanes.

Boeing is the leading exporter in the U.S. Over the past 5 years, sales outside the U.S. have accounted for 70% of Boeing commercial airplane sales. Their merger last year with Rockwell has put Boeing at the forefront of major industries such as commercial aviation, space exploration products, and defense. Their most recent merger with McDonnell Douglas made Boeing the largest aerospace company in the world. This forms a company that will design, produce, support, and expand the horizon of aerospace development well into the XXIst century.

Boeing is the number one U.S. aerospace firm in total sales, and they are the largest exporter of manufactured goods in the U.S. The company is organized into three major business groups: Commercial Airplane, Defense and Space, and Information and Support Services. They have thousands of suppliers and support hundreds of thousands of jobs in various industries. In 1996, company revenues were $35.4 billion. For

* The case was prepared by Dr. M. Reza Vaghefi, who was assisted by Pat Callahan and Bill Kelly, for classroom purposes only.

the first quarter of 1997, sales were $10.3 billion, up 70% compared with $7 billion for the same period in 1996. The revenues for 1997 are projected to be in the $48 billion range. This case will focus on Boeing's largest business segments, the Commercial Airplane Group.

Keys to Success

Phillip M. Condit became CEO of Boeing in April of 1996. He is only the seventh man to lead Boeing in its 80-year history. Condit's background makes him particularly attuned to leading the company into the next century. He has picked up the reins of the company at a time when the industry's business cycle is on a major upswing. New aircraft orders are being placed faster than the company can produce them. Condit's challenge will be to manage all the growth and merger changes simultaneously. Boeing's key objectives for continued prosperity include: continuous refining and expanding of their technical capabilities, a highly skilled and motivated workforce, and continuous improvements in quality of products and processes. The key success factors that have helped the company reach its strategic goals include the following.

Boeing as an Employer

Boeing Company employs more than 215,000 people, more than 89,000 of which are employed in the Commercial Airplane Group as of March 1997. Boeing has over 10,000 job categories, including engineering and technical, production, general office, and professional positions. Most of the jobs are located within the geographic areas of Seattle/Puget Sound, WA; Wichita, KS; Philadelphia, PA; and Huntsville, AL. Boeing places great emphasis on training and skill enhancement at all levels of employment. Boeing focuses on teamwork in areas such as problem solving and quality management.

Condit, within his first 100 days in office, announced an unprecedented $1 billion stock-grant program for all employees. This plan, called the Boeing ShareValue Trust, is a company funded, self-sufficient, irrevocable 12-year trust, designed to allow all employees to share in the results of increasing shareholder value over the long term. Boeing's airplane manufacturing capacity is at an all-time high. This means that the potential for international agreements has never been higher, for the simple reason that more companies are willing and able to participate.

The U.S. civil aircraft sector is the major contributor to the aerospace industry's positive trade balance. Approximately two thirds of commercial jet transports are shipped outside the U.S. Boeing has advanced technology, financial strengths, and a large team of knowledgeable workers. As stated by CEO Phillip Condit in a speech given in California in March of 1997, expansion in world trade has benefited the U.S. and companies such as Boeing and thousands of suppliers. At Boeing, about 70% of their commercial airplanes now sell outside of the U.S. They project that the world's airlines will add more than 16,000 new jets during the next 20 years.

Promoting Exports

The General Agreement on Tariff and Trade (GATT) and the Civil Aircraft Agreement set the rules of trade that affect the U.S. aircraft industry's ability to compete globally. The government must continue to work for a free and open climate for international trade and investment. Although virtual elimination exists in the civil aircraft industry among developed nations, many non-tariff barriers are still present, preventing some fair and free environments. The U.S. aerospace manufacturers should continue to encourage GATT for a multi-lateral trading system. World partnership and trade agreements between nations are essential for manufacturers and suppliers in international business.

A major concern to aerospace industries is the non-tariff barriers that currently exists between the U.S. and the European Community (EC). These non-tariff technical barriers weaken the trade cohesiveness throughout the North Atlantic Treaty Organization. The development of new regional standards, testing, and certification exclude participation of the U.S. and differ significantly from those imposed by the U.S. Other non-EC nations may adapt these standards as well. For U.S. manufacturers to adapt to these standards and regulations would add cost to the aerospace product. The U.S. Department of Commerce has launched initiatives for negotiations with the European Community.

Suppliers

When it comes to building airplanes, the right suppliers make a difference. Finding the right suppliers can reduce price and improve the quality of the product. Also, in order for suppliers to compete in the international arena, they need to offer economic as well as political stability. Boeing's suppliers must be reliable and deliver both high quality and absolute product safety. Boeing sees their suppliers as partners in trade.

Boeing's newest aircraft in production is the Boeing 777 (B777). With this new aircraft, Boeing has entered into a partnership not only with the supplier but also with the airline customer. Four of Boeing's B777 customers — United, All Nippon Airways, British Airways, and Japan Airways — have teams on-site at Boeing. They are a part of the designing and building process creating certain specifications for their individual needs. Rod Eddington, managing director for Cathay Pacific Airways, Ltd., in Hong Kong, noted that this was the first time an airplane was designed with substantial input from the customers. At Boeing, this concept was so successful that it has outlived the launching of the B777 to become part of the new corporate culture that Phillip Condit has initiated.

Research and Development

In 1993, the Commercial Airplane Group opened its Integrated Aircraft Systems Laboratory. This facility is the most extensive laboratory in the industry. The complex houses 53 laboratories to support the development of all Boeing commercial aircraft. Boeing's main factory is in Everett, WA, and was expanded in 1993 to accommodate the B777 production. The Everett building is the largest in the world by volume and covers nearly 100 acres. Research and development are essential to maintaining high quality and producing competitive products. With the latest system technology, Boeing remains on the cutting edge of technological advances.

Boeing 777

Boeing's new B777 underwent the most extensive flight test program in commercial aviation's history. The B777 is a wide-body, long-range, twin jet capable of carrying 305 to 440 passengers. The B777 can serve routes up to 5700 nautical miles. Several engine manufacturers, such as Pratt & Whitney, General Electric, and Rolls Royce, were involved in the testing and production of the B777. In addition to more than 4800 test flights, the B777 underwent extensive mechanical, electrical, and hydraulic systems testing to ensure a reliable, service-ready product. One of the features that customers asked for was the ability for rapid reconfiguration of the B777's interior. The Boeing engineers devised a design that allows seats, bathrooms, and galleys to be rearranged within 72 hours. The B777 made its first test flight on June 17, 1994, ironically almost 78 years to the day from Boeing's very first airplane flight on June 15, 1916.

Boeing 747

In 1996, development projects were well underway for two super-high-capacity models of the B747. These development projects were in response to demand from international carriers for airplanes that could hold more people and travel farther without refueling. It is estimated that the overall average size of airplanes will increase over the next 10 years due to an anticipated increase in long-haul travel.

Airline Industry

The airline industry is recovering from the losses suffered during the recession of the early 1990s. In 1994, an estimated $2 billion net income was reported, the first profitable year since 1989. Continued profits are expected throughout the second half of the 1990s. Other factors such as fuel prices, regulations, and infrastructure capacity are expected to remain favorable.

As profits increase, so does airline competitiveness. Current strategies are based on providing more value for travelers while bringing down cost. Airlines are adding non-stop flights and more convenient one-stop connectors for passengers. Flight schedules are becoming more flexible, and daily services to international markets are on the rise. Airlines will continue to introduce service into new market regions, and passenger convenience will be a prime target in competitive strategies. Airplanes are added to the airline's fleet to accommodate traffic growth and to replace aging in-service planes. With noise-abatement regulations being enforced in some cities, airlines are having to accommodate aircraft to comply with regulation standards. More orders for commercial planes will be placed as older aircraft are phased out and replaced by more cost-efficient aircraft.

Growth projections for the airline industry are declining, especially in the Asian-Pacific market, but Boeing expects worldwide demand for new airplanes to exceed 16,100 over the next 20 years, a demand worth over $1.1 trillion. Boeing, being the world's largest airplane manufacturer, is after 67% of that market. At the end of last year, the world's jetliner fleet totaled 11,500. 7000 of those were made by Boeing. By the end of this year, Boeing plans to deliver over 40 aircraft each month, the highest production rate in company history.

Boeing recently secured a deal with Delta Airlines that gives the company 106 firm orders for jets worth $6.7 billion. This deal makes Boeing Delta's sole aircraft supplier for the next 20 years. Also, Boeing has signed a similar 20-year contract for 103 jets, estimated at $6.5 billion, with American Airlines.

As the airline industry recovers, the growth of air travel, cost-cutting measures, and new strategic management have led to increased airline profits. Manufacturers show signs of recovery, signaled by airline requests for faster deliveries and placement of new orders. The future outlook for commercial airplanes is promising as air travel continues to grow (see table).

Many of the major travel markets are beginning to show signs of economic recovery. Although the rate of growth is declining, growth for the travel industry from 1997 to 2016 was recently estimated to be 5.1%. This year, that estimate has been revised to 4.9%. The U.S. market reported traffic growth of 4.6% in 1994. Asia and Middle East airlines show 9.4% growth, while European airlines reported 9.0% growth. The projected growth rate over the next 5 years is estimated to be 5.8%. Manufacturers should start seeing the effects of this upward trend soon. The number of global passengers each year continually multiplies. Estimates are that 73 billion revenue passenger miles will be added to the system throughout the 1990s. This is equivalent to adding one of the largest airlines with a fleet of 600 or more airplanes. Boeing recognizes that a significant number of new airplanes will be needed. In a 20-year study, more than 10,000 additional airplanes will be required to accommodate the estimated increase in travel. Boeing projects that over the next decade, the world jetliner fleet — driven by 5.5% per year growth in air travel and 6.6 % in air cargo — is expected to grow from 11,500 airplanes at the end of 1996 to nearly 17,000 airplanes in 2006.

Influences in the U.S. Market

Economic growth is essential to aircraft market recovery. The U.S. is in a recovery stage; however, restraints exist that impact a smooth recovery. Key influences that affect the aircraft market follow:

1. The rate of economic growth adjusted for inflation is expected to average 1.5 to 3.5%. This amount reflects slow growth, In order to have substantial impact, a 3 to 5% increase would be needed.
2. Tax increases reduce leisure spending, forcing people to travel less.
3. Government cutbacks in defense spending put heavy financial strains on aerospace manufacturers that are already suffering.
4. Productivity is improved, resulting in increased output at the cost of reduced job creation.
5. Low inflation levels averaging less than 4% for the next few years are bad for aircraft values, which were inflation driven through the 1980s.
6. Interest rates, both short- and long-term, are set to rise moderately, putting further pressure on airlines and straining aircraft investors' ability to finance new aircraft investment.

Global Business

The outlook for global markets is promising. International partnerships and alliances in trade have always been essential. Boeing strives to remain a dominant, globally competitive force. In 1996, Boeing announced its 20-year plan, called Vision 2016, which outlines their long-term, globally focused business path. The merger with McDonnell Douglas, one of their chief competitors, leaves only two commercial airplane manufacturers in the world.

China

In the second half of the 1990s, China is expected to lead the world in growth. An important source of economic strength is likely to come from Asia Pacific's newly industrialized economies in Korea, Taiwan, Singapore, and Hong Kong. China's economy is growing at 8.7% a year.

According to Bob Dryden, executive vice president of Boeing's Commercial Airplane Group, "The world air travel market is expected to grow about 5% per year or more in the Asian markets over the next 20 years. That will create a need among the world's airlines for about 15,000 new airplanes, worth about $1 trillion by 2014. This explains why Boeing has opened offices in China and India. The potential air travel markets in those countries are huge, but only for manufacturers willing to be partners in laying a solid foundation for healthy growth." As Boeing's CEO Phillip Condit said in his speech to the Trade Policy Conference held in Washington, D.C. in April 1997, "Currently, major trading interests, such as China and Russia, operate outside the world's trading system. This cannot continue, especially as the Chinese and Russian economies grow larger. We must work diligently to bring major trading interests into the world trading system — the sooner the better."

China now has 35 financially stable airlines in a market where traffic is growing at 20 to 30% annually. For Boeing, careful planning and strategic management will be essential to penetrate the market successfully. China's rate of expansion may soon be facing infrastructure limitations. This country had 109 airports; however, only 11 can handle widebody aircraft. The Chinese government will have to play a major role in technological advancement and airport accommodations if their travel is to continue to expand as it is expected to.

European Community

The European economic cycle is on its upward turn. Strong exports in Eastern Europe, the U.S., and Asia are a major part of this recovery. As the recession declines, European demand increases. However, this market will not be so easy to penetrate. Boeing's only other competitor in the aircraft industry is Airbus Industries. Airbus, has a firm hold on the European market. Airbus has created a new generation of aircraft that will be intense competition for Boeing's aircraft products, not only in the European Market, but also in other global markets, as well. The A330 and A340 are widebody jets that are the newest of the Airbus family. The A340 has begun operations with such airlines as Airfrance, Turkish Airlines, and Virgin Atlantic Airways, all of which have been successful.

In addition to the manufacturer competition found in the European market, there is competition from the high-speed rail. Boeing evaluated the competitive challenge posed by the high-speed rail and concluded it would be a strong competitor in local European transportation. The Community European Railway (CER) is proposing a plan that will increase the rail's share of travel up to 50% in the year 2010, while decreasing air travel from 70 to 50%.

The European Community presents several potential obstacles for Boeing and other U.S. manufacturers. Support for the U.S. Department of Commerce negotiations is needed for the removal of the non-tariff barriers that exist. If these issues are negotiated, the likelihood for Boeing to enter this market successfully is much greater.

Japan

Japan's economy seems to be moving out of recession. Industrial production is growing, inventories continue to shrink, and exports have held up despite the appreciating yen. Corporate profits and machinery orders are improving. The trade agreements that are established between Japan and Boeing are working well. This market is very valuable to Boeing, and its continued growth holds great promise.

In November 1995, Japan Airlines (JAL) announced its commitment to order five B777-300s, the stretched version of the newest Boeing jetliners. The value of this order is worth approximately $800 million. Japan Airlines' total commitment now is for 15 B777s, with options for an additional 10. In addition to other airlines' orders, 50 of Boeing's new aircraft have been ordered from the Japanese. Japan has placed more orders for B777s than any other country.

Commonwealth of Independent States

The Commonwealth of Independent States (CIS) is presently undergoing economic and political turmoil; however, its future remains bright for Boeing exports. Economic reforms will eventually bring down the inflation rate to acceptable levels. The private sector will establish a stable foundation for foreign direct investment. It is not certain, however, how quickly the CIS will emerge from the transition.

Good air transportation is essential for these nations. The territories in these states are tremendous, and other means of travel are often inadequate or unavailable. Although numerous problems exist, a few airlines are beginning to compete against those located outside the CIS.

The long-term outlook for the CIS is profitable as more foreign investments are made and air travel increases in these nations. As the CIS replaces older aircraft and technology advances, Boeing estimates by the year 2014 that revenues from these sectors could total as much as $70 billion.

From a long-term perspective, economic performance will vary worldwide. Developing countries will begin expanding their potential market share. Market reforms, trade initiatives, and infrastructure investments should provide growth in countries such as Asia, Latin America, and Eastern Europe. Reduced trade barriers, additional investment and trade, and the private sector should produce future economic growth.

Conclusion

Boeing's Commercial Airplane Group is a national leader in exports. Boeing has an excellent reputation for high-quality aerospace products. The General Agreement on Tariff and Trade should continue negotiating trade agreements across international borders in order for Boeing to compete globally. Boeing's global outlook is promising as overseas markets are growing and air travel is increasing. International trade agreements are vital to the continued success of Boeing.

Reading List

1. *AirFinance Annual 1994/95*, Boeing Commercial Airplane Group, 1995, pp. 33–34.
2. *AirFinance Annual 1994/95*, Boeing Commercial Airplane Group, 1995, pp. 31–32.
3. *Quick Facts About Boeing*, available at web site http://www.boeing.com (Nov. 15, 1995).
4. *Japan Airlines Stretches Boeing 777 Commitments*, available at web site http://www.boeing.com (Nov. 15, 1995).
5. *Boeing Executive Outlines Key Factors For Success*, available at web site http://www.boeing.com (Nov. 15, 1995).
6. *Mission, Goals and Objectives*, available at web site http://www.boeing.com (June 25, 1997).
7. *Boeing Commercial Airplane Group Overview*, available at http://www.boeing.com (June 25, 1997).
8. *Market Forces and the World Fleet*, available at web site http://www.boeing.com (June 25, 1997).
9. *Boeing Reports 1996 4th Quarter and Full Year Results*, available at web site http://www.boeing.com (June 25, 1997).

Market Outlook

	1995–1999	*2000–2014*	*1995–2014*
Average annual rate of growth			
World economic	3.6%	3.1%	3.2%
Airline traffic	5.8%	4.9%	5.1%
Commercial airplane deliveries			
Billions of 1995 dollars	$37	$52	$57
Number of airplanes	647	773	815

Source: Data from Commercial Airplane Group, Boeing Company.

10. Commercial Airplane Group, *Current Market Outlook,* May 1995, pp. 1–30.
11. Phillip Condit, *1997 First Quarter Report,* available at web site **http://www.boeing.com** (April 28, 1997).
12. Phillip Condit, *The 1997 Trade Agenda: The View From 40,000 Feet,* speech at Strategy Institute Trade Policy Conference, Washington, D.C., available at web site http://www.boeing.com (April 6, 1997).
13. P. Harris, "Future Prospects for Commercial Aircraft Values," in *AirFinance Annual 1994/95,* Boeing Commercial Aircraft Group, 1995, pp. 1–4
14. V.C. Lopez and D.H. Valdez, "U.S. Aerospace Industry in the 90s," *A Global Perspective,* September 1991, pp. 126–128.
15. Andy Reinhardt and Seanna Browder, "Booming Boeing," *Business Week,* Sept. 30, 1996, pp. 119–125.
16. "Airbus Industries," *AirFinance Journal,* July/Aug. 1997, pp. 33–38
17. Peter Flint, "Business as Usual," *Air Transport World,* February 1997, pp. 23–25.

Case 17.
History of Cellular Communications*

C ellular communication was first developed in 1947 by AT&T's Bell Laboratories. The first commercial tests of the new tech nology, however, were not performed until 1962. In 1970, AT&T proposed to build the first high-capacity cellular telephone system. While manufacturers were working on getting cellular technology up and running, the Federal Communications Commission (FCC) needed to create regulations for this new service. In 1981, the FCC granted the licensing of two cellular operators to each metropolitan statistical area (MSA), which is a region of land mass with boundaries consisting of city, county, or state lines. There are 306 MSAs and 428 regional statistical areas (RSAs) in the U.S. MSA and RSA licenses were awarded by a lottery process through the FCC. The lottery process allowed non-wire carriers, which included individuals, to obtain licenses even though they were not interested in building a communication system. Once the license was obtained, the non-builders would hold out for awhile to increase the market value of their license, then would sell their licenses to a communications system builder. This lottery process promoted an aftermarket onslaught of acquisitions and mergers from 1981 through 1986. Since 1986, there have been very few acquisitions for two reasons:

---

* The case was prepared by Dr. M. Reza Vaghefi, Mark Lado, and Bill Kelly for classroom discussion only.

cellular networks have been built in every MSA and RSA, and the market price for each MSA and RSA is much higher than the market book value.

The granting by the FCC of two licenses in each MSA effectively created a duopoly, but in 1995, because of relentless pressure from the cellular industry and consumers, the FCC finally gave up and threw in the towel. They decided on an auction process by which an MSA license would be awarded to the highest bidder. In the 2 years after making the decision to auction licenses, the FCC sold $20 billion of licenses for new segments of airwaves. The auctioning has unleashed a host of new competitors into the cellular phone industry.

Cellular Industry

The first cellular phone was introduced by Motorola in 1983 and was about the size of a brick. It could be carried around in a large briefcase and was very heavy. Today, cellular phones are small enough to fit in a shirt pocket. Since 1983, the explosive worldwide growth of wireless communications services has been fueled primarily by the skyrocketing demand for cellular phone service. In the industry's first decade (1984 to 1994), the number of cellular users jumped from fewer than 100,000 to over 19 million, according to the Cellular Telecommunications Industry Association. In the past year alone, subscribership increased at the phenomenal rate of anywhere from 35 to 70%, depending on which company you talk to. The latest industry figures set the number of U.S. cellular subscribers at just over 50 million. Industry analysts expect that by the year 2000, there will be over 90 million subscribers of cellular services.

Today, there are 13 cellular service carriers in the major markets which provide about 85% of the total cellular market. Even though a duopoly was the intent of the FCC in the beginning, the auctioning of licenses has created a purely competitive market for cellular services. The telecommunications deregulation law recently passed by Congress knocked down the barriers to competition within the cellular markets. The new law now enables cable television companies, long distance carriers, and regional telephone companies to enter one another's markets. This opened the doors for the cellular companies.

For consumers, this is good news. Pricing of cellular services has been dropping steadily since 1990. In the past year alone, prices of the new digital cellular service have fallen about 25%. The bundling of wireless services has also created a new onslaught of product offerings by the cellular companies. Not only do cellular companies offer cellular services, but they also offer, for example, pager services and electronic e-mail.

For the cellular companies, this state of affairs is not so good. The new digital companies are all vying for market share and trying to put the others out of business. Also, cellular companies are starting to shift their attention to the wired world. A study by Technology Futures, Inc., a think tank, estimates that half of the estimated 185 million cellular users could give up their land line within the next decade.

Barriers to Entry

As noted previously, in 1981, the FCC started granting a limited number of licenses through a lottery system to anyone or any company that paid the license application fee. Today, because of deregulation, market entry is limited by the number of dollars a company is willing to spend. Several of the top cellular firms are deeply laden with debt from previous MSA and RSA acquisitions and initial network system construction. The firms laden with debt may not have the capital to compete with new firms entering the market or they just may not be able to invest in future system enhancements, thereby losing market share or profits.

The shift of entry from nearly unattainable to easy entry was foreseen by many investors as a means to earn excessive market returns. As a result, cellular stock prices soared during the early 1980s. By the late 1980s, these same cellular stocks had depreciated in value compared to the market. In the 1990s, cellular companies' stock prices have remained relatively stable, although many investors are nervous about where the industry is heading in the near future.

Growth Rate

This industry is very progressive in that communication inventions and implementations of these technologies are occurring very rapidly compared to other industries. Last year the average annual growth rate was nearly 50% industry-wide. No other industry can compare to this extraordinary growth rate. The table at the end of this chapter shows a 5-year estimation of subscribers, revenues, average monthly cost, and average monthly minutes.

The demand for cellular telephones has been increasing. There are two reasons for this: the strong economy and the product offerings being made by cellular companies to increase market share. To increase growth, most cellular carriers are entering the mass market by reducing their premium usage rates and offering a variety of rate packages. Today, cellular usage rates average $74 per month compared to the wired land line household average of $30 per month.

The implementation of other system and product enhancements will also increase demand. One system enhancement that has transformed the industry is the advent of the digital network by some cellular carriers. A digital network increases transmission quality and volume, allows data to be transmitted at very high speeds, and is less expensive. Currently, many of the cellular companies are switching from older analog networks to digital technology.

The Product

The cellular telephone is differentiated by its appearance, number of caller options, quality of sound, voice activation, vehicle installation vs. being hand-held, and weight. Each subscriber (consumer) has a particular need to to be fulfilled by the use of a cellular telephone. The cellular telephone manufacturers are reproducing these telephones in as many styles as home telephones to take advantage of the disparate tastes and preferences of cellular subscribers.

Competition

Competition among cellular carriers has been somewhat fierce. Since deregulation, more and more companies are getting involved in wireless telecommunications. Operating costs have increased dramatically because of the advertising necessary to retain market share. Because of all the cut-throat pricing to gain market share, profit margins are being reduced more and more. This spells disaster for some companies. If investors feel that a company is not meeting its earnings potential, the stock value declines, which results in a selling of the stock and a greater reduction in market valuation. The biggest players stand to lose the most money; however, the relatively high concentration of firms in the cellular industry has promoted efficiencies in product development, quality, and quantity of service, and venture agreements. In the last 14 years, the cellular industry has constructed a homogeneous communication network that can be accessed just about anywhere in the U.S. Each cellular carrier profits from this standardized system.

History of McCaw Communications

William McCaw founded McCaw Communications, a cable television company in 1948. McCaw Communications was primarily family oriented. The company was very successful in running and acquiring cable businesses. By the time William's son, Craig, graduated from Stanford, the company established itself as a regional cable company. Craig began working in the business as a boy. When Craig returned to the business after college, he envisioned a much different company than did his father. After his father died in 1969, Craig assumed management responsibilities. In 1974, Craig became president and CEO of McCaw Communications. This was a time of a major company culture transition, from slow, steady, almost secure growth to becoming an aggressive, high-risk venture. Within a month, Craig executed a plan to enter the radio common carrier industry. There was great potential in this developing market. McCaw heavily invested in this industry by acquiring smaller firms and manufacturers of personal radio communications. Today this McCaw division serves approximately 320,000 paging subscribers in 13 states.

Pursue the Dream

As the possibilities for cellular communication became more probable, McCaw was faced with an uncertain opportunity — to enter the emerging cellular market or concentrate its energies and resources on its current business. There were many heated boardroom debates. The final decision was based on Craig's greed. Craig had a dream. He wanted the power, influence, and capabilities to control all of the U.S. cellular market. By the end of 1980s, McCaw's mission was to become a national provider of cellular communications. Even though Congress had instituted a lottery system for receiving cellular licenses, McCaw aggressively persuaded license holders to sell out. In fact, it was these early aggressive license buyouts that sparked the interest of the stock market in this new technology.

Pop Price Growth

Cellular license buyouts ranged anywhere from $10 to $20 a pop in 1986. The number of pops is the number of people living in the license holder's area adjusted by the percent of ownership. For example, if the Osprey Company had an 80% interest in a particular MSA with a total population of 5 million people, Osprey would own 4 million pops. McCaw knew that these pops were improperly undervalued. During the mid-1980s, McCaw aggressively sought after any cellular license in key growth areas across the country. In 1987, Craig summarized the company's vision in his letter to the shareholders: "We believe that cellular technology will help to gradually transform the way we and future generations will think about communications as well as the way we work and live. …As we (society) avail ourselves more and more of the flexibility of mobile communications, we may begin to associate a telephone number more with a person than with a place. This is the promise of cellular technology and the reason for our enthusiastic commitment to the industry." Pop prices began rising astronomically, and in 1987 Southwestern Bell paid what was then an exorbitant amount of $45 a pop. In 1988, however, Centel paid over $90 per pop. Then, in early 1989, British Telecom paid over $150 per pop. McCaw blew the market away when in late 1989 it paid over $350 a pop from LIN Broadcasting. McCaw bought out a 40% stake in LIN Broadcasting for $3.4 billion.

Stock Price Decline

Two years before the acquisition of LIN, McCaw's stock price began to fall. In fact, all cellular company stocks were being devalued by the market. To increase cash flow and reduce some of their debt. McCaw began to sell off its businesses that were not directly tied to the cellular industry. The largest sale was its cable division; in 1987, it was sold for $755 million. Also that year, McCaw sold more than 15 million shares to the public, raising $270 million. The stock market did not react much to these decisions; in fact, the stock market has not reacted spontaneously to any new developments by the cellular companies.

Internal Conflicts

Before Craig became a manager at McCaw, everyone in the company felt like they were a part of a caring, supportive family. Workers at all levels felt that they could be a part of any decision made by McCaw. Within 2 years as a manager, Craig began to develop the company's environment into more of a bureaucratic structure. The employees did not perceive the changes and were unaware of what Craig had envisioned for them. When Craig was elected as CEO, however, his bureaucratic structure immediately dissolved into an obviously rigid system. This transformation created chaos within the work force and distaste towards upper management. Several mid-level managers resigned as a result. Upper management strictly dictated and enforced their demands upon the work force. The upper management and the rest of the organization were distinctly separated. By the early 1980s, there still existed much distaste and distrust for upper management. McCaw's upper management had a mission to become the sole provider of cellular communication and would not allow any interference or detraction from their mission. As a result, the employee turnover rate dramatically increased. By the early 1990s, upper management had developed a suggestion program that allowed anonymous comments to be made about any of McCaw's decisions. This program eased much of the tension between upper management and the employees.

The Early 1990s for McCaw

In January of 1990, the employees and shareholders of McCaw were surprised to learn that their CEO earned the highest amount among similar executives in the U.S. For 1989, Craig McCaw earned $289,000 in salary and bonuses and $53 million in stock gains. This was surprising, because the company still had not earned a profit. Soon after this announcement, Craig felt the need to show his worthiness. In a television broadcast, Craig predicted five trends that would play a key role in the coming decade: quality improvement, conversion to digital, regionalization, regional Bell company activity, and knowledge navigation. It seemed that Craig had redeemed himself. By January 1991, McCaw had amassed $3.5 billion in long-term debt and had to sign up new subscribers to increase cash flow enough to pay off some of this debt. McCaw promoted its products and services heavily. Also, McCaw greatly increased cash flow when McCaw and Southwestern Bell introduced Cellular One, which provided a recognizable symbol, enhanced services, and common marketing programs. In April of 1992, nine cellular carriers agreed to form an alliance to create a common, ubiquitous, and open industry standard for transmitting data. In addition to McCaw Communications, the following companies participated:

1. Ameritech Mobile Communications
2. Bell Atlantic Mobile Systems
3. Contel Cellular
4. GTE Mobilnet
5. Nynex Mobile Communications
6. Pactel Communications
7. Southwestern Bell Mobile Systems
8. U.S. West Cellular

So far, this alliance has proven both effective and efficient for the customers. A survey was conducted to determine the needs of current cellular customers, and 90% of the survey respondents found that the alliance provided much easier access and trouble-free connections throughout the U.S. Another not surprising result of the survey was that the respondents appreciated the reduction in cellular usage rates.

1992 AT&T Buyout

On Friday November 6, 1992, *The Wall Street Journal* announced that AT&T was planning to buy out a 33% stake of McCaw Communications to gain control of the company. McCaw's stock price soared from $26.75 to $32 in one day's trading. AT&T, which planned to buy $3.73 billion of McCaw's common shares from British Telecom and the McCaw family, paid British Telecom $49 a share for all of their McCaw shares and paid the McCaw family $42 a share for the remainder. After inventing cellular communications, AT&T had put the technology aside. Now, the company was jumping back into cellular communications in a big way. AT&T operates the nation's most extensive, and arguably most technologically sophisticated, long-distance network. McCaw had cellular holdings in more than 100 markets, including top cities on both coasts, the Pacific Northwest, and southern Florida.

The Future of Communications and McCaw

Although now that Craig McCaw is one of AT&T's largest shareholders, he has refused to take a seat on the board because he has said that he cannot stand going to the meetings. He is focusing more on his future and his career. Now that the smoke has cleared from the AT&T sellout, he is getting back in the saddle and is making a run at the newest technological breakthrough. He has decided to create a celestial counterpart to the Internet, a burgeoning network to carry even a greater stream of digital data back and forth around the globe. McCaw hopes to achieve this by creating a constellation of 840 satellites that will circle the planet at low altitude, transmitting signals from any point on the planet to any other with the speed and capacity of fiberoptic cable. He calls the venture Teledesic. Others call it crazy. But, if he is as right with this vision as he was with cellular telecommunications, he just may surpass Bill Gates as the country's richest man. Speaking of Bill Gates, this time around, McCaw has solicited the financial backing of the king of Microsoft. Bill Gates has invested over $10 million of his own money in Teledesic. Gates says, "Craig is an amazing person. He thinks ahead of the pack and understands the communications business and where it's going better than anyone I know." What makes Teledesic so breathtaking is McCaw's vision, the breadth of what he wants to do with the new technology.

McCaw believes neither individuals nor technology alone drive major change. Instead, he says, "You arrive at moments in time when an entrepreneur, a technology, and the needs of people coincide. You get serendipity every once in a while. You try to be willing to accept it when it works in your behalf." Now he thinks he has a better way of linking the Internet and telephone networks around the world. Serendipity is calling again, and this time he wants to be ready.

Reading List

1. McCaw Cellular Communications, Annual Report, 1991.
2. Thomas M. Nugent, "Cellular Enters Mass Market," *Standard & Poor's Industry Surveys,* Jan. 23, 1992, pp. 32, 33.

3. L. Runyon, "Sign of the Times in Cellular Industry Report," *Kiddercom,* Jan. 27, 1992, p. 85.

4. Craig McCaw, "The Evolution of the North American Cellular Network," in McCaw Cellular Communications, Annual Report, 1987.

5. Debra Wishik, "How To Be as Smart as Your Phone," *Money,* January 1991, p. 124.

6. Louis Amato and Ronald Wilder, "Firm and Industry Effects in Industrial Economics," *Southern Economic Journal,* 57 (July), 1990, p. 93.

7. Meeds Fleming, "Winning Is Only the First Step," *Forbes,* December 25, 1989.

8. Dana Wechsler, "Just Desserts: Would Adam Smith Pay Them So Much?," *Forbes,* May 28, 1990, p. 209.

9. Bob Brown, "Cellular Nets To Use IBM for Data," *Network World,* April 27, 1992, p. 8.

10. John Keeler, "Cellular Move Underscores AT&T's Transformation," *The Wall Street Journal,* November 6, 1992.

11. Michael Fitzgerald, "MaCaw Mover Boosts Wireless," *Computer World,* April 24, 1995, p. 24.

12. Andrew Kupffer, "AT&T's $12 Billion Cellular Dream," *Fortune,* Dec. 12, 1994, pp. 100–112.

13. Dan O'Shea and Paula Bernie, "In the Groove," *Telephony,* Jan. 30, 1995, pp. 38–46.

14. Douglas Ehrenreich, "Wireless Data Gains a Foothold," *Telephony,* March 20, 1995, pp. 122–128.

Growth of Cellular Communications

Year	Subscribers (in millions)	Revenues (in billions)	Average Monthly Price	Average Monthly Minutes
1996	39.6	$20.1	$82	101
1997	50.4	23.7	$74	105
1998	63.4	30.2	$66	126
1999	77.5	38.2	$60	161
2000	90.4	46.5	$54	196

Source: Data from *The Wall Street Journal,* Sept. 11, 1997.

Case 18. Johnson & Johnson: The Global Corporation*

Introduction

Johnson & Johnson (J&J) is an international giant in the manufacture and sale of a wide range of consumer and professional, pharmaceutical, health-care, and medical products.[1] The company has established itself as a leader in the industry, and their mission is to be the best and most competitive health care company in the world.

In the mid-1880s, Johnson & Johnson developed the first ready-made, ready-to-use surgical dressings. This marked not only the birth of a company, but also the first practical application of the theory of antiseptic wound treatment. Sir Joseph Lister, a noted English surgeon, identified airborne germs as being a source of infection in the operating room.[2] Many questioned Lister's ideas except for one man — Robert Wood Johnson, who heard Lister speak in 1876. For years, Robert Wood Johnson applied his ideas to Lister's teachings, focusing on a new type of surgical dressing — ready-made, sterile, wrapped, sealed in individual packages, and suitable for instant use without the risk of contamination.

---

* This case was prepared by Dr. M. Reza Vaghefi for classroom discussion only.

Robert Wood Johnson joined with his two brothers, James Wood and Edward Mead Johnson, and formed a partnership in 1885. Operations began in New Brunswick, NJ, in 1886 with 14 employees on the fourth floor of a small building that was once a wallpaper factory. In 1887, the company was incorporated as Johnson & Johnson. With few hospitals in the U.S. in 1887 large enough to use Lister's methods of antisepsis, Johnson & Johnson (J&J) entered the surgical dressings industry.

Prior to Lister's discoveries, the postoperative mortality rate was as high as 90% in some hospitals. Surgeons could not bring themselves to believe that they were contaminating their own patients by operating without gloves and with unsterile instruments. Lister recommended a method for sterilization — spraying the room with carbolic acid — but Johnson & Johnson thought of this as impractical and cumbersome.[1] However, it was an advancement over accepted procedures; unclean cotton, collected from sweepings of the floors of textile mills, was used for surgical dressings, and surgeons operated in street clothes, often wearing a blood-spattered frock coat like a badge of honor.

Johnson & Johnson's first product was an improved medicinal plaster that used medicinal compounds mixed in an adhesive. Soon after, as noted above, they recognized the critical need for improved antiseptic surgical procedures and designed the soft, absorbent cotton and gauze dressing that would be mass produced and shipped in large quantities throughout the U.S.

By 1880, J&J was using dry heat to sterilize the cotton and gauze dressings. In 1891, a bacteriological laboratory was established, and, early in the following year, the company met accepted requirements for a sterile product by using a continuous method of dry heat, steam, and pressure throughout the manufacturing process. These new sterilization processes were the genesis of the company's slogan: "The Most Trusted Name in Surgical Dressings."[2] In 1897, J&J developed an improved sterilizing technique for catgut sutures.

From the beginning, J&J was an advocate of antiseptic surgical procedures. In 1888, the company published a book, *Modern Methods of Antiseptic Wound Treatment*, which for many years remained the standard text on antiseptic practices. That same year, Fred B. Kilmer began his 45-year career as scientific director at Johnson & Johnson. Kilmer influenced the profession's attitude through articles in J&J magazines, including *Red Cross Notes* and *The Red Cross Messenger*. In 1899, with the cooperation of several leading American surgeons, J&J developed and introduced a zinc oxide type of adhesive plaster. Because of its greater strength and quick-sticking quality, the plaster became an important part of surgery; it relieved patients of the skin irritation caused by previous methods.

When Robert Wood Johnson died in 1910 and was succeeded as chairman by his brother, James Wood Johnson, the company had become an established leader in the health care field. By 1916, demand grew so great that the company, to assure itself of adequate textile materials, purchased the Chicopee Manufacturing Corporation. The first international affiliate was founded in Canada in 1919. In 1923, the two sons of Robert Wood Johnson, Robert Wood (bearing his father's name) and J. Seward Johnson, took an around-the-world trip and became convinced that J&J must establish a strong international position. The following year, in 1924, J&J created its first overseas affiliate, Johnson & Johnson, Ltd., in Great Britain.

Also during the 1920s, the company increased its program of product diversification, introducing one of the best-known and widely used of all J&J products — Band-Aid Brand Adhesive Bandages — and a number of other new products, including Johnson's baby cream.

Robert Johnson, who later became known as the "General" after his service as a brigadier general in World War II, took over direction of J&J in 1932. He brought a vigorous new approach and philosophy of business to the organization. Under his leadership, a firm policy of decentralization was initiated, in which divisions and affiliates were given autonomy to direct their own operations.[1]

The General wrote a credo that codified the company's socially responsible approach to conducting business. The credo states that the company's first responsibility is to the people who use its products and services; the second, to its employees; the third, to the community and environment; and the fourth, to the stockholders.[2] Management believes that if the credo's first three responsibilities are met, the stockholders will be well served.

Through the years, as individual portions of the company's business grew, they were organized into subsidiaries. For example, the manufacture of disposable surgical packs and gowns evolved into Surgikos, Inc., specializing in products for hospital asepsis. The sanitary napkin line evolved into the Modess Division, birth control products became the Ortho Pharmaceutical Corporation, and Ethicon, Inc., manufactured sutures. J&J's organization also developed, as did new technologies, such as Johnson & Johnson Dental Care (1972); Critikon, Inc. (1979), a producer of critical care products; and Johnson & Johnson Hospital Services (1983).

Besides growth from within, J&J acquired established businesses that dominated its development in the health care field: (1) McNeil Laboratories, Inc. (which later became two companies: McNeil Pharmaceutical and McNeil Consumer Products Company — best known for its Tylenol pain-relieving products); (2) Iolab Corporation, producing intraocular lenses for cataract surgery, therefore opening the field to enter into other eye care areas; and (3) LifeScan, Inc., which manufactures and markets blood glucose monitoring systems.

Growth overseas was accomplished through the acquisition of existing companies and creation of new companies. J&J purchased Cilag-Chemie in 1959, followed by the purchase in 1961 of Janssen Pharmaceutica, which grew to become one of the most innovative pharmaceutical companies in the world. J&J also acquired the Dr. Carl Hahn Company (1974) and the Penaten Group (1986) — both in Germany. Overseas affiliates of J&J have been created in more than 50 countries.

In 1963, chairmanship of the company went outside of the family for the first time. Under the direction of Philip Hoffmann, who had worked his way up from a shipping clerk, domestic and overseas affiliates flourished. Hoffmann was a firm believer in decentralization and "encouraged the training of local experts to supervise operations in their respective countries. Foreign management was organized along product lines rather than geographically, with plant managers reporting to a person with expertise in the field."[1]

Currently, Ralph S. Larsen is the Chairman of the Board at J&J; he was elected in 1989. J&J has become a worldwide family of 171 companies, employing approximately 82,200 people and marketing health care products in 153 countries.

Management Philosophy

"We believe the consistency of our overall performance as a corporation is due to our unique and dynamic form of decentralized management, our adherence to the ethical principles embodied in our credo, and our emphasis on managing the business for the long term."[3]

Johnson & Johnson's mission is to make itself the best and most competitive health care company in the world. Their "single-minded goal is leadership — in every market, in every business, and in every country in which [they] compete."[4] Through research and development, J&J will enhance their commitment to excellence in science and technology, striving to be the best-cost producer in every one of their businesses. The primary interest of the company, both historically and currently, has been in products related to health and well-being.

Johnson & Johnson is organized on the principles of decentralized management — each international subsidiary is, with few exceptions, managed by citizens of the country where it is located. Believing that smaller, self-governing units were more manageable, quicker to react to their markets, and more accountable, J&J has utilized this management style since the 1930s.[5]

J&J has become a model of how to make decentralization work. However, this management style is not static; management has to fine-tune its approach over the years to achieve a balance of structure and spirit. Currently, J&J is in the middle of such an adjustment — seeking to reduce the redundancies in operations and to smooth relations with J&J's biggest customers in terms of the number of sales calls from the various business segments.

J&J is a family-friendly corporation and is committed to tying work/family agendas to their overall business strategies; J&J pioneered many of the options that are becoming more commonplace in corporations today. The return on such an investment has been in the form of increased productivity, decreased absenteeism, and increased good will.[6]

In 1988, J&J implemented a new worldwide employee training strategy. The revitalization of employee training and development is a major investment in its employees to help them achieve their full potential. The objective is to give the employees new skills and an understanding of the need to continually improve the quality of every aspect of the business. At J&J, human resources are the most important asset of the business, and it is J&J's goal to create an environment that allows these employees to contribute to their maximum potential.

Business Segments

Johnson & Johnson is divided into three business segments: consumer, pharmaceutical, and professional. The consumer segment is J&J's largest business segment and consists of toiletries and hygienic products. The pharmaceutical segment consists principally of prescription drugs, including contraceptives, therapeutics, and antifungal and veterinary products. The professional segment includes various instruments and related items used principally in the professional fields by physicians, dentists, nurses, therapists, hospitals, diagnostic laboratories, and clinics.

Marketing

Johnson & Johnson's operating units are among the most aggressive marketers in America. A strong legal department supports J&J's efforts whenever J&J feels that its patents are threatened. J&J's reputation with its retailers assures its products superior shelf space. In order to accomplish marketing goals, a significant amount is budgeted toward marketing on an annual basis.

Johnson & Johnson has many key success factors that contribute to the company's prosperity. One marketing key factor is the breadth of product line and product selection. J&J offers quite a variety of items — everything a consumer would need to use in the health care field. They also offer a full range of products for the medical profession.

Another key success factor for J&J is its recognition as a leader in the health care industry. J&J is a well-established company that has gained the respect and trust of its customers and employees. Also, J&J has numerous locations around the world making it accessible to consumers.

One skill-related key success factor is the ability to get new products developed and into the market quickly, subject to acceptance of the new product by the Food and Drug Administration (FDA). J&J's research and development department is critical to the success of the company.

Financial

Decentralization is seen as the key to J&J's yearly profit gains — averaging over 19% since 1980; annual sales have risen by more than 10% in five of those years, including each of the last two.

Worldwide sales for 1991 were $12.45 billion, which exceeded 1990 sales by $1220 million, or 10.8%. This is compared to sales increases of 15.1% and 8.4% in 1990 and 1989, respectively, due to the weaker value of the dollar relative to international currencies. Worldwide net earnings for 1991 were $1.46 billion compared with $1.14 billion for 1990 (see tables).

The record sales of $12.45 billion reinforced the company's position as the largest and most comprehensive health care company in the world. New products, a shift in product mix, and reduced operating costs contributed to the company's excellent performance for 1991. Selling in more than 150 countries, the company now generates over 50% of its revenues outside the U.S.[7]

For the first 9 months of 1991, consolidated sales of $9.30 billion exceeded sales of $8.44 billion for the first 9 months of 1990. Earnings per share on operations for the first 9 months rose 14.5%, excluding the non-recurring charge for the permanent impairment of certain assets and operations in Latin America, primarily Argentina.

Domestic sales were $6.25, $5.43, and $4.88 billion in 1991, 1990, and 1989, respectively, representing an increase of 15.1% in 1991, 11.2% in 1990, and 6.7% in 1989. Sales by international subsidiaries were $6.20 billion in 1991, $5.80 billion in 1990, and $4.88 billion in 1989; this represented increases of 6.8, 19.1, and 10.2%, respectively (see tables).

Sales of nonprescription (over-the-counter) drugs are expected to expand by about 7% during 1991 — despite the effects of the recession — which is up from the 6.1% growth recorded in 1991. Over-the-counter (OTC) drugs have grown at a compound rate of 6.7% over the past 5 years due in large part to the significant expansion in mass-merchandiser retail markets. The total OTC market is expected to expand from the present $10 billion level to $28 billion by the year 2010, benefiting from a sharp increase in sales of over-the-counter drugs previously sold on a prescription basis.[8]

Research and Development

Given top priority at Johnson & Johnson is the area of research and development (R&D). With rapid changes in technology occurring almost daily, the key to future success in the health care industry, as well as in any industry, is R&D. J&J was created because of the research and development begun by Robert Wood Johnson in an attempt to create a new type of surgical dressing. J&J's broad product line and extraordinary diversity in the health care field have provided a solid foundation for future growth.

Research expense as a percentage of sales has increased steadily over the past decade. The most noted increases are from $674 million in 1988 to $719 million in 1989 and a 16.0% increase to $834 million in 1990 over 1989. Such research activities represent a significant part of the company's business. These expenditures relate to the development of new products, the improvement of existing products, technical support of products, and compliance with governmental regulations for the protection of the consumer. Overall, industry R&D spending was expected to increase about 10% again in 1992, to $10 billion or above.

Innovation has exploded in the area of health care products in recent years. Products introduced over the past 5 years now account for 25% of sales.[5] In 1990, J&J alone introduced more than 25 new products to consumers. For example, a J&J subsidiary, Johnson & Johnson Medical, Inc., is among the leaders in developing new and improved products for infection prevention. The company is helping to improve aseptic techniques in the operating room through, for example, efficient patient draping and a system of total fluid control. Other J&J subsidiaries have introduced new products including antibacterial therapy, non-caloric sweetener, photopheresis, disposable contact lenses, monoclonal antibodies, an opioid analgesic for transdermal pain management, ovulation induction, and many, many more. Some of these products are new, some are proving themselves in clinical trials, and some are the latest research achievements in fields in which J&J has been working for more than 50 years. The creation of these products shows how J&J has brought innovation and new technology to bear across a wide range of health care applications.

Johnson & Johnson wants to continue with such innovation and has taken steps to sharpen its focus by divesting itself of businesses not consistent with that objective. For example, J&J sold the child development toy business because it was not in keeping with their health care products' objectives. In 1989, J&J sold the Lumite division of Chicopee Manufacturing Corporation, which was in the business of making special woven materials for various industrial applications. Intentions have been made known to divest the Devro sausage casing business, which has nothing to do with health care products.

The expected total for 1991 R&D was nearly $1 billion. Ralph S. Larsen said, "This investment in R&D has resulted in a steady flow of new products — with 30% of annual revenues coming from products introduced in the past 5 years."[9] In late 1991, J&J announced a worldwide licensing agreement to develop and co-market a new antibiotic compound discovered by Fujisawa Pharmaceutical Company, Osaka,

Japan.[10] Through this arrangement, J&J has the right to develop and co-market a new antibiotic compound worldwide, without having discovered and developed it.

Competition

Johnson & Johnson's main competition is with Merck & Co. and Glaxo Holdings, current world leaders. Although J&J has alliances with Merck, only some subsidiaries are involved. Due to the size of all three companies, this leaves a lot of areas uncovered. The potential for growth and prosperity is enormous. Merging companies can have positive and negative effects on J&J. Alliances with J&J would create less competition in the industry, while the merging of competitors could cause the merging companies to grow in size so much that they essentially remove J&J as a leader in the industry. If such a merger failed, though, J&J could possibly see some benefits.

The threat of new entrants does not seem to be a big concern to J&J at this time, although it should be kept in mind. Companies in this industry with the size and magnitude of J&J have taken years to develop.

The bargaining power of suppliers is also not a major concern for J&J. The companies that supply materials to J&J have had long-standing relationships with J&J and have gained the company's trust. J&J does, however, need to consider the bargaining power of customers and the threat of substitute products or services. Customers are looking for the lowest cost for the most product. Because there are many companies offering health care products to consumers, price competition is key. Many companies have cut prices by up to 50% for the Veterans Administration.[11] Glaxo and other companies make free drugs available to patients not covered by other programs. Bristol-Myers Squibb has cut the prices it charges the federal government.[12] Not only are the major competitors vying for the lowest price, but generic or store-brand products represent another significant threat (for example, C.V.S. or Eckerd brand items). These substitute products contain the same ingredients as the major companies' produts but cost less to the consumer.

The very foundation of industry growth, R&D is expected to continue to expand at strong double-digit rates in the years ahead as drug makers increase their efforts to develop new and improved drugs. The industry's ratios of research to sales ranks as the highest of all major domestic industrial groups (see tables). Bristol-Myers Squibb and the University of Mississippi recently signed a $2.45 million research and development agreement. The agreement involves a plan to produce the anti-cancer drug Taxol from ornamental shrubs. Merck and Co. planned to increase its research and development spending by 16% in 1992 to about $1.1 billion.[13]

As growth in principal domestic markets is expected to moderate, U.S. medical equipment manufacturers are increasing their focus on foreign expansion as a means to maintain historical rates of growth. Serving about 48% of the world's population, U.S. producers are the leading suppliers in the $65-billion global medical products market (see tables). Again, technological advances — the guarantee to success in this field — are expected to continue to have a critical impact on the practice of medicine in the U.S.

Environmental Issues

Technological changes are occurring every day. Product life cycles are shortening, forcing companies to introduce products aggressively to realize a quick return.[14] In 1990 alone, J&J introduced over 25 new products to the industry — new cold and flu medicines, a unique hip-replacement system, a new drug for colon cancer, women's products (Fact Plus pregnancy test and Monistat 7), new products for neurosurgeons ... and the list goes on. The marketing of these products is done in a unique manner; carefully researched advertising campaigns help in the success of these products. J&J has been a globalized business since the early 1920s, currently marketing their products in 153 countries. Glaxo Holdings is Europe's biggest drug-maker and is second to Merck in annual sales in the U.S. and worldwide.[15]

Major Issues Facing the Company

The issues facing Johnson & Johnson in the 1990s are great: lawsuits, joint ventures, awaiting approval for new products, Tylenol sales, and workplace safety. Of these, awaiting approval of new products by the FDA and joint ventures with other companies are the most important. For example, J&J developed a dental floss that would deliver sodium fluoride to the user's teeth,[16] but it took quite some time to receive acceptance. J&J has received approval for the use of the drug Levamisole for certain colon cancer patients, and the FDA has licensed J&J's new blood screening test for the hepatitis C virus. J&J said it is the first test licensed in the U.S. using multiple hepatitis C antigens, and it replaces a single-antigen test developed by J&J's Ortho Diagnostic Systems, Inc., and Chiron Corp., licensed in May 1990.

The FDA is starting to show signs of speeding up its drug approval procedures. In 1991, the FDA approved about 25 new J&J drugs, a 25% increase from the year before.[17] John Petricciani, VP for regulatory and medical affairs, said, "Over the last several years, the FDA has doubled the number of medical reviewers. It has taken time to train them, but we should [soon] see some additional output, both in older applications ... and with new submissions."[17] It currently takes approximately $245 million and 10 years to develop a new drug, test it, and bring it to market in the U.S.[17]

A joint venture between J&J and Merck occurred early in 1990. The venture was formed to develop and market over-the-counter medications to the U.S.[18] The new business will market medicines (such as the anti-ulcer treatment, Pepcid) which are currently being sold or developed by Merck as prescription drugs.[19] The venture has caused a stir in the very competitive consumer health-products business.

A federal judge issued an order to block J&J from selling the painkiller Tylenol PM in its current packaging, saying it intentionally copied the trade dress of Bristol-Myers Squibb's Excedrin PM.[20] This is not the first time that the companies have fought over these two products. In 1990, Bristol-Myers was forced to stop an aggressive ad campaign for Aspirin-Free Excedrin which claimed that the product was a better pain reliever than Extra-Strength Tylenol. In a *Wall Street Journal* issue two days later, it was reported that a federal court granted J&J a stay of the lower-court injunction against the sale and advertising of Tylenol PM.[21] The court did, however, order J&J to post a $1 million bond pending further arguments on whether the painkiller and sleeping pill unfairly copied the packaging of Excedrin PM.

Johnson & Johnson has established an intensive campaign to become number one in safety and has adopted new methods to do so, such as designing safety into production equipment, spotting accident "near-misses" and eliminating their causes, and urging workers to report safety violations.[22]

The various lawsuits involving J&J are basically over money. University Patents claimed that they were owed more than $10 million in royalties after a faculty member licensed Retin-A, originally developed as an acne treatment, as an anti-aging treatment. Other companies have claimed that they deserve the rights to a certain product or that J&J misinterpreted the contract with them.

One area J&J might want to focus on is the adult diaper market. J&J holds slightly less than 15% of the market with its 2-year-old line of Serenity products. Further R&D into this product could help J&J gain market percentage. Creative advertising plans should be designed to help J&J in its quest to be number one. In retaliation to Curad's introduction of Happy Strips, smaller adhesive bandages bedecked with McDonaldland characters, J&J brought out a similar line with Sesame Street characters and softer, thicker pads, along with a Nintendo sweepstakes. Bristol-Myers Squibb took full advantage of the power of advertising at the 1992 Winter Olympics. Before the Olympics were over, they had launched newspaper ads for Nuprin featuring figure skater Todd Eldredge and luger Erica Terwilligar as recipients of their "Comeback Award."

Summary

Johnson & Johnson will continue to succeed as an international giant in the manufacture and sale of consumer and professional, pharmaceutical, health care, and medical products. Johnson & Johnson's record stands for itself. They have the knowledge, the money, the experience, and the personnel to achieve great success. J&J will continue to amaze consumers with new developments and will remain a leader in the health care industry. There is increasing evidence that the future of health care expansion is overseas. It remains to be seen how much of that market Johnson & Johnson is going to grab.

References

1. Adele Hast, *International Directory of Company Histories*, Vol. III, St. James Press, Chicago, 1991, pp. 35–36.
2. *Brief History of Johnson & Johnson*, Johnson & Johnson, New Brunswick, NJ, 1989, pp. 2, 4–5.

3. Johnson & Johnson, Annual Report, 1988, p. 3.
4. Johnson & Johnson, Annual Report, 1989, p. 3.
5. Joseph Weber, "Johnson & Johnson: A Big Company that Works," *Business Week*, May 4, 1992, pp. 125, 127.
6. Karen Matthes, "Companies Can Make It Their Business To Care," *Human Resource Focus*, 69(2), February 1992, p. 4.
7. Johnson & Johnson, Annual Report, 1990, p. 32.
8. "Health Care: Products and Services — Basic Analysis," *Standard & Poor's Industry Surveys*, 160(34), August 20, 1992, p. H30.
9. "J&J See Big Development and Research Outlay," *The Wall Street Journal*, Dec. 9, 1991.
10. "Johnson & Johnson," *The New York Times*, Nov. 19, 1991.
11. Joseph Weber, "For Drugmakers, the Sky's No Longer the Limit," *Business Week*, Jan. 27, 1992, p. 68.
12. Harris Collingwood, "Bristol-Myers Gives Uncle Sam a Break," *Business Week*, January 20, 1992, p. 40.
13. Elyse Tanouye, "Merck To Increase R&D Budget 16% to $1.1 Billion," *The Wall Street Journal*, March 17, 1992.
14. Elyse Tanouye, "Price Rises for Drugs Cool, Manufacturers' Profits Chill," *The Wall Street Journal*, April 9, 1992.
15. Stephen D. Moore, "Johnson & Johnson's Plans," *The Wall Street Journal*, March 3, 1992.
16. Christi Harlan, "More Innovations at J&J," *The Wall Street Journal*, March 2, 1989.
17. Jane Cutaia, "1992 Will Be Easy To Swallow," *Business Week*, Jan. 13, 1992, p. 102.
18. "Johnson & Johnson," *The Wall Street Journal*, Jan. 4, 1990.
19. Michael Waldhole, "Merck and Johnson & Johnson to Form Venture for Over-the-Counter Medicines," *The Wall Street Journal*, March 29, 1989.
20. Lourdes Lee Valeriano, "Judge Blocks Tylenol PM Sale Over Packaging," *The Wall Street Journal*, Feb. 24, 1992.
21. "J&J Can Sell Tylenol PM Pending Court Arguments," *The Wall Street Journal*, Feb. 26, 1992.
22. Albert R. Karn, "This Corporate Race Belongs to the Safest," *The Wall Street Journal*, July 5, 1990.

Johnson & Johnson: 5 Years in Brief (Worldwide)

	1991[a]	1990[a]	1989[a]	1988[a]	1987[a]
Sales to customers	12,447	11,232	9757	9000	8012
Net earnings	1461	1143	1082	974	833
Cash dividends	513	436	373	327	278
Stockholders' equity	5626	4900	4148	3503	3485
Percent return on average stock-holders' equity	27.8	25.3	28.3	27.9	26.4
Per share:[b]					
Net earnings	4.39	3.43	3.25	2.86	4.83
Cash dividends paid	1.54	1.31	1.12	0.96	1.61
Stockholders' equity	16.89	14.71	12.45	10.52	20.25
Market price (year-end close)	114.50	71.75	59.38	42.50	74.88
Average shares outstanding (millions)	333.1	333	333.1	340.6	172.6
Stockholders of record (thousands)	69.9	64.6	60.5	54.5	51.2
Number of employees (thousands)	82.7	82.2	83.1	81.3	78.2

[a] Dollars in millions, except per share figures.

[b] February 1989, the stockholders voted for a 2-for-1 split of the company's common stock.

Source: Data from Johnson & Johnson Annual Reports, 1988, 1989, 1990, 1991.

Product Line Sales and Profits for Major Medical Equipment, Supply, and Service Companies

Company	Product Category	1991 Sales ($000,000)	1991 Profit ($000,000)
Abbott Laboratories	Pharmaceuticals and nutritionals	3512	993
	Hospital and laboratory products	3365	639
Allergan	Specialty pharmaceuticals	354	NR
	Surgical devices	108	NR
	Optical products	377	NR
Bard (C.R.)	Urological products	222	NR
	Cardiovascular devices	361	NR
	Surgical devices	293	NR
Baxter International	Hospital products and services	4404	525
	Medical systems and specialties	1854	233
Becton, Dickinson[a]	Medical products	1220	238
	Diagnostic systems	952	125
Johnson & Johnson	Consumer products	4584	454
	Professional products	4068	562
	Pharmaceuticals	3795	1201
Medtonic	Medical products and services	1021	196
Scimed[b]	Cardiovascular devices	184	48
St. Jude Medical	Medical products	210	101
U.S. Surgical	Wound management products	733	162

[a] Fiscal year ends September 30.
[b] Fiscal year ended February 1992.

Note: NR = not reported.

Source: Data from *Standard & Poor's Industry Surveys,* August 20, 1992.

Johnson & Johnson Consolidated Balance Sheet

	1991 ($000,000)	1990 ($000,000)	1989 ($000,000)
Assets			
Current assets	589	826	452
Cash and cash equivalents	203	105	131
Marketable securities, at cost which approximates market value	1763	1519	1320
Accounts receivable, trade, less allowances	—	—	—
Inventories	1702	1543	1353
Deferred taxes on income	238	232	196
Prepaid expenses and other receivables	438	439	324
Total current assets	4933	4664	3776
Marketable securities	276	244	254
Property, plant, and equipment, net	3667	3247	2846
Intangible assets, net	738	706	704
Deferred taxes on income	100	30	26
Other assets	799	604	313
Total assets	10,513	9506	7919
Liabilities and stockholders' equity			
Current liabilities	679	876	570
Loans and notes payable	934	829	622
Accounts payable	918	851	624
Taxes on income	158	67	111
Total current liabilities	2689	2623	1927
Long-term debt	1301	1316	1170
Certificates of extra compensation	79	75	85
Other liabilities	818	592	589
Stockholders' equity			
Preferred stock, without par value (authorized and unissued 2,000,000 shares)	—	—	—
Common stock, par value $1 per share (authorized 540,000,000 shares; issued 383,678,00 and 383,677,000 shares)	384	384	384

Johnson & Johnson Consolidated Balance Sheet (continued)

	1991 ($000,000)	1990 ($000,000)	1989 ($000,000)
Notes receivable from employee stock ownership	(100)	(100)	—
Cumulative currency translation adjustments	134	241	(9)
Retained earnings	6696	5863	5260
Subtotal	7114	6388	5635
Less common stock held in treasury at cost (50,512,000 and 50,601,000 shares)	(1488)	(1488)	(1487)
Total stockholders' equity	5626	4900	4148
Total liabilities and stockholders' equity	**10,513**	**9506**	**7919**

Source: Data from Johnson & Johnson Annual Reports, 1991, 1990, and 1989.

Research and Development Expenditures

Company	1989 ($000,000)	% Sales	1990 ($000,000)	% Sales	1991 ($000,000)	% Sales
Abbott	502	9	567	9	666	10
Bristol-Myers/ Squibb	789	9	881	9	993	9
Johnson & Johnson	719	7	834	7	980	9
Eli Lilly	605	14	703	14	767	13
Merck	751	11	854	11	988	11
Pfizer	531	9	640	10	757	11
Schering- Plough	327	10	380	11	426	12
SmithKline Beecham	772	9	759	8	808	9
Syntex[a]	245	18	271	18	316	17
Upjohn	407	15	427	14	491	14
Warner- Lambert	309	7	379	8	423	8

[a] Fiscal year ending July 31.

Source: Data from Johnson & Johnson Annual Reports, 1989, 1990, 1991.

Case 19.
Sunkyong Group*

T he Sunkyong Group is currently working on a project they call SUPEX QUEST. SUPEX QUEST is a plan to put the Sunkyong Group beyond the level of world-class enterprise and turn it into a world-leading company by the XXIst century. Sunkyong's SUPEX QUEST may appear similar to the strategy of General Electric (GE), "Possessing only the world's first and the second businesses;" however, the enterprises differ in the ways they achieve their goals. While GE has planned on constructing the world's best business structure through corporate acquisition and disposition, Sunkyong intends to maximize the abilities of its employees and make great improvements in existing businesses.

On August 8, 1994, one of Japan's most popular economic newspapers, *Nikkei Business,* introduced the Sunkyong Group as the representative enterprise which would lead the Korean economy into the XXIst century in a comparison and explanation of Sunkyong's SUPEX and GE's managerial innovations.

Sunkyong began its business in a run-down textile factory located in Suwon in 1953. Beginning with only a meager 15 machines and a total of 50 employees, by 1994 Sunkyong had become a versatile enterprise with 31 affiliated companies whose interests included oil refining, chemicals, trading, distribution, construction, hotel, pharmaceuticals, and finance and boasted 24,165 employees (including 2116 foreign employees)

* Professor Dung-Sung Cho prepared this case with the assistance of Research Associate Dong-Hyun Lee as the basis for class discussion rather than to illustrate either effective or ineffective handling of an administrative situation. Reprinted with permission.

and a total sales of $19 billion. The turning point of this spectacular transformation was its decision to undertake shares of Daehan Petroleum that were put up for sale by Gulf when it withdrew in 1980. In 1980, in terms of total sales, Sunkyong had risen from a ranking of 35 in 1976 to fifth in Korea.

The telecommunication business that Sunkyong has actively pursued in the 1990s, has different characteristics in comparison to Sunkyong's main businesses, such as its petrochemical and trading businesses. However, Chairman Chey, Jong-Hyon was confident that if Sunkyong's special management tools, SKMS and SUPEX, were well utilized, the telecommunication business would also achieve high international competitiveness, similar to their success in vertical integration of petroleum to textiles through 20 years of consistent effort.

The history of Sunkyong Group paralleled the fast economic growth of Korea which was commonly referred to as "the miracle of the Han River" in the post-war period. Current Sunkyong Chairman Chey, Jong-Hyon's brother, Chey, Jong-Gun, was the one who started the business in that textile plant in 1953. Sunkyong was later transformed into a trading company when the former Korean president Park Jung-Hee strongly drove an export promotion policy in 1960s. In 1980, Sunkyong reorganized its business structure from being textile-oriented to an energy and chemical-oriented structure by undertaking Daehan Petroleum Co. in response to the government's policy to encourage growth in the heavy and chemical industry since the mid-1970s.

The Move to Yarn Manufacturing: 1953–1972

In 1962, 10 years after the start of the business, Sunkyong was still a textile company of medium standing with only 160 weaving machines, 400 employees, and a total revenue of $2.3 million. In 1963, Sunkyong pursued a plan to increase production by adding 1000 weaving machines in preparation for increased exportation. The plan made it essential to secure a reliable raw materials source for smooth operation of the increased production facilities.

It was early 1964 when Sunkyong considered the possibility of tapping into the technology of manufacturing polyester fiber used by Teijin of Japan, which was its source for imported polyester fibers. At that time, Sunkyong Textiles had only $200 thousand in capital, and it was estimated that at least $8 million was required to construct the fiber plant. Moreover, technology had to be introduced from developed nations, and permission was needed from the government. In addition, the initial response from Teijin was discouraging. Teijin had no incentive to transfer technology to Sunkyong, because Teijin was the first company to manufacture polyester fibers in the East and monopolized the polyester fiber market in Southeast Asia.

Faced with a long wait for government approval for a construction permit and grim prospects in regard to the importation of polyester manufacturing technology, Sunkyong instead pursued acetate fiber manufacturing as a stepping stone toward polyester production. Although the acetate business was declining in the multi-national market at that time, it still accounted for 5000 tons (approximately $10 million) in the domestic market. In addition, the industry type was included in government's first 5-Year Economic Development Plan (1962–1966), which offered assistance to certain industries. In 1966, Sunkyong implemented acetate manufacturing technology from Teijin and established SK Chemical Fibres, Ltd., which oversaw the construction of the proposed plant.

In 1967, following the successful completion of its acetate plant, Sunkyong resumed efforts to construct its own polyester fiber plant. During this time, Japanese textile manufacturers had experienced many changes in the textile manufacturing environment. While Teijin had dominated the polyester market only 3 years before, many companies (including Toyobo, Nichirei, and Asahikasei) had developed their own polyester fiber technology and were operating vigorous production activities comparable to Teijin's. In response to the new competitors, Teijin began joint operations with plants in Taiwan and Thailand.

To advance into the Korean market before other Japanese competitors, Teijin agreed to negotiations with Sunkyong for a joint investment. After receiving a construction permit from the government in July 1967, Sunkyong established a 50/50 joint company with Teijin, Teijin being in charge of technology and Sunkyong in charge of management. The only remaining problem was finding funds to construct the plant. Chairman Chey, Jong-Hyon recalled the situation as follows:

> "I used a foreign currency loan instead of a government loan to construct the polyester plant. I could have also used a government loan through Teijin but as we had seen in the construction of the acetate plant, a government loan involved a complicated and difficult process, which included receiving a permission from the government and an agreement

with the National Assembly. Moreover, the information involved with the polyester plant construction did not have to be revealed if we used a foreign currency loan. We finally came up with a plan to secure funds with Japan."

The plan was as follows: Sunkyong requested that Teijin supply 10,000 pounds of polyester fiber with deferred payment over 3 years. In addition, Sunkyong requested a payment guarantee to C. Itoh to make the management of Teijin feel secure. The price of polyester fiber was $6.5/pound at that time, so $6.5 million could be obtained if the fiber was resold. But, Sunkyong was planning to apply the money that would be earned by the production and sale of textiles utilizing the polyester fiber on credit toward the required fund for the plant construction.

Sunkyong finally began the construction of an acetate plant in December 1968 and a polyester plant in February 1969, with production capacities of 5.5 tons and 7 tons, respectively. As a result, Sunkyong expanded to a group of textile enterprises including SK Chemical Fibres, Ltd., and Sunkyong-Teijin, Ltd., which produced fibers, and Sunkyong Textiles, Ltd., which produced textiles. After the construction of an acetate and a polyester plant, Sunkyong Group's sales and net income grew rapidly from $2.3 million and $0.2 million, respectively, in 1962 to $50 million (31% by Sunkyong Textiles, Ltd., 10.5% by SK Chemical Fibres, Ltd., 42% by Sunkyong-Teijin, Ltd., 16% by others) and $3.7 million, respectively, in 1972.

Oil Business: 1973–1978

Decision to Move to Petrochemicals and Oil Refining

In the 1970s, the Korean government announced its third 5-Year Economic Development Plan (1972–1976), which involved focusing on strengthening the chemical and heavy industry policy by shifting the existing light industry-oriented exportation structure into the heavy chemical industry. Large domestic enterprises acted in concert with the government and quickly advanced into the heavy and chemical industries. Lacking skills and experience in the heavy industry, Sunkyong showed more interest in the petrochemical industry which supplied raw materials for synthetic fiber.

In 1973, Sunkyong together with investments from C. Itoh and Teijin, planned to build an oil refinery plant which was to possess a capacity of 150,000 barrels a day. Sunkyong began a full-scale entry plan in the petrochemical industry which included obtaining a construction permit from the government for the petrochemical industry complex and getting a promise from Saudi Arabia to supply 150,000 barrels of oil a day. As Sunkyong was busy with plans, the world was hit with the first "oil shock". Sunkyong's plan to enter the petrochemical industry was put on temporary hold.

Strategy of Vertical Integration: From Petroleum to Textiles

The strategy of vertical integration began to actualize when the new chairman — Chey, Jong-Hyon — took office after the sudden death of his brother. In his 1975 New Year's resolution as chairman of Sunkyong, he presented a vision for a complete vertical integration from petroleum to textiles:

> "I wish to clearly present two strategies for Sunkyong to grow into one of the major companies in the world. First goal is to achieve vertical integration from petroleum to the textiles industry. I believe that in order to both strengthen and sustain the group's competitiveness in textiles in the 21st century, the group needs to expand into the petrochemical industry and even further into the oil refinery industry. That's the way to secure the supply of required raw materials in textile industry and guarantee low costs. Second is to cultivate management skills coupled with company expansion. In order to successfully operate enormous capacities from textile to oil refinery business, Sunkyong not only needs millions of dollars of financial power, high degree of specialized knowledge, and technology, but also management skills comparable to those of international enterprises."

Establishment of SKMS

Chairman Chey often compared the enterprise management to a computer. In his corporate management and computer metaphor, he always emphasized the importance of software as much as hardware:

> "Constructing the management structure that has been vertically integrated from petroleum to textiles means acquiring hardware in an analogy with computers. As software is needed in order to operate hardware of a

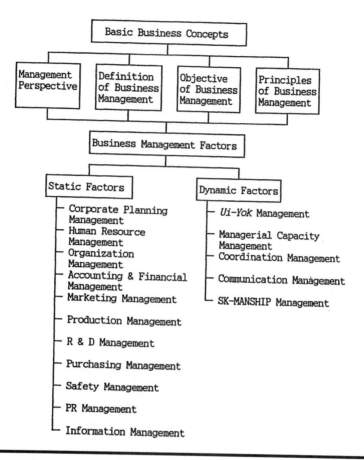

Figure 1 Sunkyong Management System (SKMS)

computer, Sunkyong needs new software for corporate management which would suit the new business structure of 'from petroleum to textiles'."

Chairman Chey's ideal management system (his software to manage Sunkyong Group) is clearly evident in the Sunkyong Management System (SKMS) which was launched in 1975 and completed in 1979. As shown in Figure 1, SKMS is composed of two sections: the basic business concepts, which outline the outlook of an enterprise, the definitions and goals of the corporate management, and the management principles, and the business management factors, which are concrete functions to realize the former. Chairman Chey intended to improve Sunkyong Group's competitive advantages through SKMS:

"In 1975, I thought about how the Sunkyong Group would change by the year of 2000. With competition from western companies increasingly more aggressive, the business climate in the year 2000 will be quite different from present conditions. Hence, I thought about which of Sunkyong's advantages would compete best against western companies. Marketing, finance, and R&D, where western companies were already gaining an advantage, could not become Sunkyong's competitive advantages. I decided to solve the problem which could not be solved by Western business management for 300 years: the very problem of utilizing capabilities of human resources through SKMS."

In SKMS, much emphasis was placed on maximizing both the physical employment and the brain engagement of the workforce. The current chief of the management planning office, Son, Kil-Seung (the present vice-chair), who primarily conducted the operation of SKMS explained the core idea of SKMS as follows:

"According to traditional management theory, physical employment is often discussed but there is no mention about the brain engagement. Hence, management skills that draws self-motivation to enable brain engagement were not developed. Sunkyong decided to utilize previously untapped parts of human resources that others were not using sufficiently in order to sustain greater competitiveness. We researched a method that could elevate the brain engagement of company members voluntarily and willingly. The result was the birth of SKMS."

SKMS classified the business management factors into two categories of factors: static and dynamic. It combined the static factors of traditional management methods (production, marketing, and finance) with dynamic factors (motivation [*Ui-Yok*], managerial capacity capability, coordination, and communication). SKMS's "dynamic factors" categories reflected a deficiency in traditional management methods.

The Importance of Communication

Chairman Chey pointed to the idea that the human is not a conductor but rather a semiconductor and stressed the importance of communication among dynamic factors:

"It was in the early 1970s when I supervised a production meeting of Sunkyong Textiles. While I was attending numerous meetings participated by three stations including production, sales, and marketing, I discovered that the meetings did not progress because everyone had different understandings of the word 'full capacity'. While one person defined 'full capacity' as the previous production record, another person defined 'full capacity' as production in 24 hours' full operation of weaving machines. I then realized that the confusion and dispersed power were a result of the varying knowledge and judgment criteria among the members in management. Coming from various backgrounds, specialties, and departments, each participant was perceiving things based on his own respective orientation. I knew that any decision-making process was in danger of failure unless fundamental elements of management could be agreed upon. In case of Sunkyong Textiles, production capacity increased from 500,000 Ma/month to 800,000 Ma/month within only three months after we defined the term 'full capacity' to be the maximum capacity of production that could be reached theoretically by removing obstacles one by one in order to reach the goal."

Chairman Chey, Jong-Hyon believed that people with heterogeneous talents could be united into one homogeneous power if communication among corporate members could be facilitated by a uniform definition of every word used in the work place. SKMS became a management system unique to Sunkyong that was established on the basis of the actual experiences of Chairman Chey, Jong-Hyon and his systematic research.

Can Meeting

Sunkyong Group formulated a unique meeting system called the Can Meeting. The Can Meeting was a gathering of all department members and chiefs. Can Meetings were held in places outside of the everyday work areas, and everyone talked freely about things inside and out of the company, without regard to one's position or post. Obviously not all of the organization's problems were solved by one Can Meeting. Hence, numerous Can Meetings were held to listen to the opinions of employees and create a sense of unity under one goal by encouraging relationships between members through unreserved discussions. Chairman Chey commented on the effects of the Can Meeting system as follows:

"The Can Meeting was not popular at first because it was misused as meetings to denounce department heads. But as the Can Meeting system was continued, the original purpose was realized and many problems began to get solved. Also, it created a harmonious atmosphere in the work place. Sunkyong was formatting a management culture of participation and agreement based on an expansion of the Can Meeting system."

Second Oil Crisis and Yukong: 1979–1988

The Second Oil Crisis

Sunkyong's strategy to enter the oil refinery industry began to materialize at the time of the second "oil shock", which, in 1979, led to the government passing an oil supply and demand regulation order. The detailed plan was to allow an oil refinery company to import crude petroleum, to allow domestic general trading companies (GTCs) to introduce crude petroleum on a private basis, and to provide government aid for the required fund. These actions were to open more channels for oil importation, as government-based oil importation was limited. In response, private companies actively began to negotiate with oil-producing nations. To qualify as a fifth oil refinery company,[*] companies were required to show proof of an oil supply to the Department of Energy and Resources. Hyosung, Hyundai-Yanghang, Dong-A Construction, Korean Air, and Hyundai Construction were quick to seek oil supplies. Moreover, Ssangyong and Samsung were also negotiating for oil with Iran and Malaysia, respectively. But, the desperate efforts of many Korean companies were thwarted: long-term contracts of crude oil were unthinkable. With an increase in prices from $12/barrel up to $34/barrel within only 3 months, even a spot contract of one shipment capacity was difficult to attain. Under these extreme conditions, Sunkyong was the only company able to secure a long-term supply contract.

Sunkyong signed a long-term oil importation contract with Saudi Arabia and finally began to supply imported crude petroleum to domestic oil refinery companies on July 17, 1980. Details of the contract between Sunkyong and the Oil and Mineral Corporation, owned by the Saudi Arabian government, included supplies of 50,000 barrels per day in the first year (1980), 70,000 barrels per day in the second year (1981), and 100,000 barrels per day in the third year (1982), with a price of $31 to $32 per barrel.

---

[*] There were four oil refinery companies at that time: Korea Oil Corporation (1962, joint venture with Gulf), Honam Refinery Company, Ltd. (1967, joint venture with Caltex), Kyungin Energy Company, Ltd. (1968, joint venture with Union Oil), Ssangyong Refinery Company, Ltd. (1976, joint venture with National Iranian Oil Company).

Yukong Acquisition

In October 1980, the Korean government announced its decision to privatize Daehan Petroleum Corporation in response to Gulf Oil's withdrawal from Korea on August 19, 1980. Gulf Oil, with Yukong, was supplying 100% of necessary crude oil to Korea. Considering Yukong's position as both a key industry of the nation and an oil refinery business, the government proposed the following qualifications for applicants who wished to acquire Yukong:

1. Securing a long-term and stable crude petroleum supply
2. Fund-raising ability to complete expansion and storage on schedule
3. Investment capability as an oil-producing country
4. Management skills necessary for an oil refinery company
5. Fidelity as a company that can carry out its social duties as a key industry
6. Negotiation skill and past accomplishments with oil-producing companies

Sunkyong, along with Samsung and Nambang Development, jumped into competition for Yukong. Vice-Chairman Kim Hang-Duk recalled his experiences with the Yukong acquisition as Sunkyong's 38-year-old managing director:

> "No one at that time expected that Sunkyong would acquire Yukong. Sunkyong was seen to be inferior to Samsung in every aspect including company size, manpower, business experience, and sponsorship. However, we had thought differently. The core ability which was required to undertake Yukong was perceived to be an ability in securing both crude oil and funds. Sunkyong had met these two constraints since the 1970s. Top executives including Chairman Chey told staffs in the field not to worry because they placed a net so that fish could not escape."

Sunkyong's outstanding capability in oil importation and their plan to introduce the oil dollars of Saudi Arabia through a loan were recognized. Sunkyong finally acquired Yukong in November 1980. Yukong was known at that time as the goose that laid golden eggs. Sunkyong Group was only ranked number ten among large domestic enterprises, with a revenue of $764 million in 1979, and leaped suddenly to a rank of fifth, with a total revenue of $8.3 billion in 1981.

After Sunkyong acquired Yukong, it pursued the massive investments required to facilitate vertical integration of petroleum and textiles. Sunkyong completed the construction of a new aromatics plant in 1986, followed by the start of a DMT/PTA plant construction in October 1987 and completion of the construction of new ethylene and polyollephine plants. The plant constructions of PO/SM and OX/PT were finalized in June and July of 1988, respectively.

Long-Term Strategic Planning

Along with the Can Meeting system, the establishment of long-term strategic planning was developed in the Sunkyong Group. It was the first domestic company to establish a 10-year long-term strategy. Chairman Chey especially emphasized the fact that every business required shrewd and accurate planning:

> "Whatever we do in the future, we must seek a technology-oriented business that is not easily approachable by others. Based on my 20 years of experience, business that others find hard to initiate is more profitable even though it requires a longer period of time to develop. In preparing early, we could be ahead of the competition, making it difficult for them to catch up. Therefore, those of you in business affairs, look 5 years into the future, presidents of affiliated companies should seek management 10 years in advance, and as chairman I will make plans toward 30 years into the future."

Business affairs were supervised by the management planning office, but the members of the planning office were in charge of technical tasks, including a reference publication which contained the performance of each affiliated company, estimations of future business environments, and preparations for the Can Meeting for each post and station. The actual activities of long-term strategic planning, which were connected to the vision, goals, business strategies, and functional strategies of the group were materialized through the Can Meetings held over 100 times.

A Can Meeting was subdivided into three groups. The first group was the presidency Can Meeting, supervised by Chairman Chey, which shaped the path that the Sunkyong Group would take over the next 10 years. In 1979, the total revenue of the Sunkyong Group was $766 million. In a Can Meeting in 1979, Sunkyong set the goal to reach a total revenue of $4471 million within the next 10 years, by 1989. This goal was criticized as being unreasonable considering the current situation. However, the optimistic view that the goal might be reached — once Chairman Chey's vision ("from petroleum to textiles") was to be realized — was exactly what happened.

Based on results from the presidency Can Meeting, the second group, the executive Can Meeting, was held at each of the 20 affiliated companies and was supervised by the president. At these meetings, topics of discussion included how to allocate responsibility for achieving the goal between each of the affiliated companies, how to increase existing businesses in order to achieve the goal, and what kind of new business should be developed.

With the results from the executive Can Meeting, the third type of Can Meeting, the business division Can Meeting, was held at each of the business stations and was supervised by each section's chief. The purpose was to review details of existing and new businesses and make business plans. The results of the business division Can Meeting were then relayed to the executive and the presidency Can Meetings so that the final 10-year long-term strategic planning was established. All members of Sunkyong, which exceeded 13,000 from the chairman to new staffs, participated in Can Meetings more than once and had a chance to make a statement about the projections of the group, goals, and strategies for the next 10 years. Sunkyong's 10-year long-term strategic planning was the first attempt by a Korean domestic company in strategic planning and became a popular guide to other large domestic groups or companies in establishing long-term plans.

Vice-chairman Kim Hyang-Duk, who was in charge of management at Yukong, said the following about the importance of long-term strategic planning:

> "The business structure of Sunkyong had been vertically integrated with Yukong Company at the center. The oil refinery company, Yukong Company, which held the most weight in the Sunkyong Group, required especially careful investment decisions because the investment capacity was not only enormous but it also required an average of 5 years before one investment was to be completed due to the characteristics of the oil refining industry. Establishing and carrying out long-term plans for a 10-year period, medium-term plans for a 5-year period, and annual business plans were systematized at Yukong."

Diversification Strategy Into Related Businesses

During the 4 years beginning in 1983, after acquiring Yukong in 1980, Sunkyong sold half of its affiliated companies that had been showing poor results, a total of 11 affiliated companies that included foods and beverages, lumber, machinery, and semiconductors. After Sunkyong initiated a re-energizing effort at its 11 remaining affiliated companies, it pursued an active business diversification effort centering around the petrochemical industry, beginning with the acquisition of Hungkuk Sangsa in 1980 which sold petroleum products. It also established Yukong Line for oil transportation in 1982, Yukong Gas for LPG supply in 1985, and Yukong Arco Chemical in collaboration with Arco Chemical of U.S. in 1987. Among the 13 new affiliated companies during the 1980s, 11 companies were directly related to Yukong.

Other than Yukong, Sunkyong pursued diversification in surrounding focused businesses including Sunkyong Industry and SKC. Moreover, in 1980, SKC, which developed polyester films for the first time in 1978, succeeded in the independent development of videotapes, achieving a position of fourth behind the U.S., Germany, and Japan, and the company began production of computer floppy disks in 1981. SKC supplied polyester films to another affiliated company, SKM, which produced audiotapes.

Sunkyong Industry, which produced mainly polyester fibers, diversified its business, moving into precision chemistry, modern fibers, new materials, and the life sciences on the basis of its core abilities in the chemical field and entered into the pharmaceutical industry on the basis of research accomplishments in the field of life sciences. (The sales composition of the Sunkyong Group is summarized in Tables 1a and 1b.)

SUPEX QUEST: 1989 and beyond

Sunkyong Group's unique management techniques included SKMS and SUPEX QUEST. At SKMS, emphasis has been placed on fully utilizing the physical employment and brain engagement of their human resources. SKMS is designed to induce the highest possible level of volunteering and willingness of Sunkyong's workforce.

SUPEX QUEST is a guideline to maximize the benefits derived from the practice of SKMS. It stems from the belief that maximum effort should be put forth to achieve the highest humanly possible level of performance, the level of "super excellence", which, applied to work processes and methodology, could help Sunkyong become a world-class enterprise. The essential goal of both SKMS and SUPEX is to optimize human resources performance.

Origin and Concept

Sunkyong introduced its new management tool, SUPEX QUEST, in 1989. Chairman Chey, Jong-Hyon explained the motives of the SUPEX QUEST as follows:

> "The ultimate objective of SKMS was to push Sunkyong to world-class status. But even after 10 years of implementation, we had not accomplished much of our anticipated goal. We researched possible reasons for our poor performance and found that the problem was not in SKMS but in the difficulties of implementation of SKMS. After much careful consideration, we formulated SUPEX QUEST and the pursuit of super excellent goals, which was a plan to execute SKMS in a more effective and efficient manner."

The "super excellent" level is the optimal level that can be reached by the maximum utilization of human abilities. SUPEX QUEST is a critical task-processing method that enables the realization of "super excellent" goals. Vice-President Kim, Soo-Gill of SKC made this comment regarding the strategic meaning and implications of SUPEX QUEST:

> "For Sunkyong to become a world-class company, the present speed of development has to be surpassed. The usual method that others are using is to follow the shadow of developed companies. This method of operations relegates us to second-position status always chasing behind other companies. For instance, when we used the present world-class enterprises as our model, although we made improvements in management, those enterprises were also concurrently improving and developing thus making our advancements insufficient. Super excellent levels will allow us to better focus our collective energy and resources to reach our goals."

A comparison between SUPEX and benchmarking is provided in Figure 2.

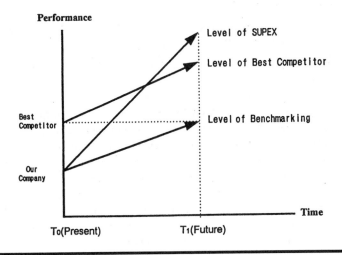

Figure 2 Comparison Between SUPEX and Benchmarking Performance

The Five-Step Approach to SUPEX QUEST

Sunkyong thought of a method that could implement a shrewd and solid working process for SUPEX. As illustrated in Figure 3, a required task is accomplished in a defined five-step approach. First, the factors related to the profit maximization are sought, then the SUPEX level of attained Key Factors for Company Success (KFS) is determined, and

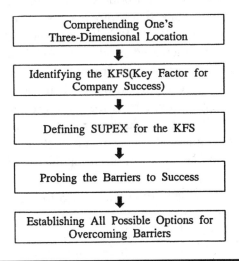

Figure 3 Five-Step Approach to SUPEX QUEST

barriers between the present level and the SUPEX level are probed and solved step by step. Han, Bong-Hee, the managing director of SKC, who led the SUPEX team, explained the essentials of the five-step approach to SUPEX QUEST as follows:

> "The core concept of SUPEX QUEST is to move beyond a normal level of KFS, step 2, and aim towards the super excellent level — or the maximum humanly possible utilization of resources and skills. In addition, once the SUPEX level is achieved, constraint factors that produce differences between the SUPEX level and present level are determined and these points undergo a process of analysis and modification in 'Can Meetings'. SUPEX QUEST is not only more simple compared to benchmarking or MBO [management by objective], but it also helps members to widen their perception and create competitive advantages."

MPR/S/T

When the polyester plant, SKC, was pursuing SUPEX, the Sunkyong Group discovered an instance where profit maximization could not be achieved with the five-step approach and SUPEX QUEST alone. The production capacity was at 51,000 tons annually before the pursuit of SUPEX. After the amount of 178,000 tons was set as the SUPEX level and barriers were removed one by one, production increased to 65,000 tons. However, soon after that products were not being sold, and inventories started to accumulate. Sales were poor because only the production department was pursuing SUPEX. The marketing department could not keep up with the increased production following SUPEX. Later, once the marketing department commenced SUPEX QUEST, production could not meet the increased demand. In order to increase the annual production quantity, efforts from the production department and R&D were needed. At last, Sunkyong realized that the profit could not be maximized unless all departments including marketing (M), production (P), and R&D (R) were all simultaneously pursuing SUPEX.

Since then, Sunkyong installed SUPEX QUEST in the marketing, production, and R&D departments and also in the staff departments (S), which included finance, human resources, and planning to assist M, P, and R. Furthermore, SUPEX QUEST was overseen by top management (T), who led, helped, and checked line and staff departments in concert. Divisions separating each department were removed, concentrating power centrally.

Kim, Tae-Hyuk, who worked as the head of the SUPEX QUEST team, explained the factors that allowed SUPEX QUEST to succeed:

> "The very reason that SUPEX QUEST was implemented successfully was the persistent interest of and rewards to the top manager. SUPEX case studies from each affiliated company were directly reported to Chairman Chey under the name SUPEX Briefing, and a group reward was given if a case was to be recognized as a successful SUPEX case."

Director Hyun, Sun-Yeop who was the member of SUPEX QUEST team, emphasized the fact that SKMS and SUPEX QUEST were complementary:

> "When SUPEX QUEST was introduced, many people thought that it was resulted from the failure of SKMS. But then we realized that all solutions were summarized in SKMS while we were in agony trying to resolve management problems through SUPEX QUEST."

EMD (Executive Management Development)

Sunkyong planned to train leaders who could carry out SUPEX QUEST by developing and utilizing an Executive Management Development (EMD) program. Chairman Chey wanted to build a base on which both the company and every individual could grow simultaneously by supplying outstanding managerial techniques to many people, including members of Sunkyong:

> "Once, I met people from General Electric (GE) and heard them reiterate the idea 'GE is not for everybody'. But I wanted to say 'Sunkyong is for everybody'. No matter how smart or stupid, anyone could become an executive manager at Sunkyong by following SKMS and SUPEX QUEST."

Diversification into Information and Telecommunications Businesses

Sunkyong Group's business structure went through a restructuring by diversifying around focused businesses and downsizing unrelated business in 1980s. In the 1990s, Sunkyong attempted to diversify toward new areas in order to improve its business structure, which gave too much importance to its oil and chemical businesses. After entering the financial industry by acquiring a stock company in 1991, Sunkyong decided to pursue information and telecommunication as its new core business.

Among ten companies which have been either newly established or acquired in the 1990s, seven have been in the fields of finance, information and communication, and logistics. As a consequence of Sunkyong's efforts, revenue from the oil and chemical businesses, which represented 74% of the group's revenue in 1981, decreased to 64% in 1993. (The changes in Sunkyong's businesses are summarized in Tables 2a and 2b.)

Entering Mobile Telecommunications

Sunkyong's advancement into the information and telecommunication industry was part of the group's management strategy that Sunkyong was planning since the early 1980s. From the mid-1980s, when Sunkyong's long-term vision from petroleum to textiles was completed, Sunkyong decided upon entering the information and telecommunication industry as its next management goal. Sunkyong set up a telecommunication team in the management planning office in the U.S. to establish a long-term management plan, complete research in technology, and secure competent employees. Chairman Chey, Jong-Hyon explained the position and determination of Sunkyong to enter the information and telecommunication business in his 1992 New Year's address:

> "Ever since the completion of vertical integration from petroleum to textiles, I have been considering what kind of business Sunkyong should pursue next. Although I contemplated the entry into the home electronics and automobile industries, which were very popular then, there already existed sufficient competition. Increased competition in an already competitive industry would not benefit the country, thus I investigated industries which would avoid unnecessary competition with existing companies and could contribute toward the development of the nation. Considering its growth capability in the globalization era, I chose the information and telecommunication business as Sunkyong's next business and decided to pursue it as the group's new core business. We decided to advance first toward the service and software fields which would enable us to compete fairly. Also, I felt that Sunkyong could succeed in this field comparatively easily as opposed to entering in hardware since this field was already filled with competition from electronics companies."

Sunkyong established its corporation — Yukronics, Inc. — in New Jersey in October 1989; a software company — Sunkyong Information

System — in May 1990; and a workstation company — YC&C — in October 1990. Sunkyong entered the information and telecommunication business through Daehan Telecom in April 1991 to acquire a license for the Second Mobile Communication. In particular, Yukronics, Inc., invested $2.12 million in Unidata, which retained core technologies in the information and telecommunication business including voice digitization and compression.

The Ministry of Communications, a Korean government office which was in charge of communications, decided to introduce competition to the monopolized mobile telecommunication field and announced an outline of the procedure to select new businesses in mobile telecommunications and pagers in April 1992.

According to the Korea Information Society Development Institute (KISDI), the growth rate of the mobile telecommunication service has been estimated to be 44.9% annually from 1991 to 2000; also, the number of registrations was expected to increase from 20,000 registrations in 1991 to 4,500,000 by the year 2000. Market capacity of the mobile telecommunication was anticipated to reach $2.5 billion by the year 2000.

According to the deadline set by the Ministry of Communications, on June 25, 1992, six business groups, including Daehan Telecom of Sunkyong, Dongboo, Dongyang, Ssangyong, Kolon, and Posco, applied for a license to start the Second Mobile Telecommunications Corporation as a consortium. The consortium of Daehan Telecom was organized with a total of 16 companies in collaboration with 13 domestic companies including Yukong, Korea Electric Power, Korea Computer, Kyongin Electronics, Daehan Education Insurance, Naewae Semiconductor, and three foreign companies including GTE (U.S.), Bodaphone (U.K.), and Hutchison (H.K.).

The results of the first evaluation were announced by the Ministry of Communications on July 29, 1992: three companies including Daehan Telecom, New World Mobile Telecommunications, and the Second Mobile Communication were selected out of the six applicants on the basis of their fund-raising ability, technology plan, and sales plan.

On August 20, 1992, the Ministry of Communications announced its final decision on 36 items including a base design plan, a construction plan of the telecommunication network in a specific region (Seoul), and a telecommunication development plan. Daehan Telecom of Sunkyong Group, with 8388 points/10,000 total, was selected as the final candidate, a decision based particularly on its R&D plan, network structure, and design ability. Daehan beat out New World Mobile Telecommunications and the Second Mobile Communication, who attained 7496 points and 7099 points respectively.

However, presidential candidate Kim, Young-Sam of the government party requested that residing president Rho, Tae-Woo postpone the decision until after the presidential election to avoid criticism of minority parties on the fairness of the decision process. After only 2 weeks, Sunkyong decided to give up the license and notified the government of its decision. Chief Sohn, Gil-Seung of the management planning office held a press conference and explained Sunkyong's position and reasons regarding the voluntary action:

> "We will not pursue the telecommunication business under the current government; however, we will certainly compete again if circumstances permit when the new government begins its term. As an enterprise which contributes to the nation's economy, Sunkyong cannot just ignore social controversy, and we have decided that we should not do anything that might disrupt harmony in the nation based on our management ideology. We wish to participate in the business only after Sunkyong's capabilities are fairly recognized under a different political power without the possibility of misunderstanding.

A New Opportunity

Chairman Chey applied for the license for the Second Mobile Telecommunications again in February 1993 as President Kim, Young-Sam was inaugurated. The Ministry of Communications announced its plan to select a new business entity in Second Mobile Telecommunications in connection with privatization of Korea Mobile Telecommunications Corporation (KMTC) and officially made a request to the Federation of Korean Industries for a list of potential candidates. In connection with this, consortiums were formed around six companies including Sunkyong, Dongboo, Ssangyong, Kolon, and Posco, just as in 1992.

The reason that the Ministry of Communications delegated the problem of selection to the Federation of Korean Industries (FKI), which represented all Korean enterprises, was for the business world to display a unified front and to earn the credibility of the government as well as the citizens. However, the fact that the current chairman of the FKI was Chairman Chey, Jong-Hyon of Sunkyong was a coincidence. As a result, it was expected, from past experience in 1992, that Sunkyong would face trouble in gaining complete credibility from both the government and citizens even if Sunkyong was to be chosen on the basis of its capability.

Consequently, Chairman Chey sought possibilities regarding First Mobile Telecommunications. By purchasing Korea Telecommunications in the mobile communication business in 1984, Sunkyong could easily accumulate know-how and gain advantage in the telecommunications field. However, the acquisition of First Mobile Telecommunications posed many problems. GTE, Bodaphone, and Hutchison had participated in a joint consortium in First Mobile Telecommunications since 1992. Divided by 10%, these companies were entitled to claim a sum conservatively estimated at $162 million for their technology collaboration and business infrastructure construction in the form of sending engineers and establishing corporations in Korea.

In addition, if Sunkyong's decision to acquire the KMTC was publicized, the expected increase in stock prices could become a serious financial burden. In order to secure a strong management position in First Mobile Telecommunications through stock purchases, at least 23% of the total stock had to be purchased in order to attain a strong position. Assuming a current price of KMTC stock of $336, a minimum of $423 million was necessary as a stock purchasing fund, which was ten times the amount of what was needed for purchase of Second Mobile Telecommunications.

Moreover, the expected price would generally be determined by a weighted average of transactions for 30 days in the stock market, but an increase in stock price would result from announcement of Sunkyon's intent to acquire First Mobile Telecommunications, and even more burden would be put on funding. Furthermore, KMTC, as a reinvestment in a government-owned monopoly, lacked competitiveness and a customer-service orientation and was plagued by various structural problems.

In contrast, Sunkyong could become a dominant stockholder with only $75 million in Second Mobile Telecommunications, although full-scale operations could only commence 5 years after investments in facility and technology development. First Mobile Telecommunications was already operating the paging business, unlike the Second Mobile Telecommunications (see Table 3).

Despite its political controversy, should Sunkyong pursue Second Mobile Telecommunications and utilize its most advantageous technology? Or should Sunkyong choose to invest in First Mobile Telecommunications, a considerably safer investment, with the aid of the Federation of Korean Industries, although it would require about $500 million, which was a quarter of Sunkyong's annual investment capacity?

Table 1a. Major Companies of Sunkyong Group (1994)[a]

Business	1962	1972	1979	1981	1987	1993
Trading[b] (including textiles)	2.3	16	423	1495	2110	3773
Chemical fiber	—	26	180	258	258	700
Chemical	—	—	11	38	340	807
Construction	—	—	39	55	227	868
Hotel	—	—	34	19	43	90
Petrochemical[c]	—	—	—	4235	3694	8697
Shipping	—	—	—	—	112	703
Finance	—	—	—	—	—	114
Other	—	—	79	23	2	219
Total	2.3	42	766	6123	6786	15,971

[a] Units are in millions of dollars.

[b] In 1976, Sunkyong Textile was transformed into a general trading company titled Sunkyong, Ltd.

[c] This business includes oil refining and distribution of oil and LPG gas.

Table 1b. Major Companies of Sunkyong Group (1994)

Business	Company	Sales ($million)	Total Assets ($million)	Profit ($million)	Number of Employees
Trading and distribution	Sunkyong	4381	1135	11	1263
	Sunkyong Distribution	221	133	−18	430
Petro-chemical	Yukong	7406	8148	67	5935
	Hungkuk Sangsa	1591	844	0.1	1043
	Yukong Gas	562	227	8	217
Chemical	Sunkyong Industries	841	1344	13	3875
	SKC	680	797	9	3401
	Yukong Oxichemical	169	519	0.4	123
Construction	Sunkyong Engineering and Construction	1163	1436	7	2461
Shipping	Yukong Line	787	624	2	488
Hotel	Sheraton Walker Hill	9	164	3	1502

Table 2a. Sales and Total Assets of Sunkyong Group

Items	1950s-60s	1970s	1980s	1990s
Entry, number of	7[a]	18	13	10
Exit, number of	0	0	14	0
Number of businesses	7	22[b]	21	30[c]

[a] This number includes the mother company, Sunkyong Textile.

[b] Sunkyong, Ltd., merged two companies and Sunkyong-Teijin, Ltd., merged SK Chemical Fibres, Ltd.

[c] In 1992, Sunkyong Magnetic (SKM) was separted from Sunkyong Group.

Table 2b. Sales and Total Assets of Sunkyong Group[a]

	1979	1980	1981	1982	1983	1984	1985	1986
Sales	765	5019	6123	6271	6245	6543	6376	6030
Total assets	699	2596	2560	2545	2468	2513	2545	2830

	1987	1988	1989	1990	1991	1992	1993	1994
Sales	6786	7761	9021	10,732	12,985	14,186	15,971	19,528
Total assets	3386	4663	6771	9172	12,388	13,528	24,048	19,201

[a] Units in millions of dollars.

Table 3. The Situation of Korea Mobile Telecommunications Corporation

	1984	1985	1986	1987	1988	1989	1990	1991	1992	1993
Sales[a]										
Total	4.9	8.0	10.2	17.0	165.5	540.9	1014.1	2009.5	3307.3	5331.3
Mobile	4.7	6.9	9.1	14.6	82.1	251.9	470.3	933.1	1664.5	2672.5
Wireless	0.2	1.1	1.1	2.4	83.4	289.0	543.8	1076.4	1642.8	2658.8
Profit	0.4	1.5	0.7	1.3	37.2	150.5	276.8	582.5	623.6	957.7
Total assets	4.3	6.0	9.3	13.5	610.1	1326.4	2420.9	4092.7	5975.8	9364.9
Subscribers (unit)										
Mobile	2658	5685	7093	10,265	20,353	39,718	80,005	166,198	271,868	471,784
Wireless	15,647	18,782	37,794	60,200	100,373	198,286	417,650	850,515	1,451,710	2,262,256

[a] Figures in millions of dollars.

Index

Index